God and the British Soldier

'There is no book which seriously competes with this . . . it is likely to become the standard work on the subject.'

Prof. Richard Holmes, *Cranfield University*

'An excellent piece of research and writing that will change how we think about both the motivation of the army and young men's religious life.'

Dr Dan Todman, *Queen Mary University of London*

Historians of the First and Second World Wars have consistently underestimated the importance of religion in British society in the first half of the twentieth century. In this compelling and fascinating study of the role of religion in the British army in both World Wars, Michael Snape shows that religion had much greater currency and influence among British soldiers than has previously been recognised.

By drawing on a wealth of new material from military, ecclesiastical and secular civilian archives, Snape re-evaluates the complex religious attitudes of the British soldier, the role of the army chaplain and the wartime work of civilian religious agencies such as the Salvation Army and the YMCA. In doing so, he shows that religion was a key component of British national identity and that it served as a major buttress to British military morale during the two World Wars.

Rejecting the myth that religion was unimportant to the soldiers of this era, *God and the British Soldier* demonstrates how the British soldier of 1914–18 and 1939–45 was far from being the irreligious product of a fundamentally secular society. Indeed, and contrary to the widely accepted view that war helped to advance the secularisation of British society, Snape argues that the nation's religious culture emerged intact and even strengthened as a result of the citizen soldier's experience of the two World Wars.

Michael Snape is Lecturer in Modern History at the University of Birmingham and a member of the University of Birmingham's Centre for First World War Studies. He is author of *The Redcoat and Religion* (Routledge 2005) and *The Church of England in Industrialising Society* (2003).

D1453391

Christianity and society in the modern world
General editor: Hugh McLeod

Also available:

The Reformation and the visual arts: the Protestant
image question in Western and Eastern Europe
Sergiusz Michalski

European religion in the age of great cities
Hugh McLeod

Women and religion in England, 1500–1720
Patricia Crawford

The reformation of ritual: an interpretation of
early modern Germany
Susan Karant-Nunn

The Anabaptists
Hans-Jürgen Goertz

Women and religion in early America, 1600–1850:
the puritan and evangelical traditions
Marilyn J. Westerkamp

Christianity and sexuality in the early modern world:
regulating desire, reforming practice
Merry E. Wiesner-Hanks

The Redcoat and religion: the forgotten history of the
British soldier from the age of Marlborough to the eve
of the First World War
Michael Snape

God and the British Soldier

Religion and the British Army
in the First and Second
World Wars

Michael Snape

Routledge
Taylor & Francis Group

LONDON AND NEW YORK

D
639
.R4
S55
2005

First published 2005
by Routledge
2 Park Square, Milton Park, Abingdon, Oxon OX14 4RN

Simultaneously published in the USA and Canada
by Routledge
270 Madison Avenue, New York, NY 10016

Routledge is an imprint of the Taylor & Francis Group

Typeset in Bell Gothic and Perpetua by
Florence Production Ltd, Stoodleigh, Devon
Printed and bound in Great Britain by
Antony Rowe Ltd, Chippenham, Wiltshire

British Library Cataloguing in Publication Data
A catalogue record for this book is available from the
British Library

Library of Congress Cataloging in Publication Data
A catalog record for this book has been requested

ISBN10: 0–415–19677–9 (hbk)
ISBN10: 0–415–33452–7 (pbk)

ISBN13: 978–0–415–19677–2 (hbk)
ISBN13: 978–0–415–33452–5 (pbk)

In memory of my grandfather, Francis Snape

By the way, just in case I depart this life during the coming war you can be quite sure that I shall die in a state of grace. That after all is the *only* thing that matters. Whether one dies now or in 50 years time doesn't matter a jot. Compared to Eternity Life is too short to worry about leaving it. So *should* anything happen please don't worry or be sad. Really I shall be much better off than you!!

(Second Lieutenant Peter Sutton, Royal Tank Regiment, 3 September 1939)

CONTENTS

PREFACE

Like many historians of the two World Wars, I bring to this study a very personal interest. As a child growing up in the 1970s, I was close to my paternal grandfather, a veteran of the First World War. Although his service in the army represented less than five years of a remarkably long life, the legacy of those years was apparent to me even as a child. In material terms, the war's long shadow was evident in a series of seven photographs which, mounted in a single frame, greeted all who entered his living room. One of these photographs was a portrait of my grandfather; a small, scowling figure dressed in crumpled khaki serge. Another five portraits were of his brothers, similarly attired. The seventh and largest photograph was of two figures, one of them my great-grandfather, laying the first wreath on Clitheroe's cenotaph, an honour that was his by dint of losing four sons to the Great War. Although my grandfather served as an infantryman on the Western Front from 1915 to 1918, unlike most of his siblings he emerged physically unscathed. Nevertheless, his wartime experiences were reflected in other ways, from the troubled nights he suffered in my father's childhood to the unease with which he viewed toy guns and toy soldiers in my own.

On becoming aware of Wilfred Owen, Siegfried Sassoon and Erich Maria Remarque in my early teens, I inevitably associated my grandfather's generation with a loss of idealism and with a dramatic, tragic and far-reaching experience of disillusionment. Consequently, and as I began to study the religious history of modern Britain at university, I quickly absorbed the commonplace view that a haemorrhaging of religious faith was, like the loss of patriotism, part and parcel of the collective experience of this generation. Still, and at the same time, my knowledge of my late grandfather gave me grounds to doubt this assumption. Far from lapsing into an embittered agnosticism or atheism, my grandfather remained a churchgoer all his life. Clearly, the war had left its mark upon his faith, a fact reflected by the leaves from Delville Wood that he kept pressed in a Douai Bible and also by the offerings that he gave towards Masses for the souls of his brothers. As I began to delve into the subject of religion and the soldier, I imagined that this might have been a Catholic peculiarity – an example, in my grandfather's case, of how Lancashire Catholicism had survived the carnage of the Western Front as it had the racks and dungeons of penal times. However, and as I examined the survival of Catholic piety among British soldiers in the context of the First World War, it became increasingly clear that this resilience was common to most religious traditions and, furthermore, that it obtained in the Second World War as well. As I became acquainted with the work of new generations of religious and military historians and delved deeper into a greater variety of sources, it became increasingly clear that the presumed connection between the experience of modern war and the secularisation of British society was fundamentally misconceived and that it required radical revision. In attempting this revision, it also became evident that this task had been unnecessarily delayed, the all too obvious gulf between the military and religious historians of modern Britain having enabled a mutually congenial amnesia to settle upon the subject of religion and the twentieth-century British soldier. Certainly, this was convenient for all concerned; after all, since the 1960s the increasingly pacifist mood of the British churches and the strongly secular outlook of its military historians have ensured that neither constituency really wants to be reminded of an obvious aspect of twentieth-century British history, namely that religion and religious agencies served as vital forces in inspiring and sustaining the British army and its citizen soldiers throughout both World Wars.

Readers will note that, in exploring these themes, I have been quite lavish with the use of illustrations and examples. This is quite intentional, as it seemed to me that only a barrage of evidence would make an adequate impression on the myths and prejudices that are entrenched around so many of the issues raised in this book. However, the problem of representativeness is inherent in this study's extensive use of personal testimony, a problem that is compounded by the fact that much of it was yielded at a later date in the form of memoirs and oral history interviews. Conscious of the problems that this situation involves, I have endeavoured to balance this later testimony with contemporary material from personal letters and journals, from the secular and religious press and from ecclesiastical and military archives. This mix of evidence has been further enriched by the findings of contemporary surveys conducted by the churches and also by those undertaken by distinctly secular organisations such as Mass-Observation and the *Daily Mirror*. The result, I hope, is a persuasive and objective analysis that has not been dominated by the voice of interested 'upper middle-class subalterns', a problem that is present and confessed in Richard Schweitzer's very recent study *The Cross and the*

Trenches: Religious Faith and Doubt among British and American Great War Soldiers (2003).[1] Heavily dependent on personal testimony, Schweitzer's study is a tribute to his remarkable industry as a researcher but this very reliance deprives it of some valuable perspectives provided by other sources. Hence, Schweitzer's study goes little beyond proving that 'on balance, Great War soldiers were more religious than not'[2] and demonstrating the truth of Richard Holmes' observation that 'Religion and those who championed it divided men's opinion, but there was a far more powerful spiritual undertow on the Western Front than we sometimes think'.[3]

Lastly, a note on the parameters of this study. Throughout this book I am dealing exclusively with Christianity and Judaism, which were the only major religions to have a significant following in British society and in the British army at this time. Furthermore, and for the sake of coherence, I have focused on soldiers of the British army who were natives of the British Isles, thus excluding Commonwealth troops and a relatively small proportion of men and women who, though born overseas, served in the British army. I have also confined my studies to Britain's full-time soldiers (thus excluding the Home Guard in the Second World War) and I have not attempted to address the role of religion in the Royal Navy, in the RAF or in the latter's predecessors, the Royal Naval Air Service and the Royal Flying Corps. Hopefully, this attempt to reappraise the religious experience of British soldiers in the two World Wars will encourage others to reconsider the role of religion among British civilians, among Britain's other armed services and among their Commonwealth comrades in arms.

ACKNOWLEDGEMENTS

In researching and writing this book I am extremely grateful to Professor Hugh McLeod for inviting me to contribute a monograph on war and religion to the Routledge series on Christianity and Society in the Modern World. I am also grateful for his unstinting support and encouragement over many years, and not least in guiding this project to completion, a task that has also been patiently and generously shared by Vicky Peters, the History Editor at Routledge, and by Philippa Grand. In addition, I am very deeply indebted to Dr John Bourne, Dr Bob Bushaway and Dr Stephen Parker for many lengthy and useful discussions on the salient themes raised in this volume. I am also very conscious of the more occasional but still invaluable help given to me by other scholars, in particular by Dr Stuart Mews, Dr John Walsh, Prof. David Hempton, Prof. Callum Brown, Prof. Clyde Binfield, Dr Sarah Williams, Dr Alan Wilkinson, Dr Mark Smith and Dr Katherine Finlay. I must extend my collective thanks to the members of the University of Birmingham's History of Religion, War and Society and Open End seminars, as well as to its Centre for First World War Studies. I would especially like to thank those veterans of the Second World War, namely Mr Charlie Wakeley, Prof. John Hick, Dr Colin Starkie, Mr Tony Foulds and Mr Michael Sutton who kindly agreed to be interviewed by me. All of these have proved a fund of references and inspiration; the mistakes that my endeavours may have led to are entirely my own. Naturally, I owe a great deal to the staff of many libraries and archives, but in particular I would like to thank Miss Melanie Barber of Lambeth Palace Library, Fr John Sharp of the archives of the Archdiocese of Birmingham and Major Margaret Easey of the Royal Army Chaplains' Department Archive at Amport House. It is, of course, a truism that research can be a lonely business. Over the past few years I have had the great good fortune to have the firm support of my parents, brothers, friends and colleagues. However, my chief support has come from my wife, Rachel, and from my daughter, Katy. Without the love and happiness that they have given me, this book could never have been written.

COPYRIGHT ACKNOWLEDGEMENTS

The author gratefully acknowledges the help of Mrs Clare Adams, Mr Anthony Bennet, Mr John Crosse, the Revd Owen Eva, Mr Fred Gee, Mrs Marjorie Jones, the descendants of the Revd W.H. Miller, Captain J.R.T. Pollard and Mr John Scollen in giving their permission to quote from copyright material currently held in the Department of Documents at the Imperial War Museum. He is also grateful to Mr Michael Sutton for permission to quote from Peter Sutton's letter of 3 September 1939. He would also like to thank the Trustees of the National Library of Scotland for their permission to quote from the Haig papers and the Trustees of the Liddell Hart Centre for Military Archives for permission to quote from the manuscript memoirs of Sir E.H.L. Beddington. He is indebted to the Trustees of Lambeth Palace Library for access to material in their library's care. All material from George MacDonald Fraser's *Quartered Safe Out Here* is reprinted by kind permission of HarperCollins Publishers Ltd © (George MacDonald Fraser, 1993). Material from *The Recollections of Rifleman Bowlby* is reproduced by kind permission of Pen and Sword and extracts from all Mass-Observation material is reproduced with permission of Curtis Brown Group Ltd, London, on behalf of the Trustees of the Mass-Observation Archive, Copyright © Trustees of the Mass-Observation Archive. Every reasonable effort has been made to contact the owners of copyright material cited in this book but this has proved impossible in some cases. The author would be grateful for any information that might lead to further copyright acknowledgements in future editions and extends his apologies in advance for any omissions which it may contain.

ABBREVIATIONS

ABA	Archdiocese of Birmingham Archives
ABCA	Army Bureau of Current Affairs
AChD	Army Chaplains' Department
ATS	Auxiliary Territorial Service
BBC	British Broadcasting Corporation
BEF	British Expeditionary Force
CIGS	Chief of the Imperial General Staff
CMS	Church Missionary Society
CO	Commanding Officer
CVWW	Council of Voluntary War Work
CWL	Catholic Women's League
EEF	Egyptian Expeditionary Force
ENSA	Entertainments National Service Association
FAU	Friends Ambulance Unit
GHQ	General Headquarters
GOC	General Officer Commanding
HQ	Headquarters
IWM	Imperial War Museum
LPL	Lambeth Palace Library
MC	Military Cross
MO	Mass-Observation
NAAFI	Navy, Army and Air Force Institute
NCO	Non-commissioned Officer
NSL	National Service League
POW	Prisoner of War
PP	Parliamentary Papers
PRO	Public Records Office
RAChD	Royal Army Chaplains' Department
RAF	Royal Air Force

RAMC	Royal Army Medical Corps
RAP	Regimental Aid Post
REME	Royal Electrical and Mechanical Engineers
RSM	Regimental Sergeant Major
SPCK	Society for Promoting Christian Knowledge
Toc H	Talbot House
VC	Victoria Cross
WAAC	Women's Army Auxiliary Corps
YMCA	Young Men's Christian Association
YWCA	Young Women's Christian Association

INTRODUCTION

The secularisation debate, war and the soldier

'MEN IN UNIFORM CAN'T REALLY be considered religious, unless it be a Christian profundity that makes a Gunner say Jesus Christ! when he drops a shell on his foot.'[1] These words from Spike Milligan's memoirs of his service in the Royal Artillery during the Second World War express some important assumptions as to the state of religion in British society and in the British army at this time. Religion, it is claimed, was an irrelevance, particularly for a generation of young men trained to deliver destruction through the most modern means that the industrial age could supply. Implicit also in this claim is the common view that the life of the soldier is in itself profane and defies the norms of respectable civilian society. Ironically, and although he may not have realised this, Milligan was fully in concurrence with the churches in holding this opinion, for the lifestyle of the common soldier had vexed and concerned Christian moralists since the seventeenth century. In fact, by the late nineteenth century, the British army had become a mission field in its own right, this status being symbolised by the numerous soldiers' homes run by Christian philanthropists in garrisons throughout the British empire.

By this time, of course, most of the nation's religious commentators were also convinced that the churches faced the much broader challenge of an ever-encroaching tide of popular irreligion. From their perspective, it appeared that the intellectual climate engendered by the Enlightenment and the economic, social and demographic effects of the Industrial Revolution had been inimical to the interests of the churches. They had led to an urban and class-ridden society in which the seemingly natural and consensual religiosity of the pre-industrial age had been shattered by economic, social and demographic upheaval and by the overarching and inexorable progress of modern science, technology and intellectual inquiry. Informing this view of secularisation was a growing body of national and local evidence. This demonstrated that, whatever the perplexities of the educated classes, it was the teeming multitudes of the urban working classes who were most alienated from the churches and who presented them with their most formidable pastoral and missionary challenge. In the immediate aftermath of the First World War, this problem was underlined in the form of *The Army and Religion* report of 1919, a report that addressed the religious impact of army life and of industrialised warfare on the mainly working-class soldiers of the British army. Drawing on an impressive range of chaplains' and soldiers' testimonies collected during the latter stages of the war, the report drew conclusions that were largely negative and equally predetermined. David Cairns, the Scottish Presbyterian academic who authored the report, had declared as early as January 1917 that:

> My feeling is that what the Churches need is to have brought before them the real state of matters, viz. that they have lost, or are in danger of losing the faith of the nation, and that they have got to look deeply into the matter and set their hearts and minds to the problem of how the situation may, by God's grace, be retrieved before it is too late.[2]

The view that British society was secularised as a consequence of the Enlightenment and of the Industrial Revolution has been strongly held in ecclesiastical and academic circles. In the former, it has instigated a mournful rhetoric of defeat and, in the latter, a pronounced and occasionally obsessive interest in statistics of religious practice and in the chronology of this decline.[3] Despite some robust challenges and extensive fine-tuning over the years, the view that the secularisation of British society was driven by a 'working-class evacuation of the churches'[4] that was complete by the turn of the twentieth century has assumed the status of a historical orthodoxy. Much like Milligan's comments on religion, this view has at its heart a fundamental paradox. If Milligan was quick to dismiss the importance of religion for his fellow soldiers, his memoirs of life in the army are curiously riddled with religious incidents, jokes and reflections.[5] In a similar manner, the literature that has traced and debated the chronology of the secularisation of Britain from the Industrial Revolution to the first half of the twentieth century has great difficulty in reconciling falling levels of public religious observance with other indicators of the enduring strength of Christian belief and practice among Britain's urban working classes.

These indicators have become apparent from various oral history projects and their implications have been comprehensively explored by Sarah Williams in her seminal study *Religious Belief and Popular Culture in Southwark c.1880–1939* (1999). However, if this local study constituted a serious enough challenge to received wisdom, Callum Brown produced a full-scale critique of the classic view of secularisation in the form of his book *The Death of Christian Britain* (2001). In this radical reassessment of the place of religion in British society since 1800, Brown emphasised the enduring cultural strength of Christianity in British society from the Industrial Revolution to the 1960s, reinterpreting the British as 'a highly religious nation, and the period as [Britain's] last puritan age'.[6] Focusing on the massive, sustained and multi-faceted missionary endeavour of the churches (an enterprise that was itself born of fears of burgeoning godlessness), Brown underlined the pervasive influence of religion in the British media and in British popular culture, arguing that Britain's 'salvation industry' created 'a unifying Christian environ-ment which commandeered the vehicles of public discourse, penetrating home and office, school and hospital, street and pub, parliament and town hall'.[7] In reviewing the superficially damning statistics of regular churchgoing, Brown stressed the significance of habits of occasional churchgoing, of Sunday school attendance and of the British people's 'very strong attachment to religious baptisms, marriages and funerals'.[8] While conceding that the unskilled work-ing classes were the social constituency that was least disposed to public religious practice, Brown stressed that the demography of British society still ensured that 'The working classes made up the majority of churchgoers in virtually every denomination in every period from 1800 to the 1960s, with the skilled working class of artisans and tradesmen being particularly numerous in congregations'.[9] Rather than accepting the primacy of social class in deter-mining the place and fate of religion in national life, Brown underlined the importance of gender in popular religious culture. In doing so, he stressed the potency and prevalence of a church-sponsored discourse that became dominant in the nineteenth century and that laid equal stress on 'the essential femininity of piety and the essential irreligion of masculinity'.[10] Within a religious culture shaped by these ideas, male piety was subordinate and even problematic. It was female piety, especially in the home environment, which formed the bedrock of popular religiosity and it was women's abandonment of their ascribed religious role and identity that drove the relatively sudden and dramatic secularisation of British society from the 1960s.[11]

This book seeks to present new perspectives and new evidence on the role and importance of religion in British society in the first half of the twentieth century by focusing on two generations of British soldiers and their religious experiences in the two World Wars. Consequently, it will draw on the revisionist work of Sarah Williams and Callum Brown as well as on the more traditional interpretations of those who have championed the classic view of secularisation in modern Britain. Remarkably, and despite their perennial interest for British historians, no major study has yet been published on the religious impact of the two World Wars upon the British people. This situation has not been helped by the fact that military and religious historians of modern Britain tend to inhabit separate and mutually uncomprehending worlds. While the former have largely failed to recognise the underlying importance of religion in these conflicts, the latter have proved distinctly squeamish about studying the religious dimensions of the two World Wars. On the basis of the existing literature, for the majority of church historians these dimensions seem to consist of the positions and perplexities of prominent churchmen and of the history and heroes of Christian pacifism.[12] Notwithstanding the importance of religion for such growing areas of academic interest as the rise of the cult of remembrance in the inter-war period, the lack of detailed research into popular religious life during the war years remains a major lacuna in the extensive historiography of British society in the First and Second World Wars.

A lack of serious research has not, however, prevented some bold assertions from being made as to the adverse effects of these conflicts in religious terms. In *Church and People in an Industrial City*, a classic study of the role and decline of the churches in industrial Sheffield, E.R. Wickham argued that the First World War had a 'catastrophic' impact on the churches and 'devastating effects on the religious life of the nation' at large. Ultimately, it heightened religious doubt and scepticism among 'the more serious-minded' and triggered a popular reaction 'against "organised religion"'.[13] Similarly, the most ambitious statistical study of the process of secularisation in modern Britain perceived the two World Wars as having a disastrous effect on pre-war patterns of religious observance and attachment.[14] However, such conclusions are highly questionable, ignoring as they do the existence of compulsory religious observance in the armed forces, the palpable sense of moral and religious purpose engendered by the two World Wars and even the widespread damage and destruction caused to church buildings in urban areas between 1940 and 1945. In fact, and far from viewing the First and Second World Wars as calamitous for religious life in Britain, more recent studies have begun to reveal a complex and multifaceted *revival* of religion in British society as a result of these conflicts.[15] In this respect, such studies parallel and complement recent research into the French experience of the First World War and the Soviet experience of the Second. This research has demonstrated how, even in these aggressively secular and atheistic modern societies, religious life flourished amidst wars of unparalleled destructiveness and intensity.[16]

In studying the religious experience of the British soldier in the two World Wars we are by implication addressing the strength and significance of religion in contemporary British society as a whole. Not only was the army the largest of the nation's armed forces in both World Wars but it was also recruited from all social classes, from every corner of the British Isles and (increasingly) from both sexes. However, given its overwhelmingly male composition and the structure of a society in which more than 70 per cent of the male workforce were classed as manual workers,[17] we are largely concerned with the wartime attitudes and behaviour of young, working-class males – men who were the citizen soldiers of a modern, industrial and urbanised society. If class, gender, war and the varied influences of modernity can be argued to have been crucial factors in the process of secularisation, their collective experience can tell us much about the strength, influence and dynamics of contemporary British religion. It can also provide some key insights into other variables in British religious life – variables such as age, ethnicity, denomination and locality. However, and before throwing ourselves into this study, it is necessary to note some important contextual points concerning the development of the British army during the two World Wars and the formidable military challenges that it had to overcome in the bloody and prolonged course of each.

The British army in two World Wars

Between 1914 and 1918 and 1939 and 1945, the professional 'peacetime' character and composition of the British army was transformed by the mobilisation of its Territorial and Reserve forces and by a massive influx of wartime volunteers and conscripts. Between 4 August 1914 and 11 November 1918 (and in addition to the 800,000 men of the pre-war regular army, Territorial Force and the Army and Special Reserves) more than 4,970,000 men volunteered or were called up for the army, a figure that represented 22 per cent of the male population of the United Kingdom.[18] In addition, thousands of women swelled the pre-war ranks of the regular and Territorial nursing services. From March 1917, the other roles that female volunteers were playing in army work were recognised and extended with the creation of the Women's Army Auxiliary Corps, which counted more than 40,000 women in its ranks at the peak of its strength in November 1918.[19] Although the army's expansion during the Second World War was rather less dramatic, its eventual wartime strength still ran into millions. At the outbreak of war in September 1939, the army's regular, Territorial and Reserve forces numbered just over 892,000 men plus nearly 23,000 women of the Queen Alexandra's Imperial Military Nursing Service and the newly formed Auxiliary Territorial Service. By the end of the war in Europe, and with the army at the peak of its wartime expansion, this number had risen to 2,920,000 men plus just over 200,000 women, the vast majority of whom were serving in the ATS.[20] Although this total was significantly less than the 3,500,000 men and 64,000 women mustered by the army in November 1918,[21] the army nevertheless accounted for more than 62 per cent of the fighting strength of the nation's armed forces in the summer of 1945.[22]

In addition to the substantial development of the army's female services, the massive growth of the army during the two World Wars was accompanied by a significant broadening of its social composition. Despite sustained attempts by the War Office to enhance the quality of its recruits, in 1914 and in 1939 the ranks of Britain's regular army were still largely filled by unskilled men from the lowest strata of the urban working classes. Despite the mass unemployment of the inter-war period, the unattractiveness of army life was reflected in the fact that, in 1939 as in 1914, the regular army was still significantly under strength.[23] Although the Territorial Force (or Territorial Army as it was renamed in 1921) proved somewhat better at attracting a higher standard of recruit from its creation in 1908,[24] even part-time soldiering failed to attract an adequate number of enthusiasts.[25] Thus, the creation of citizen armies in the course of the two World Wars was accompanied by a massive influx of men from social groups that had traditionally shunned the army as a career and that had proved only slightly more susceptible to the Territorial system. This broadening of the social profile of the rank and file was also reflected among the army's regimental officers. High casualty rates in the First World War and the political pressures of a 'people's war' in the Second helped to generate a wartime officer corps that, in its lower echelons at least, was more socially diverse than that which had led the pre-war and inter-war regular army.[26]

If the army became more broadly based in gender and in social terms during both World Wars, in ethnic terms the composition of its British component was somewhat narrower in the Second. Relative to their share of total population, at 8.6 and 2.4 per cent respectively, the Scots and the Welsh had been under-represented among the rank and file of the regular army in 1914. However, the English were somewhat over-represented at 79.4 per cent and the Irish had more or less broken even at 9.6 per cent.[27] Of the army's 4,970,000 wartime recruits, 80.6 per cent were English, 11.2 per cent were Scottish, 5.5 per cent were Welsh and only 2.7 per cent were recruited in Ireland.[28] Chronic problems in Irish recruitment in the First World War were, of course, largely attributable to the disaffected state of Nationalist Ireland. The turbulent state of pre-war Irish politics ensured that the Territorial Force had not been established in Ireland in 1908 as it had been in mainland Britain. Although the Military Service (No. 2) Act of April 1918 notionally extended conscription to Ireland's male population, its terms were not implemented before the end of the war. Despite the magnanimous stance adopted by the leaders of the Irish Parliamentary Party in the light of the promise of Home Rule, and a consequent surge of recruits for Kitchener's New Armies in the early months of the war, Nationalist Ireland was to prove highly resistant to calls for more men in the longer term. This situation was exacerbated by the growing strength of Republicanism in the aftermath of the Easter Rising of 1916 and by the contemporary threat of conscription. Following the Anglo-Irish War of 1919–21 and the subsequent creation of the Irish Free State, five of the British army's Irish infantry regiments were disbanded, though not before some Irish troops had evinced worrying signs of disaffection.[29] By 1922, the Irish proportion of the regular army had fallen to 3.1 per cent – only a third of what it had been prior to the First World War.[30] However, and despite this dramatic fall in the army's proportion of Irish soldiers, the Irish Free State continued to furnish a trickle of recruits for the regular army throughout the inter-war period.[31]

The continuing links between the British army and southern Ireland were clearly exposed during the Second World War, when around 43,000 men and women who had been born in Eire voluntarily joined the British armed services.[32] By 1944, nearly 28,000 (or just over 1 per cent) of the army's officers and other ranks had been born in southern Ireland, with a further 3,060 Irish women serving with the ATS, a figure that represented 1.5 per cent of its total strength.[33] Largely at Churchill's instigation, an 'Irish brigade' was created in 1942 that harked back to the exploits of the 'Wild Geese' and that underlined the continuing association of Irishmen with the British army notwithstanding the official neutrality of Eire.[34] In the longer term, the reduction of Ireland's contribution to the British army helped to ensure that the predominance of its English constituency was even more marked in the Second World War than it had been in the First. Exclusive of the ATS, by 1944 82.9 per cent of all British soldiers who had been born in the British empire were English, while only 9.6 per cent had been born in Scotland and 4.4 per cent had been born in Wales.[35]

If the ethnic profile of the British army was quite different in the two World Wars, then so too were the means by which the army was expanded. In 1914–15, Lord Kitchener, then Secretary of State for War, created a 'New Army' of thirty divisions that was to take its place alongside the Regulars and the Territorials. Like their Territorial counterparts, many New Army units had strong local and regional connections, the apotheosis of this phenomenon being the scores of locally raised 'Pals' battalions that figured so prominently among the later New Army divisions.[36] Although popular as a recruiting strategy, the raising of the New Army and of its Pals battalions arguably had the effect of preventing the army from using the skills of its individual recruits to the full. Furthermore, the enormous casualties that the Pals battalions incurred brought terrible tragedy to many communities across the British Isles. During the course of the First World War, and particularly after the commencement of the battle of the Somme in the summer of 1916, the original identity of New Army units was inexorably diluted by casualties, by conscription, by transfers and by the wholesale reorganisation of the BEF on the Western Front in early 1918.

The New Army experiment of the First World War was not to be repeated in the Second. From the early 1920s, it was envisaged that the Territorial Army would provide the basis for any future wartime expansion of the army. Existing Territorial units constituted 'First Line' Territorial divisions and provided cadres for second and third lines where necessary.[37] Although limited conscription for the army commenced in May 1939, on the outbreak of war in September a much wider National Service (Armed Forces) Act ensured that conscription provided the bulk of the army's manpower for the duration of the war.[38] Particularly in view of the army's relative unpopularity alongside the Royal Navy and RAF, conscription was certainly necessary.[39] Furthermore, and as the war progressed, a closely regulated wartime economy ensured that the army found itself in fierce competition for manpower and skills with Civil Defence, war-related industries and the other armed services.[40] Consequently, from 1941 a determined attempt was mounted from within the army itself to make more effective use of its personnel. In the post-Dunkirk period, Sir Ronald Adam, the General Officer Commanding Northern Command, encouraged an army psychiatrist to undertake experiments among men in his training units. The results were not encouraging, demonstrating that unsuitable men were routinely being sent to the army. However, the blame did not lie entirely with civilian bureaucrats. In September 1941, a committee chaired by Sir William Beveridge found that the army was widely misusing the talents of its skilled tradesmen.[41] The army's efforts to improve the situation were led by Adam after he became adjutant-general at the War Office in June 1941. His campaign was spearheaded by a new Directorate of Personnel Selection that determined the attributes required for the various jobs in the army and devised intelligence and aptitude tests for new recruits in order to fill them. From the summer of 1942, all recruits were also required to spend the initial period of their basic training in the General Service Corps. From here, after being tested and subjected to infantry training, recruits were dispatched to training centres appropriate for their allotted branch of service.[42] Although scientific in its procedures and necessary in itself, this system inevitably developed at the expense of the cultural and regional homogeneity that had characterised much of the British army in the early years of the First World War.

Perhaps the greatest difference between the British army of the two World Wars lay in the mechanisation of the army in the inter-war period, a process that was not solely the consequence of technological progress. As a result of the army's sanguinary experiences on the Western Front, Britain's military theorists and the army's General Staff looked with horror upon the prospect of another static and attritional conflict and came to favour a dependence on mechanised firepower and mobility in the event of another European war.[43] By the late 1930s, therefore, the internal combustion engine had virtually superseded the horse for military purposes. Throughout the years of the Second World War, its own doctrine dictated that the British army should fight 'using the maximum quantity of machinery and the minimum number of men in the front line'.[44] However, mechanisation did not simply involve a greater provision of lorries and the exchange of horses for armoured vehicles in cavalry regiments. The technical and logistical requirements of a mechanised army and the doctrine of combined arms by which it sought to bring its various components into battle accelerated the diversification of the soldier's trade. As Correlli Barnett has observed, 'Whereas for centuries a "soldier" had been a man with a musket or a sabre or a cannon, he could now be an electrician, a typist-clerk, a telecommunications expert, an accountant, an industrial craftsman'.[45]

The diversification of the British army was inevitably accompanied by the reduction of its front-line strength and by the commensurate expansion of its technical, logistical and administrative 'tail'. In 1914, 74 per cent of its soldiers had served in fighting units but by 1935 this percentage had fallen to 58 per cent. A contemporary calculation even estimated that each vehicle supplied to the army added 2.5 soldiers to its maintenance echelons. In January 1941, the burden of maintaining the army in the Middle East was reflected in the fact that each division of 18,000 men required a further 41,000 men engaged in maintenance and supply work to keep it in the field.[46] During the Burma campaign, where the local infrastructure was even less developed, this figure soared to 56,000.[47] Even in the conventional infantry division, which by the middle of the war had its own lavish supply of vehicles, front-line infantrymen comprised only a quarter of the division's total strength.[48] Galled by such statistics, Churchill raged that there was too much 'fluff and flummery' behind the fighting troops[49] and sourly claimed that the army was far more likely to crowd dentists' chairs and YMCA institutions than fighting men into any future bridgehead in Europe.[50] The cutting edge of Churchill's army was reduced still further by the major anti-aircraft role that the army had acquired prior to the Second World War. At its peak, Anti-Aircraft Command had a strength of several thousand anti-aircraft guns and around half a million personnel, including 170,000 women.[51] Despite being enhanced by the presence of the ATS, life in Anti-Aircraft Command was not characterised by its activity or excitement and the caricature of an isolated gun-site between the villages of Great and Little Snoring was one that would have been familiar to many hapless gunners.[52]

Despite the great discrepancy in fatal casualties incurred by the British army during the two World Wars (approximately 705,000 in the First as compared to 144,000 in the Second),[53] both World Wars represented a significant departure from earlier conflicts insofar as enemy action accounted for far more fatalities than did disease. Obviously, there were some local exceptions to this general rule. In Salonika, Mesopotamia and East Africa during the First World War disease still proved a far greater killer than the enemy.[54] Moreover, in Burma during the Second World War, the ratio of sick to battle casualties never fell below 10:1 and in 1942 it was in excess of 250:1.[55] Nevertheless, by the end of the Second World War, the British army had clearly benefited from a twentieth-century revolution in military medicine, with the British soldier being in no more danger of dying of disease in 1943 than his civilian counterpart at home.[56] Furthermore, medical and surgical advances in the inter-war period also served to reduce mortality among the wounded. In the Second World War, the widespread use of penicillin, sulphonamides, blood transfusions and air evacuation ensured far higher survival rates than those which had been obtained thirty years earlier. In 1914–18, the mortality rate for chest wounds was 54 per cent and for amputees 70 per cent; during the Second World War these figures were reduced to 5.7 per cent and 20 per cent respectively.[57]

Despite being separated by only a single generation, the character of the British army and the circumstances in which it fought the Second World War were therefore often strikingly different from those of 1914–18. The army's Irish component was much reduced and the British army in the Second World War did not cultivate the same degree of regional association which it had in the First. Far from being a largely infantry force, as it had been in 1914, the British army between 1939 and 1945 was a highly mechanised entity. Front-line troops were in a minority and it sought to fight battles as economically as possible in human terms. This cardinal military doctrine of the British army, as well as its lengthy vacation from mainland Europe between 1941 and 1943, ensured that its casualties were much fewer than those that it had incurred on the Western Front between 1914 and 1918. Furthermore, whereas the British army had played the leading role in the defeat of the German army on the Western Front in 1918, its contribution to Allied victory in 1945 was dwarfed by the Soviet and American armies and at least matched by the Royal Air Force and the Royal Navy. Quite apart from these tactical and strategic considerations, life expectancy was also enhanced by key advances in medical science that rendered soldiers far less susceptible to fatal diseases or to premature death from wounds received. As we shall be seeing, the generations that fought these wars were also regarded as being temperamentally very different from each other and as requiring rather different handling.

The challenge of the two World Wars

In August 1914, and in response to the German invasion of Belgium, the original British Expeditionary Force of four infantry divisions and one cavalry division sailed for northern France. On 23 August, and in conjunction with their French allies, the regulars and reservists of the BEF fought their first major battle of the First World War around the Belgian town of Mons. Driven back by the sheer weight of the German offensive, the BEF conducted a desperate fighting retreat deep into northern France before turning to play a significant part in the successful counter-offensive mounted by the French on the river Marne in early September. The subsequent German retreat to a defensible line on the river Aisne triggered the so-called 'race to the sea', during which both the Allies and the Germans attempted to manoeuvre around each other's western flank. In its closing stages, the BEF successfully held the Belgian town of Ypres against a succession of German attacks in October and November. By the end of 1914, the war of manoeuvre on the Western Front had effectively ceased and a state of prolonged and largely static trench warfare had been inaugurated that was to last until the German spring offensive of March 1918. Whatever the strategic consequences of the inconclusive fighting of 1914, the effects on the BEF had been shattering, its 90,000 casualties being more than the original number of British soldiers who had landed in France that August. Inevitably, from the First Battle of Ypres onwards, the non-professional soldiers of the Territorial Force and the New Army were to play an ever-increasing role in Britain's burgeoning military effort on the Western Front and elsewhere.

If the latter months of 1914 frustrated hopes of a swift Allied victory, then the next three years were also plagued by strategic failure on the Western Front. As the relatively inexperienced BEF grew in the course of 1915 (repulsing a further German offensive around Ypres in April and May), successive if comparatively minor British offensives failed at Neuve Chapelle, Aubers Ridge, Festubert, Givenchy and Loos. Moreover, a combined Allied military and naval offensive against Turkey, Germany's ally since October 1914, met with dismal and bloody failure along the shores of the Dardanelles, culminating in wholesale evacuation in January 1916. By this point, it was abundantly clear that only conscription could meet the army's manpower needs for the duration of the war. However, and despite the passage of two Military Service Acts in January and May, the weight of the mainly British offensive on the Somme in the summer and autumn of 1916 was still largely borne by the volunteers who comprised the army's Regular, Territorial and New Army divisions. If 1916 saw defeat in the Dardanelles and disappointment on the Somme, the year also saw stagnation in Salonika (to which British forces had been sent in the autumn of 1915 in order to assist Serbia) and the most humiliating British defeat of the war at Kut-el-Amara in Mesopotamia, where an invading Anglo-Indian force was compelled to surrender to the Turks after a four month siege.

Despite the offensive failures of the previous two years on the Western Front, the spring and early summer of 1917 witnessed progress of sorts in British offensives at Arras and Messines. Although no breakthrough was achieved in either case, the British line was appreciably advanced and British success (however limited) contrasted sharply with the near-catastrophic failure of the French offensive on the Chemin des Dames. This failure triggered a wave of mutinies in the French army and shifted the greater weight of the offensive burden on the Western Front onto the shoulders of the BEF for the remainder of the war. However, the glow of earlier British successes in 1917 was dimmed by the Third Battle of Ypres of July to November. Although Sir Douglas Haig had initially envisaged a sweeping advance out of the Ypres salient and towards the Flanders coast, the offensive stalled due to heavy German resistance, adverse weather and appalling ground conditions. The furthest extent of the British advance was the Passchendaele ridge, a few miles north-east of Ypres, which fell to the BEF's Canadian corps in early November. If there is evidence that British morale was sorely tried by the experience of Third Ypres, the much smaller offensive at Cambrai later that November restored some hope of better things to come – at least initially. Using an unprecedented concentration of tanks (which the BEF had used in smaller numbers and with mixed success since September 1916) the British ploughed through the formidable Hindenburg Line in a surprise attack that met with considerable success in its opening phase. However, Haig's decision to prolong the offensive despite a lack of reserves proved mistaken and a devastating German counter-attack at the end of November drove the British back to their original positions. By the end of 1917, British setbacks on the Western Front were yet again compounded by the misfortunes of its allies. In addition to the Russian collapse on the Eastern Front in the wake of the Bolshevik revolution, the autumn of 1917 saw the rout of the Italian army at Caporetto, a calamity that prompted the dispatch of five badly needed British divisions from the Western Front to north-eastern Italy. Despite this gloomy situation, the British army enjoyed better success in 1917 in its subsidiary theatres of war. In Mesopotamia, the British defeat at Kut was avenged by the recapture of the town and by a successful drive upon Baghdad, which fell to the British in March. More success was enjoyed against the Turks in Palestine, where the Egyptian Expeditionary Force, which was commanded by Sir Edmund Allenby from June 1917, eventually broke through the Turkish lines at Beersheba at the end of October. In the wake of the Turkish retreat, Jerusalem fell to the EEF in early December.

Notwithstanding the arrival of increasing numbers of American troops, 1918 saw the war very nearly lost on the Western Front. With the transfer of large numbers of seasoned troops from the Eastern Front, the Germans enjoyed the strategic initiative at the beginning of the year and launched a massive and devastating offensive against the right flank of the British line in northern France on 21 March. Thrown into disarray by the extensive use of new German infiltration tactics, the right flank of the BEF was subsequently driven back some forty miles. However, and after incurring heavy losses, the German advance eventually petered out amidst the wastelands of the former Somme battlefield and subsequent offensives directed at the Allies in April and May failed to revive its early momentum. By late July, the initiative again lay with the Allies, who were ready to go onto the offensive under the overall command of the French general Ferdinand Foch. Following the success of a Franco-American counter-offensive near Soissons, Foch and Haig launched a spectacular counter-strike by the BEF near Amiens in early August. Supported by hundreds of British tanks and by nearly 2,000 Allied aeroplanes, Canadian and Australian infantry smashed into the German positions and initiated a steady British advance that was to last until the end of the war in the west on 11 November. However, the forward momentum of the 'last hundred days' was maintained at very heavy cost and generally without the lavish scale of tank and air support available at Amiens. British casualties (excluding Australian and Canadian) numbered nearly 275,000 in the last four months of the war. Nevertheless, the British army's contribution to Allied victory cannot be gainsaid, the BEF being primarily responsible for the emphatic defeat of the German army in the field. Elsewhere, in the Middle East, Salonika and on the Italian Front, the closing months of the war were also marked by ultimate if still costly success. In September 1918, Allenby resumed his advance in Palestine, the British and their Arab allies having captured Damascus and Beirut by the time of the Turkish armistice on 30 October. In Salonika, British forces played a major supporting role in breaking through Bulgarian lines in September and, in Italy, the mainly British Tenth Army formed much of the cutting edge of the concluding Italian offensive of the war at Vittorio Veneto.

If the First World War had been a terrible trial for the British army, its experiences between 1939 and 1945 were arguably worse in some respects. Despite fewer fatal casualties, the prestige of the army was battered by recurrent catastrophes between 1940 and 1942. On the outbreak of war in September 1939, a BEF was once again dispatched to France. Originally consisting of four regular divisions, its size had been augmented by an incomplete armoured division, another regular and eight Territorial infantry divisions by the time the 'Phoney War' in the west came to an abrupt end with the German invasion of the Low Countries and France in May 1940. With elements of the British army having already shown themselves to be inferior to the Germans in Norway, the BEF was badly mauled and very nearly annihilated by the Germans in the Franco-Belgian campaign of May–June 1940. Although the rapid collapse of French, Belgian and Dutch resistance added greatly to its misfortunes, the campaign nevertheless exposed serious defects in the British army's pre-war training, equipment, systems of command and tactical doctrine. Furthermore, and despite the tenacity of certain units, the ratio of fatal losses to prisoners of war (some 3,500 to 40,000) suggested an emphatic refusal on the part of the British soldier to fight to the last man and the last round. If the reputation of the army was partly redeemed after the Norwegian and French fiascos by successive British triumphs against the Italians in Libya and East Africa, these victories brought with them a nagging awareness that British and Commonwealth troops were here confronting an enemy that was decidedly inferior not only to themselves but also to the Germans.

Whatever encouragement could be garnered from victory over the Italians in the opening months of 1941, the following spring brought further disaster in the wake of renewed contact with the German army. Not only did the dispatch ooff British and Commonwealth troops from North Africa to Greece in March prevent the destruction of the Italians in Libya, but the campaign in Greece ended in yet another ignominious evacuation April and in the German invasion and capture of Crete in May. Meanwhile, the arrival of General Erwin Rommel and his *Afrika Korps* in Libya that February not only guaranteed Italian survival but also signalled the commencement of two further years of campaigning in North Africa for Britain's hitherto victorious Western Desert Force. The first eighteen months of warfare against Rommel was a searing experience for British and Commonwealth arms, months that underlined continuing weaknesses in British command, tactics, equipment and morale. If partially redeemed by the successful defence of Tobruk from April to December 1941, the overall performance of the Western Desert Force (which was re-designated Eighth Army in December 1941) was decidedly lacklustre in this highly fluid campaign. Indeed, the fall of Tobruk and the retreat to Egypt in the face of a renewed Axis offensive in the early summer of 1942 marked the nadir of British military fortunes in the Second World War. Although Rommel's attempts on the Suez Canal were checked at the First Battle of Alamein in July and at Alam Halfa in September, it was not until late October that the Eighth Army went onto the offensive once more. Under the vigorous leadership of its new commander, Lieutenant-General Bernard Law Montgomery, the Eighth Army's deficiencies had been substantially remedied and the success of Montgomery's methods was demonstrated in the Second Battle of Alamein which, though bloody and essentially attritional, saw the near destruction of Rommel's *Panzerarmee Afrika*. Despite this crushing victory, Hitler's decision to reinforce and hold Tunisia in the face of the Eighth Army's advance from the east and of Anglo-American landings in Morocco and Algeria prolonged the war in North Africa until May 1943, when nearly 250,000 Germans and Italians finally surrendered at Cape Bon.

While the pendulum of victory swung to and fro in North Africa, the British army was also coming to grips with a formidable new adversary in the Far East. Here the burden of campaigning fell largely on the shoulders of the vastly expanded Indian army. However, there was still a substantial presence of British units on the ground, with most Indian brigades containing a British battalion and some wholly British divisions serving in this theatre of war. The entry of Japan into the war in December 1941 found British and Indian forces poorly prepared and unduly self-confident, their spectacular discomfiture being marked by the rapid fall of Hong Kong, Malaya, Singapore and Burma, a period of defeat that concluded with Japanese forces establishing themselves on the north-eastern borders of India. Significantly, and whatever reverses the Germans succeeded in inflicting on the British army in Europe and North Africa, it was in the Far East that the British army experienced the worst defeat in its history in the fall of Singapore and its longest retreat in the evacuation of Burma. Although attempts to counter-attack from the Indian border along the Arakan coast failed in late 1942, a moral if costly victory was achieved through Orde Wingate's first long-range Chindit expedition of February to May 1943, an expedition that saw British, Gurkha and Burmese troops raid deep into Japanese territory. The following year saw a second and much larger Chindit expedition into Burma, this foray coinciding with two Japanese offensives that marked their long-awaited invasion of India. However, the Fourteenth Army, which had been under the command of the formidable Lieutenant-General William Slim since its creation in the autumn of 1943, showed that months of further training, re-equipment and growing confidence had paid off. These twin Japanese offensives were emphatically defeated between February and July 1944 in the Arakan and around the Indian border towns of Imphal and Kohima.

If the course of 1943 and 1944 saw the revival of British fortunes in the Far East, then this period also saw the return of the British army to coalition warfare on the continent of Europe, although by this stage its primacy in Western Europe had been ceded to the Americans. After absorbing the First Army, which had arrived in Algeria the previous November, the Eighth Army landed in Sicily in July 1943, subsequently playing a major role in the invasion of Italy in September and in the ensuing Italian campaign. Although the Eighth Army bore the brunt of Britain's ground war in the Mediterranean and furnished Montgomery and some of its veteran divisions for the invasion of France, the cross-Channel invasion of June 1944 and the subsequent campaign in north-west Europe was undertaken by the largely untried troops of the Second Army. With its commanders constrained by nagging concerns over morale, a chronic shortage of replacements and by the resultant need to keep human losses to a minimum, the Second Army's operations in north-west Europe bore the hallmark of lessons learned in the First World War and of experience gained in North Africa and elsewhere. They were, in fact, characterised by heavy artillery support, close liaison with the RAF, better systems of command and by a marked preference for carefully controlled, set-piece battles in which combined arms and material superiority would ultimately prevail over German tenacity. Despite some setbacks (not least of which was the virtual destruction of the 1st Airborne Division at Arnhem in September 1944) the Second Army proved fit for its offensive purpose and succeeded in sustaining its advance through France, Belgium, southern Holland and Germany until Germany's surrender in May 1945. While the Eighth Army slogged its way up the Italian peninsula until the end of the war in Europe, the Fourteenth Army also showed its offensive mettle during the later stages of the Burma campaign, its steady advance from the Indian border commencing in December 1944 and continuing until the surrender of Japan nine months later.

As this necessarily brief outline will have shown, the two World Wars were hardly years of unbroken triumph for the British army and ultimate success in its operations was due to a variety of factors. Victory on land depended on the successful implementation of difficult and potentially costly offensive strategies in both World Wars. In pursuing these strategies, the British army was heavily dependent on Allied and Commonwealth support and on the effective co-operation of land, sea and (increasingly) air power. Although Britain's land operations clearly required the enormous material resources of an advanced industrial society to sustain them, the army was also compelled to remove senior commanders and regimental officers who were not up to the mark and to constantly adapt its organisation, tactics, weaponry and operational planning to current needs. Finally, and most crucially from the point of view of this study, because it was reliant on non-professional soldiers, the army also had to pay very careful attention to the mood and motivation of its civilians in arms. As the following chapters will show, this consideration had major ramifications in religious terms, demonstrating and underlining the importance of religion and of religious agencies in relation to the all important morale of the British soldier.

Chapter 1

'DIFFUSIVE CHRISTIANITY' AND THE RELIGION OF THE SOLDIER

Introduction

BY 1914 MANY OF MAINLAND BRITAIN'S Protestant clergy were uncomfortably aware of declining levels of church membership and church attendance. Although habits of non-attendance were entrenched in many urban working-class areas, by this time the decline of religious practice among the middle classes was also becoming apparent.[1] The problematic findings of the parliamentary Census of Religious Worship of 1851 had caused consternation by suggesting that less than half of the population of England and Wales were churchgoers (statistics from Scotland were more fragmentary).[2] By 1914, however, the figures seemed much worse. According to the most comprehensive statistical study of churchgoing in modern Britain, the major Protestant denominations in England, Scotland and Wales had approximately 5,682,000 official adherents out of a total population of nearly 42 million. This figure comprised 2,437,000 Anglican communicants (including those of the Scottish Episcopal Church), 1,242,000 Scottish Presbyterian communicants and 2,003,000 members of the larger and more established Nonconformist denominations, which included the Baptists, the Congregationalists, the English and Welsh Presbyterians and the various branches of Methodism. By 1946, however, the tally of committed Anglicans and Non-conformists had declined markedly both in absolute and in relative terms, developments such as the union of the Wesleyan, Primitive and United Methodist churches in 1932 doing nothing to reverse this trend in the longer term. In 1946, and out of a population of nearly 48 million, the principal Protestant denominations now counted only 5,030,000 members and communicants, comprising 1,987,000 Anglican and 1,297,000 Scottish Presbyterian communicants and 1,746,000 members of the major Nonconformist churches.[3]

However, this overall picture (and the churches' longstanding preoccupation with statistics of formal religious affiliation and observance) should not blind us to the fact that, even at this later date, British society was still identifiably and self-consciously Christian. Besides the existence of established or national churches in England and Scotland, the monarchy provided the focus for a British civil religion which was expressed in the development of a national cult of remembrance in the aftermath of the First World War, by the holding of national days of prayer during the war years and by stirring radio broadcasts by King George VI during the Second World War, broadcasts that made heavy use of religious and patriotic rhetoric.[4] As in the Victorian era, religious values and churchgoing habits continued to be inculcated among Britain's governing classes in the nation's public schools. For the middle classes, churchgoing still remained emblematic of respectability, notwithstanding declining levels of church attendance and an increase in civil marriage among them. Even in the roughest areas of urban Britain, occasional churchgoing was fairly commonplace and a strong church presence was maintained through a vast network of church and Sunday schools, welfare agencies and voluntary societies.[5] Despite inter-war disquiet within the churches over the spread of artificial birth control, the liberalisation of the nation's divorce laws and the impact of organised leisure on Sunday observance,[6] the norms of Christian morality were still very much embedded in British law on questions such as abortion and homosexuality. The influence of these norms on the national consciousness was, of course, vividly demonstrated in the public debates surrounding Edward VIII's relationship with Wallis Simpson and the whole abdication crisis of 1936.[7] Finally, Christianity continued to exert a profound influence on popular culture. This influence was reflected in the teaching of scripture in non-denominational council schools, in the churches' near monopoly of the rites of passage and in a widely shared passion for hymnody that transcended the boundaries of denomination and social class.[8] In terms of the media, the influence of the churches was reflected in the wide circulation of literature ranging from the ubiquitous parish magazine to the famous *Boy's Own* paper, a magazine published under the auspices of the Religious Tract Society.[9] From the early years of the 1920s, the churches' influence in the media was substantially enhanced by the advent of the BBC and by the rise of religious broadcasting under the patronage of John Reith, the Corporation's first director-general and a staunch Scottish Presbyterian.[10]

Notwithstanding signs of change in the nation's moral climate and a downward trend in church membership and churchgoing among British Protestants between 1914 and 1945, these developments concealed a number of important regional and denominational variations. In Scotland, Wales and Ireland, the melding of ethnic, political and denominational identities in the nineteenth century ensured higher levels of churchgoing and church membership until well into the twentieth century.[11] Even in England, where levels of church attendance and membership were historically lower, there were significant regional and local variations. As late as the 1950s, a comprehensive survey of English society and culture found that the North West and the South West had higher levels of church affiliation and public religious practice than did the rest of England. The same survey also confirmed that those who had 'no religious affiliation at all' were far more likely to be found in large urban areas than in smaller towns and villages.[12] Nor did decline afflict all of the many denominations represented in mainland Britain. Whereas the period 1914–45 saw numbers of communicants and church members fall in many mainstream Protestant churches, the period was one of significant growth for Roman Catholicism, Judaism and newer and more marginal Protestant groups such as the Jehovah's Witnesses and Seventh Day Adventists.[13] Whereas there were 2,389,000 Roman Catholics in 1914, by 1946 their numbers had risen to 3,094,000, this growth being assisted by continuing immigration from Ireland.[14] Similarly, the Seventh Day Adventists increased their membership from 2,671 in 1914 to 6,268 in 1946.[15] Although Roman Catholicism was evidently buoyant and expansive in many working-class districts of industrial Britain, even in urban England there were Anglican parishes and Nonconformist congregations that, by dint of local circumstance, bucked the prevailing trend of decline.[16] Lastly, factors such as gender and social class clearly influenced patterns of religious affiliation and public worship. Women tended to be more closely involved in church life than men and members of the unskilled working class were less susceptible to churchgoing habits than were those of higher social groups.[17]

In sum, the religious configuration and development of Britain between 1914 and 1945 was characterised by variety and complexity rather than by blanket decline. Indeed, national totals of Protestant church members and communicants even enjoyed a short-lived resurgence in the 1920s, a resurgence that was repeated in the 1950s.[18] Despite long-term indicators of the decline of mainstream Protestantism in the inter-war period, the churches remained strong in large parts of Britain and the cultural influence of Christianity remained robust in society at large. As John Drewett, a Sheffield clergyman and an astute religious commentator, described the situation in 1942:

> About one-quarter of the adults and rather more children are attached to a religious denomination. In some parts of the country church attendance is more common than in others; generally speaking, the proportion of practising Christians in the large cities is less than it is in the country and in the smaller towns. It is also true that the influence of the Church is greater in some of the old cathedral cities than it is in the modern industrial areas. We observe, furthermore, that in some parts of the country Non-conformity is much stronger than in others, and that, particularly in the 'Celtic fringe,' there is a strong Puritan tradition which still has a considerable influence on the social customs of the people.[19]

Diffusive Christianity

The continuing strength and influence of Christianity in Britain was demonstrated not so much by habits of regular churchgoing (which were confined to as little as one-fifth of the population in 1914 and one-sixth by the mid-1940s) but in a phenomenon that churchmen were describing as 'diffusive Christianity' as early as the turn of the twentieth century.[20] This prevalent, if somewhat elusive, form of belief is perhaps best described as an ethically based and non-dogmatic form of Christianity, one which derived its currency from a sense of religion's social utility and from an almost universal (if generally limited) measure of religious education. This form of religion seems to have pervaded all levels of British society and, as Callum Brown has observed, 'What made Britain Christian' was not levels of churchgoing but 'the way in which Christianity infused public culture and was adopted by individuals, whether churchgoers or not, in forming their own identities'.[21] According to Drewett, this kind of Christianity was nurtured from an early age. In terms of the public school system, and ever since the reforms of Thomas Arnold in the early nineteenth century:

> [T]he middle-class Englishman ha[s] been trained [in] Christian-Humanist values. He has learnt from the sermons in his school chapel and in the general atmosphere of its community that he must shoulder the responsibilities of government as well as accept the privileges of a ruling class. The conception of the English gentleman is a product of classical humanism and liberal

Christianity. Its essence is a code of behaviour, an ethical system and not a religious faith.

Clearly evolved 'to meet the needs of a world-wide Empire', Drewett maintained that this form religion was more akin to notions of 'blood and soil', with their National Socialist overtones, than to any of the specific creeds of Christendom.[22] Nevertheless, and as Drewett explained, its currency did have advantages for the churches:

> The diffused Christianity of the ruling class is not without its effect in many departments of our social life. Without it there could hardly be an Established Church or bishops sitting in the House of Lords. It influences our state educational system and the administration of justice. It is the religion of many of our judges, executive and civil service chiefs, and of high officers in the services. It ensures that Christian opinion will receive, at any rate, a courteous hearing in the affairs of state. It means, in general, that this country may in some sense be called Christian, and that up to now no rival philosophy has been accepted as the basis of our national life.

However, this form of belief also posed problems because:

> The diffused Christian of the educated classes is almost proud of his ignorance of theology. His religion is one of works: he believes in giving the other fellow a helping hand; he is, or tries to be, a good neighbour. He is friendly to the Church and admires the work of many of the clergy, but he has little patience with doctrine or dogma. The practice of Christianity seems to him to be a straightforward business, and the Church seems to exist largely to make straight ways crooked and light places dark.[23]

Far removed from this privileged milieu, a comparable situation also obtained among the nation's working classes. Mediated through Sunday and elementary schools and through the churches' extensive network of youth and charitable organisations, the 'diffused Christianity of the working classes' manifested itself in a 'moral code' rather than in a firm attachment to the churches:

> Unlike that of the ruling class, with its insistence upon service, that of the workers is mainly concerned with personal abstention

from drink, bad language, gambling and sexual vice. The 'diffused Christian' usually informs you that he is as good as his acquaintance who goes to church . . . Like his brother in the middle class, he believes in *practical* Christianity and will often quote from the Sermon on the Mount to show that in this matter he is on the side of the Master and the Samaritan, whereas the Church is too often 'priestly and levitical.' There is no doubt that the average working man looks upon the Church as a club for the good people. He will not join because he thinks he will fail to 'live up to it,' and he expects (and rightly) a higher standard of goodness from those of his mates who are known to attend church.[24]

Whatever the Christian inspiration of its respective moral codes, the problems posed by diffusive Christianity were real enough. Although challenged by Puritanism and Evangelicalism in previous centuries (and even supplanted in those parts of the British Isles where these took root) the survival of this form of religion into the twentieth century implies that the historic religion of the mass of the English in particular was little more than an invincible if unconscious Pelagianism.[25] Certainly, it was resilient enough to be seen as an obstacle to the inculcation of orthodox Christianity – by contemporaries as well as by historians.[26] As Drewett put it, and once again alluding to the spectre of Nazi Germany:

Since most Englishmen think themselves Christians because they give a cup of cold water to a stranger, they are in a sense spiritually inoculated. The more they do in the way of social service . . . the more self-satisfied they become and the further are they from that sense of need and dependence upon God which only comes as a result of conviction of sin . . . this kind of 'love your neighbour' religion, when divorced from faith in God, is gravely in danger of becoming a 'folk religion' which may call itself 'positive Christianity' and institute schemes of winter help.[27]

Evidently, the dominance of this kind of religion said little for the effectiveness of historic and contemporary methods of religious education in inculcating sound Christian doctrine among the young. One of the most common complaints of Protestant chaplains during the First World War concerned the doctrinal ignorance which was manifest in the ranks of the nation's citizen army. Although allowing for certain exceptions, P.C.T. Crick (in civilian life chaplain to the Archbishop of York and a Fellow of Clare College, Cambridge) wrote in 1917:

A very short experience of work among soldiers seems to lead inevitably to the conclusion that the chief element in the situation is an almost universal lack of religious education. It would not be too much to say of the great majority both of officers and men that they are frankly ignorant of most of the intellectual propositions of Christianity; and in consequence there is also found a very general absence of what may be called conscious churchmanship.[28]

If the scale of officer casualties had notably weakened the historic connection between the public schools and the officer corps by 1917, according to Crick the baneful legacy of the public schools was still very evident among officers from this milieu. As Crick put it, 'the monotony of public worship during school-days, combined with the absence of the corrective of simultaneous and real religious education' accounted for a very large number of old public school boys who were 'not predisposed to be regular or enthusiastic in their attendance at church'.[29] Unfortunately, the state of 'conscious churchmanship' among the other ranks was equally deplorable. Because council schools were expected to teach scripture from a non-denominational perspective (an expectation that acquired the force of law in 1902)[30] the nation's council schools could never be a source of doctrinal instruction for those children who attended them. Naturally, this was a worsening problem given that the proportion of English and Welsh children in council elementary schools rose from 50 per cent in 1900 to nearly 70 per cent in 1938.[31] As Crick observed, the nation's Sunday schools were hardly the place to remedy this deficiency. Although they still enjoyed an impressive following among the working classes, their curriculum was undemanding (concentrating principally on the teaching of Bible stories, prayers and hymnody)[32] and parents' motives in sending their children were mixed, not least among them being the chance of spending a quiet Sunday without the lively company of their progeny. Moreover, Crick remarked that Sunday schools frequently suffered from lax discipline and from an unimaginative teaching style that was all too redolent of normal school hours.[33]

Crick's verdict as to the wholesale failure of religious education was confirmed and developed by a survey of Anglican chaplains in 1916 and, more importantly, by *The Army and Religion* report of 1919. Confronted with a mass of evidence to this effect, the report contained a whole chapter entitled 'The Failure of Education' and lamented that:

Throughout our evidence two complaints recur (1) that there is an absence of serious thought about religion, and (2) that there is ignorance of the facts and truths of Christianity . . . When one thinks of the amount of time and labour which has been spent in the last half-century on religious education in day schools and Sunday-schools, the result seems strangely small and must inevitably lead us to the question [of] whether our methods are sound.[34]

If the report provided abundant proof of the failure of religious education in England, evidence from north of the border also gave 'grave cause for disquietude'.[35] According to Church of Scotland sources:

Men who have been years in Sabbath schools have no real grasp of religion . . . The percentage of men in the Army who are hostile to religion is small, but among them there is the most amazing ignorance of the fundamental ideas of our religion.[36]

Even Roman Catholic schools in mainland Britain, with their strong and sometimes coveted catechetical emphasis, were shown to be wanting in the context of war. Fr Charles Plater's *Catholic Soldiers*, a report compiled and published in parallel with *The Army and Religion* report, revealed strong regional variations in the effectiveness of Catholic elementary education, with nominal Catholics from the south of England (i.e. London) often being ignorant of the rudiments of their faith.[37]

If current means of religious education were deemed inadequate for the generation that fought the First World War, the situation no doubt deteriorated in the inter-war period. Besides the continuing increase in the proportion of children educated in non-denominational council schools, levels of Sunday school attendance also began to fall, a development which was related to the gradual displacement of the austere 'Victorian Sunday' by the recreationally oriented 'continental Sunday'.[38] Furthermore, and besides the modest inroads of secular ideologies such as Fascism and Communism, the inter-war period also saw the growth of certain heterodox religious movements, the most conspicuous of which was Spiritualism. By the 1940s, symptoms of religious ignorance and confusion among the British army and the British public were all too evident. As one Anglo-Catholic army chaplain said of the conscripts of 1939:

One has had to face the hard fact that the vast majority of nominally 'C. of E.' men do not attempt to *practise* the Christian Religion. For them, 'Christianity' means merely their acceptance as ideals of a code of morals described by respectability. They have no realisation of all that is implied by their duty to God, and no consciousness of their need for grace. We are dealing with a pagan generation.[39]

Five years later, and in more measured tones, Mass-Observation, a relatively new social survey organisation, sought to analyse the religious outlook of the population of 'a typical London borough'. Among its 'scientifically selected sample of residents', it found that:

> The keynote of the whole investigation was confusion. The ordinary person has not a logically arranged system of beliefs and doubts, things which he is prepared to accept and things which he feels he must deny . . . His beliefs are a mixture of convictions and habits, independent thought and the relics of what he was taught as a child . . . These beliefs and prejudices are often put into narrow pigeon holes so that one scarcely influences another.[40]

If 'only one person in twenty was willing to say frankly and definitely that he believed there was no God', even among atheists and agnostics 'over a quarter said they prayed on occasions to a God whose existence they doubted. One in twelve had been to church within the past six months [and] over half thought there should be religious education in schools'.[41] A similar chaos prevailed among Anglican churchgoers, a quarter of whom did not believe in an afterlife while a similar proportion rejected the divinity of Christ.[42] What still shone through, however, was a fundamentally ethical conception of religion:

> To many people . . . religion means neither belief in a particular doctrine, nor going to church, nor even a belief in God. To these, religion consists of living a good life, irrespective of what you believe. It is the Christian ethic they speak of, which has become so much a part of the ideas of this country that it is taken for granted.[43]

On the basis of the evidence yielded by this survey, it was argued that 'The chief problem [for the churches] is surely not the 5% who disbelieve, but the 32% who are not quite certain and the still larger number who do believe but are confused about the implications of their belief'.[44] These problems, however, were already apparent to a new generation of army chaplains. In 1943, and with major educational reform in the offing, a conference of Methodist chaplains in the Eighth Army emphasised the desperate need for proper religious education in all British schools:

We have found painful evidence in our work as Chaplains of the failure of our educational system in both Day and Sunday schools – not only to produce a Christian philosophy of life, but even to lay the minimum foundation of religious knowledge . . . We do not want sectarian teaching. But we should insist on a proportion of teachers, in all grades of schools, qualified to teach the fundamental facts of religion. The Churches must choose either to come to terms on an agreed syllabus of religious instruction or perpetuate the present ignorance and agnosticism.[45]

Fatalism

Although fatalism is a perennial feature of military life,[46] this tendency could well have been accentuated in the two World Wars by the unprecedented range and apparently random power of modern artillery, factors which rendered men vulnerable to death or wounding even out of the font line. Nevertheless, the fatalism of the British soldier in the early twentieth century appears to have been less solidly grounded in a Christian view of providence than was the fatalism of his eighteenth- or nineteenth-century forebears.[47] As one Anglican chaplain admitted in 1917, because its symptoms were essentially the same, the metaphysical basis of soldiers' fatalism was extremely difficult to ascertain.[48] Apparently, soldiers variously chose to see human destiny as governed by providence, or as subject to the brutal material forces of the modern age or even, among the more educated at least, in terms of the agnostic nihilism of Omar Khayyám. In fact, it was not unknown for these convictions to be held in tandem and without any real sense of their incompatibility.[49] Traditional forms of fatalism also thrived in this context. If the ancient Highland notion of being 'fey' (or doomed) was liable to manifest itself among Scottish troops,[50] a Scottish Presbyterian chaplain claimed of his ministry to two Scottish infantry battalions:

Almost every soldier in the line has become an Ultra-Calvinist – if not a man of faith, at least a man of fatalism. He believes that he will die only 'when his number's up', and that his bullet has his name on it. I have had more talks on Predestination and God's ordering of lives with soldiers than with Christian people during all my ministry.[51]

Between 1939 and 1945, this widespread fatalism was again very much in evidence, particularly among front-line soldiers. For example, the soldier-poet Keith Douglas revised his poems and arranged for the disposal of his royalties prior to the invasion of France in 1944.[52] These measures were not merely prudential, for Douglas's chaplain recalled how Douglas had received Holy Communion and had told him that he expected to die in France just before he embarked for Normandy. The same chaplain buried Douglas only four days after the invasion.[53] Likewise, Tony Foulds, an officer with a battery of self-propelled guns in Normandy, remembered how one of his sergeants 'came to see me to say that he didn't think he was going to survive the attack on the following day and he left me various personal effects to send back to his wife'. Although Foulds tried to remonstrate with him, 'He was shot through the head the following day [and] he was one of only, I think, three casualties'.[54]

In some cases, this widespread fatalism appears to have been inspired or expressed by premonitory dreams. During the Third Battle of Ypres, Hugh Quigley of the 12th Royal Scots wrote:

> Last night I had a strangely poignant dream: I was lying in hospital, trying madly to move my legs, both tied down in splints, and biting my lips to overcome pain coming from the right groin. A comfortable wound might be the outcome of the premonition. Let us hope so: then I can see again the Old Country . . .

A few days later, Quigley was seriously wounded and sent back to Britain.[55] However, such dreams could have less favourable outcomes. In October 1917, Lieutenant William St Leger of the 2nd Coldstream Guards dreamed recurrently of his own death. In the first of these dreams, St Leger saw himself among the 'spirits of the officers and men of the regiment who had been killed' and who helped assist its survivors repel a German attack. In the second, he dreamed that he was locked in a hand-to-hand struggle with an enormous and apparently invulnerable German and woke convinced that he would not survive the following spring. St Leger was killed the following April during the battle of the Lys.[56]

Inevitably, a strong Christian corollary of this sense of fatalism was the belief among many pious or awakened soldiers that they had been – or might be – spared by God for a special purpose. At Toc H between 1915 and 1918, the celebrated Anglican chaplain 'Tubby' Clayton sought to capitalise on this sentiment in order to recruit clergymen for the post-war Church of England. Clayton even introduced a pledge for prospective ordinands that read: 'If God decides to bring me through this war, I vow to take it as a hint from Him that I shall help and serve the Church in future throughout the life that He gives back to me.'[57] In the context of the Second World War, this tendency naturally resurfaced. Deep in the hold of a 'hell-ship' filled with prisoners of war sailing from Singapore to Saigon in February 1945, Owen Eva, who later became an Anglican priest, felt that surviving this ordeal would be a hopeful sign of God's future plans for him. As Eva remembered of a tortured night spent waiting for the ship to be torpedoed:

> Praying in the hold . . . I became very conscious of the presence of God, and with it the certainty of being safe in his care. This was not a sort of feeling that we would survive; it was the certainty that if I lived it would be because God still had work for me to do in the world and if I died then I was safe in his care. I knew I could let go of fears and worries and trust in God's love and power. Then I went off to sleep and had my one and only good sleep of the voyage.[58]

In the case of Robert Runcie, a future Archbishop of Canterbury, it was a need for reparation which helped to confirm his intention to become a priest after the war. While a tank commander in the 3rd Scots Guards in Normandy, Runcie encouraged a comrade to go forward to identify the position of an enemy tank, a mission that resulted in his death. As Runcie later confessed to a biographer, 'I won't say that incident led directly to my becoming a priest, but it had a lot to do with it. I thought, "I'll make up for that some day."'[59]

A more heterodox and less altruistic indication of the soldier's preoccupation with the future was a widespread interest in fortune telling. Although divination is a perennial aspect of popular culture,[60] during the years of the First World War a prevailing atmosphere of uncertainty and insecurity conspired to push fortune telling to the fore. In 1917, an Anglican chaplain wrote scathingly of 'the reputation enjoyed in London and elsewhere by persons who profess to foretell the future, with especial reference to the course of the war, by "occult" methods of various kinds'.[61] Although clearly present in the First World War, this interest may have grown with the burgeoning of the inter-war leisure industry and it was possibly much greater in 1939 than it had been in 1914. Certainly, for many anxious soldiers fortune-tellers were an obvious resort and Colin Starkie, who commanded a field hygiene section in North Africa and Italy, remembered that many of his men visited fortune-tellers while stationed in North Africa.[62] Ironically, by the years of the Second World War, even chaplains could seek reassurance from clairvoyants. Prior to the Arnhem landings of September 1944, one parachute chaplain consulted a fortune-teller who told him that she saw him with 'a tray of dentist's instruments'. At the same time, 'she also got a terrible pain in her thigh'. In the event, the chaplain in question was captured at Arnhem and witnessed a fellow prisoner being shot through the groin by their trigger-happy German captors.[63]

Given the theologically dubious nature of fatalism and fortune telling, devout soldiers as well as chaplains could be unsettled by this kind of phenomenon. Indeed, in the winter of 1917–18, one Baptist private was deeply troubled (on theological as well as on personal grounds) by a sense that he was going to be killed.[64] Such were the misgivings caused by conspicuous wartime trends in popular belief that in 1917 the Church of England's venerable Society for Promoting Christian Knowledge published a pamphlet entitled *Fatalism*. Written by R.H. Malden, an academic and naval chaplain, the pamphlet attacked popular fatalism and a cluster of associated phenomena such as belief in luck, mascots and fortune telling. Identifying fatalism as 'the temper which asserts that things are "inevitable"',[65] Malden argued that such an outlook was fundamentally 'incompatible with Christianity', whether it was expressed in Christian and providential or in secular and deterministic terms.[66] Whatever the guise fatalism assumed, Malden pointed out that it was both immoral and heretical by implication because it denied human responsibility and precluded a filial relationship with God. In fact, even a fatalism which was couched in Christian terms denied the efficacy of prayer and implied that God 'cannot love us or be loved by us'.[67] Similarly, in 1941, the Revd C.F. Rogers, Professor of Pastoral Theology at King's College, London, devoted a substantial pamphlet to deprecating 'Superstition' of all kinds. His targets included the 'flourishing trade in mascots', the popular interest in 'dream books' and the 'so-called Science of Astrology', phenomena that he saw as scientifically absurd, theologically objectionable and part of a wider reversion to 'paganism'.[68] Within months, Canon Roger Lloyd of Winchester had returned to the attack on this raft of beliefs and attitudes in the pages of the *Expository Times*, a journal widely read by the Anglican clergy. Describing Fatalism as 'Public Enemy Number One', Lloyd condemned not only 'astrological soothsaying, which is the disreputable charlatanry of Fatalism' but also the manner in which Fatalism (in the spurious guise of 'Destiny') had been harnessed by the leaders of the Axis powers in their monstrous bid 'to be the rulers of the world'.[69]

Although orthodox religious opinion was clearly disturbed by sundry manifestations of unorthodox and even non-Christian belief, many army chaplains preferred to interpret these phenomena in more acceptable theological terms. This tendency was very much to the fore in the *Catholic Soldiers* report of 1919. As one of its clerical informants claimed:

> The fatalistic expression, 'My name may be on it,' was very common, and thoroughly accepted as true, but the men had only

a vague notion of what it meant really, and if you pressed them, you found that their fatalism was, after all, Divine and Providential.[70]

Despite the concern which they provoked (and even attempts by certain soldiers to give their denomination as 'Fatalist')[71] the mishmash of fatalistic sentiments and practices that were so evident in wartime was neither appealing nor coherent enough to amount to anything like an alternative creed. While acknowledging the widespread existence of fatalistic attitudes in the trenches of the Western Front, E.C. Crosse was consoled by the fact that this 'shallow philosophy of life' failed to provide any real insight into the future.[72] Geoffrey Gordon, another First World War chaplain, made the telling observation that 'intellectual fatalism' did not have 'the effects upon conduct which logically it should'; certainly it did not give a man 'the recklessness of the Dervish' and still less did it 'prevent him from making superhuman efforts to save or to help his friends in difficulty or in danger'.[73] Far from commanding universal credence among the troops themselves, the prevalence of fatalistic sentiments and attitudes even came to be the subject of some self-deprecating army humour. In 1916, a Private J. Hodson wrote a piece for the *Daily Mail* about the 'sure-to-be-hit sensation'. According to Hodson:

> Sometimes a very vivid dream that you are being killed will do it, or maybe a letter from some one at home saying that they are convinced they will never see you again . . . everything you do seems to make death doubly certain [and if] the news that one is for leave comes in the trenches, most of us, I imagine, are certain that we shall be killed before we get out of them.[74]

Given the ubiquity of fatalism, its variable provenance and widely disputed significance, *The Army and Religion* report could only conclude that:

> Our correspondents differ a good deal in their interpretation of this sudden apparition of an ancient creed. Some associate it simply with current materialism. Some associate with it the remarkable popularity of Omar Khayyam among the better educated men. Several are struck by its resemblance to the fighting creed of Islam, and one Scottish Presbyterian chaplain thinks it due to a re-awakening of the Calvinism which has been the hereditary creed of Scotland . . .[75]

Amulets

The manifold stresses of war also ensured that there was a considerable degree of divergence from orthodox prescription and usage in relation to Bibles, prayer books and other religious artefacts. While G.A. Studdert Kennedy, the famous 'Woodbine Willie' of wartime legend, detected an 'inherited respect for the Bible' among British soldiers of the First World War, he was sure that such respect was seldom born of fervent piety. While the Bible had 'an enormous circulation in the trenches', relatively few had a real knowledge of its contents and the majority attitude towards it was betrayed by soldiers' comments made while he was distributing New Testaments at Rouen. These comments included such pearls as 'Yes, I'll 'ave one, sir; you never know your luck; it may stop a bullet' and 'I'll 'ave one, too, so long as you're giving 'em away. I left my old one at 'ome as a souvenir'.[76] If this mix of 'superstition and sentiment' seemed to characterise the majority attitude towards the Bible during the First World War, Ernest Gordon of the 2nd Argyll and Sutherland Highlanders recalled that the Bible became an object of intense if unorthodox scrutiny among many of his fellow prisoners of war after the fall of Singapore in 1942:

> The Bible they viewed as having magical properties; to the man who could find the right key all would be revealed. One group assured me with absolute certainty that they knew that the end of the war was at hand. When I asked them for proof they told me that they had found it in the books of Daniel and Revelation. They went on to demonstrate mathematically how they had arrived at this conclusion. They had manipulated numbers and words from these two books in a way that seemed convincing enough to them . . .[77]

If a fascination with holy writ was in this case stimulated by despair and by a lack of information from the outside world, the greatest attraction for the carrying of scripture and the wearing of religious medals was the supernatural protection that they were often thought to bestow. Among front-line soldiers in particular, belief in the talismanic properties of the Bible appears to have been endemic. At Gallipoli, for example, one soldier showed a Presbyterian chaplain a Testament which he had given him some months earlier. In William Ewing's words, 'He had carried it in his pocket constantly' and:

> A Turkish bullet had ploughed its way right through the book, but did not quite reach his side. He showed me the bullet, and

where it had lodged harmlessly inside his belt. He felt, he said, as if he had been struck by a sledge-hammer; he was, however, only 'winded' for the moment. There is no doubt that the Testament saved his life.[78]

This temptation to ascribe survival to the supernatural power of the Good Book was also shared by Arthur Smith, who served as a staff officer on the Western Front throughout much of the First World War. Although Smith claimed that he never treated his pocket Bible as a talisman, he was firmly convinced that it had saved his life in a dramatic fashion. Presented to him by his father and bearing on its flyleaf a text from the 91st Psalm ('Because thou hast made the Lord thy refuge. There shall no evil befall thee. For he shall give his angels charge over thee to keep thee in all thine ways'), Smith had been hit by a piece of shrapnel that had 'cut right through the Bible until that page in the Psalms from which that text was taken'. According to Smith, 'that to me was a very significant thing and encouraged my faith'.[79]

Naturally, chaplains were inclined to take a dim view of such conclusions. One Wesleyan chaplain remarked upon the tragic irony of one soldier – the son of 'a famous Greek scholar' – who had been killed by a bullet that had gone straight through 'the Greek Testament in the boy's breast-pocket'.[80] William Ewing was also dismissive of the preservative powers of the Good Book, observing that 'A small Bible was brought to me one day through which a hole was fairly drilled by the bullet that killed its owner.'[81] When symptoms of the abuse of the Bible by soldiers re-emerged during the Second World War, Ronald Selby Wright, the celebrated 'Radio Padre', felt disposed to tackle these issues over the airwaves. In an address on the Bible entitled 'My Portable Library', Selby Wright insisted that 'There is nothing superstitious about the Bible' and asked:

> Are you one of these superstitious people, for example, who likes having a Bible with you for luck and hoping that the bullet will be deflected by the 'Bible-next-your-heart' business? One of these people who thinks that every time you open your Bible, close your eyes and put your finger down, you will get a text that is going to mean something to you that day – a most untrustworthy, extra-ordinary idea. You know the story about the man who once did that, and the text he found was 'Judas went and hanged himself' . . . and the next text he got was 'Go and do thou likewise'.[82]

Despite the cautionary humour of the 'Radio Padre', it seems likely that a heavy wartime emphasis on providing soldiers with devotional items actually encouraged their appropriation for uses which the churches deemed superstitious. Quite clearly, there was a tendency in Catholic circles to flood the army's Catholic constituency with rosaries and miraculous medals. As one Catholic chaplain noted in the First World War, 'men, like boys, like anything they can get. You can't load them up with too many scapulars, crucifixes, medals, etc.'[83] During the Second World War, this lavish distribution of devotional artefacts clearly resumed. John Scollen, a Roman Catholic artillery officer, noted of the midnight Mass he attended at Christmas 1941: 'Our chaplain, a Lancashire man from Rochdale, said the Mass and preached a short sermon. Afterwards he distributed "Cardinal's crosses" to those who did not have them and rosaries to everyone, whether they already had them or not.'[84]

An inevitable consequence of this scale of distribution was that large numbers of rosaries, medals and other Catholic artefacts found their way into non-Catholic hands. In fact, just six months into the First World War, one Catholic chaplain was trumpeting in the Catholic press the definite demand for miraculous medals among Protestant soldiers.[85] By 1917, Fr William Doyle, an experienced Catholic chaplain, could write, 'there are few men, no matter what their belief, who do not carry a rosary or a Catholic medal round their necks. I wonder what the non-Catholic Padres think of this fearful increase of Idolatry!'.[86] Objectionable or not, the wearing of rosaries and Catholic medals by Protestant soldiers was endemic, a situation reflected by the fact that Edward Lovett, a London folklorist of the time, was often given Catholic medals for his collection of charms following 'personal conversations with troops in London' between 1914 and 1917.[87] Plater's report of 1919 even concluded that the practice was so widespread by the end of the war that it had nullified Catholic distinctiveness in this regard.[88] Inevitably, the practice recurred as a widespread phenomenon between 1939 and 1945. Although he looked askance at his Roman Catholic sergeant's 'gaudy pictures of saints', Raleigh Trevelyan, an Anglican infantry officer, still wore a medal of St Christopher throughout the Italian campaign.[89] In Catholic countries or regions, of course, such means of protection were readily available. Private Charlie Wakeley of the 1st Worcestershire Regiment was given a rosary by a Dutch youth during the liberation of southern Holland in September 1944, a rosary that he kept until the end of the war.[90] Although Catholic sources were keen to insist that Catholic soldiers did not regard or use their rosaries and medals as protective 'charms',[91] the truth of this assertion is questionable, particularly given that one infantry chaplain of vast experience in the First World War admitted 'I suppose uninstructed soldiers regard them more or less as charms' – a category which embraced all Protestants as well as many Roman Catholics.[92]

In addition to the use of sacred artefacts, there was also a common tendency for secular artefacts to be pressed into service as protective amulets, among these being rabbits' feet, lucky coins, trinkets, sheep's cauls and even pieces of coal and shrapnel, the latter being seized upon in the belief that like repelled like.[93] So widespread was this practice that Geoffrey Gorer's *Exploring English Character*, a comprehensive survey of English attitudes and practices conducted in the mid-1950s, found that 'roughly one serving man or woman in three had his or her private means of solid magic' during the Second World War. Although individuals were often reticent about their possession of mascots,[94] Gorer found that the concentration of wartime mascot owners was strongest among 'married men aged 25 to 34'.[95] Secular mascots were even carried alongside artefacts of an explicitly religious nature. In 1917, for example, Edwin Campion Vaughan, a Roman Catholic infantry officer, braved the front line complete with his rosary, his miraculous medals and a lucky sovereign.[96] Indeed, the difference between a religious artefact and a magical charm was easily blurred. While in France in 1915, for example, John Reith received a signet ring from his parents, a ring that was in the shape of a shield and which arrived inscribed with the words 'God our shield-Father-Mother'. Though Reith came from a strongly Presbyterian background, and even if his parents were not disposed to regard their gift as a charm, Reith confessed that 'I was glad to have it and it seemed a protection against danger'.[97]

A significant variation on the appropriation of religious artefacts for protective use was the common belief that the theft or misuse of such objects was inherently unlucky. Robert Graves remembered a fellow officer taking a piece of stained glass from a ruined church in France in 1915. However:

> As we went out, we met two men of the Munsters. Being Irish Catholics, they thought it sacrilegious for Jenkins to be taking the glass away. One of them warned him: 'Shouldn't take that, sir; it will bring you no luck.' (Jenkins got killed not long after).[98]

These beliefs were also current during the Second World War, especially in the Catholic context of the Italian campaign. While billeted in a church in northern Italy, Macpherson Knowles, an atheist and a medical officer with the 3rd Grenadier Guards, carelessly left his washing basin on the altar. Soon after, a bursting shell blew shrapnel into the church, piercing the basin and spilling its contents over the altar. As Knowles recalled, 'the medical sergeant said – in fairly sharp language – that that would teach me a lesson to put a washing bowl on the altar'.[99] Similarly, while billeted in a cardinal's villa, Alec Bowlby helped himself to some liturgical items that he had found hidden in a cupboard. On exhibiting his spoils, the reaction of an Irish comrade was one of alarm rather than envy, the soldier in question reminding him that 'It's unlucky to take holy things'.[100]

Whether secular or religious in origin, personal mascots were not necessarily inanimate objects. In the First World War, Guy Chapman's experience of a colonel of the 13th Royal Fusiliers convinced him that this officer was preternaturally lucky. After a bombardment in which this officer had correctly anticipated the fall of the final shell he became to Chapman a human 'talisman which could soothe frayed nerves and call up new strength'.[101] Likewise, Macpherson Knowles recalled the tendency among infantrymen in the Second World War to regard some young officers as 'lucky', i.e. 'they could do anything and didn't seem to get hit'. Like Chapman's colonel, these officers were prized commodities because men in their platoons considered themselves 'covered' by their good luck.[102] As with religious artefacts, even chaplains could be seen as providing a certain amount of extra protection. For example, William Doyle, who served with the 16th (Irish) Division on the Western Front, noted a tendency for men to converge on his dugout during bombardments and to ascribe their survival to his proximity.[103] Even more striking was the experience of the Revd R. Bulstrode, an Anglican brigade chaplain with the 20th (Light) Division, who noted how in the Ypres sector early in 1916:

> A strange yarn grew up about Bridge 6 [on the Ypres canal], that I (of all people) had knelt in prayer on the bridge while my men passed over to an attack, apparently greatly cheering them . . . Even the Chaplain General had heard of it, and reminded me of it with a smile on my next leave. But I assured him that I had never done, or thought of doing, anything so dramatic, and that I was only too glad to get across those bridges with a whole skin. The bridges were narrow and frail, and a kneeling figure would soon have been made to realise that his presence was the reverse of 'cheering' to those who wished to pass to the shelter of a trench or sunken road.[104]

In addition to artefacts and individuals, an enormous variety of personal rituals (traditional or otherwise) were also widely employed to fend off bad luck. Robert Graves, for example, noted how an allusion to his battalion's lack of officer casualties sent fellow officers rushing to touch wood early in 1916.[105] Similarly, and while moving up for an attack in Italy in 1944, Alec Bowlby remembered that a fellow soldier buoyantly announced that there would be another Military Medal in the platoon by the time it was all over.

As Bowlby recalled, 'We were horrified. If we'd been Catholics we would have crossed ourselves.'[106]

As in the case of fatalism (with which ideas of luck were commonly entwined)[107] some chaplains were uncomfortable with the habits of mind and body which belief in luck entailed. As one chaplain wrote in a regimental magazine in 1915: 'It is high time that attention be drawn to the childish belief in "mascots". It is nothing less than rank paganism and silly superstition to believe that the "lucky charm" is going to protect one from danger.'[108] In addition to being both 'puerile and pagan', R.H. Malden pointed out that such 'childish' beliefs betrayed a neutered view of the Almighty:

> Careless semi-Christians [he averred] will always accept a much smaller conception of God, and will not believe that the relationship between Himself and His creation is really an uninterrupted intimacy. They will then call in Luck to fill the gaps which God has left.[109]

However, and as with fatalism and its sundry manifestations, too much significance should not be attached to this common preoccupation with lucky mascots and rituals. As the First World War went on, the anxieties of many chaplains may even have been allayed in this respect. As one Catholic chaplain put it: '[The men] laugh at charms. Too many people with charms get killed.'[110] Again, the essentially superficial nature of belief in luck was the subject of some army satire, a contemporary list of 'Soldiers' Superstitions' pronouncing that 'It is considered very unlucky to be killed on a Friday' and averring that 'To drop your rifle on foot of a second lieutenant is bad luck – for him. To drop ditto on foot of sergeant major is bad luck – for you'.[111]

Spiritualism, ghosts and visions

Besides their other proclivities, soldiers of the First World War in particular often claimed to have seen ghosts and to have beheld visions of angels and of Christ himself. Although Jay Winter has seized upon this evidence to argue that Spiritualism was very much 'in vogue' among the British army of 1914–18,[112] there is in fact little evidence to support this view, notwithstanding a growing interest in Spiritualism among bereaved civilians at home.[113] Significantly, the most famous book on Spiritualism to emerge out of the soldier's experience of the war was *The Road to En-Dor*. This book described how enterprising prisoners of war in Anatolia were able to present themselves as mediums in order to win various privileges and eventual repatriation from their credulous Turkish captors. As its author – Lieutenant E.H. Jones of the Indian Army – freely admitted, the book was published not with the intention of promoting Spiritualism but of exposing its fraudulent character.[114] Despite the fact that wartime Spiritualist publications were awash with unattributed stories from the trenches, the compilers of *The Army and Religion* report (who were not usually slow to expand upon depressing aspects of the soldier's religious and moral condition) found that only three out of nearly three hundred memoranda which they received mentioned 'the presence of spiritualistic ideas' in the army. In fact, even one of these qualified its presence with the remark that 'There is some interest in spiritualism, but not so much as there is outside the Army'.[115] Although there were no doubt interested Spiritualists in the army, soldiers' séances appear to have been extremely rare. This was partly due to the fact that mediums tended to be women but it was also because (true to the radical political ethos of their forebears) many secular Spiritualists associated with the Lyceum movement opposed the war and became conscientious objectors following the introduction of conscription in 1916.[116]

The fact that soldiers claimed to have seen ghosts did not in itself betoken a sympathy for Spiritualism. Robert Graves thought the wartime Spiritualism he found among civilians at home to be both pitiable and off-putting[117] but even he was convinced that he had seen a ghost in France. As Graves maintained:

> At Béthune [in 1915], I saw the ghost of a man named Private Challoner, who had been at Lancaster with me, and again in 'F' Company at Wrexham. When he went out with a draft to join the First Battalion, he shook my hand and said: 'I'll meet you again in France, sir.' In June he passed by our 'C' Company billet . . . I could not mistake him, or the cap-badge he wore; yet no Royal Welch battalion was billeted within miles . . . I jumped up, looked out of the window, and saw nothing except a fag-end smoking on the pavement. Challoner had been killed at Festubert in May.[118]

Overall, it seems likely that Winter has overstated the strength of Spiritualism by treating manifestations of an enduring popular cosmology as expressions of Spiritualism per se. This is a fundamentally unsound interpretation because the Spiritualist doctrine 'of another world from which spirits of the dead returned to help and console the citizens of this world' fed on traditional beliefs in ghosts and other spirits. In fact, as Jennifer Hazelgrove has shown, Spiritualism's chief asset in the inter-war years was precisely its 'capacity to incorporate and co-ordinate traditional thoughts and beliefs' within the context of a popular culture that was still very much 'steeped in supernatural signs'.[119] Pre-war British society also had a voracious appetite for ghost and fairy stories, the years before the First World War being marked by the popularity of M.R. James's ghost stories and of J.M. Barrie's *Peter Pan*.[120] If the publication of Arthur Machen's sensational story of the bowmen of Mons in the London *Evening News* of 29 September 1914 highlighted the contemporary taste for such fiction, then it also served to expose a subsequent and perplexing readiness among soldiers and civilians alike to protest the truth of essentially fictional events around Mons in August 1914.[121] Despite the spurious credentials of the legend of the 'Angels' or 'Bowmen' of Mons (there are, in fact, no reliable first-hand testimonies from soldiers as to the appearance of angels or spectral bowmen at Mons that pre-date the publication of Machen's story), there were less spectacular stories of apparitions which had an unambiguously Christian and indeed prophetic character.

One story published in the *Irish Times* during the war recounted how a senior officer of the Irish Guards had been visited by a nun while working late in his office in Flanders. His unexpected guest told him that 'the war would continue so long as the inhabitants of EUROPE remained in a callous state and failed to prostrate themselves collectively and absolutely before GOD'. In order to prevent further disruptions of this kind, the officer in question visited a local convent, where he was assured that no nun had been out that night. The sisters were duly paraded before him but he could not recognise his visitor among them. However, when leaving the building he saw a portrait of a late Mother Superior hanging on the wall and instantly identified her as his visitor. With reference to this incident, one chaplain commented: 'That this remarkable story is genuine I have not the slightest doubt. Whether the nun's message really came from the dead nun or was evolved out of the gallant officer's inner conscience is another question.'[122] Stirrings of conscience were also in evidence in another officer's account of how he beheld a vision of the crucifixion in a squalid railway wagon en route for Germany. Thomas Butt, a subaltern in the 2nd King's Own Yorkshire Light Infantry, was captured at the battle of Le Cateau in late August 1914 and subsequently mistreated by his captors. Lying wounded in a horse truck fouled by piles of manure, Butt had what he described as 'an interesting and awe-inspiring experience'. As Butt recalled: '[S]uddenly I had a vision of the Cross at the far end of the truck and a voice crystal clear said "What do you think your suffering is compared to that?" as the figure pointed to the crucifix.' According to Butt, the effect of this vision was instantaneous and 'From that moment fear went'.[123]

Significantly, Butt was by no means alone in beholding visions of Christ in such circumstances. By 1915, numerous stories had begun to circulate about the so-called 'White Comrade' or 'Comrade in White' who ministered to British wounded in no-man's land. Because these stories were largely popularised by imaginative civilian poets and essayists (who were working as far apart as Aberdeen and Australia),[124] their precise origins are hard to locate. Nevertheless, and in parallel with more spectacular stories of supernatural intervention at Mons, they were eagerly taken up by soldiers and civilians alike. When the Anglican chaplain C.E. Doudney visited his parishioners at Bath in the summer of 1915, he insisted that:

> Men whose lives have not been known to be religious in the least, upon whose lips perhaps blasphemy has been more frequent than any decent words, men who have been known perchance to their comrades as 'a bad lot' have, in their agony on the battlefield, known the presence of the White Comrade.[125]

However extravagant such claims may appear, and whatever they may reveal about the Victorian iconography of Christ, the army of 1914–16 contained (as we shall be seeing in Chapter 4) a much higher proportion of church members and churchgoers than did the army of 1917–18. Furthermore, 1915 was the high point of a discernible religious revival which affected many units and soldiers of the British army. If visions of the 'White Comrade' may have been no more than culturally conditioned responses to extreme trauma and suffering, they were no doubt more likely to occur and to gain credence at this stage of the war than at any other. In any event, a real sense of the protective presence of Christ endured among religious soldiers throughout the course of the war. In this respect, it is instructive to note how one pious but nervous young soldier described his experiences of an attack at Ypres in the summer of 1917. Writing to his fiancée, Basil Lawrence of the 1/21st London Regiment remembered how:

> We were in the assembly trenches, and then zero moment arrived announced by two deafening explosions followed by all the guns opening. Fritz was dropping his heavies near by and we dreaded the walk across the open to get to the other trenches, but during the intervening time I got one of those wonderful visions of Christ – of His Passion and Crucifixion – of His great Love, and by just fixing my eyes on that vision of the Cross I was calmer than ever before . . . [T]he following evening we were subjected to the worst bombardment I had ever been in, during which I was able

to pass humorous remarks with the others. Why? Because I had had a vision of Christ with extended arms in front of us all and instead of bearing our sins, He was bearing all the harm from the shells, and I knew they would be diverted from us . . . Sure enough, and to me it was only because of faith, two dropped on the parapet and *were duds*, otherwise we should have been 'goners'.[126]

In a more abstract sense, soldiers of the Second World War were also prone to perceive Christ in the suffering world around them. For Ken Tout, the sight of a motorcyclist blown into a hedgerow in Normandy stirred images of Calvary.[127] Likewise, for Alec Bowlby, the sight of a wounded soldier perched, arms outstretched, on top of a tank in Italy proved particularly unsettling. After being raked by the fire of a German machine gun that Bowlby and his companions had declined to deal with, Bowlby admitted that the sight of the tank and its human cargo made him feel 'sick with guilt' and that 'The Christ-like rifleman made it worse'.[128] However, for others there was still a sense in which the image of the suffering Christ could prove consoling. Indeed, as one officer wrote to his family from Normandy:

As I write . . . I can sense the presence of Jesus on the Cross; so that I know his unbounded love and suffering compassion for all this waste of his work and so that I receive at this moment his strength and blessing on us all for what we may face.[129]

Calvaries and Leaning Virgins

What no doubt encouraged this sense of the presence of Christ during the First World War was the sacred landscape of northern France and Belgium, a region that was thickly planted with roadside calvaries. Although by no means absent from soldiers' reflections on the Normandy campaign of 1944,[130] the longevity of the army's stay in this region from 1914 to 1918 ensured that the impact of these calvaries was much greater upon this generation. In these four years, Protestant Britons encountered a Catholic landscape in numbers unprecedented since the Reformation but there was little or no animosity towards a symbol that was historically alien to the landscape of Protestant Britain. In fact, and as sundry witnesses testified, Protestant soldiers betrayed 'no dogmatic aversion' towards them and they often bought miniature crucifixes as souvenirs or for use as amulets.[131] Given the prevailing wartime rhetoric of sacrifice, and sensitised as they were to the power of Christian iconography by the paintings, prints and lantern slides to which they had been exposed at Sunday school,[132] it is hardly surprising that a great many should have proved susceptible to the images of the suffering Christ that they encountered on the Western Front. Although its redemptive overtones were generally obscure, this was an image with which ordinary soldiers could readily identify. As one officer put it:

> Men have noticed the crucifixes they have passed in France. It is a symbol which they like. It bears possibilities. Not much is yet attached to it, but it is the Crucified Christ rather than the Risen Christ which appeals.[133]

If Christ as the heroic epitome of patient and purposive suffering struck a chord with ordinary soldiers and furnished chaplains with the inspiration for many of their sermons, the presence of wayside calvaries was not unproblematic. Quite apart from the appropriation of crucifixes as amulets, the survival of these calvaries posed potentially awkward questions concerning the providential immunity of the sacred. Certainly, observations as to the widespread survival of these calvaries were commonplace during the war and they sometimes inspired a strong if implicit belief that they were the subjects of divine protection. As Frank Meryon Chance, a subaltern of the 1/24th London Regiment, wrote from France in April 1915: 'I think that quite the most remarkable feature of the war is the standing up of the cross with our dear Lord upon it amidst scenes of terrible strife & distress . . .'[134] Likewise, J.F.R. Modrell, yet another soldier of the London Regiment, observed that as late as 1917 and in those areas which the Germans had recently laid waste in their withdrawal to the Hindenburg Line, calvaries still remained immune to the destruction that surrounded them:

> Every house in every village had been blown up, until there was not one brick on top of another, even the churches had suffered the same fate . . . the only things which had escaped this wholesale destruction were the crucifixes or shrines which stand at the entrance to every French village. That this was not due to any special consideration on the part of the Bosche was evident, as where a crucifix stood at [a] cross roads the cross roads had still been blown up, and although in some cases the crater made by the explosion extended right to the bottom of the shrine, it still stood upright . . . The curious way in which these shrines escaped destruction was the subject of a good many heated arguments, but although fellows never agreed as to the reason, nobody ever denied on all parts of the battle front the same thing had happened.[135]

Despite such claims, the immunity of these calvaries was clearly more imagined than real. Significantly enough, Modrell defined 'destroyed' as toppled rather than blown to pieces and even he ultimately conceded that there had been cases in which these calvaries had been completely obliterated.[136]

The same ability of the British soldier to endow the sacred with the improbable was further demonstrated in the case of the 'Golden', 'Leaning' or 'Hanging' Virgin of Albert, a large gilded statue of the Virgin and child that had originally crowned the dome of the town's nineteenth-century basilica. Dislodged from its original position by a German shell in January 1915, this representation of Notre Dame de Brebières had been partly secured by French engineers but it remained in its precarious and highly visible situation throughout the Somme fighting of 1916.[137] In April of that year, Rowland Feilding remarked that the statue had moved to a point at which it was 'poised horizontally in mid-air, in the attitude of diving' and Feilding aptly observed that:

> As with many religious emblems in the fighting line, the chance action of the shells has rather added to, than detracted from the impressiveness of this one, and as one looks up at it today, the Child, with its hands outspread, seems to be looking down from the Mother's arms in blessing on our soldiers, in the ruined square below.[138]

The 'Golden Virgin' certainly provided chaplains with food for thought. Thomas Tiplady, a Wesleyan chaplain who was notably impressed by the Catholic culture of northern France, viewed the situation of the 'Golden Virgin' as a metaphor for that of contemporary Christianity:

> Most of us felt alarmed for Christianity when the war broke out . . . It seemed as if it were falling to the ground . . . Was not the outbreak and continuance of barbarism a sign that Christianity had failed? Then came the magnificent and voluntary rally to the flag in defence of Belgium . . . Never before had so many offered to die for the ideals of Christianity. We saw that Christianity had stooped from the sky to the street. It had become incarnate.[139]

Not only this, but, observing that the Virgin was sculpted to appear lame, Tiplady was moved to reflect that:

> She upholds and exalts Christ, but the strain causes lameness . . .
> The sculptor has preached better than he knew. His statue in

the heart of the Somme has become more than the artistic expression of the unselfish service of the Virgin Mother. It has become the spiritual interpretation of the great struggle on the Somme front.[140]

Most soldiers, however, appear to have read less exalted meanings into this striking spectacle and a great many stories circulated as to the significance of the Virgin and its wartime situation. Although these stories were common to the British, French and German armies alike,[141] the most widely accepted account among British soldiers was that the war would end when the statue finally fell. As Bernard Martin remembered, the currency of this story rested not only on an inclination among soldiers to believe tales of the miraculous but also on a rather limited range of conversation:

> [A] superstition arose which everyone who fought on the Somme wanted to believe – that when another shell chanced to hit the pendant statue, bringing the Virgin and child crashing into the street below, the war would end. Nonsense, of course, impossible without a miracle, but men like us who lived alongside fear needed miracles. Such superstitions and rumours were always welcome in the restricted conversation of a small mess and, if a bit thin, could be nourished with a little imagination before being passed on to new-comers.[142]

In any event, this story proved to be incorrect when the statue was at last toppled by British artillery fire during the German spring offensive of 1918.[143]

Emergency religion and its meanings

Whatever the vagaries of the soldier's imagination, there can be no way of disputing the veracity of the First World War aphorism that 'there are no atheists in the trenches'.[144] Undoubtedly, fear of death and the proximity of the enemy provoked a recourse to the sacraments on a very large scale in both World Wars. Naturally, the eve of battle was a time in which religious sentiments often came to the fore. For many Roman Catholics, it was a time for confession and for Holy Communion, with chaplains of Irish units usually reporting busy periods as soldiers prepared for an attack or for embarkation to an active theatre of war.[145] As one chaplain said of Roman Catholic soldiers: 'Speaking roughly, the fervour of the men's Catholicity was at any moment proportioned to the amount of danger that was to be faced.'[146] *The Army and Religion* report confirmed that this phenomenon was broadly true of Protestant soldiers as well.[147] Even among nominally Anglican soldiers, most of whom were either unconfirmed or normally reluctant to communicate, the prospect of action could see demand for Holy Communion soar. Studdert Kennedy was tempted to ascribe this phenomenon to the words of administration used by the Book of Common Prayer, 'The Body [or Blood] of our Lord Jesus Christ, which was given for thee, preserve thy body and soul unto everlasting life.'[148] However, and despite this suspicion that the sacrament was being treated as a mere preservative, it is equally possible that traditional lay attitudes to Holy Communion were in fact asserting themselves under these circumstances. During the latter decades of the nineteenth century, many Anglican clergymen had made determined but largely unsuccessful efforts to popularise frequent communion among their parishioners and to turn their parishes into what were effectively 'eucharistic communities'.[149] However, such efforts ran contrary to the entrenched attitudes of the Anglican laity, which were that Holy Communion should only be taken by those who lived exemplary lives or by those who were on the point of death.[150] Although Anglican chaplains may therefore have been mistaken in perceiving a craven attitude to Holy Communion in times of danger, there can be no doubt as to the appeal of the sacrament at such times. Under normal circumstances, Maurice Murray, a brigade chaplain with the 12th and 13th Royal Sussex Regiment in 1917, could expect around twenty-five communicants from each of these battalions. However, preparations for their attack at Pilckem Ridge on 31 July 1917 saw these numbers rise dramatically. As Murray wrote in his diary for Sunday 29 July:

> There were so many communicants that Crawley [the senior Anglican chaplain to the 39th Division] and I decided to have the Holy Communion (a veritable viaticum) in the big Church Army hut adjoining. I went back on [a] bicycle to my tent and got my robes and helped to administer to over 200 communicants, and Thom gave out hymn after hymn and took some prayers.[151]

Soldiers were also inclined to come to Holy Communion in larger numbers while on active service during the Second World War, no doubt being impelled by the same desire to be spiritually prepared for – and perhaps even preserved from – fear, danger and death. From the perspective of its Anglican padre, church life thrived among the men of the 43rd Reconnaissance Regiment during the north-west Europe campaign, with large attendances at voluntary services and higher numbers of communicants being clear evidence of its flourishing state.[152] For George MacDonald Fraser, active service in the latter stages of the Burma campaign also proved to be a spiritually galvanising experience:

I'd been given the hand of fellowship by the Scots Kirk at Deolali (mainly because it would be welcome news to my father), and had accidentally strayed into a C. of E. communion service at Meiktila, receiving wafers and wine to which I obviously wasn't entitled, and escaping detection only by copying the actions of the other communicants. Also, after being an agnostic from the age of ten, I'd started saying my prayers again – there's nothing like mortal danger for putting you in the mood; as Voltaire observed, it's no time to be making enemies.[153]

Holy Communion was not the only sacrament that could be in demand at such times. W.H. Miller, an Anglican chaplain with the 2nd King's Own Royal Lancaster Regiment, was prevailed upon to baptise a soldier on Imphal airstrip just before the departure of the second Chindit expedition in 1944. As Miller remembered:

I baptised a man who came to me with this special request. Normally I would not take such a step without enquiry and preparation, but under such unusual circumstances I felt it was right to admit him to the fellowship of the Church. The baptism was as simple as could be; a mess-tin filled with water from some-body's water-bottle served as our font. A few of his personal friends stood with him. At the same time we had some prayers. At such a critical time as that, no-one found it easy to pray; but who shall question that it gave us the strength and comfort which we all needed so badly?[154]

However difficult it may have been for soldiers to participate at this impromptu baptismal service, there can be no doubt that soldiers prayed very widely and very readily both before and during periods of action. As Geoffrey Gordon observed in 1917:

[T]here is no doubt that, in the hour of danger the great majority of men pray; it is not perhaps a very high type of prayer, it is purely individual, self-centred and inspired by fear . . . There is a story that during a lull in a heavy bombardment, a man emerged from a dug-out and shouted inquiries to a neighbouring shelter: 'You all right in there, mate?' 'Yes – so far, but some of them b– shells come b– close.' 'What have you been doing while it was going on?' 'Well, as a matter of fact, we've all been saying our prayers.' 'So've we – we've been praying like hell.'[155]

Understandably, this phenomenon appears to have survived throughout the First World War, with *The Army and Religion* report eliciting plenty of evidence to show that very few soldiers did not pray at all and that 'Prayer as a natural cry for help and security has greatly increased'.[156] During the Second World War, of course, the same phenomenon was very much in evidence. At Anzio for example, where the whole Allied beachhead was subjected to heavy German artillery fire, Church Army workers found an unusual but gratifying interest in their prayer meetings, particularly among those who had 'fallen from the Faith'.[157] For Charlie Wakeley of the 1st Worcestershire Regiment, the circumstances of active service gave him a dangerous insight into the strength of his RSM's atheism, an atheism that he was wont to advertise when forming the battalion up for church parade. Sent as company runner to locate RSM Hurd on one occasion during the Normandy campaign, Wakeley found him in his slit trench on his knees in prayer, a situation that Wakeley was reluctant to disturb or talk about for fear of possible repercussions – 'He'd never let that story have got round, but since he's been dead I've told it a good many times.'[158] If heavy fighting in the Normandy *bocage* awakened the religious sensibilities of RSM Hurd, fighting a literally merciless enemy in the jungles of Burma also helped to create a mood of sober piety among the men of at least one column of Chindits in 1944. Although more formal services were impossible, Cecil Johnston, a missionary-turned-chaplain, recalled how, at night, when a pivot tree was selected for the column's 'clock' formation:

> I'd walk to the centre and take off my cap – that meant every-body knew I was leading in prayer [and] praying for them. Then I had a little Scripture Gift Mission book which I'd read two or three verses [from] under a theme and say a short – a very short – prayer, we'd all put our caps on (though most of them had not heard the prayer) and we'd proceed.[159]

If the readiness of soldiers to pray in certain circumstances was never in doubt, chaplains could evince very different opinions as to its moral quality and religious significance. For many relatively callow chaplains on the Gallipoli peninsula in 1915–16, this widespread recourse to prayer seemed to be symptomatic of a definite religious awakening.[160] However, during the subsequent months and years of the war, and with the prospects of a general religious revival in recession, many chaplains became more circumspect if not openly sceptical about this phenomenon. By the spring of 1917, James Black, a Scottish Presbyterian brigade chaplain, was only prepared to confirm for the civilian readership of a church magazine that 'It is a truism to say that many men have learned to pray' and that 'Some have learned prayer's passion and power'.[161] However, by 1917 other chaplains were prepared to be more forthright in their opinions. Studdert Kennedy was typically trenchant in his verdict on prayer arising from what was sometimes described as 'the emergency religion of the trenches'.[162] In a wartime talk addressed to soldiers entitled 'Why doesn't God answer Prayer?', Studdert Kennedy saw fit to clear up a few misconceptions about its nature, pointing out that:

> When Christ said 'Whatsoever ye ask in My name I will do it for you,' He did not mean that if you just tacked His name on to any request you made you would be sure to get it from God. Praying isn't like getting things out of a penny-in-the-slot machine: drop in a prayer and get a bit of chewing gum, or a blighty, or the end of the war.[163]

Moreover, in his insistence on the need to pray in a Christ-like spirit of heroic selflessness, Studdert Kennedy declared his contempt for prayers for mere self-preservation:

> I remember once in the line, when we were being shelled very heavily, I stood beside an enormous sergeant who was a great friend of mine, and on the other side of me somewhere was a chap that had lost his nerve and was whining out prayers for protection: 'O God, keep me safe!' 'O God, save me!' The sergeant was looking after his men, shouting out warnings to us, and swearing steadily all the time. This fellow's prayers were getting on our nerves, and at last the sergeant turned to me and said, 'That chap's saying his prayers, isn't he, sir?' I said, 'No, he isn't, sergeant, that's not prayer, its "wind".'

In Studdert Kenendy's opinion, this was not prayer because it was 'purely selfish prayer, and selfish prayer is not prayer at all . . . The words without the spirit are as useless and as vain as the mumbo-jumbo of a conjuror before he does the trick.'[164]

Significantly, rigorist views of this kind were not foreign to the more thoughtful soldier. As one young officer reasoned:

> I had given up asking God to see that I wasn't killed soon after I reached the front in 1914. It seemed selfish and unreasonable to expect him to take special steps on my behalf when I was only one in about ten million soldiers in the various armies.[165]

Similar reservations were aired by Burgon Bickersteth, who wrote to his father, the vicar of Leeds, in the spring of 1917:

Religion which suddenly bubbles to the surface at the moment of danger is very healthily considered to smack too much of the death-bed confession and to be about as valuable (which does not mean to imply that it is valueless). Many of us have had that determined, half-sporting feeling that we will be especially careful not to be extra-religious because we are in an extra-dangerous spot.[166]

Although the spiritual worth of prayer which arose out of a context of terror clearly divided informed opinion, one of the more astute conclusions reached by David Cairns for *The Army and Religion* report was that 'To talk slightingly of "funk religion" is to begin at the wrong end, and to miss the meaning of what is going on'.[167] As Cairns viewed the evidence:

Most men . . . pray before they go over the parapet, or advance in the face of machine guns, and they thank God when they have come through the battle. It is possible to make too much and too little of this. Granting that it is at best a very elementary form of religion, and that it is usually evanescent enough, it is none the less very significant. It means that in presence of the most terrific display of material force that human history has ever seen men believe that there is an Unseen Power, inaccessible to the senses, which is yet mightier than high explosives, which knows all and which hears prayer . . .[168]

It does in fact seem clear that in these situations many soldiers were either returning to old habits or else demonstrating the presence of existing ones. Although regular churchgoing was a minority pursuit for the generations which fought both World Wars, habits of personal prayer were still very wide-spread, being commonly taught and fostered at home as well as at Sunday school.[169] During the war years, the appeal of prayer was underscored by the evident popularity of national days of prayer, these national occasions producing attendances at church that could be significantly higher than those normally produced by the great Christian festivals.[170] If MO found in 1943 that around half of its National Panel 'of 1500 voluntary informants' never prayed,[171] there is a good deal of evidence to indicate that this group was not representative of the nation at large. As late as the 1950s, Geoffrey Gorer found that only 14 per cent of the English people claimed that they never prayed. Moreover, among those then aged 65 or over, 71 per cent still claimed to pray once a day or more often, an interesting reflection of how resilient habits of personal piety proved to be among the generation that had fought the First World War. Although Gorer found that habits of personal prayer were less marked among the generation that fought the Second, even at the mid-point of the twentieth century 31 per cent of all English males still prayed at least once a day or more often and only 21 per cent declared that they never prayed at all.[172] Illustrative of the scope and quality of this popular culture of prayer were Neville Talbot's comments regarding the Lord's Prayer, a prayer that he described in 1917 as 'the one island of religious ground, amid marshes of ignorance, common to Englishmen' and which he dubbed 'the padres' great stand-by'.[173]

Clearly, it would be misleading to imagine that the periodic popularity of the sacraments, voluntary services or private prayer simply derived their appeal from a craven self-interest in moments of peril. As chaplains recurrently noted in both World Wars, the sick and wounded proved remarkably receptive to their spiritual work[174] and voluntary thanksgiving and memorial services in the aftermath of battle were generally well and reverently attended by front-line troops. Indeed, these tendencies no doubt informed the outlook of Montgomery's favoured chaplain, Frederick Llewelyn Hughes, who instructed his chaplains to treat 'Thanksgiving and Memorial Services' as no less important than 'Eve of Battle Services' and 'Voluntary Companionship at Zero Hour'.[175] As Alec Bowlby remembered, one such memorial service (and the words of Psalm 121) seemed to provide the balm which his battalion badly needed following a bungled assault on an enemy position in Italy in 1944:

> In the late afternoon, when the air was soft and infinitely peaceful, the Battalion padre held a service for the dead. Several hundred men attended, and we stood in line facing the same hills . . . 'I will lift up mine eyes unto the hills from whence cometh my strength,' read the padre . . . I looked at the hill, thinking of the men who had died there, and how close I had come to it myself. But as the padre read on it became more and more difficult to think of the dead as dead. The words of the psalm, the serenity of the hills, the touch of the sun on my face, confused them with the living to such an extent that for a moment I felt sure there was a God.[176]

An identical mood was also apparent among men of the 11th Royal Scots Fusiliers following heavy fighting in Normandy. As one of their veterans described a post-battle service:

> [We sang] 'There is a small corner of a foreign land' [and] 'Praise my soul the King of Heaven' and the 23rd Psalm. The Colonel

read the lesson followed by a lusty response of 'Onward Christian Soldiers'. We prayed for our dead comrades, for the wounded and for those posted as missing. The service ended with a lone piper playing the lament, 'Flowers of the Forest' and the blessing. The singing had silenced the noise and battle.[177]

A firm sense of the value and efficacy of prayer seems to have been a constant rather than an occasional factor for many soldiers, with front-line soldiers in particular being fortified by the knowledge that others were praying for them at home. Walter Shaw, a Methodist soldier of the West Yorkshire Regiment who was killed on 1 July 1916, was grateful that he was being prayed for by relatives and well-wishers alike.[178] Similarly, Michael Joseph Lavin, a Roman Catholic of the same regiment who was also killed in 1916, wrote home that September thanking his parents for the prayers they had offered on his behalf while on pilgrimage to Holywell.[179] This tendency had not diminished a generation later. As a Second World War chaplain noted, the prayer cards which he distributed to the men of the 43rd Reconnaissance Regiment in the early summer of 1944 were soon in great demand, a demand that was fuelled by the King's broadcast of 6 June which called upon British women to follow the example of the Queen in praying for their menfolk involved in the invasion of France.[180] As Eric Gethyn Jones remembered:

> Within a week there were hundreds of requests for a second card, the first having been sent to wife or sweetheart, and plans having been made to say the same prayers every night at, if possible, the same time. The card was reprinted and this daily link worked in many instances and was, I believe, helpful.[181]

It is also significant in this respect that Kate ter Horst, the famous Dutch heroine of the battle of Arnhem, owed part of her fame as a benevolent mother figure to reading the Bible and praying with the British wounded who had been deposited in her large Oosterbeek home.[182] Besides the prayers of civilians, J.A. Sime, a chaplain who worked at 21st Army Group's psychiatric hospital in 1944–5, was even struck by the readiness with which front-line soldiers would pray for each other. According to Sime:

> Many patients asked for prayer, and nearly always requested that the men from the Line and their own particular friends should specially be remembered. The comradeship amongst these men was striking, and many instances of their sheer goodness to one another I shall always remember.[183]

In addition to this widespread resort to prayer, another significant indicator of the strength of diffused Christianity among the soldiers of both World Wars was the phenomenal popularity of hymn singing. As John Wolffe has argued, the nineteenth century was marked by the 'general triumph of the hymn' in British cultural life, so much so that a fondness for hymnody spread beyond church circles and became 'part of the folk tradition'.[184] As Sarah Williams has shown, among the working-class residents of Southwark between the 1880s and 1930s hymns were strongly associated with childhood, with the maternal influences of home and with fond memories of Sunday school. To the natural potency of nostalgia was added the appeal of rousing melodies and the power of exalted sentiments and aspirations that few could find their own words to express.[185] Among British soldiers in the First World War, the centrality of hymns in popular culture was partly reflected by their misappropriation. Although there are numerous examples of this phenomenon,[186] the 2nd Royal Welch Fusiliers sang a ribald song to the tune of 'O God, our Help in Ages Past', with each verse being 'a little more racy than the first'.[187] In addition to such subversion, a common wartime conceit involved the setting of hymns to the various stages of a soldier's day, from reveille ('Christians, Awake!'), to inspection of the guard ('Sleep on, beloved').[188] However irreverent these adaptations may have appeared, they nevertheless reflected a genuine and profound fondness for hymnody among this generation. As E.C. Crosse observed from his experiences as a chaplain in the First World War, soldiers' hymn singing constantly reminded him that hymns 'rather than the Bible, now provide the one popular devotion of the average Englishman'.[189] The veracity of this observation can be clearly demonstrated by the experiences of Julian Bickersteth, who spent one fateful night in July 1917 ministering to a deserter awaiting execution. Although a hardened criminal in civilian life and a habitual deserter since joining the army, the soldier in question spent his last night singing hymn after hymn with Bickersteth. As Bickersteth wearily noted:

> I think it was a distinct effort on his part to give religion full play. To him, hymn singing meant religion. Probably no other aspect or side of religion had ever touched him, and now he was 'up against it' he found real consolation in singing hymns learnt in childhood – he had been to Sunday school up to twelve or thirteen. Anyhow, that was the point of contact I had been seeking for.[190]

Twenty years on, and among a new generation of citizen soldiers, hymnody had lost little (if any) of its appeal. Since 1927, the singing of

'Abide With Me' had been a feature of every FA Cup Final and audience research during the 'Phoney War' period showed the BBC that hymn singing would provide most of the appeal for any religious services broadcast on its Forces Programme.[191] Indicative of the power of hymnody, particularly when allied to the heady occasion of a national day of prayer, are Tony Foulds's recollections of a service that was broadcast from Lincoln cathedral on the third anniversary of the outbreak of the Second World War. With the microphones and 2,000 servicemen present, Foulds was struck by the 'tremendous atmosphere' of the occasion and by the feelings of 'togetherness' and of 'loyalty to the crown' which the service engendered. As Foulds remembered:

> [I]t was a wonderful occasion and very spiritually uplifting . . .
> I think that even the other ranks who had had to polish up to
> go on church parade . . . were impressed . . . Obviously, that
> number of people singing together the well-known hymns which
> most of them had known from childhood . . . took the rather
> lofty rafters off![192]

Naturally, hymns once again came almost instinctively to soldiers in the front line. Hundreds of recently captured British wounded sang 'Abide With Me' as defeat engulfed the 1st Airborne Division at Arnhem in September 1944 and, several months earlier in the Burmese jungle, a chaplain and his batman turned to hymnody during fighting around the Chindit stronghold of 'Blackpool', their 'great favourite' being 'Guide me, O Thou Great Jehovah'.[193] Similarly, and painfully conscious of the threat of anti-personnel mines while advancing towards the German border early in 1945, Peter White, a young officer of the 4th King's Own Scottish Borderers, drew comfort from the chillingly apposite words of a hymn by Mary Baker Eddy, 'I will listen for thy voice lest my footsteps stray'.[194]

Telling evidence of the power of hymnody was also evident among those who were suffering from more enduring afflictions than the hazards of the front line. J.A. Sime noted how some dimly remembered hymns provided the first evidence of the improving state of a soldier who was suffering from severe battle exhaustion.[195] Likewise, for Douglas Firth of the Royal Army Service Corps, who worked on the infamous Burma–Thailand railway, the words of familiar hymns proved a vital means of solace during months of privation and horror in the Thai jungle. As Firth, a devout Baptist, remembered:

> With clear memories of playing the Chapel organ, I would use
> my battered miniature *Ancient and Modern* hymn book and sing

over my tenor part to myself and [I] reflected on favourite hymns, 'Abide with me'. Third verse – 'I need thy presence every passing hour'. 'Jesus stand among us' and 'O God our help in ages past' with its fourth verse – 'A thousand ages in thy sight are like an evening gone' . . . this book took me away from the terrible daily happenings, beatings [and] daily funerals of my fellow prisoners . . .[196]

Evidently, Firth was by no means alone among British prisoners of war in the Far East in drawing solace and inspiration from hymnody. As another prisoner recalled of evenings at Chungkai, a camp on the Burma–Thailand railway:

At irregular intervals there was community singing. We passed our requests to the master of ceremonies beforehand. Usually we asked for the songs of childhood ['Tipperary', 'Under the Spreading Chestnut Tree'] . . . When the singing was at its height the requests would shift to songs of a more inspirational character: 'The Lord is My Shepherd' . . . 'Abide With Me', 'Jerusalem the Golden' and 'Lead, Kindly Light' . . . The last chords ended, the prisoners, with spirits refreshed, moved back to their huts in a state of peace they had not known for a long time.[197]

As these cases of the sacraments, prayer and hymnody may have already suggested, a conspicuous disparity could exist between the religious susceptibilities of front-line soldiers (and, indeed, certain prisoners of war) and the religious susceptibilities of lines of communication troops. During the First World War, the general calibre of the latter was not held in high esteem. According to the war correspondent C.E. Montague, the typical French base was simply a 'tainted backwater in which the swelling flotillas of the unfit and the unwilling were left to rot at their moorings'. In Montague's memorable description, towards the rearmost areas of the BEF,

gravitated most of the walking wreckage and wastage, physical and moral, of active warfare: convalescent, sick and wounded from hospital, men found too old or too young for trench work, broken-nerved men smuggled out of the way before disaster should come, and malingerers triumphant and chuckling, or only semi-successful, suspect, and tediously over-acting.[198]

Widely regarded as the natural habitat of the shirker and the malingerer, the moral tone of the army's overseas bases during the First World War was lowered still further by the ready availability of drink and prostitutes. Given this context, and without the proximity of the enemy to act as a religious stimulant, chaplains often despaired of the moral and religious condition of troops in these areas. The situation was summed up for *The Army and Religion* report in the following terms:

> Combatants are infinitely more responsive, of course, than non-combatants. Even at the Base, in the reinforcement camps where the men are congregated before being drafted up to the Front, a good chaplain can get any number of candidates for Confirmation or men wishing to make their Communion, Confession, etc. [However,] units permanently on the Line of Communication or at Base would break the heart of almost any priest.[199]

If lines of communication troops were less susceptible to religious influences, even otherwise receptive front-line soldiers could be corrupted by exposure to the pernicious influences of bases like Rouen. As David Cairns explained in 1919:

> The Line was a very much cleaner place than the Base. At the Bases we have had the conditions of barrack towns at home reproduced, with the immense accentuation of the evil which is caused by the absence of [soldiers'] own women folk, and by the reaction of a population [which is] essentially civilian against the restraints of discipline . . . We must add to this also in the case of many units the extreme reaction from the nervous tension and excitement of the Line, the presence of licensed facilities for vice, and the almost incredible temptation to which the men are subjected under these conditions by the cunning and shameless ingenuity of those who make a trade of vice.[200]

These general differences between front-line and rear-area troops were, of course, largely replicated in the Second World War, during which the number of rear echelon troops was proportionately much greater. In 1943 a MO report on religious life in the army discerned definite symptoms of 'some sort of "religious revival"' among British soldiers on active service in the Middle East, indications that were wholly absent among those troops who were yet to go abroad.[201] Again, however, even veterans of hard fighting could be spoiled by prolonged exposure to inaction and one Roman Catholic chaplain of the 16th Infantry Brigade found his flock to be wholly unresponsive to his ministry following the brigade's transfer from the Middle East to garrison duties in India in 1942. In fact, it was positively inimical to religious work when the town of Bangalore transpired to be much like 'Blackpool or Southend during holiday time'.[202]

Conclusion

Given the mass of contradictory evidence which confronted them, contemporary churchmen were probably too disposed to take a pessimistic view of the religious condition of British society in general and of the British soldier in particular. In view of the paradoxical and even elusive nature of the supernatural attitudes and practices that they faced, some of the more candid and informed religious observers of the British soldier in the First World War could only admit their confusion and frustration. As D.S. Cairns wrote in *The Army and Religion* report, a state of 'spiritual anarchy' had been 'created and revealed by the war', a view that confirmed an earlier verdict that although 'The soldier has got religion, I am not sure that he has got Christianity'.[203] If chaos appears to have been the salient feature of the supernatural outlook of most British soldiers during the First World War then this was equally true of British society during the Second. Between 1939 and 1945, successive MO reports noted how, within a broad theistic consensus, orthodox Christian beliefs and practices co-existed with a widespread belief in luck, in astrology and in Spiritualist conceptions of the hereafter.[204] Inevitably, this eclectic outlook was also common to Britain's contemporary citizen soldiers. Remarkably, and despite its inherent subjectivity and incoherence, it could even provide a shared supernatural understanding between soldiers and civilians that defied the orthodoxies of the mainstream churches. Illustrative of this is the case of Stanley Whitehouse of the 1st Black Watch who, on the night of his eighteenth birthday in November 1944, found himself locked in a murderous embrace with a German soldier at a crossroads in Holland. As Whitehouse recollected:

> Three years after that fierce little battle of the crossroads . . . my family and I were celebrating my twenty-first birthday. We were discussing the war years and where we were on particular birthdays when my mum revealed a most singular occurrence. On the night of my eighteenth birthday she had a vivid and frightening dream in which she saw me scrabbling in the mud. Then she heard me cry 'Oh Mum' and sat up in bed, covered in sweat. She was unable to eat or sleep for days – until she had received a letter from me, indicating that I was safe. I was stunned by this revelation, all the more so because I had told no one at home

about my frantic skirmish that night. Undoubtedly psychic powers were at work on my eighteenth birthday, collaborating closely with my guardian angel.[205]

If many churchmen were discouraged by this kind of evidence and attributed such vagaries to the inadequacies of religious education, then they were also too readily inclined to dismiss symptoms of more orthodox religiosity among soldiers as worthless manifestations of emergency religion. However, these verdicts generally ignored the profound influence that Christianity continued to exert upon British culture. Quite clearly, and however much secular and heterodox ideas may have impinged upon the beliefs of some, for the vast majority of soldiers Christianity remained dominant in shaping their moral and spiritual universe. In the latter respect, the predominance of Christianity is evident from the reactions of successive generations of British soldiers to Christian artefacts and iconography. Furthermore, and notwithstanding low levels of formal religious practice in civilian society, it is clear that hymn singing and personal prayer served as unobtrusive common denominators in popular religious life. In short, and notwithstanding its many complexities and attendant vexations for the churches, in the first half of the twentieth century 'diffusive Christianity' remained the principal characteristic of Britain's religious landscape and the significance of this fact should not be underestimated. Far from symbolising the decaying remnant of a once great religious culture, the prevalence of 'diffusive Christianity' reflected the existence of a broad expanse of common ground between the churchgoer and the non-churchgoer and an enduring bond between the churches and the mass of the British people. Moreover, and as we shall be seeing in Chapter 3, 'diffusive Christianity' embraced an array of deeply entrenched beliefs and convictions to which the British army could usefully appeal amidst the many trials of the two World Wars.

Chapter 2

GOD AND THE GENERALS

Introduction

THE RELIGIOUS BELIEFS AND CONVICTIONS of the army's senior officers during the two World Wars have tended to be studied only in relation to a handful of controversial figures whose wider reputations have made them the subject of intense scrutiny and debate. In this regard, the religious beliefs of Douglas Haig, Bernard Montgomery and Orde Wingate have been closely examined by their biographers. As a result of these studies, one may be tempted to conclude that the militant Protestant religiosity of these men was at best nothing more than a colourful anachronism and at worst a dangerous eccentricity. Indeed, among critics of all three there is the strong suspicion that many of their judgements in military matters were as questionable as the religious faith that underpinned and sometimes informed them.[1] However, what these largely unconnected biographical studies tend to obscure is the remarkable currency of a practical, patriotic and theologically unsophisticated Protestant piety among senior general officers of the First and Second World Wars. In part, this phenomenon was a function of the social and religious milieu in which most of them had been born and bred. Not only were a significant proportion of regular army officers the sons of clergymen but, as John Terraine has rightly emphasised, practically all of the men who fought the First World War were '19th Century people, men born in the age of Queen Victoria'.[2] Thus, and because the British army's regimental and junior staff officers of the First World War were the army's senior commanders in the Second, many of the attitudes and mores of the late Victorian generation continued to make their presence felt in the army throughout the Second as well as the First World War.

Among the overwhelmingly Protestant upper- and upper-middle-class families from which the late Victorian and Edwardian officer corps was primarily recruited, regular churchgoing was practically universal, a thorough knowledge of scripture was commonplace and family prayers were a normal feature of domestic routine.[3] Furthermore, at least until the Second World War Britain's public schools continued to perform their Victorian function of 'adhering the upper classes to Christianity',[4] essentially by promoting a conformist and uncomplicated religious outlook among boys from this milieu.[5] At Eton as late as the 1930s, for example, all boys were required to attend chapel two or three times on Sundays and at least once on each weekday.[6] In addition to their experiences at home and at school, the regular army also did much to shape the conformist religious outlook of its junior officers. As John Baynes has observed:

> [Regimental officers] might not have taken their religion very seriously, but they were not likely to doubt that the teaching they had been subjected to in their youth, and still had drummed into them each Sunday on Church Parade, was fundamentally true. The complete dissenter was therefore a rare bird . . . A regular officer who paraded his doubts on religion in 1914 would be thought unreliable by his superiors, and an appalling bore by his equals.[7]

The life and career of Sir Frederick Ivor Maxse, who began the First World War as the commander of the BEF's 1st Guards Brigade and who ended it as the BEF's Inspector-General of Training, illustrates the ambivalent situation of the military atheist. The son of an aristocratic but radical naval officer who harboured a profound contempt for Christianity, Maxse loathed church parade while a cadet at Sandhurst in the early 1880s. Nevertheless, and despite his lack of enthusiasm for organised religion, Maxse could not escape the influence of his profession, class and education in this respect. At Sandhurst he submitted to church parades notwithstanding his distaste for them and went on to marry a keen churchwoman, the Honourable Mary Wyndham, in 1899. Moreover, when appointed to oversee military training in France in 1918, he looked to reforming figures of the church for inspiration, assuring his wife that his approach to this role would be that of 'a Savonarola or a LUTHER!'[8]

As Maxse's sentiments may suggest, regular officers of his generation had a high estimation of the professional value of religion. This was an institution over which the heroic example of soldier saints such as Sir Henry Havelock and Gordon of Khartoum cast a long shadow and in which the contribution of religion to the army's internal discipline was recognised in the promotion of the temperance cause and in the sponsorship of 'soldiers' homes' by many senior officers. Indeed, until his death while visiting Indian units of the BEF in November 1914, the British army still possessed its own incarnation of the Christian hero in the form of the hugely popular Field Marshal Lord Roberts VC, its last commander-in-chief, who took it upon himself to extol the merits of reading the New Testament to the men of the Ulster Volunteer Force who enlisted in the British army in the late summer and autumn of 1914.[9] The prevalence of a strongly religious cast of mind among many of the army's most senior officers in the two World Wars was, as we shall see, reflected in the importance that they came to attach to military chaplaincy. However, their religiosity also had much broader ramifications, not least in providing many of them with a much-needed sense of divine guidance and inspiration, one which was often couched and rationalised in terms of a deeply Protestant theology of providence and election.

Haig and religion

Given the scale of bloodletting on the Western Front between 1916 and 1918, Sir Douglas Haig undoubtedly serves as the most famous and controversial illustration of the godly GOC, not least because his sense of divine election and providential purpose deepened as the First World War went on and his burden of personal responsibility increased. Raised by a devout mother, under her tutelage Haig developed a habit of prayer, a sense of divine oversight and a great familiarity with scripture from an early age, being required to send her commentaries on selected biblical passages every week while at school.[10] Despite his Presbyterian background, Haig appears to have attended Church of England services for much of his professional life, a consequence of the Anglican milieu of Clifton College, of his student days at Brasenose and of the immediate circumstances of army life in England and India.[11] If Haig was not unduly bound by denominational ties earlier in life, then his attitudes towards denominationalism appear to have hardened under the impact of the First World War, during which he appears to have become convinced of the pressing need for 'a great Imperial Church to which all honest citizens of the Empire could belong'. Fearful of a Russian-style revolution, Haig could see no alternative to an even closer integration of church and state and he held fast to his vision for the ecclesiastical future of the empire until his death in 1928.[12] However, if Haig's pre-war and essentially pragmatic non-denominationalism was not untypical of his social and professional milieu, then the same could also be said of his pre-war interest in Spiritualism, an interest encouraged by his youngest sister, Mrs Henrietta Jameson. In a manner that prefigured his later tendency to harness supernatural power for his own purposes, during one séance at the time of the Haldane reforms Haig dutifully sought advice on the best means of expanding the Territorial Force. On this occasion, the medium assured him of the benign interest in his career of 'a small man named Napoleon [who] had become changed for the better in the spirit world'.[13]

If Henrietta Jameson continued to urge upon her brother the influence of Napoleon as late as June 1916 (by which time Napoleon had, apparently, been seconded by God to serve Haig in an advisory capacity),[14] Haig's beliefs had already assumed their definitive wartime form. As GOC of First Army in 1915, Haig's new religious seriousness was already in evidence. Besides praising the work of his chaplains prior to the battle of Loos, during the subsequent fighting Haig had visited the HQ of Hubert Gough, then one of his corps commanders, and had consoled him with the conviction 'that we shall win "Not by might, nor by power, but by *my spirit*, saith the Lord of hosts" [Zechariah 4.6]'.[15] By the time he supplanted Sir John French as commander-in-chief of the BEF in December 1915, Haig was already fully convinced that he was an instrument of divine providence. As he confided to his wife at the time: 'All seem to expect success as the result of my arrival, and somehow give me the idea that I am "meant to win" by some Superior Power.'[16] If Haig had rediscovered a vivid belief in divine providence and election, within weeks he had stumbled upon a congenial prophet in the form of the Revd G.S. Duncan, a junior Presbyterian chaplain at St Omer, who was to become 'his faithful chaplain' for the remainder of the war.[17] Although, by his own admission, Duncan was an academic whose pastoral experience was almost nil,[18] Haig found Duncan's personality and preaching very much to his taste. Curiously enough, their first encounter was on the first Sunday of 1916, an occasion which King George V had appointed as a national day of prayer.[19] Treating the occasion with 'all due solemnity', Duncan's sermon on prayer left an indelible impression on Haig and apparently confirmed his inclination to return to the bosom of the church in which he had been raised. Already disillusioned with the Church of England, whose worship he had found wanting and whose chaplains he perceived as being plagued by a divisive spirit of party,[20] Duncan immediately impressed Haig with his delivery and with his demeanour, which Haig tellingly described as 'quite after the old Covenanting style'.[21] If Duncan's enduring emphasis on prayer and providence never lost its appeal to Haig, Duncan's eloquence no doubt contributed to his developing view of the chaplain's role in the army. Indeed, as Haig remarked of his first encounter with Duncan:

> He told us that in our prayers we should be as natural as possible, and tell the Almighty exactly what we feel we want. The Nation is now learning to pray! And that nothing can withstand the prayers of a great united people . . . The congregation was greatly impressed, and one could have heard a pin fall during his prayers and sermon. So different to the coughing and restlessness which goes on in church in peace time.[22]

From the early weeks of 1916, Haig grew increasingly dependent on Duncan's sermons and upon his consistent preaching of 'a fine manly Christianity'[23] for both inspiration and solace.[24] Certainly, and with the notable connivance of Dr Simms, the senior Presbyterian minister on the Western Front,[25] Duncan appears to have become 'generally accepted (unofficially) as the Commander-in-Chief's chaplain'.[26] In August 1917, and prompted by Duncan's alarming suggestion that he be relieved and moved closer to the front line, Simms wrote to Duncan in highly revealing terms: 'I beg of you to steady your brain. I look on you as a gift of God to our great Chief. Do you not think that that is duty grand enough for any chaplain, to stay & strengthen & uphold his hands in this titanic struggle?'[27] Clearly, and as Simms implied, Duncan's support for Haig was directly comparable with Aaron's support for Moses during Israel's battle against the Amalekites, a battle described in Exodus 17. As Simms put the situation in a further letter to Duncan:

> I feel very sure that Aaron had no greatness of conscience as to the propriety of his actions when he st[oo]d on the mountain top upholding his great leader's arms while the battle raged below. Stay & strengthen your soul with that old world story. No one in this Campaign has the sacred claim to our very best as [does] our Chief, for he bears a well nigh crushing burden, & I bless God day and night that he has found a chaplain who he is not afraid to say does help him to bear up under this load. And how mortal man can desire a better, nobler, greater task for his war work I cannot imagine. That the man he delights to honour is a Presbyterian is to me a double cause of thanksgiving for I look upon it as the noblest, strongest form of religious influence that I know on this earth.[28]

In view of the nature of their relationship, it is hard to escape the conclusion that Haig saw in Duncan the epitome of what he wished a military chaplain to be. Haig had a habit of describing Duncan as somebody who 'could make anyone fight' and it was with this pointed encomium that he introduced Duncan to General John Pershing in July 1917, Pershing being the commander of the American Expeditionary Force, another raw host of largely citizen soldiers who were about to experience the fiery trials of the Western Front.[29] During 1917, and as Haig's capacity for command was thrown into question by a succession of indecisive offensives and by the evident mistrust of Lloyd George, his relationship with Duncan became even closer. As Duncan recalled: 'During those anxious and arduous months in 1917 my relations with Haig, always pleasant, became much more intimate and personal.' Indeed, by the end of the year, Haig was even allowing Duncan to peruse portions of his diary, a journal in which Haig was prone to record the events of the day and his own religious reflections on the current situation.[30]

If Haig's religiosity served to define his relationship with Duncan then it also helped to set the tone of life at GHQ, which Duncan described as 'monastic' in temper, not least because of Haig's prompt ban on female visitors.[31] However, the prevailing moral and religious tone at GHQ was that of the kirk rather than the cloister. In April 1917, Haig's chief intelligence officer, John Charteris, who was both a fellow Scot and a son of the manse, described one Sabbath as 'a regular Scottish Sunday', in which he and Haig had discussed the day's sermon 'as one used to do as a boy in Scotland'.[32] Given this milieu, it is scarcely surprising that at least one senior staff officer, namely J.F. Birch, Haig's protégé and artillery adviser, should have chosen to abandon the Church of England for the Church of Scotland for the duration of the war.[33] Even amidst the turmoil of the German spring offensive of 1918, Haig remained punctilious in his attendance at church, Duncan admitting his surprise at seeing Haig's car appear 'as usual' on the Sunday after the storm had broken.[34] Indeed, in August 1918, and with his great riposte at hand, Haig instigated a special service of thanksgiving at GHQ:

> [Haig] summoned the appropriate Staff Officers and directed them to make arrangements for a Special Thanksgiving Service to be held at Montreuil on August 4th to give thanks to God for the guidance of Providence which had brought the Empire and the Army through these four years of toil and strain, and to entreat that it might not be withdrawn until final success crowned their efforts.[35]

As this thanksgiving service indicated, Haig's regular religious observance and his close relationship with Duncan was reflective of a strong and deepening sense of divine purpose and of his own dependence on God. Although Haig was widely considered to have been uncommunicative on matters of faith even in private conversation or correspondence,[36] his closest associates were under no illusion as to the influence that his faith had upon him. On the eve of the Somme offensive, Haig wrote to his wife:

> I note what you wrote in Tuesday's letter that 'for this coming offensive ask for God's help.' Now you must know that *I feel* that every step in my plan has been taken with the Divine help and I ask daily for aid, not merely in making the plan, but in carrying it out, and this I hope I shall continue to do until the end of all things which concern me on earth. I think it is the Divine help which gives me tranquillity of mind and enables me to carry on without feeling the strain of responsibility to be too excessive . . .[37]

Towards the end of 1917, when the fortunes of the Third Battle of Ypres had affected even the mood at GHQ,[38] in the light of a sermon from Duncan on Luke 22.41–3 Haig was moved to break his customary silence on matters of faith in order to confide to Charteris: 'When things are difficult, there is no reason to be downhearted. We must do our best, and *for a certainty* a ministering angel will help.'[39] Likewise, in April 1918, Haig received a message from Duncan reminding him that 'There is no man under heaven for whom these days a greater volume of prayer ascends to heaven than for you. May the knowledge of that strengthen you.' Haig's reply was characteristic: 'I am very grateful for your thinking of me at this time, and I *know* I am sustained in my efforts by that Great Unseen Power, otherwise I could not be standing the strain as I am doing.'[40]

While Haig appears to have been reluctant to partake in Holy Communion,[41] the Bible featured heavily in sustaining his personal, theologically unsophisticated and supremely practical religious faith. As Duncan noted, Haig's ready familiarity with its contents was not unusual, a working knowledge of scripture being merely an accepted part of 'an intelligent person's education'.[42] Illustrative of the solace that the Bible afforded Haig were the words spoken to King Jehoshaphat of Judah, then faced by a coalition of Moabites and Ammonites, in 2 Chronicles 20.15: 'Thus saith the LORD unto you, Be not afraid nor dismayed by reason of this great multitude; for the battle is not yours, but God's.' Haig fervently invoked these words both before and during the long expected German offensive of March 1918, referring to them in a letter to his wife in February of that year and admonishing Duncan with them on the sombre morning of Sunday 24 March.[43] Seven months later, and in the more favourable circumstances of impending Allied victory,

Haig was tempted to draw a comparison between the fate of Germany and the humbling of ancient Assyria, writing in his diary on 20 October:

> Colonel Wigram . . . states that a telegram just rec'd states that cholera in a bad form has broken out in Berlin. It looks as if the prophecy of II Kings is to be fulfilled re the Assyrians being slain in battle and many thousands by the Lord in pestilence![44]

If the contents of the Bible inevitably confirmed Haig's faith in the overriding care and purposes of providence, as with so much else the impact of this faith on his exercise of command has become a matter of dispute between Haig's admirers and critics. Acknowledging that Haig felt himself to be an instrument of providence, Duncan maintained that this conviction was held 'in all humility, not out of egotism or wishful thinking, but with a sober grasp of the situation as he saw it'. Duncan also rejected the suggestion that an overwhelming spiritual conceit had closed Haig's mind and clouded his military judgement. As Duncan put it:

> With some men, no doubt, belief in a divine 'call' leads easily to fanaticism. But Haig was no fanatic. There was about him a mental balance which was associated not a little with his stern sense of duty; and like other devout men down the ages he heard in the call of duty the voice of God. He takes his place with those heroic figures (like Moses and Joshua in the Scripture records, or like Cromwell and Lincoln in the story of the nations) who in some critical hour of history begin by recognising the need for action in the situation which confronts them, and then, in a spirit of obedience and faith in God, find themselves braced to meet it with courage and resolution, and in so doing draw strength from unseen sources.[45]

Seen from this perspective Haig's religious faith was a positive asset to the British war effort, a personal gift that enabled him to surmount all military and political adversity until final victory was achieved on the Western Front.[46] Nevertheless, even Haig's friends could feel uneasy about its influence. Charteris, for example, was wary of its 'fatalistic' undertones and remarked that, because the will of providence as to the outcome of the war was far from clear, the same sermons that Haig found so inspiring could quite easily have given heart to Hindenburg.[47] In addition, Gerard DeGroot has drawn attention to the emphasis on the sacrificial, purgative and regenerative aspects of the war which featured prominently in Duncan's preaching.[48] Although the texts of Duncan's sermons have not survived,[49] these themes were commonly employed by army chaplains of the day and it is possible that Haig garnered from these sermons (whose content he routinely summarised in his diary) the view that human suffering invariably tended towards higher ends.[50] Furthermore, DeGroot has criticised Haig for being too disposed to rely on blind faith rather than hard evidence in his overall vision of the war. As DeGroot put it:

> Haig's religious faith did occasionally obscure the real war. If intelligence from the front conflicted with his vision of the war, he often either ignored or subconsciously misinterpreted it . . . With the end predetermined, events along the way diminished in importance. If data was occasionally ignored, it was because Haig believed that the goodness of God was the most reliable indicator of the way the war would be resolved.[51]

If DeGroot was nevertheless ultimately prepared to grant the 'sad fact' that, 'in order to win, Britain needed Haig and Haig needed religion',[52] more hostile critics have maintained that Haig's faith helped to weaken the competence of Haig's command. According to Basil Liddell Hart, whose influence on the study of British generalship in the First World War has been immense,[53] the nature of Haig's religiosity precluded a sober and objective handling of the BEF on the Western Front.[54] Moreover, for Denis Winter, the crystallisation of Haig's religious views during the war years merely represented 'an unhealthy development in a man already tending towards delusions of infallibility'.[55]

Haig's lieutenants

Compelling though it is, the continuing controversy over Haig's command of the BEF should not obscure the vitally important fact that Haig was far from being alone among senior British commanders on the Western Front in drawing inspiration from a similar type of religion and in viewing his own part in the war in explicitly providential terms. As we shall see, from early 1916 the BEF's army commanders were active in their promotion of the chaplains' work and this appears to have stemmed, as much as anything else, from a sincerely felt piety on their part. As Bishop Gwynne, the senior Anglican chaplain on the Western Front, testified from his own experience, generals Horne (First Army), Plumer (Second Army), Byng (Third Army), Rawlinson (Fourth Army) and Gough (Fifth Army) were remarkable for the earnestness of their religious faith.[56] Certainly, Plumer's religious habits and convictions were much commented upon, with Archbishop Lang extolling him as 'a great soldier, a great Englishman, and a true-hearted Christian'.[57] Similarly, Gwynne likened Plumer to Lord Roberts in view of his piety and his popularity with the men under his command.[58] Although best remembered for his support of the chaplains' school at St Omer and for his association with Talbot House and the Toc H movement, Plumer's Anglican piety was such that even his private devotions were worthy of note. According to Charles Harington, who served as Plumer's chief of staff for much of the war, prior to the attack on Messines ridge in June 1917 Plumer felt the compulsion to pray. As Harington remembered:

> Zero was at 3.10 a.m. We all had breakfast at 2.30 a.m. with the Army Commander. The rest of us went to the top of Cassel Hill to see the mines go up. Five hundred tons of explosives. I can see the glow in the sky as I write. Not so the Army Commander. He was kneeling by his bedside praying for those gallant officers and men who were at that moment attacking.[59]

As was the case with Haig at GHQ, Plumer's faith helped to set the tone at the HQ of the Second Army. As one Canadian staff officer later wrote:

> I always like to think of General Plumer in his attitude towards religion. It seemed to be just a part of himself. He was a devout Christian gentleman and it seemed to form a very important part of his personality, his perspective and his background. This was well known amongst his Staff officers at Army Headquarters and all through the [Second] Army. I think it had the effect of interesting many of his Staff officers in that side of their personal life . . . This, to me, was one of my greatest prides; to serve under and in close staff contact with a Christian man of this kind.[60]

General Sir Henry Sinclair Horne, the GOC of the First Army from September 1916 until the end of the war, was, like Plumer, a devout Anglican and liked to attend church twice on Sundays. If Gwynne regarded Horne as on a par with Plumer in terms of his efforts to promote the work of chaplains in the BEF,[61] in January 1917 Horne was one of three army commanders to write public letters in support of the Church of England's National Mission of Repentance and Hope on the Western Front:

> I have [he wrote] a firm belief in prayer as a support always and an inspiration often. I am convinced that prayer puts the

finishing touch to our sense of duty, and provides a stimulant that carries us through danger and difficulty . . . History tells us how men fight for a cause which concerns their religion. If we have religious enthusiasm, with the high standard of devotion to duty and self-sacrifice which inspires our troops, we gain a great deal.[62]

Similarly, and at the height of the Third Battle of Ypres, Horne spoke with obvious effect at a general conference of First Army chaplains. As G.S. Duncan recalled:

The Conference owed much to the presence and the Christian utterances of Gen. Horne at the opening session . . . Gen. Horne, speaking as the Army Commander, said just the right things in his short 10 minute address. Morale and religious emotions, he reminded us, are very closely bound up, and while we are out to beat the Germans, we must be in all earnest in seeking to qualify ourselves to best them. Every blow at the Germans is a blow for the Kingdom of Christ. He recalled the great work which had been done last winter in his army in connection with the National Mission, and said he wanted this winter's campaign to be prosecuted with even more thoroughness than last year's.[63]

For his part, Sir Julian Byng also proved forthcoming in expressing his thoughts on the war's religious dimensions. Promoted to the command of the Third Army in June 1917, Byng put his views to Gwynne in a private meeting three months later. As Gwynne noted in his diary:

It was quite a short interview but that gave me an insight into what some of our best believe. He began by asking whether I thought that the clergy were seeing the great vision of what was in front of them – the great difficulties and at the same time the grand prospects. He also went on to say that even this great material force was an expression of the spiritual power behind the material and thought that all the big men here were called out by God for this work; that God gave him his present job and though he did not feel big enough or good enough for it, he felt he had a claim on God for equipment for the work given to him. I came away feeling that if this is the spirit of our leaders then we need have no fear about the ultimate victory.[64]

Sir Hubert Gough, a particularly controversial general who was sacked in March 1918 for the failure of his Fifth Army to stem the German spring offensive, was another strong advocate of the Church of England's National Mission, declaring at Christmas 1916 that 'Our success in this great struggle depends entirely on whether God is on our side. He certainly will not be unless we are his servants.'[65] Furthermore, and whatever his flaws as a commander, in his recollections on his service as a chaplain on the Western Front, E.C. Crosse praised Gough as 'a true friend of padres' in the Fifth Army.[66] Indeed, Gough and Crosse shared the same views as to the moral and religious qualities that would ensure victory. In his preface to Crosse's pamphlet *The God of Battles* (1917), Gough concurred with Crosse's claim that 'Moral qualities are of primary importance in a soldier's life, and that God is the Lord and Giver of these . . . It is therefore upon moral qualities that the issue of the war must in the long run depend.' Furthermore, Gough went on to aver:

> A real Faith in God and His justice and His Power in the end, whatever happens, to make Right conquer, is a very great support to courage; in fact I might say without exaggeration it is an absolute necessity for the maintenance of our courage.[67]

The third of the BEF's army commanders to offer his public support for the work of the National Mission in the winter of 1916–17 was Sir Edmund Allenby,[68] who was removed from the command of the Third Army in order to take command of the EEF in June 1917. Although this was something of a demotion, six months later Allenby redeemed himself in spectacular fashion through the long-awaited capture of Jerusalem. Such was the public enthusiasm for Allenby's triumphant campaign in the Holy Land (and for his entry into the Holy City on foot) that he felt the subsequent adulation of his religious admirers rather embarrassing.[69] However, and notwithstanding the general's blushes, Allenby rather courted celebrity of this kind. In his fervent message of support for the National Mission, Allenby had pronounced:

> We are called to make the act of Repentance; to look for and to throw away whatever can divert our energies and lessen our powers . . . we must bare our hearts before God, then purged of every base motive we may go forward in high hope to the sure triumph awaiting us.[70]

In addition to his stirring support for the National Mission on the Western Front, in 1918 Allenby penned an enthusiastic preface for an official history of the work of the Young Men's Christian Association with the EEF. As Allenby once again enthused:

No one has more reason than I to be grateful to the YMCA for its work in connection with the army . . . Broad-minded Christianity, self-regardless devotion to work, a spirit of daring enterprise, and sound business guidance have built an organisation which has earned the gratitude of the Empire.[71]

If strong religious beliefs were characteristic of the BEF's army commanders during the First World War then the same was no doubt true of its corps and divisional commanders. Like their better known superiors, as a body they were very much children of the Victorian era and products of the late Victorian regular army, the average age of divisional commanders being fifty-one years and six months on appointment.[72] Lord Cavan, who was widely regarded as the best corps commander on the Western Front,[73] ascribed his success in this capacity to an inspirational period of prayer in the Upper Room at Toc H just after taking command of XIV Corps in the Ypres salient. Speaking at a public meeting in Woolwich in 1936, Cavan explained how he went to Toc H after a miserable day spent noting the weaknesses of the Allied position in and around this critical sector. According to one historian of Toc H, Cavan went on to describe how:

He knelt down himself and prayed, as he had never prayed before, that Almighty God would give him comfort, self-reliance, courage, and would take away despair . . . He felt as if an overwhelming burden had been lifted from him and that he was free and strong once more. He rose from prayer, refreshed, renewed; knelt again to render parting thanks, descended the stairs, went out into the darkness and walked alone back to his Corps Headquarters. From that day until this meeting in Woolwich, he had made no mention of that visit to Talbot House. But now, as Chief of the Imperial General Staff, he felt that it was right and fitting that he should publicly declare that he owed the whole of his subsequent career to that one visit to the Upper Room.[74]

There were also many keen churchmen among the army's divisional commanders. In September 1917, one major-general delivered an address at a First Army chaplains' conference that G.S. Duncan described as 'a master-piece of genuine Christian thought & sentiment, its earnestness being reinforced by the genuine humility and unaffected tenderness of the man'.[75] Further-more, William Temple noted that meetings of the progressive Life and Liberty movement 'roped in Major-Generals in shoals' in France and Belgium in 1919.[76] However, if front-line soldiers were largely oblivious to the consolation and inspiration which their army and corps commanders derived from religion, then its effects on their divisional commanders could be more obvious. Given the politics of the army's ethnic divisions, in December 1915 Lord Kitchener thought it prudent to replace the GOC of the 16th Division, Lieutenant-General Sir Lawrence Parsons, with a Roman Catholic, Major-General W.B. Hickie. The division had not yet been committed to battle and Kitchener chose Parsons' successor with the aid of a list of Roman Catholic officers furnished by John Redmond, then leader of the Irish National Party.[77] If sectarian issues impinged on the officers and men of the 16th Division (who seem to have reacted indignantly to the manner of Parsons' removal)[78] for soldiers of other divisions the pious foibles of their commanders could prove a source of irritation and even scorn. Lieutenant Bernard Martin of the 1st North Staffordshire Regiment remembered how his battalion was berated on church parade by their divisional GOC on account of the foulness of their language, a habit which he decried as 'a disgrace to the whole Division'.[79] Likewise, Major-General Sir Reginald Pinney, who successively commanded the 35th and the 33rd Divisions on the Western Front, was known as 'a devout, non-smoking teetotaller' who abolished the rum ration as a routine issue for the men of the 33rd Division after his arrival in September 1916.[80] For his notorious 'edict against the rum ration',[81] Pinney earned the enduring hostility of one regular soldier who remembered that:

> Our Division was the worst in the whole of France for rum issues: if we got any at all we were issued with half a ration instead of a whole one. In lieu of the half ration of rum the Divisional General, Major-General Pinney, erected places a couple of miles from the front line where men returning from the line could have a cup of hot tea and one small biscuit. In his comfortable quarters many miles from the Front I expect he couldn't see what benefit rum was to any man . . . He was called a bun-punching crank and more fitted to be in command of a Church Mission hut at the Base than a division of troops.[82]

Monty and religion

Unquestionably, religion was very important for many of the army's general officers during the First World War and this was also true of the Second. However, the very different outlook of the British army's rank and file in the two World Wars called for rather different styles of command and leadership, a fact which led senior general officers of the Second World War to be more communicative about their religious beliefs to the men under their command. The most important exemplar of this development was, of course, Bernard Law Montgomery. The grandson of the eminent Anglican divine Frederick Farrar and the son of Henry Montgomery (the first bishop of Tasmania and one-time secretary of the Society for the Propagation of the Gospel) the young Montgomery was originally intended for the church and grew up in a household dominated by the influence of his pious and puritanical mother.[83] Given the manner of his upbringing, Montgomery had a ready familiarity with the Bible from an early age and, by his own admission, scripture was the only subject at which he excelled during his schooldays at St Paul's.[84] Montgomery's religious upbringing, his populist style of leadership and his concern for military effectiveness came into their own after he assumed command of the Eighth Army in August 1942 and his religious convictions exerted an enormous influence on his personal philosophy of command. As Montgomery wrote in his *Memoirs*:

> I do not believe that today a commander can inspire great armies, or single units, or even individual men, and lead them to achieve great victories, unless he has a proper sense of religious truth; he must be prepared to acknowledge it, and to lead his troops in the light of that truth. He must always keep his finger on the spiritual pulse of his armies; he must be sure that the spiritual purpose which inspires them is right and true, and is clearly expounded to one and all. Unless he does this, he can expect no lasting success. For all leadership, I believe, is based on the spiritual quality, the power to inspire others to follow . . .[85]

A number of factors conspired to ensure that full rein was given to these personal convictions after Lieutenant-General Montgomery took command of the Eighth Army in the fateful summer of 1942. First, there was the experience of the First World War and the fact that its course and its outcome had seemed to confirm, as we shall see, the significance of religion as a positive influence on the morale of citizen soldiers. Second, there was the fact that, since the dark days of 1940, a growing emphasis had arisen in British society on the moral dimensions of the war and on the importance of the nation's Christian heritage and identity. Third, there was the fact that, in an increasingly democratic age, Britain's citizen army had 'to be led rather than driven' and general officers were thus obliged to persuade and cajole the ordinary soldier as never before.[86] As Correlli Barnett has put it, the most able of British generals in the Second World War felt compelled to work on their public relations and to become 'immediate and personal figures to the troops, not merely remote embodiments of command to whom was owed unquestioning respect and obedience'.[87] In combination, these factors allowed Montgomery to reinvent himself as a latter-day John the Baptist, an oddly attired figure preaching inspiration and hope in the desert.

Convinced of the religious foundations of good morale and of God's oversight of British military fortunes, Montgomery marked the Eighth Army's defensive victory at Alam Halfa with a service of thanksgiving that was held at his main HQ at Burg-el-Arab on Sunday 6 September 1942.[88] Thereafter, and as part of his remarkable transformation of the Eighth Army's self-confidence, Montgomery regularly invoked the aid of the Almighty in personal messages that were 'To be read out to all Troops'.[89] The first of these messages was issued on 23 October 1942, on the commencement of the great offensive at Alamein. As Montgomery's message concluded:

> Therefore, let every officer and man enter the battle with a stout heart, and the determination to do his duty so long as he has breath in his body.
> AND LET NO MAN SURRENDER SO LONG AS HE IS UNWOUNDED AND CAN FIGHT.
> Let us all pray that 'the Lord mighty in battle' will give us the victory.[90]

Similar messages were issued by Montgomery at Christmas 1942, after the Eighth Army's victory at Medenine in March 1943, and prior to and during the Eighth Army's campaign in Sicily in the following summer.[91] Moreover, Montgomery extended this tried and tested practice to the forces of the 21st Army Group, which he commanded in North West Europe in 1944–5. In May 1945, and on the conclusion of the war in Europe, Montgomery turned in a sombre mood to the theme of those who had been killed but here again the theological prognosis was decidedly upbeat:

> I would ask you all to remember those of our comrades who fell in the struggle. They gave their lives that others might have freedom, and no man can do more than that. I believe that He would say to each and every one of them:-
> 'Well done, thou good and faithful servant.'[92]
>
> [Matthew 25.21]

Although Montgomery transformed the morale of the Eighth Army through a variety of means that included the ruthless dismissal of inadequate officers, an intense emphasis on training and the careful nurturing of a habit of victory, it is important not to downplay the influence that Montgomery's militant religiosity had on the men and women under his command. Certainly, there is considerable evidence to show that it made a strong impression on many, with the person of Montgomery himself being often seen in quasi-religious terms. As Captain Warwick Charlton remembered of Montgomery's advent in the desert:

> There was this extraordinary little man whom nobody knew anything about, really. And what he did was a sort of Wesleyan thing . . . It was a revival thing . . . The first thing he did was to preach a sermon, about victory and success . . . he knew where he was going and what he wanted to do. And he preached at us, and people felt impelled to go out and carry this message . . .[93]

Clearly, Montgomery seems to have had a similar effect upon the units of the Second Army which were visited during a 'preaching tour' of south-east England early in 1944.[94] As the official history of the 43rd (Wessex) Division put it:

> He [Montgomery] appeared in person to inspect the greater part of the Division, drawn up in a hollow square at Rye on 4th February in the early winter dawn. All had risen long before daylight. As he walked along the ranks, snow began to fall. Finally, he mounted a jeep and, calling on the men to break their ranks and gather round, addressed the troops all around him . . . [H]e resembled one of the great missionary Bishops of the Middle Ages, calling upon the soldiers to embark upon a Crusade. His bearing with the troops at this time always contained a hint of the ecclesiastic. If he had been born in another age, he would probably have been a towering figure of the Church. As a great political Cardinal of the later medieval period, he would have been thoroughly at home.[95]

According to a chaplain present at Rye, 'The effect of [Monty's] speech, especially on the [other ranks], was very considerable'.[96] If, on the eve of D-Day, a trooper of an armoured regiment reacted to a similar pep talk with the words, 'It's like the coming of the Messiah',[97] those who knew Montgomery well were especially prone to place him in more exalted company than mere cardinals or revivalist preachers. For one staff officer who accompanied Montgomery to the headquarters of the American First and Ninth Armies in the wake of the German breakthrough in the Ardennes in December 1944, Montgomery arrived at his new command 'like Christ come to cleanse the temple'.[98] Likewise, Sergeant Norman Kirby, who was in charge of intelligence and security at the Tactical HQ of Montgomery's 21st Army Group, remembered it as an 'almost monastic establishment' and that the mobile church which was eventually attached to it was unavoidably 'reminiscent of the Ark of the Covenant which accompanied and comforted the Israelites on their long journey in the wilderness'.[99] Naturally enough, Montgomery's overweening vanity and his constant invocations of the Almighty could give rise to a certain scepticism on the part of more seasoned soldiers. Whatever the feelings of the other ranks, certain officers of the 43rd Division regarded his speech at Rye as 'a gross example of showmanship'[100] while Geoffrey Picot, who served as an officer in the 1st Hampshire Regiment, remembered one particular conference held in southern Holland later in 1944 for officers of the 50th Division:

> [A]t eleven o'clock the short, slight figure of Montgomery strode on to the stage. Everything was going well, he announced, he was in complete control of the campaign, making the enemy dance to our tune, and in any case the Lord mighty in battle was on our side. Throughout a thirty minute talk there was not the slightest noise apart from his voice. Afterwards some of my friends reminded me that when a battalion went into battle the orders clearly stated whether supporting arms like tanks and artillery were 'in support' or 'under command'. In the first case the battalion commander told them what support he wanted and they decided how to give it (if possible) and in the second case the battalion commander gave them orders which they had to obey whether they liked it or not.
>
> 'We're all right now,' my pal reckoned. 'The Lord's not just in support. Monty's got Him under command.'[101]

Monty's contemporaries

Orde Wingate was another controversial and demonstratively religious officer who did much to boost the battered morale of the British army in the middle years of the Second World War. Although a much younger man than Montgomery, the army's leading proponent of irregular warfare was the product of a Plymouth Brethren upbringing, a background that endowed Wingate with a fascination with scripture to rival that of the victor of Alamein. If Wingate's prodigious knowledge of the Bible informed his passionate Zionism as well as his approach to irregular warfare, his youth, eloquence and evident desire to repeat the exploits of his Old Testament heroes won him some important political and military patrons.[102] Convinced of God's providential plan for his life, it was a crisis of personal faith as much as anything else that led to Wingate's attempted suicide in Cairo in 1941.[103] However, his survival appears only to have deepened an already profound belief that divine providence was intimately involved in the course of his life. Notwithstanding his remarkable convictions and charisma, the direct impact on British troops of Wingate's colourful Old Testament religiosity was of course more limited than that of Montgomery. When he was killed in an air crash in March 1944, Wingate was still only a major-general and his Chindit expeditions of 1943 and 1944 contained a substantial component of Gurkha, West African, Burmese and even American personnel.[104] Still, and despite the multi-national and multi-religious composition of the forces that he led into Japanese-occupied Burma, Wingate could not resist issuing orders of the day which reflected his own fiery brand of Christianity. As the first Chindits set out for Burma in February 1943, his order of the day concluded with the exhortation: 'Finally, knowing the vanity of man's efforts and the confusion of his purpose, let us pray God may accept our services and direct our endeavours so that when we shall have done all, we shall see the fruit of our labours and be satisfied.'[105] Similarly, for Operation Thursday, the second Chindit expedition of the following year, Wingate developed a strategy of fortified bases – or strongholds – to be used in the coming operations deep behind Japanese lines. In typical style, Wingate outlined this doctrine in a memorandum headed by a text plucked from Zechariah 9.12, 'Turn you to the strong hold, ye prisoners of hope.'[106]

Less flamboyant than Montgomery or Wingate, although no less earnest in terms of his piety, was Lieutenant-General Sir William Dobbie. A distinguished officer of the Royal Engineers, Dobbie had joined the Plymouth Brethren while still a student at Woolwich and was related to Wingate by marriage. A capable staff officer, Dobbie had served on Haig's staff in the First World War and was well known in evangelical circles in the inter-war period.[107] Given his religious views and recurrent strokes of good fortune throughout his military career, Dobbie was very much inclined to view his life in terms of a personal history of providential care. However, the events of the Second World War – and not least his own experiences as governor of Malta from April 1940 to May 1942 – persuaded Dobbie to embark upon a veritable campaign of evangelism in the latter half of the war. In 1943, one observer reported Dobbie as being 'on a tour of military camps [in the Middle East] emphasising divine intervention at Malta'.[108] By 1945, Dobbie felt compelled to present his views to a wider public in the form of an autobiography entitled *A Very Present Help* in which he strongly asserted the power of prayer and the continuing relevance of the Bible in both personal and national life, recalling the events of the Second World War and emphasising the providential nature of the 'tremendous and wonderful years' of Malta's long siege.[109]

Dobbie's immediate successor as governor of Malta was the redoubtable Viscount Gort VC, previously commander-in-chief of the BEF during the Franco-Belgian campaign of 1940. In August 1940, and with the salutary experience of the fall of France behind him, Gort was invited to address the nation in a Sunday evening service which was broadcast to commemorate the outbreak of the First World War. As a staunch churchgoer, and with the Battle of Britain still in the balance, Gort seized the opportunity to deplore the decline of Sunday observance in inter-war society and to proclaim that:

> [I]t is a plain fact that unless a country bases its life on a religious faith it cannot endure . . . to-day it is evident to every one of us that we are engaged not only in a fight for democracy, but over and above that in a crusade for the maintenance of those religious principles which we were taught by our mothers . . . This is our strength and our sure guarantee that with God's help and with the aid of the sister nations of the Empire our cause will prevail.[110]

Interestingly, Gort had earlier cornered a leading politician in their London club and had spoken 'vehemently on the theme that a religious revival was vital to the salvation of the country'.[111]

In addition to the demonstrative figures of Montgomery, Dobbie and Gort, there were other senior general officers whose personal religiosity was no less real for being more reserved. Highly introspective and temperamentally very different from Montgomery the showman, Lieutenant-General Kenneth Anderson was a devout Presbyterian who was very much disposed to ponder the mysterious workings of providence. A Scot who had served his military apprenticeship in the Seaforth Highlanders before and during the First World War, Anderson commanded the 3rd Division at Dunkirk and a corps in England before being appointed to command the First Army in August 1942. In November 1942, and in a message addressed to the men of the First Army prior to their descent on French North Africa, Anderson intoned:

> Our fathers of old were never ashamed to ask God's blessing on their enterprises, but openly acknowledged there were many things man cannot do by his own unaided strength. In spite of the wonderful machines and inventions of to-day, that still is true. Whether we admit it openly or not, we all know in our hearts that there is above us a Power who made this world and all that is in it, including mankind. Let us, therefore, unashamedly and humbly ask God's help in our endeavours, and strive to deserve it.[112]

Evidently lacking the exuberance and audacity of Montgomery's pre-battle exhortation to the Eighth Army before its attack at Alamein, Anderson's comparatively muted rhetoric was at one with his rather plodding style of command. Labouring under the unflattering sobriquet of 'Sunshine' and all too aware of the meagre success of the Tunisian campaign which followed the successful invasion of Algeria, Anderson wrote to Sir Alan Brooke on Christmas Day 1942 confiding that he had seen 'the hand of God' in recent events and that the fulfilment of plans was not always to be expected because 'The Almighty is much too wise to spoil us mortals that way'.[113] Although the Axis surrender in Tunisia in May partly redeemed Anderson's earlier perform-ance, he was to be denied the opportunity of leading the Second Army into Normandy in 1944 and eventually ended the war as GOC in East Africa.

Besides these fighting generals, it is worth noting that the two men who held the exalted post of CIGS from June 1940 to the end of the war also harboured strong religious convictions. Sir John Dill and Alan Brooke clearly had much in common – both were Ulster Protestants and both had been corps commanders in Gort's original BEF. Although Dill had transferred his allegiance to the Church of Ireland following the death of his father in 1894, he was descended from a distinguished family of Ulster Presbyterians. Further-more, after serving with distinction as a staff officer during the First World War,[114] he became an enthusiastic supporter of the Toc H movement, acting as the first chairman of its Aldershot branch.[115] Brooke, Dill's friend and successor as CIGS from December 1941, was the son of a leading family of Ulster landowners and very much the epitome of a Christian gentleman of the old school.[116] In addition to his puritanical sensibilities, Brooke clearly retained throughout the war a powerful belief in the benign and governing hand of providence and in the efficacy of prayer. Pondering the death of Lieutenant-General W.H.E. Gott, who was en route to take command of the Eighth Army in August 1942 when his aircraft was shot down by a lone German fighter, Brooke mused:

> It seemed almost like the hand of God suddenly appearing to set matters right where we had gone wrong. Looking back on those days with the knowledge of what occurred at Alamein and after it I am convinced that the whole course of the war might well have been altered if Gott had been in command of the 8th Army. In his tired condition I do not think that he would have had the energy and vitality to stage and fight this battle as Monty did . . .[117]

Similarly, the end of the war in Europe on 8 May 1945 moved Brooke to confide in his diary:

I remember the night Winston offered me the job of C.I.G.S. in the large smoking room at Chequers, he went out of the room shortly afterwards. I was so overcome that my natural instinct was, when left alone in the room, to kneel on the sofa and pray to God for his assistance in my new task. I have often looked back, during the last 3½ years, to that prayer, and thanked God for the way he had listened to me and provided me with the help I had asked for, and without which I should have foundered in the first year. I am not a highly religious individual according to many people's outlook. I am however convinced that there is a God all powerful looking after the destiny of this world. I had little doubt about this before the war started, but this war has convinced me more than ever of this truth. Again and again during the last 6 years I have seen His guiding hand controlling and guiding the destiny of this world toward that final and definite destiny which He has ordained. The suffering and agony of war in my mind must exist to gradually educate us to the fundamental law of 'loving our neighbour as ourselves'. When that lesson has been learned, then war will cease to exist.[118]

A third high-ranking Ulsterman, Lieutenant-General (later Field-Marshal) Harold Alexander, was of a similar stamp. As the GOC of the 1st Division in France during the 'Phoney War', Alexander was punctilious in attending Holy Communion on Sundays in a makeshift chapel on the Franco-Belgian border. Not only this, but the Anglican chaplain at 1st Division HQ remembered Alexander being present at a large open-air communion service during the retreat to Dunkirk, a debacle from which Alexander emerged with an enhanced reputation as a fighting general.[119] However, although Alexander was an Ulster Protestant, his natural affability and his service in the Irish Guards during the First World War rendered him unusually sympathetic to Roman Catholicism. Whereas Dill had blanched at the prospect of his only son's conversion to Rome and Brooke, after attending Mass at Lille cathedral in March 1940, had wondered 'how such ritual should have survived with the progress civilization has made',[120] Alexander clearly found much that was comforting in Catholic ritual and devotion. Rudesind Brookes, a Benedictine monk who had served with him as a subaltern in the Irish Guards on the Western Front in 1917–18, remembered Alexander as being 'very sympathetic to Catholicism and very much aware that the Regiment was a Catholic one'. Moreover, Alexander made a point of carrying a small crucifix inside his tunic throughout the Second World War.[121] Undoubtedly, Alexander's quiet religiosity seems to have made his decision to sanction the bombing of the ancient monastery of Monte Cassino in 1944 especially painful. As Brookes, who was then serving in Italy as chaplain to the 1st Irish Guards, remembered:

> Alex invited me to accompany him on a visit to view Monte Cassino . . . the abbey was a sanctuary of enormous prestige and antiquity, venerated by the Faithful of all nations on both sides . . . As we gazed at the ruined monastery, Alex told me that giving the order to bomb the abbey had been the most difficult decision he had ever had to make, but that he had finally decided that men's lives must come before stones however holy.[122]

However, and notwithstanding this pronounced sympathy for Catholicism, like so many of his peers Alexander was remarkably adept at citing the King James Bible. In March 1943, and with the Tunisian campaign approaching its climax, Alexander warned Montgomery of the frenzied resistance that he was to expect along the Mareth Line: 'The devil is come down unto you, having great wrath, because he knoweth that he hath but a short time [Revelation 12.12].'[123]

In addition to Anderson, Dill, Brooke and Alexander, the scholarly but taciturn Sir Archibald Wavell, who served as commander-in-chief in the Middle East and in India during the war years, was also remarkable for his understated faith and for his unusual academic interest in biblical history. As a staff officer in the Middle East in 1917, Wavell had made a study of the Greek Bible as Allenby's EEF had advanced inexorably through the Holy Land. Although famously reserved in conversation, Wavell clearly had the capacity to inspire an audience given the right material. After delivering a morning lecture on Allenby's campaigns at a conference of regular and Territorial chaplains in 1939, Wavell was hailed by a senior chaplain as 'one of the greatest Christians in the British Army', a reputation he then vindicated by delivering a further address to the assembled chaplains. As Eric Gethyn-Jones recalled:

> In the afternoon, Wavell talked of the work of the chaplain in War . . . The General repeatedly stressed the fact that much would be expected of us. He pointed out that a chaplain whose foundations were solid was of inestimable value both to individual and unit, but that one who was found wanting as a man of God was depriving the men of their right to spiritual strength, support and guidance. It was a clear directive to remember our Lord's warning that to whom much has been committed; of that

person much would be required. I have on many occasions heard bishops and inferior clergy speak on this subject at theological lectures, diocesan synods and chaplains' conferences, but never have I experienced so great an impact and such manifest sincerity . . . It was a humbling and salutary experience.[124]

Conclusion

Although necessarily selective, it is clear from the preceding discussion that a great many senior officers in both World Wars attached considerable importance to religion. To a large extent, this situation was dictated by prevailing patterns of religious belief and practice among Britain's upper classes. However, it also reflected the professional culture of Britain's regular army at the turn of the twentieth century, an institution which regarded religious officers and religious agencies as important sources of inspiration and discipline. Commanded in both World Wars by men who were largely the products of the late Victorian and Edwardian middle and upper classes, the uncomplicated religion which they acquired as children in the home was reinforced by their experiences at public school and by the professional ethos of the late Victorian and Edwardian officer corps. Naturally, when placed in positions of critical importance and heavy responsibility, as Protestants and patriots they were tempted to see their own careers – as well as the history of their homeland and, indeed, of British arms – in providential terms. As we shall now see, their exalted positions and their sense of the importance of religion also enabled them to revolutionise the role of army chaplains in relation to the citizen soldiers whom they came to command.

Chapter 3

COMMAND AND THE CLERGY

Generals, chaplains and morale

Introduction

DESPITE THEIR IMPORTANT POSITION throughout the war years, the nature and significance of the role of army chaplains during the two World Wars has been deeply and repeatedly misunderstood. This misunderstanding arises from a number of factors. First, there is the highly coloured but influential literary legacy of the First World War. Most conspicuously, Robert Graves, in his iconoclastic memoir *Goodbye To All That* (1929), contrasted the figure of the combative and courageous Catholic chaplain with the caricature of his ineffectual and ultimately superfluous Anglican counterpart. With the latter in mind, Graves claimed that:

> For the regimental chaplains as a body we had no respect. If the regimental chaplains had shown one tenth the courage, endurance, and other human qualities that the regimental doctors showed, we agreed, the British Expeditionary Force might well have started a religious revival.

As Graves alleged:

> The fact is that [Anglican chaplains] were under orders not to get mixed up with the fighting, to stay behind with the transport and

not to risk their lives. No soldier could have any respect for a chaplain who obeyed these orders, and yet there was not in our experience one chaplain in fifty who was not glad to obey them. Occasionally on a quiet day in a quiet sector the chaplain would make a daring afternoon visit to the support line and distribute a few cigarettes, and that was all . . . Sometimes the colonel would summon him to come up with the rations and bury the day's dead, and he would arrive, speak his lines, and hastily retire.[1]

This caricature of the useless Anglican chaplain was reinforced by the figure of the Revd Elliot Warne, the central character in Charles Benstead's sensational novel *Retreat: A Story of 1918* (1930). Warne's brief career on the Western Front culminates with his loss of faith, his loss of sanity and an unheroic death from influenza. In 1933, Guy Chapman's memoir *A Passionate Prodigality* reiterated the charges made by Graves as to the respective merits of Rome and Canterbury, Chapman declaring that:

[O]ur bluff Anglicans . . . had nothing to offer but the consolation the next man could give you, and a less fortifying one. The Church of Rome sent a man into action mentally and spiritually cleaned. The Church of England could only offer you a cigarette. The Church of Rome, experienced in propaganda, sent its priests into the line. The Church of England forbade theirs forward of Brigade Headquarters, and though many, realising the fatal blunder of such an order, came just the same, the publication of that injunction had its effect.[2]

Notwithstanding the growing rebellion among military historians against the manifold literary myths that have obscured and even perverted historical understanding of the British army in the First World War,[3] Graves's damning verdict on the army's chaplains remains largely uncontested. Although the complex and colourful figure of G.A. Studdert Kennedy has attracted perennial interest, his biographers have never succeeded in properly locating him in the context of wartime chaplaincy, his personal cult demanding that he be treated as a unique and prophetic figure among the Anglican clergy of his day.[4] Challenges have even been forestalled by the internal politics of the Church of England. If Roman Catholics were naturally pleased by the plaudits their chaplains received, these favourable verdicts also represented for Anglo-Catholics a clear vindication of sacramental religion, thereby furthering the Anglo-Catholic agenda within the Church of England in the inter-war years. While crude impressions of Anglican and Catholic chaplaincy have lingered on unchallenged, no major published study has ever appeared of the hundreds of Presbyterian or Free Church chaplains who served in the British army during the First World War. Presumably, this deafening silence is attributable to the power of pacifist sentiment in Britain's Protestant churches during the inter-war years and during the Cold War era, sentiment which has no doubt served to hinder any positive reappraisal of this branch of army chaplaincy.

For Christian pacifists, whose influence grew far beyond the confines of their Free Church stronghold in these years, the concept of military chaplaincy has (at best) been viewed as an embarrassing aberration and (at worst) as a blatant and even blasphemous travesty of the gospel of peace. Indeed, during the 1930s, and no doubt capitalising upon the calumnies contrived by Graves and Benstead, Christian pacifists made a concerted attempt to revolutionise the nature of chaplaincy in the British army. In 1931, during the annual parliamentary debate over Army Estimates, three Free Church MPs led an unsuccessful attempt to abolish chaplains' salaries and thus end their compromising subservience to the military authorities. Four years later, in his *We Say 'No': The Plain Man's Guide to Pacifism*, Canon 'Dick' Sheppard, the leading demagogue of Christian pacifism in the inter-war era and the originator of the Peace Pledge Union, reconceived chaplains as a new generation of 'missioners' who would not be compromised by formal ties to the military.[5] Although this rhetoric quickly evaporated during the Second World War, during the 1960s, and under the influence of the Cold War, Vietnam and other post-colonial conflicts, it re-emerged with a vengeance. In 1969, Gordon Zahn, a Roman Catholic priest and a veteran American pacifist, published his *Chaplains in the RAF: A Study in Role Tension*, a book that investigated the position and attitudes of RAF chaplains in the light of current circumstances and of the campaign of obliteration bombing that had been mounted against Hitler's Germany during the Second World War. In the course of his investigations, Zahn came to the arresting (if unsurprising) conclusion that judging the essential morality of military policies and actions was 'not generally regarded as part of the job' by his subjects and that chaplains 'would view such action as highly inappropriate and a distinct threat to the effective performance of their ministry'.[6] In 1981, Alan Wilkinson, an Anglican clergyman of a Free Church background, resumed this refrain by extending this scrutiny to the British army in an article entitled 'The Paradox of the Military Chaplain'. In this essay, Wilkinson identified eight paradoxes and tensions inherent in the role of the padre and highlighted the constraints upon the chaplain exercising a suitably 'prophetic role' in his milieu.[7] A decade and a half later, Stephen Louden, a senior Catholic army chaplain, developed these lines of analysis and criticism into a full-length book entitled

Chaplains in Conflict: The Role of Army Chaplains since 1914.[8] In this study, Louden concurred that, in the work of the army chaplain, 'Synchronous engagement by two organisations [i.e. the church and the army], whose purposes are not immediately reconcilable, have been shown to create tensions from conflicting loyalties'. Indeed, he found that the evangelical and pastoral ministry of the army chaplain had been largely subverted and 'subsumed into a latent function of providing practical support for the specifically military objective of the host organisation'.[9]

Inevitably, such arguments and recrimination from within the Christian tradition have helped to maintain the status of the military chaplain as an Aunt Sally for a new generation. While they have heavily influenced Richard Schweitzer's interpretation of British military chaplaincy in the First World War[10] they have also impressed Joanna Bourke. In her sensational and highly reductive study *An Intimate History of Killing: Face-to-face Killing in Twentieth-Century Warfare* (1999), Bourke developed the stereotype of the chaplain who readily and cheerfully embraced the business of wholesale slaughter. While ignoring the moral force of the just war tradition and its profound significance for historically Christian societies, Bourke sifted through a miscellany of largely unconnected evidence from the two World Wars and Vietnam in order to arrive at the conclusion that the purportedly uncritical attitude of chaplains towards government-sponsored killing boiled down to a primordial enjoyment of killing itself, an enjoyment that chaplains shared with the mass of their fellow soldiers:

> From their pre-eminent positions as moral arbiters in civilian society, during times of war the chaplaincy reached an all-time low . . . reconciling combat with Christianity was remarkably non-controversial. Indeed, in wartime, many clergymen longed to take part in the blood-letting and, frustrated in their ambitions, sanctified the slaughter and surrendered themselves to the cult of arms.[11]

Not surprisingly, an accumulated mass of selective, self-righteous and lurid writing on the subject of military chaplaincy in Britain and in the wider English-speaking world has obscured rather than clarified the history and purpose of British army chaplaincy during the two World Wars. Although far more balanced and helpful historical inquiries emerged as doctoral theses in the 1990s,[12] these had the disadvantage of being written from within the constraints of an ecclesiastical (and often purely denominational) perspective, thus overlooking the significance of army chaplaincy in the wider contexts of British military needs and British cultural history. Thus, in her study of

Anglican chaplains in the First World War, Alison Brown came to the mistaken conclusion that 'the Army clearly did not know what to make of uniformed chaplains on active service',[13] while Alan Robinson, in his more comprehensive study of army chaplaincy in the Second World War, was tempted to view the chaplain's duty of promoting good morale as somehow separate and distinct from his more 'religious' duties of holding services, visiting the hospitalised and counselling soldiers with personal problems.[14] In contrast with previous studies, it is the purpose of this chapter to go beyond highly subjective debates on the morality of army chaplaincy and the relative strengths of its denominational manifestations in order to place the subject in its proper, i.e. military, context. In doing so, it will demonstrate that the development of British army chaplaincy was driven by compelling military and, indeed, cultural considerations, that the army's expectations of chaplains of all denominations were remarkably uniform and that the principal architects of contemporary army chaplaincy were not churchmen at all but the most distinguished commanders of the British army.

The First World War and the revolution in army chaplaincy

By the outbreak of war in 1914, the role of most regular army chaplains was geared to ministering to the needs of professional soldiers and their families in home and overseas garrisons. In contrast to the army's Presbyterian and Roman Catholic chaplains, who were generally attached to individual battalions of the army's Scottish and Irish regiments, the members of the Anglican majority in the Army Chaplains' Department were posted to principal garrisons in Britain and the colonies rather than to individual units. Embarrassingly enough, and in combination with their limited numbers, this pattern of deployment had ensured that regular army chaplains had often been conspicuous by their absence in the many colonial campaigns of the late Victorian period. In post-Mutiny India, the army's Anglican chaplains were not even members of the AChD, military chaplaincy being one of the responsibilities of the Indian Ecclesiastical Establishment, which was maintained by the Government of India. Outside India, and especially in its African campaigns, the army was forced to make extensive use of the local clergy, many of whom were missionaries who chose to volunteer their services as acting chaplains. The army's historic indebtedness to Britain's overseas missionaries was reflected by the appointment of Bishop John Taylor Smith, the bishop of Sierra Leone, as chaplain-general in 1901. Although not even a member of the AChD up to this point, Smith had the good fortune to minister as an acting chaplain to Queen Victoria's ailing son-in-law, Prince Henry of

Battenberg, during the Ashanti War of 1895–6.[15] Significantly, it was Taylor Smith's missionary ardour which persuaded him to accept his new role. As one staff officer recalled of the circumstances of this appointment:

> It was put to him that, being a great missionary, he might be nominated to a position which would give him the best chance of dealing with the largest missionary society in the world – namely, the soldiers of the British Army, who go into all countries and are watched by the believers in Moslem and Hindu faiths as an example of what Christianity is. It is obvious from this that if the soldier is brought to the knowledge of Jesus Christ he and his fellows become members of a very fine missionary society scattered throughout the world.[16]

The outbreak of a major European war and the subsequent creation of a vast new citizen army did much to alter the nature, organisation and scale of the army's chaplaincy arrangements. Inevitably, existing models of garrison chaplaincy were rendered all but redundant as the regular army was deployed to the continent and its numbers swamped by millions of Territorials, volunteers and conscripts. In the context of the pastoral needs engendered by a national emergency and the phenomenal growth of the British army, Britain's leading Free Churches were persuaded to put aside their historic suspicion of state-sponsored religion and to accept commissions for their chaplains in the same manner as the Church of England, the Church of Rome and the British Presbyterian churches. In January 1915, a further step was taken towards the diversification and equalisation of affairs within the AChD when a Jewish chaplain went overseas for the first time.[17] If the denominational profile of the Department was greatly extended in the context of the First World War, then so too were official contacts between the War Office and Britain's principal religious denominations, the appointment and work of army chaplains being largely co-ordinated by a clutch of new and often fractious denominational and inter-denominational committees. In addition to its expanded confessional profile and the enhanced involvement of the British churches in chaplaincy affairs, the AChD also experienced a phenomenal growth throughout the course of the war. In August 1914, the Department comprised 117 commissioned chaplains, thirty-six acting chaplains (most of whom were either probationers or Wesleyan chaplains) and four honorary chaplains. However, by August 1916 the Department had grown to number no fewer than 2,143 chaplains (all commissioned) and by November 1918 this number had risen to 3,475 (see Tables 1 and 2). Impressive though they are, because of the existence of annual and even shorter contracts, these figures actually under represent the total number of British clergymen who received temporary commissions as army chaplains during the First World War. Although it is impossible to judge at this stage what this number actually was, Bishop Gwynne, the bishop of Khartoum and the Church of England's deputy chaplain-general on the Western Front from the summer of 1915, estimated in December 1917 that at least 300 Church of England chaplains had returned to England each year since 1915.[18]

Despite the phenomenal growth of the AChD, its record during the early stages of the war was inauspicious to say the least. Due to an administrative error, the sixty-six regular chaplains of the original BEF were all but excluded from its mobilisation tables, and thus found themselves without horses, field equipment or even maps.[20] If the chaplains of the Territorial Force proved difficult to even mobilise,[21] controversy soon arose over the organisation of army chaplaincy on the Western Front, the key issue being the propriety of Anglican chaplains serving under a principal chaplain who was in fact a Presbyterian.[22] As a result of mounting criticism from within the Church of England, the War Office was persuaded to appoint Llewelyn Henry Gwynne (the bishop of Khartoum, who was then serving as a brigade chaplain on the Western Front) to the new office of deputy chaplain-general in July 1915, a development that had the effect of creating 'a dual organisation of Chaplains in France'. Under this arrangement (which remained unique to the Western Front) the deputy chaplain-general's branch of the AChD oversaw military and spiritual matters relating to Anglican chaplains while the principal

Table 1 The expansion of the AChD, 1914–18[19]

Denomination	August 1914	August 1915	August 1916	August 1917	August 1918
Church of England	89	620	1,270	1,850	1,941
Presbyterian	11	110	175	273	298
Roman Catholic	17	250	400	583	643
Wesleyan	–	100	160	219	256
United Board*	–	75	125	205	248
Welsh Calvinist	–	7	10	11	11
Jewish	–	2	3	13	14
Salvation Army	–	–	–	–	5
Total	117	1,164	2,143	3,154	3,416

Note: * Comprising Baptists, Congregationalists, United Methodists and Primitive Methodists.

Source: *Statistics of the Military Effort of the British Empire During the Great War*, London: HMSO, 1922 (1992 reprint by The London Stamp Exchange), 190.

Table 2 The deployment of British army chaplains on 11 November 1918

Denomination	Home stations	France and Flanders	Egypt and hospital ships	Salonika	Mesopotamia, Bombay and hospital ships	East Africa	Other foreign stations	Italy	Total
Church of England	709	878	134	93	62	30	21	58	1,985
Presbyterian	75	161	19	22	11	–	6	8	302
Roman Catholic	78	389	54	45	38	2	13	32	649
Wesleyan	60	127	20	14	17	–	6	12	256
United Board	60	126	19	13	15	1	4	12	251
Welsh Calvinist	4	5	1	–	–	–	–	–	10
Jewish	4	8	3	1	–	–	–	–	16
Salvation Army	–	4	1	–	–	–	–	–	5
Total	989	1,698	251	189	143	33	50	122	3,475

Source: *Statistics of the Military Effort of the British Empire During the Great War*, London: HMSO, 1922 (1992 reprint by The London Stamp Exchange), 190.

chaplain's branch of the Department under Dr J.M. Simms managed the military affairs of chaplains of all other denominations.[23] In addition to these inter-denominational tensions, Anglican chaplaincy was also marred by jealousy and squabbling between the Church of England's various church parties, with the chaplain-general, a strong Evangelical, arousing suspicions of discrimination against those Anglo-Catholic clergy who sought commissions as temporary chaplains.[24]

Though ecclesiastical politics were problematic enough, divisional Church of England chaplains did not inherit an established tradition of regimental chaplaincy from the pre-war army (a problem which they shared with the English and Welsh Free Churches) and were under orders to remain with their field ambulances when their respective brigades were in the line. In fact, they were permitted to venture into forward positions only when summoned to bury the dead. In such circumstances they were more or less compelled to develop their work in rear areas, establishing numerous canteens and organising sports and other recreational activities. While this rear area work was no doubt good for soldiers' morale (and it must be remembered that the legendary Talbot House at Poperinghe, which was opened in December 1915, was a fruit of such endeavour) the lot of chaplains in general was not helped by the absence of any guidelines for their work other than those contained in King's Regulations, injunctions that baldly required them to conduct parade and voluntary services and to perform burials. Perversely enough, and despite their ill-defined role, there was no lack of chaplains in France by the end of 1915. Owing to extensive and relentless denominational lobbying, the allocation of chaplains per infantry division nearly trebled from five in August 1914 to fourteen in March 1915 and was to be further increased to seventeen in the winter of 1916–17. Over the same period, increasing numbers of chaplains were also allotted to the hospitals, bases and lines of communication of the burgeoning BEF. Such was the proliferation of chaplains that in August 1915, when the Church of England's Advisory Committee sought to raise the quota of Anglican chaplains to nine per English division, the BEF's adjutant-general complained that there were already too many chaplains in France and that most seemed to have little or nothing to do.[25]

Despite widespread evidence that Anglican chaplains were reluctant to remain in the rear by the end of 1915, the issue that revolutionised the position and role of Anglican and other brigade chaplains in the winter of 1915–16 was the vital question of military morale ('that mysterious quality', so one chaplain aptly described it, 'without which an army was like a machine without fuel').[26] Although a somewhat elusive term that can be variously analysed and defined, military morale fundamentally represents the overall willingness of individual units and the soldiers which comprise them to endure the manifold hazards and discomforts of war. Inevitably, a wide range of factors will influence this willingness and not all of these factors will operate with constant or equal force. Nevertheless, it is possible to assert that, for the soldiers of a modern democratic society, high morale is fostered by belief in a cause, by good training, by confidence in one's leaders, by the existence of adequate supply and support services, by loyalty to one's immediate comrades and by a habit of victory.[27] As John Baynes put it in his classic study of the 2nd Scottish Rifles at the battle of Neuve Chapelle:

> High morale . . . is a quality of mind and spirit which combines courage, self-discipline, and endurance . . . In time of peace good morale is developed by sound training and the fostering of esprit de corps. In time of war it manifests itself in the soldier's absolute determination to do his duty to the best of his ability in any

circumstances. At its highest peak it is seen as an individual's readiness to accept his fate willingly even to the point of death, and to refuse all roads that lead to safety at the price of conscience.[28]

Despite the fact that their morale is of paramount importance to the military success of citizen armies, only limited studies of its sources and significance in the British army of 1914–18 have yet been published and none has fully appreciated the significance of chaplains in this respect. Since John Baynes analysed the motivation and performance of the regulars and reservists of the 2nd Scottish Rifles at Neuve Chapelle in March 1915, David Englander has written an excellent survey of discipline and morale in the British army in 1917–18 and Gary Sheffield has stressed the importance of officer–man relations in contributing to the resilience of the British soldier throughout the First World War. According to Sheffield, the paternalist ethos of the regular officer corps was successfully transmitted to temporary officers during the war years and this ethos played 'a crucial role in sustaining the morale of the British army through four years of gruelling attritional warfare'.[29] Similarly, in an important study of soldiers' life behind the lines, J.G. Fuller emphasised the importance of civilian recreational culture in maintaining the morale of British and Dominion soldiers. Using their own magazines and newspapers as barometers of their mood and as sources of information on activities behind the lines, Fuller argued that concerts, sports, canteens and even organised excursions played an invaluable role in helping citizen soldiers adjust to 'the new world in which they found themselves'.[30] Finally, a recent study by Timothy Bowman of discipline and morale in the army's Irish regiments has averred that morale was maintained by an *esprit de corps* inculcated by the army's regimental system, by organised sports and recreations at a regimental and divisional level, by the generally good state of officer–man relations, by the visit of high-profile politicians and by organisations such as the YMCA, the AChD and the Orange Order, all of which had a peculiar significance for the army's more devout – and not to say sectarian – Irish constituency.[31] However, what these factors had in common was that they all fundamentally operated at the local or micro level. As Bowman argues in an echo of Englander, 'during the Great War there were very few initiatives taken at the High Command level to foster morale; instead, regimental officers were largely left to use their own initiative'.[32]

Although not recognised in any previous study of British military morale or of British army chaplaincy in the First World War, from December 1915 onwards the work of the army's chaplains was systematically harnessed to the maintenance and promotion of the army's morale, a process which was initiated and closely monitored from the highest levels of the army's command. In order to understand the dynamics of this development it is necessary to consider the situation of the British army on the Western Front at this point of the war and also the tactical orthodoxies which prevailed among its senior officers. As a result of the inter-Allied Chantilly conference of December 1915, British military commitments were set to grow significantly on the Western Front during the course of 1916, with a major Anglo-French offensive being planned in the region of the Somme from that February. However, the much-expanded BEF was by this time largely composed of wartime volunteers and the mettle of Britain's citizen soldiers, although tested on a limited scale in 1915, had yet to be tried to the full. Although, in strategic terms, an offensive posture was thrust on the Allies by the continuing German occupation of Belgium and much of northern France, it was also conventional military wisdom that the key to success in modern warfare lay in the attack. Despite the unprecedented killing power of magazine-loading rifles, machine guns and artillery, it was still a widely held view among Europe's military elite that victory would ultimately fall to those who pressed their attacks with the greatest vigour, a view that appeared to be borne out by Japanese success in the Russo-Japanese War of 1904–5. Indeed, far from shattering the 'cult of the offensive', the unprecedented weight of twentieth-century firepower was seen as facilitating its application. However, defensive firepower was recognised as posing some problems for the attacker, demanding greater self-discipline and higher morale in advancing through the fire-swept zone. For British military theorists in the pre-war years, the problem of cultivating these virtues was complicated by a lack of faith in the human material which would be placed at the army's disposal in the event of a major European war, a lack of faith exacerbated by the debate over 'national efficiency' that had been prompted by the sobering lessons of the Boer War. As Tim Travers has put it: 'The desire to stress the offensive spirit was exacerbated . . . by a pessimistic or anti-modern strain of thought that revolved around a deep suspicion of the likely behaviour of the new urban recruits when under fire.'[33] Even before the war, therefore, British military thinking had underlined 'the centrality of human qualities in war' and it had constructed what Travers has termed 'the image or paradigm of the psychological battlefield', a paradigm that 'stressed the importance of morale and the human dimension in resolving tactical problems'.[34] If Ferdinand Foch, who was to lead the Allied armies to victory on the Western Front in 1918, popularised the dictum 'War = the domain of moral force. Victory = Will',[35] this was a premise that also held sway among the British army's senior commanders both before and during the war years. Notwithstanding the sobering tactical lessons of previous months, in August 1915 the BEF's General Staff could still collectively assert that 'human nature is the dominant factor in war, and no arguments to the contrary, however specious, can alter this fact'.[36]

At the beginning of 1916, the BEF was confronting its severest test to date while being largely composed of the suspect members of the pre-war civilian population. This citizen army, although wholly composed of volunteers, contained significant elements such as trade unionists and Irish Nationalists whose long-term staying power could not be relied on. More worrying still, the imminent Military Service Acts seemed set to dilute the quality of the BEF still further by filling its ranks with conscripts whose motivation was naturally open to question. Inauspiciously enough, 1916 began under the long shadow of the offensive failures of previous months. Besides the abortive campaign against the Turks in the Dardanelles, 1915 had seen a succession of failed British offensives on the Western Front at Neuve Chapelle, Aubers Ridge, Festubert and Loos. By early 1916, therefore, the underlying question of how to motivate and sustain the fighting spirit of Britain's citizen army had become one of critical military importance. At this juncture, a firm conviction emerged among the General Staff of the BEF that chaplains had a key role to play in helping to sustain the morale of the fighting troops. Although it must be re-emphasised that good morale was promoted by a wide variety of means (means which ranged from a policy of aggressive trench raiding through to the provision of adequate leave and the maintenance of an efficient postal service)[37] there can be no doubt as to the central place that was assigned to chaplains in this regard, and not only in the provision of rear area canteens and entertainments that were of obvious practical use to the troops. From the winter of 1915–16 onwards, chaplains were expected to play a direct and sustained role in motivating soldiers to fight.

However naive the faith of key general officers in the power of chaplains to inspire the fighting spirit of the troops may appear to us, from the perspective of their time it could hardly be described as delusory. For Bible-reading Christians of their generation, this conviction had an obvious scriptural foundation in Deuteronomy 20.1–4:

> When thou goest out to battle against thine enemies, and seest horses, and chariots, and a people more than thou, be not afraid of them: for the LORD thy God is with thee, which brought thee up out of the land of Egypt. And it shall be, when ye are come nigh unto the battle, that the priest shall approach and speak unto the people, And shall say unto them, Hear O Israel, ye approach this day unto battle against your enemies: let not your hearts faint, fear not, and do not tremble, neither be ye terrified because of them; for the LORD your God is he that goeth with you, to fight for you against your enemies, to save you.

However, the new role that came to be ascribed to chaplains was not simply a function of excessive wartime piety and biblical zeal among Sir Douglas Haig and his principal subordinates. The role outlined in Deuteronomy was already being discharged by many high-profile clergymen at home, the famously belligerent Bishop of London, Arthur Winnington-Ingram, being only one of many Anglican, Roman Catholic and Free Church clergy who embraced this particular task.[38] In fact, these churchmen's antics were not simply a deviant phenomenon precipitated by the trauma of war. As Anne Summers has demonstrated, the British churches were key contributors to a popular militarist culture in Edwardian Britain, not least through their quasi-military youth organisations and in the widespread support that many of their members gave to the cause of conscription in the pre-war years.[39] The advent of war, in other words, simply moved existing sentiments and activities among the churches into a higher gear.

Besides the weight of scriptural prescription and the fitness of the churches for their militant role, the British army at this stage of the war was highly amenable to religious influences. As we shall be seeing in Chapter 4, the Territorials and Kitchener volunteers who comprised the bulk of the British army at the beginning of 1916 contained a disproportionate number of church members and churchgoers whose zeal had already been manifested in widespread if now forgotten religious revivals among British troops at home and abroad. On professional grounds as well, the generals had good reason to be optimistic about the military value of their chaplains and of the inculcation of a militant religiosity among their troops. In addition to the stirring examples of the Crusades and the Hundred Years War (which had been brilliantly reappraised for this generation by Charles Oman in his *Art of War in the Middle Ages*) and the more recent precedent of Cromwell's New Model Army, even the European, trans-Atlantic and colonial wars of the nineteenth century demonstrated how formidable and resilient non-professional soldiers could be, particularly when motivated by a cause that was anchored in strong religious conviction. In the Napoleonic Wars, this lesson had found its ultimate expression in Spain's war of liberation of 1808–14 but it had also been manifest in the Tyrolean revolt of 1809, in Russia in 1812 and in the Prussian-led war of German liberation of 1812–14. Notwithstanding the supposedly secular *zeitgeist* of nineteenth-century European culture, subsequent decades had continued to demonstrate the military potential of popular religious fervour, notably in Spain's Carlist Wars of the 1830s, in the wars of the Italian *Risorgimento* and in the Franco-Prussian War of 1870–1. If the American Civil War had also witnessed this phenomenon on a massive scale outside Europe,[40] its validity had also been demonstrated more recently to the British army by the Boxers in China, by the tribesmen of the North West Frontier, by the Mahdists of the Sudan and, most significantly of all, by the devoutly Christian Boers of South Africa. Critically, and as we have already seen, religion still exercised a profound influence on British society's ethical view of the world. Even among the industrial working classes, where regular contact with the churches often ceased with attendance at Sunday school, Christianity was inextricably linked to a code of behaviour and morality whose terms condemned the aggression and atrocities of imperial Germany while vindicating the reasons for British intervention in the war. Finally, there were no other figures in the British army endowed with the same moral and religious authority as its chaplains, men who had been hitherto widely regarded as numerous and under-employed functionaries who were performing a role that was at best vague and ill-defined.

Above anyone else, it was Sir Douglas Haig who was the driving force behind revolutionising the role of army chaplains. Haig was a man of deep personal faith and a professional soldier who, since his Staff College days in the 1890s, had accepted the primacy of 'human nature and morale as deter-minants of victory'.[41] As Travers has argued, in Haig's view 'victory almost always went to the side with the highest morale, discipline and offensive spirit, and these were qualities that the infantry needed above all, for they were the only arm that could actually force the decision'.[42] As commander-in-chief of the BEF, Haig consistently sought to ensure that his chaplains made a concerted and systematic contribution to bolstering morale in the pursuit of victory, particularly among front-line units.[43] Within a month of his being appointed commander-in-chief on 19 December 1915, Haig invited Bishop Gwynne to dine at GHQ and announced to him that 'A good chaplain is as valuable as a good general', sentiments which he acted upon by having Gwynne's rousing Christmas sermon of 1915 published and circulated among the troops. Furthermore, Haig averred that 'no one could do more than a chaplain to sustain morale and explain what our Empire is fighting for' and he urged Gwynne to dismiss chaplains who were lacking in what he termed 'spiritual force'.[44] Haig himself noted of his conversation with Gwynne, 'I spoke to him regarding the importance of sending a message to all the clergy to preach of the great object of the war viz. the freedom of mankind from German tyranny.' The chaplains, so Haig thought, 'were too narrow in their views. They must be enthusiasts to do good.'[45]

However much they may have been based on his deepening regard and even dependence on the ministry of G.S. Duncan, the Presbyterian chaplain at GHQ, Haig's convictions were by no means the product of his recent promotion. Prior to the battle of Loos, and as commander of the First Army, Haig had met Harry Blackburne, then the Church of England's senior chaplain in the 1st Division, and had spoken 'most appreciatively of the chaplains' work'.[46] Nor was Haig's confidence in the importance of chaplains unique among army commanders in the winter of 1915–16. Of General Sir Herbert Plumer, who was then commanding the Second Army, Gwynne maintained that 'Being a deeply religious man himself, [Plumer] knew that for rein- forcement of nerve power and endurance there was nothing that kept up the hearts of men so much as religion'.[47] It was symptomatic of the importance of such attitudes among the most senior officers of the BEF that, on 15 January 1916, a conference of army commanders at Cassel progressed from a discus- sion on training, gas attacks and resting tired divisions to addressing the future role of military chaplains. According to Haig, the meeting recognised that 'Every effort must be made to raise the "moral" [sic] of the troops. Amuse- ments, games, etc. etc. must be organised.' Furthermore, and as Haig noted in his diary:

> I also called attention to the large number of clergymen who are now being sent to join the army. Army [commanders] must look to the efficiency of these men as well as to any other part of their commands. We must have large minded, sympathetic men as Parsons, who realise the *Great Cause* for which we are fighting, and can imbue their hearers with enthusiasm . . . Any clergyman who is not fit for this work must be sent home.[48]

While endorsing the value of chaplains' existing work in rear areas, the Cassel conference also proved crucial in helping to establish a front-line role for chaplains in the long build-up to the Somme offensive. Although their admis- sion to the forward trenches was by no means instantaneous, some weeks before the offensive began, and in order to clarify some existing confusion in Fourth Army, a circular was issued by the BEF's adjutant-general confirming that all earlier restrictions on the movements of chaplains had been lifted and that chaplains 'should be encouraged to go where the Senior Chaplains . . . of divisions . . . decide that their services can be most advantageously employed, and where they can be of most use to the troops'.[49]

   The significance of the new dispensation was soon apparent. As the newly appointed assistant chaplain-general of the First Army, Harry Blackburne's first interview with Haig's successor at army HQ, Sir Charles Monro, was immediately encouraging. Blackburne recalled:

> My first interview with him was most entertaining . . . he talked about my future work and said he would do all he could to help me, as indeed he did. He himself took me round in his

car, to introduce me to the generals of corps and divisions as well as many others who would be able to help me in this new appointment.[50]

This new spirit of co-operation between chaplains and general officers was also very much to the fore when the Archbishop of Canterbury, Randall Davidson, visited the Western Front in May 1916. Invited to visit by Gwynne with 'the warm concurrence of Sir Douglas Haig . . . and of the other Generals, with whom [Haig] had talked it over',[51] Davidson received a warm welcome at the hands of the General Staff. At GHQ at Montreuil, Davidson 'could not elicit anything except laudation' from the commander-in-chief on the question of chaplains, Haig being

> strong on the great value of the changed administrative order which now encourages the chaplains to go forward into the trenches, if they will do so, instead of being, as formerly, kept behind at the casualty clearing stations, or even further back.

Besides speaking warmly of Gwynne's work, Haig was notably 'enthusiastic about the fine type of young Padre now at work in all parts of the line'.[52] If Davidson was both pleased and flattered by what he found at GHQ, Haig had a characteristically blunt recollection of their meeting:

> Sunday 21 May [1916] . . . We had quite a large party of clerics at lunch . . . The Archbishop was very pleased with all he had seen and the work the various chaplains are doing. The latter told him how much they have been helped in their work of late by *all* Commanders, 'So different to the old days' whatever that may mean . . . In reply to a question, I told the Archbishop that I had only two wishes to express and I had already explained them to Bishop Gwynne, and these are:
> *First* that the chaplains should preach to us about the objects of Great Britain in carrying on this war. We have no selfish motive, but are fighting for the good of humanity.
> *Secondly*. The chaplains of the Church of England must cease quarrelling amongst themselves. In the field we cannot tolerate any narrow sectarian ideas. We must all be united.[53]

Well received though he had been at Montreuil, Davidson derived additional satisfaction from the reception that had taken place on the previous day at Béthune, where Harry Blackburne had organised a meeting for the archbishop that had been attended by around forty general officers from Monro's First Army. As Davidson recalled:

> I was immensely struck with the keen appreciation shown by everyone of these leading officers as to the first-rate character, capacity, courage and perseverance of the chaplains and how very much has now come to turn on their work. Nearly every General spoke of them as being just the men who ought to be there and of having got a real grip upon their troops and cheering them in every way.

The occasion was, he claimed, 'a striking instance of the pulling together of padres and officers and their mutual appreciation of one another'.[54] Significantly, this appreciation was paraded on other occasions and not only before distinguished visitors. In a telling anecdote, Michael Adler, the BEF's senior Jewish chaplain, remembered being with an Australian brigade when it was unexpectedly visited by Haig in the spring of 1916. As Adler remembered:

> We three Chaplains stood at the end of the line, and Sir Douglas rode up to us and, shaking hands, asked which denominations we represented. 'I am glad to see you working so well together,' he said, 'as you can help us greatly by teaching the men about the noble cause for which we are fighting'.[55]

By the time of the commencement of the Somme offensive, Haig appears to have been well pleased by the way in which his chaplains had embraced their new role. In a private letter to King George V dated 28 June 1916, Haig wrote with evident satisfaction:

> Everywhere I found the troops in great spirits and full of confidence of their ability to smash the enemy when the moment for action arrives. Several officers have said to me that they never have known troops in such enthusiastic spirits . . . We must, I think, in fairness give a good deal of credit [for] this to the parsons. I have insisted on them preaching about the cause for which we are all fighting and encouraging the men to play their part. Some parsons too that were no use have been sent home. But, taken as a whole, they have done well and have been a very great help to us commanders.[56]

Although the close relationship between the BEF's General Staff and its chaplains was born of the circumstances of early 1916, the most public indication of the high command's appreciation of the chaplains' contribution to military morale came during the subsequent winter of 1916–17, when the Church of England's National Mission of Repentance and Hope was preached among the officers and men of the BEF. Although its goals were poorly defined and its penitential tenor provoked some fierce criticism at home,[57] the National Mission attracted considerable support from within the higher reaches of the army. Sir William Robertson, then CIGS, expressed his warm approval of the National Mission in a public letter to the Bishop of London in which he confessed:

> I am old-fashioned enough to think that this great war, like those
> of which we read in the Old Testament, is intended to teach us
> a necessary lesson, and if this be so it follows that we ought to
> examine ourselves and take the lesson to heart.[58]

As we have seen, the work of the National Mission on the Western Front was also publicly endorsed by three out of the BEF's five army commanders; Generals Horne, Allenby and Gough all declaring their strong support for it. These declarations were published in 1917 in a pamphlet entitled *Religion and Morale: The Story of the National Mission on the Western Front*, a pamphlet that was largely the work of Bishop Gwynne. Whatever ambivalent or self-critical note the National Mission may have struck on the home front, this was apparently not the tone of the mission as it was preached in the BEF by its Anglican chaplains. In a deliberate echo of the Boer War, copies of Lord Roberts' celebrated prayer of 1900 were 'widely distributed' among the troops[59] and the whole venture was regarded as a positive exercise in pointing the troops towards the twin prospects of victory and a better post-war society – 'a great spiritual offensive against the powers of evil' as one chaplain described it.[60] The fulsome support of the generals for the National Mission was certainly recognised by chaplains themselves. At a planning conference for the mission at Amiens in December 1916, Oswin Creighton noted that:

> [Bishop Gwynne] told us a lot of what had been said to him by
> different Generals about their appreciation and the importance of
> the chaplain's work – really very striking. It is certainly encour-
> aging to find that most of our chief men are really religious. We
> all felt stirred up generally to try and carry on the work of the
> Mission out here.[61]

Such high-level and public support for chaplaincy work did not end with the work of the National Mission, however. Later in 1917, the new importance of the chaplain's work in fostering the morale of the army was reflected in E.C. Crosse's pamphlet, *The God of Battles: A Soldier's Faith*. With the encouragement of General Gough, who wrote its preface, Crosse maintained that the work of the eponymous deity was to be found not in spectacular and providential interventions but in those moral qualities that, if properly cultivated, ultimately brought victory. With respect to the famous medal struck to commemorate the fate of the Spanish Armada bearing the legend 'The Lord sent the wind and they were scattered', Crosse argued that it was not so much a Protestant wind that had providentially saved England from invasion but the fact that 'God found a more congenial home in the reformed England of the sixteenth century than He did in the corrupt and decadent empire of Spain'.[62] At the very first course of the new 'Chaplains' School', which belatedly commenced at St Omer early in 1917, General Horne of the First Army spoke to the chaplains in attendance about 'chaplains' work from an Army Commander's point of view'.[63] For his part, General Plumer not only provided the premises for this establishment but also addressed several of its courses. As Gwynne recalled, the advice Plumer gave to chaplains on these occasions was wholly geared to the chaplain's role in sustaining morale: 'Identify yourself with your Units as much as possible, do what they do. If you can play games play with them, march when they march – make them your friends and let them feel you are their own padre.' As for the business of preaching, Plumer admonished:

> Prepare carefully, give of your best, for congregations in the Field are paraded to attend. Be brief. Tell them at the start what your message is about and stick to the point, prepare well the prayers, put yourselves in their place and ask yourselves what would help most and what they would like you to ask for them.[64]

In addition to stimulating a closer alliance between the commanders of the army and its chaplains, the reformulation of the chaplain's role from the winter of 1915–16 also led to dramatic innovations in the methods and deployment of the BEF's brigade chaplains. In accordance with the adjutant-general's circular as to the deployment of padres, planning for the Somme offensive saw senior chaplains initiate the practice of assigning 'battle posts' to all chaplains in their divisions. In an offensive action, this meant that one of a division's three brigade field ambulances would be designated the main dressing station and would remain well behind the line, while the other two would be positioned close to the fighting.[65] Usually, the senior chaplain would allocate a chaplain to each forward field ambulance and two to the main dressing station 'as it was here that most of the deaths from wounds occurred, and the mere task of burying the dead was often very heavy'.[66] Although technically non-combatants, the balance of a division's chaplains were generally encouraged to accompany the attacking battalions, their presence being important for morale 'because they alone were not under orders to be there, and as such they could hardly fail to encourage the rest, who had no option in the matter'. As Crosse put it: 'From a religious point of view it showed to the men far better than any preaching could do God's care for each.' However, those chaplains who accompanied the forward battalions generally elected to stay with their regimental aid posts where a padre 'could find nearly all he wanted to do in directing the wounded, or in getting a hot drink going'. Occasionally, chaplains would help stretcher parties locate the wounded, stretcher-bearers being apparently glad 'to have some one to give them a lead'.[67]

A significant corollary of this front-line role was the growing number of decorations awarded to members of the Chaplains' Department, a development which not only recognised individual bravery but that also served to lend chaplains greater credibility among front-line troops. Edward Noel Mellish, attached to the 4th Royal Fusiliers, became the first chaplain VC of the war after tending and rescuing wounded men under fire at St Eloi in March 1916.[68] Two VCs and a host of lesser decorations were to follow. By April 1918, Taylor Smith could note that 195 awards had been made to Anglican chaplains alone, 145 of these being Military Crosses and bars.[69] Such was the flood of awards that Julian Bickersteth confessed his unease about the MC that he was awarded in January 1918:

> I am honestly sorry about it. I hold, and shall continue to hold, strong views about chaplains' decorations. They never have 'to go over the top'; they have a comparatively easy job from the military point of view. I could in fact name hundreds of officers in this division still undecorated who more than deserve a decoration.[70]

These reservations were also shared by the Roman Catholic chaplain William Doyle, who wrote to his father: 'I am sorry these rewards are given to chaplains, for surely he would be a poor specimen of the Lord's Anointed who would do his work for such a thing.'[71] Despite such qualms, these decorations were not cheaply obtained, not least because the formal extension of a front-line role to chaplains naturally led to a sharp rise in casualties among them. A confidential return to Lambeth Palace dated October 1916 listed fourteen Anglican chaplains as having been killed in action or as having died on active service; three of them having been killed in the Fourth Army since the beginning of the Somme offensive.[72] By October 1917, the number of fatalities among Anglican chaplains had risen dramatically, with thirty-nine being listed as having died or been killed on active service.[73] According to official sources, a total of 166 army chaplains died as a result of the war – this number comprising ninety-eight Anglican, eleven Presbyterian, thirty-four Roman Catholic, ten Wesleyan, twelve United Board and one Salvation Army chaplain. Of these, ninety-seven were killed in action or else died of wounds received.[74]

In view of these figures, the idea that one denomination's chaplains were deficient in personal courage is clearly one of Graves' grosser calumnies. In fact, it is all too clear that among some brigade chaplains the imperatives of their front-line role engendered a spirit bordering on the foolhardy. In November 1916, for example, Julian Bickersteth accompanied a wiring party into no-man's land – 'a most interesting experience', he wrote, 'I was glad of it because I do so dislike the men to have to listen to someone who has not been with them under all conditions'.[75] Other chaplains chose to go into attacks with the first wave of the attacking troops. On 31 July 1917, the first day of the Third Battle of Ypres, a corporal of the 1/1st Hertfordshires noted the outstanding if prosaic courage of a brigade chaplain who began to distribute cigarettes to an attacking battalion which had been stalled by heavy machine gun fire. He recalled:

> We were all lying there and I suddenly felt an object fall at my side. I looked around and it was a tin of Woodbines. I looked again and there was a padre. I'd never seen a padre taking part in an attack and whoever he was he was worthy of the very highest praise because he was in a very dangerous position.[76]

For one Wesleyan chaplain of the 2nd Royal Welch Fusiliers, such enthusiasm was to prove fatal. After making a favourable impression while assisting with the battalion's wounded in an earlier attack on a German position, he was killed while participating in an assault on the village of Villers-Outreaux in October 1918. According to the battalion's medical officer, J.C. Dunn:

> The padre should not have gone with 'A' Company in the early morning. He was told that he would be an embarrassment to them; but he was impulsive, he insisted on going, and was killed when seeking an M.C. to please some fool of a girl in Liverpool who had taunted him with having no decoration.[77]

Naturally, besides being an inspiring and consoling presence among the fighting troops, chaplains were also expected to aid morale by burying the dead. The interment of the dead was one of the few specific duties expected of a chaplain throughout the course of the war and, during its first sixteen months, the otherwise unhelpful terms of King's Regulations helped to ensure that this was the only pretext by which most chaplains could gain access to the front line.[78] Amidst the trench warfare that characterised most of the fighting experience of the British army on the Western Front, the presence of large numbers of erstwhile comrades lying unburied and in various states of decomposition was seen not only as a danger to health but also as a very real threat to morale. On one occasion, E.C. Crosse remembered being 'roundly abused' by one general who had seen 'a large number of unburied dead in front of our line'. In the circumstances, Crosse had been compelled to reply that it was impossible to bury them 'without adding to their number'.[79] Besides being a dangerous occupation in itself, the work of burial was also deeply unpleasant, a task made worse by the fact that chaplains were not only responsible for conducting burial services but were also involved in the collection and identification of human remains. In September 1916, David Railton was involved with his whole battalion in clearing part of the Somme battlefield. In a troubled letter to his wife, Railton confided:

> No words can tell you all I feel, nor can words tell you of the horrors of clearing a battlefield. This Battalion was left to do that, and several men went off with shell shock and two were wounded. I am certain the shell shock was caused not just by the explosion of a shell near by, but by the sights and smell and horror of the battlefield in general. I felt dreadful, and had to do my best to keep the men up to the task.[80]

The force of King's Regulations also provided chaplains with their best opportunity to provide explicit moral and religious justifications for the war effort. In the sermons given at parade services (occasions that remained, theoretically at least, compulsory for all troops in rear areas throughout the course of the war), the chaplain had a delicate balance to strike. According to E.C. Crosse, bloodthirsty exhortations had little effect on the usually humane Tommy and sermons on the terrors of death were both resented and counter-productive, making 'the worst possible subject for a sermon'.[81] Good chaplains were, however, equal to the task. In an impressive church parade of men of the 16th (Irish) Division at St Omer prior to the Third Battle of Ypres and more than a year after the Easter Rising in Dublin, William Doyle preached a sermon which enthused his listeners by appealing to their strong Nationalist convictions. Invoking the exploits of the 'Wild Geese' in Flanders two centuries earlier, Doyle went on to deliver a skilful exposition of the reasons behind the Irish Parliamentary Party's support for the war. According to Doyle's biographer:

The men of the 8th Dublins declared that Fr. Doyle 'ought to get into Jim Larkin's shoes!' It appealed to others for a different reason. General Ramsay (a Protestant) stated afterwards that it was one of the most tactful and impressive sermons he had ever heard, and General Hickie said that he was intensely pleased with the way in which 'dangerous' topics had been handled without offending anyone. It certainly required some diplomatic skill to appeal to Irish regiments in the British Army by evoking memories of the Irish Brigade which fought against England. Nor was it easy, without hurting English susceptibilities, to convey the fact that the Irish soldiers who were listening were fighting for what they believed was Ireland's cause as well as Belgium's.[82]

If not normally confronted with such a delicate situation, chaplains were certainly expected to kindle fire in the bellies of their listeners and to provide the same kind of reassurance before battle as that required of the priests of ancient Israel. In this respect, Victor Tanner, an Anglican chaplain who served with the 2nd Worcestershire Regiment throughout 1917 and 1918, clearly lived up to expectations. In a pre-battle sermon in September 1917, Tanner took as his text 'the Lord God's exhortation to Joshua before the crossing of the river Jordan ("Be strong and of a good courage; be not afraid, neither be thou dismayed [Joshua 1.9]")'.[83] A year later, with the German army in retreat on the Western Front, Tanner took the opportunity to remind his battalion that this was no time for slacking:

> We're out here to do a certain job – a difficult job – and it's still unfinished and we, as England's sons, are charged to see it through. To falter or give way to war weariness at this stage would be to betray our trust. A cancer is eating out the heart of Europe, and it's got to be cut out and we have to take our share in doing it, or else our pals will have died in vain and our children will have to endure a war even bloodier than this one . . . Not only England but the whole civilised world is watching us, yes, and depending on us. So let's get to work again with renewed vigour and determination and do our bit and do it well, for the sake of the Regiment, for the sake of our homes, and of the boys and girls growing up in them, and, last but by no means least, for the honour of God and the triumph of right . . .[84]

Significantly, COs were not above prescribing the content of chaplains' sermons. For example, one Anglican chaplain remembered being among sixty others summoned to Béthune to hear their new corps commander address them on 'the work of a chaplain, as it strikes a layman'. As the chaplain in question recalled:

> It was a remarkable effort. The point I chiefly remember was his admonition to us to avoid Bible History and Dogma and to preach constantly on 'Honour, Duty, and Discipline . . . You chaplains,' he concluded, 'are regarded by those in Authority as absolutely essential to the success of the British Expeditionary Force. The Army has a soul as well as a Body. We look after its body but we shall not win this war unless the Army's soul is cared for too. High ideals of Honour, Duty, and Discipline are the life of an army and you are the best people to inculcate them. Ring the changes on these and you will find the men will listen to you.'[85]

In a similar vein, Major-General Sir William Thwaites, an officer who is credited with having transformed the 46th (North Midland) Division after successive failures at Loos and on the Somme,[86] recalled that before an attack he would assemble his chaplains and instruct them in what he wanted his soldiers to hear. On one occasion he declared that what he wanted was 'a bloodthirsty sermon next Sunday, and would not have any texts from the New Testament'. On the Sunday in question he remembered that 'I got hold by accident of a blushing young curate straight out from England – but he preached the most bloodthirsty sermon I had ever listened to'.[87] Of course, for those chaplains who consistently failed to satisfy there was always the threat of removal. When a new GOC, Major-General W.G. Heneker, and senior staff officer, Lieutenant-Colonel E.H.L. Beddington, were appointed to the 8th Division in the winter of 1916–17, they agreed that their new division had 'a poor record and poor morale' and embarked upon a purge of its senior officers. One of the first heads to roll was that of its Anglican senior chaplain. As Beddington remembered:

> I went in to GHQ to see Mike Furse, the [Assistant] Chaplain General [of Fourth Army] . . . He asked me the reason for my request and I said that our Chaplain would stress all the time that unless you were really good your chances of going to Heaven were poor, whilst the doctrine needed for men of an infantry division, whose expectation of life was bound to be short, should in my view approximate to that of the Mohammedan religion, i.e., he that dies in battle goes to Heaven. Mike nodded assent, but asked what I thought should happen to our Chaplain. I suggested

duty at a Base Hospital. Mike grinned broadly and agreed: he sent us Stafford Crawley (afterwards Canon of Windsor), a quite first-class [Senior] Chaplain in every way, whose only drawback was that I had to put a Military Policeman on sentry over him to see that in [an] attack he did not go over the top with the leading wave.[88]

Despite some strong competition and his reputation for composing popular verse and doling out cigarettes, the most celebrated clerical morale-booster in the BEF during the later years of the war was none other than G.A. Studdert Kennedy. An experienced parish priest and gifted public orator, Studdert Kennedy had spent most of his clerical career evangelising among the urban working classes before he arrived in France in the winter of 1915–16. After distinguishing himself in his unenviable posting as a base chaplain at Rouen in the early months of 1916,[89] Studdert Kennedy was given a succession of postings to brigades and training establishments across northern France. In the addresses which he gave at various locations on the Western Front and that were subsequently published as *Rough Talks of a Padre* towards the end of the war, Studdert Kennedy's skill as an orator was demonstrated in the clarity of his message and in the pungent and even vulgar style of his prose.[90] There can be no doubt that Studdert Kennedy's public ministry was perceived as having a significant military value, particularly in the light of the chaplain's role as it came to be conceived by Haig and his subordinates from early 1916. Following his service as a brigade chaplain with the 46th (North Midland) Division in 1916, Studdert Kennedy's subsequent postings to front-line divisions were to formations whose performance and condition was considered to be lacklustre. In 1917, Studdert Kennedy served with the 24th Division, a New Army division which had faced recrimination and reorganisation after its perceived failure at Loos in September 1915.[91] Similarly, in 1918, Studdert Kennedy served with the 42nd (East Lancashire) Division, a dispirited Territorial division that, since its arrival on the Western Front in 1917, had earned itself the nickname of 'the windy Forty-Second' and that was the subject of a raft of measures aimed at raising its morale in the winter of 1917–18.[92] In addition to these postings, Studdert Kennedy was used as a principal missioner for the National Mission in France and was successively attached to three infantry training schools which were part of a network of specialist training establishments that arose during the course of the war and that were 'designed to bring all ranks up to the high standards demanded by modern warfare'.[93]

While attached to the Fourth Army Infantry School at Flixecourt in the autumn of 1917, Studdert Kennedy famously made the acquaintance of

Lieutenant-Colonel R.B. Campbell, who was then responsible for the BEF's notorious School for Physical and Bayonet Training, a semi-itinerant establishment which Studdert Kennedy subsequently joined as chaplain.[94] One of the major aspects of the work of Campbell's school was to tour the BEF with the aim of promoting the best spirit and method behind the use of the soldier's most visceral weapon, the bayonet. As Philip Gibbs, one of the army's official war correspondents, testified:

> Colonel Ronald Campbell was a great lecturer on bayonet exercise. He curdled the blood of boys with his eloquence on the method of attack to pierce liver and lights and kidneys out of the enemy. He made their eyes bulge out of their heads, fired them with blood-lust, stoked up hatred of Germans – all in a quiet, earnest and persuasive voice and a sense of latent power and passion in him.[95]

Campbell's troupe of experts and assistants included champion boxers and a non-commissioned officer whose principal claim to fame was that he had dispatched no fewer than eighteen Germans in hand-to-hand combat.[96] Studdert Kennedy's contribution to this enterprise was, first, to inject a little humour into the proceedings by sparring with the boxers of the troupe and, second, to raise the tone of the exhibition towards its close, although not at the cost of mitigating its effects. As Gibbs put it:

> They gave pugilistic entertainments to tired men. Each of them had one thick ear. Woodbine Willie had two. They fought each other with science (as old professionals), and challenged any man in the crowd. Then one of them played the violin, and drew the soul out of soldiers who seemed mere animals, and after another fight Woodbine Willie stepped up and talked of God, and war, and the weakness of men, and the meaning of courage. He held all those fellows in his hand, put a spell on them, kept them excited by a new revelation, gave them, poor devils, an extra touch of courage to face the menace that was ahead of them when they went to the trenches again.[97]

Although an extreme example of the degree to which an army chaplain was prepared to adapt his ministry and his pronouncements to the interests of military morale, Studdert Kennedy's priorities were shared by most if not all of his fellow chaplains in the BEF. Apart from their own sermons, chaplains often found other means of ramming their message home. For example,

Fr R.H.J. Steuart, a Jesuit who served on the Western Front from 1916 to the end of the war, ensured that the men of his battalion were regularly exposed to the fiercely patriotic rhetoric of Lord Northcliffe's *Daily Mail* while they were in the line. As Steuart remembered, 'I arranged for these papers, five copies to each company, to be brought up every evening with the rations, and on the following morning I took them round.'[98] Bishop Gwynne, however, preferred to instruct the soldiers of the BEF more directly. In August 1916, Gwynne published a *Letter to the Church of England Troops on the Second Anniversary of the Commencement of the War*. In this fierce, four-page rallying cry amidst the trials and tribulations of the Somme offensive, Gwynne declared that:

> The Master said: 'They that take the sword shall perish with the sword.' Those who had resort to brute force and ordeal by battle, and chose their own time and place, are now meeting their match. We are now starting the last lap . . . For us there is no stopping; we are trustees for the blessed dead. Every dead soldier, every maimed and broken warrior, calls out to us never to lay down our arms . . . The cloud of witnesses, Lords Roberts and Kitchener, Generals, their officers, non-commissioned officers, men, some near and dear to us, others our close friends, comrades, are looking on. They look to us to carry on the struggle. They desire earnestly that we should not lay down our arms until the Cause for which they died triumphs.[99]

However, by the autumn of 1917, Gwynne's tone had changed from one of exuberant defiance to one of profound concern at what he perceived to be the declining morale of the BEF. Although the accuracy of this perception has been questioned by historians, it was certainly widely shared among the BEF's General Staff at this time. This perception was encouraged by large-scale disturbances among British troops at Etaples in September 1917 and by the promulgation of a record number of death sentences for desertion and other military offences in the same troubled month.[100] With the spirits of hundreds of thousands of British soldiers sinking into the liquid mud of the Ypres salient, Gwynne was increasingly worried by 'a certain unrest in the minds of some of our soldiers'. According to his own estimation, this unrest was 'brought about by a kind of fedupedness about the war', a sentiment fuelled by 'disloyal people at home' and by 'a certain number of men who are brought into the army against their will and try to spread discontent among the troops'.[101] Naturally, the fate of Britain's closest allies in recent months gave further cause for concern, the adverse course of the war having already provoked revolutionary turmoil in Russia and wholesale mutiny in the French army. Consequently, in mid-October, Gwynne convened a small inter-denominational conference of chaplains at St Omer in order to address the problem of the army's morale. After much discussion, the improvement of social conditions after the war was recognised as a salient issue in soldiers' minds. Although 'There did not appear [to be] any violent revolutionary ideas among the men', it was a matter of debate as to 'how far such thinking' could be 'guided and controlled'.[102] The consequences of this meeting were twofold. First, it was agreed that a leaflet should be written and circulated which would clarify British war aims, including that of social reconstruction at home. Second, it was decided that the army's chaplains should organise a far-reaching programme of social education, with the Chaplains' School training chaplains for this purpose and civilian speakers and YMCA facilities being used 'to hold conferences among the men'.[103]

The matter of the leaflet was relatively unproblematical. On 22 December, Gwynne and Simms visited a receptive Haig at Montreuil 'and talked over the question of reconstruction after the war'. Not only did the commander-in-chief 'take a real interest in it, but promised to write a few words himself to back it up'.[104] Eventually, Gwynne produced a text which declared the nation's aspirations for post-war society as being:

> Better homes where children could grow up healthy and strong; better education which gave a child full opportunity for developing the faculties implanted in him by God; a fair deal for labour, giving to the worker a fuller life; justice for women and a resolute stand against prostitution; a discipline which keeps a man at his best and maintains holy matrimony as the ideal of family life.[105]

The matter of the chaplains' 'Scheme of Reconstruction' was, however, much less straightforward. If in many ways it merely developed issues which had been raised by the National Mission twelve months earlier, by the end of 1917 talk of outside speakers and soldiers' study circles apparently raised the spectre of soldiers' soviets and total military collapse. In view of determined opposition led by the Adjutant-General G.H. Fowke, in early February Haig gave permission for the scheme to go ahead providing soldiers' study circles were eschewed and that a chaplains' co-ordinating committee vetted prospective speakers. Furthermore, all lecturers were to be approved in advance by 'the Military Authorities at the Front or at the Bases'.[106] If nothing else, the inaugural meeting of the co-ordinating committee several days later was a great success. With even the Roman Catholics represented, Gwynne was of the opinion that the Chaplains' Department had never before seen such unanimity.[107] However, it was all downhill from there. On 21 March, the Germans launched their long awaited and initially very successful spring offensive, among their trophies being 'hundreds of thousands' of copies of the chaplains' war aims leaflet stockpiled for distribution to the army.[108] Not only this, but the desperate and unusually fluid nature of the fighting throughout the spring and summer of 1918 did little to help the Reconstruction Scheme get off the ground. By the autumn of 1918, the Reconstruction Scheme had been eclipsed by a parallel but secular initiative, the Educational Training Scheme, which also had its roots in a desire to inoculate the citizen soldier against revolutionary socialism and to strengthen his morale through a careful programme of education.[109]

Despite the confidence of the army's commanders as to the importance of chaplains in relation to morale, the task of chaplains in this respect was beset by some fundamental pastoral and ethical problems. Inevitably, the chaplain's 'complete deference to the cause'[110] was a position that gave rise to certain moral and theological difficulties for some,[111] particularly given the strongly ethical dimension of popular Christianity to which chaplains made their primary appeal. In certain cases, chaplains could be confronted with some difficult questions about the interpretation and circumstances of the war. E.C. Crosse, for example, remembered how men constantly 'witted' him with 'the essentially unchristian nature of their occupation' and how he was compelled to fall back on some schoolroom repartee:

> 'Come on, Padre, what is your answer to this? "Thou shalt not kill." What do you make of that commandment now?', a soldier once remarked to me on my way up to the trenches at Meaulte. The only reply I could think of at the time was 'Well, I hope that you are getting equally busy about the other nine.' Public opinion seemed quite satisfied that I had won that bout.[112]

Similarly, one artillery chaplain was challenged by the following observations of a Canadian gunner:

> Well, when we enlisted everybody told us that this was a righteous war, and that we were fighting on the side of God. We believed it then, but if it's God's war why does he send rain up North, and spoil the show? If it's God's war why doesn't He send good weather and let us have a decent smack at the Boche?'[113]

Besides the Ten Commandments and the vagaries of the weather, deeper questions of theodicy also troubled many. As Studdert Kennedy apprehended,

'The first great difficulty of the private soldier is war . . . It is, of course, the old problem of evil in an acute form, and there is no complete and logically perfect solution of it.'[114] In 1920, Philip Gibbs observed that:

> God and Christianity raised perplexities in the minds of lads desiring life and not death. They could not reconcile the Christian precepts of the chaplain with the bayoneting of Germans and the shambles of the battle-fields. All this blood and mangled flesh in the fields of France and Flanders seemed to them – to many of them, I know – a certain proof that God did not exist, or if He did exist was not, as they were told, a God of love but a monster glad of the agonies of men.

This, claimed Gibbs,

> was the thought which our Army chaplains had to meet from men who would not be put off by conventional words. It was not good enough to tell them that the Germans were guilty of this crime, and that unless the Germans were beaten the world would lose its liberty and its life.[115]

Indeed, if chaplains' words were insufficient to resolve this difficulty then so too was their overall demeanour. Stephen Graham, a private soldier who met 'some ten or twelve chaplains' while serving in France with the 2nd Scots Guards, was unimpressed by their close relationship with the military authorities:

> What struck me most about them was the extraordinary way they seemed to make their minds fit to the official demands made upon opinion. They always rapidly absorbed the official point of view about the war, and often the officers' point of view as well.[116]

As Graham also went on to remark:

> The men, while they liked those who talked to them of home, were cold towards [chaplains] in the matter of religion. For the chaplains did not live the Christian life in any pictorial or dramatic way. The men no doubt thought that as servants of God they should be angels of mercy and light. They expected them to stand out in extraordinary contrast to the ugliness of war.[117]

As Gibbs summarised the situation:

> The devotion of military chaplains to the wounded, their valour,
> their decorations for gallantry under fire, their human comrade-
> ship, and spiritual sincerity, would not bridge the gulf in the minds
> of many soldiers, between a gospel of love and this argument by
> bayonet and bomb, gas-shell and high-velocity, blunderbuss, club
> and trench shovel.[118]

Although Gibbs believed that soldiers were generally reluctant to express
such views to their chaplains, there is no shortage of evidence that they were
in fact aired quite widely. As early as January 1916, Christopher Stone, a
practising Anglican and an officer in the 22nd Royal Fusiliers, wrote home
to his wife:

> I have argued with the Chaplain out here about Christianity and
> the War, and have maintained that the war is *not* Christianity's
> chance at all, as some thought it would be. It is opposed to war
> and no juggling with texts will make it approve of war. If it means
> anything it means peace on earth, good will towards men; it means
> war on evil things, on the Devil; but it doesn't mean stick that
> man with a bayonet because he's wearing a German uniform.[119]

Similarly, one Roman Catholic chaplain admitted that:

> Men often used to ask me to explain why it is that God should
> seem, as it were, to destroy His own work and allow evil to
> conquer. So many priests were killed, the church was the first
> place to be hit and destroyed, good Catholics were driven from
> their homes never to return again. True, sin is a great offence
> against God, but was not suffering too awful for words, and more
> often than not, it was a good fellow who was knocked out in
> the fight.[120]

Significantly, Fr Francis Drinkwater noted in his diary how he was challenged
on the subject of the war as early as August 1915: 'It's rather a bad time
for you gentlemen, isn't it, sir? Difficult to believe in Almighty God with all
this going on.'[121] If the wounded soldier who asked these questions was 'very
cheerful' and the two 'parted friends', by July 1916 Drinkwater was himself
beginning to entertain doubts, writing after the 46th Division's disastrous
attack on Gommecourt:

I shall soon be a pacifist and a conscientious objector – to modern warfare anyhow. It becomes more impossible every month, and the ghastly mangling of human beings en masse seems disproportionate to any conceivable object. 'A bloody mug's game' said a stretcher bearer.[122]

Despite these symptoms of moral disquiet among some junior officers and other ranks, from the point of view of the BEF's commanders, the performance of their chaplains from the winter of 1915–16 appears to have been very satisfactory. As we have seen, from this point through to the end of the war, Haig and many other senior generals of the BEF were consistent and enthusiastic in their support of chaplains' work, a support which was dictated by their understanding of the crucial importance of good morale in Britain's citizen army and by their grasp of its religious and moral dimensions. The army's ultimate success on the Western Front demonstrated to their satisfaction that the efforts of its chaplains had not been in vain and that they had played a full part in sustaining the army's morale throughout the longest and bloodiest campaign in its history. In an official dispatch to the War Office dealing with the battles of 1917, Haig described the value of chaplains' work as 'incalculable'[123] and he undoubtedly clung to this view until the end of the war. On the Sunday following the Armistice, Haig wrote effusively to J.M. Simms, the BEF's principal chaplain, expressing his profound appreciation for the work of the army's chaplains on the Western Front:

Strengthened as I know I and the whole Army have been by the Divine Power, I cannot adequately express the gratitude which I owe to you and all our chaplains for the grand work which they have rendered to our Cause. – And to you in particular, my dear Dr. Simms, I thank you with all my heart.[124]

Four months later, in March 1919, the recent 'splendid work' of the Chaplain's Department was acknowledged by the bestowal of the title 'Royal' at the behest of the king himself.[125] Indeed, General Plumer was so convinced of the contribution that chaplains had made to the success of the war effort that he later credited Bishop Gwynne with having done more than any other individual to secure eventual victory.[126] In 1932, Sir J.E. Edmonds, the official historian of the war, wrote: 'Nothing can be truer than that the troops liked having chaplains with them . . . they were a potent influence in the domain of morale, and often a useful link between the man in the ranks and his officer.'[127] This faith in the military worth of the army's chaplains was not confined to the king, to the commanders of the BEF and to sympathetic historians of Edmonds' stamp. For Lieutenant-Colonel W.D. Croft, who commanded the 11th Royal Scots and the 27th (Lowland) Brigade on the Western Front, the military value of the padres he had encountered while a battalion commander had proved immense. One Presbyterian chaplain, an Ulsterman popularly known as 'Corky', had done a huge amount of work 'among the men in a quiet, unassuming way', proving 'an excellent intelligence officer, enabling one to keep a sure finger on the pulse of the battalion'. Likewise, a Roman Catholic colleague had exerted 'a tremendous influence' for good on the same unit.[128]

Although such views helped to define the role of the chaplain and came to enjoy the status of a military orthodoxy, how accurate was the fundamental assumption that the morale of the British soldier in the First World War was in some way related to the strength of his religious and moral outlook? If there is little evidence to suggest that many soldiers shared the apocalyptic view that Germany was the Anti-Christ (a view that was widely current in clerical circles)[129] there does appear to have been a strong if generally implicit sense among them of the manifest justice of Britain's cause, one which was no doubt underpinned by Germany's invasion of Belgium and by the lurid catalogue of atrocities perpetrated by Germany, Austria-Hungary and Turkey. As Brian Bond has observed, the sense of moral purpose with which Britain went to war in 1914 was shared 'by all social classes and persisted to a remarkable extent for much of the war, even after the appalling costs had become clear'.[130] Likewise, and despite the depressing autumn of 1917, Gary Sheffield has argued that this sense was shared by the great majority of Britain's citizen soldiers throughout the First World War.[131] Because the morale of any group is to a large extent an aggregate of that of its individual members, a telling insight into the underlying attitude of many (and perhaps most) Tommies is provided by one chaplain's account of an encounter between an American doctor and a wounded British soldier during the Third Battle of Ypres:

> The American doctor, who was just having his first experience of war, was bending over one of our wounded boys: 'Ah, my poor man, you are badly hurt,' said he. 'Well, sir', was the response, 'it's in a righteous cause.' 'Well,' said the doctor, 'let's hope it is. I don't think any cause can justify this.'[132]

Crucially, the British army proved to be the only army of the major powers that entered the war in 1914 and which did not experience a widespread failure of morale in 1917 or 1918. Although a host of other factors were undoubtedly at work in ensuring that the army's fighting spirit remained intact, it would be wrong to conclude that the underlying moral and religious consciousness of the British soldier (and the systematic endeavours of thousands of army chaplains in sustaining it) made no contribution to this vital prerequisite of Allied victory. In conversation with G.S. Duncan in April 1917, Haig alluded to this fact when he ascribed the recent failure of the Nivelle offensive to the moral state of the army of France's secular Third Republic. As Duncan noted in his diary, '[Haig] said that the French as such were bound to fail in an offensive . . . they are a decadent race. They haven't it in them.'[133] From his own experiences on the Western Front, Lieutenant-Colonel W.D. Croft was firmly convinced that religious conviction had been the most important mainspring of good morale. In his history of the 9th (Scottish) Division, Croft averred that:

> In war, in order to stick it out day after day, winter and summer, in face of set-backs and disasters, religion is essential. This fact has been proved again and again in all wars. To quote but a few cases: What made the warriors of Saladin invincible? Their religion. What made the Ironsides of Cromwell the terror of Europe? What made the Fuzzy Wuzzy break a British square? And, in the present war, why were the Scottish troops the best fighting material in the world? The same answer – Religion. Whether a man be a Ghazi or a Gloucester, a Hottentot or a Highlander, provided he is soaked with religious fervour which makes him forgetful of self, ready to offer himself willingly as a sacrifice, taking no account of his body as compared with his immortal soul, that man is invincible in battle, and an army of such men can rule the world. But this religion must be no affair of mushroom growth – the religion which comes to a man who hears a crump for the first time. No, no; it must be ingrained; taught from babyhood. Oh, make no mistake about it, religion is the mainspring of the Happy Warrior.[134]

Although extravagantly phrased, it is nevertheless significant that the basic premise of Croft's argument has been accepted by several leading historians of the British army in the First World War. As John Keegan and Richard Holmes have wisely cautioned, it would be 'rash, even in an age when religion may seem relatively unimportant in the West, to ignore its influence upon men in battle'.[135] Similarly, in his famous study of the 2nd Scottish Rifles at Neuve Chapelle, John Baynes accepted that, even among the hardened regular soldiers of 1914–15, 'Religion was not an essential factor in morale, though a valuable help in many cases'.[136]

Chaplains, morale and the Second World War

Although the months following the Armistice led to rapid demobilisation and the virtual reversion of army chaplaincy to its pre-war character and role, the inter-war period did see some important organisational changes within the RAChD. Besides the creation of a small body of reserve chaplains for both the Regular and Territorial armies, an official quota of one chaplain per 1,100 co-religionists was established in 1920, a ratio that corresponded quite closely to the ratio of chaplains to soldiers in the British army in November 1918 (which stood at approximately 1:1,025).[137] Owing to a shortage of chaplains, this ratio had to be adjusted to one chaplain per 1,250 co-religionists following the outbreak of the Second World War.[138] Given the smaller size of the British army during the Second World War, the quota system and the fact that temporary or 'emergency' commissions were granted for the duration of the war, far fewer chaplains served in the British army between 1939 and 1945 than had served between 1914 and 1918. Although the RAChD grew dramatically in the months following Britain's declaration of war, doubling its size from just over 800 Regular, Territorial and Reserve chaplains in September 1939 to 1,623 chaplains by January 1941,[139] only 3,692 chaplains of all denominations served between 1939 and 1945, just fractionally more than the total number of commissioned chaplains serving with the British army in November 1918.[140] However, and despite the higher overall ratio of soldiers to chaplains and their smaller numbers in absolute terms, the outbreak of a new European war in September 1939 ensured that the model of army chaplaincy forged in the crucible of the First World War remained substantially the same in the Second. As in the First World War, chaplains were deployed to bases, hospitals, lines of communication and fighting divisions, most of the latter having an establishment of around sixteen chaplains of all denominations by 1943.[141] However, an important new addition to the Department's burden were the personnel of Anti-Aircraft Command, whose numerous batteries and installations were scattered across the length and breadth of Great Britain and for whose benefit Ronald Selby Wright, a Church of Scotland Territorial chaplain, took to the airwaves in 1942 as 'the Radio Padre'.

If the general morale of a citizen army had concerned Haig and his generation a quarter of a century earlier, this issue was perhaps even more pressing for the army's general officers between 1939 and 1945. Notwithstanding the impact of mechanisation and the huge material superiority which the Allies came to enjoy over Germany and Japan in the latter stages of the war, the human factor remained vital to the ultimate success of British and Allied arms. As the British official history of the Second World War put it, until the very end of the conflict the war 'was still basically a matter of flesh and blood'.[142] Unfortunately, this truism held little comfort for senior officers during the early years of the war for, as David French has observed, during the inter-war period the legacy of the First World War had only served to deepen professional military concerns as to the reliability of a citizen army:

> The next generation of soldiers, better educated than their fathers and full of folk memories of the holocaust of the Western Front, were likely to be frankly sceptical of the military abilities of their leaders. They would not offer unquestioning obedience to their officers, a quality that senior officers believed was indispensable if troops were to be called on to endure heavy losses without flinching. Furthermore, after 1930, senior officers knew that if their soldiers did disobey they no longer had the right to shoot some to encourage the others. In such circumstances, officers would have no option other than to carefully study the moods of their men and lead them by negotiation. Casualty consciousness and the overriding need not to overtax their troops' morale was, therefore, deeply embedded in the thinking of senior British officers long before the Second World War.[143]

The misgivings of the inter-war period were horribly vindicated by the succession of defeats which the British army suffered at German and Japanese hands between the spring of 1940 and the summer of 1942. Indeed, by the time of its withdrawal from Crete in June 1941 the British army was already known in certain quarters as 'the evacuees'.[144] Disregarding the army's defective tactics, its inferior equipment and their own fallible leadership, Britain's military commanders were not slow to cast the blame for these humiliating setbacks on a flaccid generation whose spirit had been sapped by the burgeoning leisure culture and the fashionable pacifism of the 1930s. After the catastrophic fall of Singapore in February 1942, Winston Churchill could only conclude that his soldiers were not the men their fathers had been and, after the humiliating loss of Tobruk later that year, senior commanders recurrently lobbied for the restoration of the death penalty for cowardice and desertion.[145]

Naturally, there was a determined effort to identify and remedy what was amiss with the current generation. As Secretary of State for War, Sir James Grigg ruminated on the 'pansydom' of the inter-war period and its debilitating effect on those who were its products.[146] In July 1942, Sir Alan Brooke, then CIGS, confided to Sir Archibald Wavell:

> I agree with you that we are not anything like as tough as we were in the last war. There has been far too much luxury, safety

first, red triangle, etc., in this country. Our one idea is to look after our comforts and avoid being hurt in any way'.

Wavell did not demur.[147] As the army's forward-looking adjutant-general from the summer of 1941, it fell to Sir Ronald Adam to devise a systematic means of monitoring and addressing the state of morale among soldiers in Great Britain, men who not only played a crucial role in home defence but who also constituted a reservoir of reinforcements and replacements for other theatres of war. In the aftermath of Dunkirk, the term 'browned off' had come to epitomise the state of mind of the average soldier, his despondency being fed by recurrent defeat overseas and by the oppressive weight of parades, fatigues and other army 'bullshit' at home.[148] Convinced that 'This war is going to be won or lost on morale',[149] from January 1942 Adam authorised the compilation of regular reports on military morale in Great Britain, reports which were scrutinised and acted upon by a specially created Morale Committee at the War Office. Over subsequent months, grievances ranging from the state of officer–man relations to the inadequacy of separation allowances were gradually addressed, these developments, in conjunction with much-needed victories in North Africa and Italy, doing much to lift the spirits of Home Forces prior to D-Day.[150] Nevertheless, and despite this progress, the army's morale remained a fragile commodity. For example, although the home army was to provide the bulk of the divisions for the invasion of France, there was widespread resentment among those seasoned formations which were recalled from the Mediterranean to assist with the operation. One such regiment was regarded as being in a state of near-mutiny after its return to England and even daubed the walls of its barracks with such worrying slogans as 'No Second Front'.[151]

Although concerns over the state of the army's morale may well have been exaggerated, with senior officers tempted to misread the truculence of a more egalitarian and less military generation, it remained very much part of the padre's task to support and promote soldier morale. In fact, from the army's point of view, it remained his defining role. Quite simply, and as in the First World War, from a military perspective the whole of the chaplain's ministry stood to benefit soldiers' morale, whether it was in terms of providing an invigorating service, a reassuring presence in the front line, a decent burial for dead comrades or a cup of tea and a chat in the canteen. As one veteran chaplain put the situation in the mid-war period:

[T]he Army's chief interest in the R.A.Ch. Department is an interest in morale; in my case I was practically told that this was so. I was useful to the Brigade, I became a sort of mascot, I was good for morale.[152]

In a society in which Christian and public morality were still closely intertwined, the assumption that good morale had a strong moral and there-fore religious basis continued to prevail. As Sir Francis Fremantle put it in a parliamentary debate in 1943:

> [T]hose who take a long term view of the matter and are in command are fully aware that the essential thing at the bottom of victory is the morale of the men . . . The Army [has] done great things in the direction of morale in this war, not only through generals whose names and their encouragement of religion are household words to us, but we have also the Army Welfare Department, which has done so much to help on and encourage this line of thought and feeling in the Army. But at bottom it is worth nothing unless you have a moral basis. It is the religious basis which is the only thing that is behind and above and over everything.[153]

Certainly, religion did play an important role in national morale during the Second World War, shaping British propaganda and exercising a defining influ-ence on contemporary perceptions of the war. In this respect, the sacredness of Britain's cause was reflected in recurring national days of prayer, in the anti-Nazi pronouncements of the churches, in the widely acclaimed 'miracle' of Dunkirk and in the celebrated image of the dome of St Paul's cathedral standing untouched in the midst of the London blitz.[154] As the war progressed, and no doubt with the secular ideological motivation of the *Wehrmacht* and of the Red Army in mind, it would appear that even some civilian commen-tators were prepared to identify a militant Christianity as the best equivalent and counterpoise to Nazi indoctrination. This was certainly the case with A.D. Lindsay, a leading Christian educationalist and the master of Balliol. For *The British Way and Purpose* (a series of pamphlets published from 1942 by the Directorate of Army Education in order to support army education in citizenship), Lindsay wrote:

> If a cause is worth fighting for, it must matter more than the men who fight for it . . . We want a faith that is as good as the Nazi faith is evil, without being in any way less dynamic . . . Christianity teaches a faith in God conceived as justice, and goodness, mercy and love . . . this faith has been powerful in our civilisation . . . it has, in fact, made this country what it is.[155]

Even before the calamities of 1940–2, the legacy of the First World War ensured that the army's view of the chaplain's functions was very much geared towards his influence on morale. One exposition of the role of the chaplain from the 'Phoney War' period maintained that, with respect to morale:

> It is the chaplain's work to raise this essential part of the all-round fitness of the soldier to its highest pitch . . . The work of the chaplain cannot be too strongly emphasised and the interest of the nation in this department cannot be too highly stressed.[156]

As British military fortunes fell in the course of 1940, the army's stress on morale and the efforts of the RAChD rose in proportion. In October 1940, Sir Archibald Wavell addressed a chaplains' conference in Cairo, in which, as one chaplain recalled, 'He pointed out that this was a war of morale and of the spirit, more than any other war in history. Our task, he said, was to strengthen the spirit of the men.'[157] Five months later, in March 1941, a collected volume appeared entitled *Front Line Religion*. Edited by Ronald Selby Wright, the book comprised an essay by Lord Gort, then Inspector-General of Training, and twenty further essays by army chaplains past and present. Direct and uncompromising, the essays covered a range of stirring topics including 'The Christian Knight', 'St. George of England' and 'The Guarantee of Victory' and all purported to be 'short talks given by Padres to some of the thousands of men of the British Army'.[158] Naturally, the addresses reflected and emphasised some powerful religious themes in contemporary British propaganda, notably Britain's role as the last defender of 'Christian civilisation' in Europe, an idea emphasised by Winston Churchill in his legendary 'Finest Hour' speech of 18 June 1940.[159] As R.F.V. Scott of the London Scottish reflected in 'The Sword of the Lord', Europe should not be abandoned to the unholy alliance of Nazi Germany and the Soviet Union:

> [W]ho could contemplate with an easy conscience the thought of another dark age in Europe . . . It is very easy to say that God would make it all right in the end, but what of the generations in between? Have we the right to hand them over to a dark bondage that might well be worse than death – to forces that more surely than bombs would make havoc of all that is finest and best in civilization? Surely it were better to die defending them, than to be damned for deserting them . . . the day has come when the Faith must be defended. And we will defend it, as the military textbook baldly puts it, 'To the last round and to the last man'.[160]

Such eloquence, of course, proved insufficient to stem the tide of defeat that swept over the British army in Greece, North Africa and the Far East in subsequent months, defeats for which successes against the Italians hardly compensated. Nevertheless, the RAChD continued to urge upon its members the importance of their role in relation to morale. Mgr Coghlan stressed that Roman Catholic chaplains were expected to 'sustain the Morale of their men and be ready to meet adverse situations with calmness and equanimity. They should never be guilty of passing on alarmist rumours.'[161] More positively, Percy Middleton Brumwell, the deputy chaplain-general, devoted a substantial portion of a pamphlet entitled *The Army Chaplain* to the subject of morale. Written in 1942, Middleton Brumwell gave a brief moral history of European warfare and reminded his readership of Napoleon's famous dictum that, in warfare, 'The moral is to the physical as three to one'.[162] With a view to more recent events, he pronounced that the nation's morale had deterred German invasion after Dunkirk and had kept Britain in the war notwithstanding the grim ordeal of the blitz and the scourge of the U-boat. The course of the war, he claimed, had conclusively proved that 'Notwithstanding the tremendous power of the opposing machine, morale is all important, pre-eminent and pre-dominant'.[163] Addressing how the chaplain could strengthen morale, Middleton Brumwell identified four 'moral qualities' which particularly concerned the army chaplain given that religion underpinned them all. The first of these was the 'The Will to Win', a determination grounded in a sense of the rectitude of the national cause. As Middleton Brumwell urged:

> This sense of the right must animate all the thought of our manhood and womanhood, and give strength of will and power of resistance, and a full and thoroughgoing determination to win. This is the first great basis of high morale.

In addition, there was the promotion of 'Self-Respect', a virtue that promoted the reputation of the army and of the nation overseas and that avoided the debilitating 'shadow of scorn or contempt' which was so damaging to a soldier's sense of self-worth. Third, 'Self-control' was vitally related to self-respect and again the chaplain had a key role to play in ensuring 'that every lower instinct' was properly restrained, not least because habits of self-control were vital to proper conduct in action. As the deputy chaplain-general intoned, in battle 'self control is vital – vital. Courage is not the absence of fear but the control of fear. Panic spreads like a forest fire . . . One man may lose control and a whole line be affected.' The fourth and last component of good morale was the development of 'a high sense of honour', a virtue which enabled the ordinary soldier to act without the need for supervision:

It is the greatest compliment that the nation can pay a man — England *expects* that this day and every day each man will do his duty. It will affect behaviour everywhere, and cause a man to exercise all those qualities of a great manhood which the stern duties of the present time demand.[164]

Although Middleton Brumwell envisaged the forging of a new generation of Christian warrior, he had no specific advice to offer on how this end might be achieved. However, the chaplain's promotion of morale did come to assume a more explicit character in 1942 with the advent of 'Padre's Hour', a hugely popular initiative which originated in the newly formed Airborne Division. As an elite formation that would undergo unusual hazards as the spearhead of many future operations, its GOC, Major-General F.A.M. Browning, was anxious to ensure a high level of motivation among his men and that their 'religious instruction . . . should not be neglected'. Hence, with the co-operation of the division's senior chaplain, a weekly period of religious instruction for all soldiers was established as part of the division's training routine.[165] Unlike church parade, the ethos of Padre's Hour was essentially informal; chaplains took men of their own denomination, gave a short talk on a particular subject 'and then let the men raise any points which they had not fully grasped, or on which they needed further enlightenment'.[166] From being a modest innovation confined to the Airborne Division, Padre's Hour quickly spread throughout the British army both at home and overseas, attracting moral and material support from the interdenominational Church Committee for Supplementing Religious Education Among Men in HM Forces. Within months of the inauguration of Padre's Hour, this committee had produced a pamphlet entitled *The Padre's Hour: Technique of Adult Religious Education* and also two further booklets entitled *The War within the War* and *Thinking Ahead*, both of which provided chaplains with topics for discussion, bibliographies and suggestions for external speakers.[167] Part of the appeal of Padre's Hour lay in its informality, an approach which was already paying dividends for the army's own 'Radio Padre', Ronald Selby Wright. As Selby Wright put it, Padre's Hour enabled men to 'heckle and argue, as they couldn't do in church — they could get points cleared up or refuse to be satisfied as they chose'.[168] The popularity of Padre's Hour also owed something to a strong body of wartime support for public religious education, support that was in part a reaction to the godless totalitarian ideologies of Fascism and Communism and which came to be enshrined in the new religious provisions of the 1944 Education Act.[169] Finally, Padre's Hour also appealed to a spirit of inquiry and discussion that was already abroad in the British army. Indeed, it is hard not to see Padre's Hour as the religious equivalent of the compulsory discussion groups which had been launched under the aegis of the leftward-leaning Army Bureau of Current Affairs in 1941.[170] As compulsory weekly gatherings, both Padre's Hour and ABCA meetings fed an impression that the British army was alive with creative discussion and that, as A.D. Lindsay put it, 'there had not been an Army in England which discussed like this since that famous Puritan Army which produced the Putney Debates and laid the foundation of modern democracy'.[171]

If the army in Great Britain was placing an ever-increasing emphasis on the role of the chaplain between 1940 and 1942, it was the Eighth Army in North Africa which first saw this heightened emphasis applied in the context of active service. As is widely recognised, it was Montgomery who stressed the role and status of the chaplain among British troops in this theatre of war. Although Montgomery's enthusiasm for the RAChD has often been attributed to his singular upbringing and to his personal religiosity, it must be stressed that his idealisation of the role of chaplains was also heavily influenced by the philosophy of the BEF's General Staff in the First World War and by recent developments in the Home Forces. In all probability, the value of meticulous planning was not all that Montgomery learned as a staff officer on the Western Front. When Archbishop Davidson noted the 'mutual appreciation' of chaplains and First Army officers that had been evidenced at the joint meeting held in his honour at Béthune in May 1916, he noted that Bernard Montgomery was among the officers present on this occasion.[172] Similarly, when Montgomery left England to assume command of the Eighth Army, he was coming from a home context in which the role of the chaplain was already acquiring greater significance in terms of military morale. While still with the Home Forces in England, Montgomery had already pronounced at one briefing conference that:

> The most important people in the Army are the Nursing Sisters and the Padres – the Sisters because they tell the men they matter to us – and the Padres because they tell the men they matter to God. And it is the men who matter.[173]

Although the situation in the Western Desert had stabilised with Rommel's repulse at the First Battle of Alamein, when Montgomery assumed command of the Eighth Army in August 1942 it was still very much under the shadow of a string of successive defeats, the worst of which had been the loss of Tobruk to the Axis in June. According to the editor of *Crusader*, the Eighth Army's weekly newspaper, by the time of Montgomery's arrival in Egypt the standing of its senior officers had fallen so low that 'the most popular general in the Eighth Army was probably Rommel'.[174] Montgomery's shake-up of personnel, training and morale in the Eighth Army is the stuff of legend, a legend assiduously cultivated by Montgomery himself. One of his first steps was to secure the dismissal of D.A. Duncan as the Eighth Army's assistant chaplain-general, ensuring that he was replaced by Frederick Llewelyn Hughes, who was then serving as deputy assistant chaplain-general of XIII and XXX Corps.[175] Characteristically, Montgomery remained convinced of the wisdom of this choice, describing Hughes as 'the ideal of what an Army padre should be'.[176] Certainly, the two had much in common; both came from clerical families and both had served as infantry and as staff officers in the First World War.[177] Moreover, they clearly had very similar views regarding the status of religion as the foundation of good morale. According to Hughes' own account, he managed to strike the right note with Montgomery from the outset. At their very first interview in Montgomery's famous caravan, Montgomery pronounced that 'Everybody ought to know at all levels what is the thing in his job which matters most'. Having said this, Montgomery inquired of Hughes, 'Now Padre, in your job and at your level, what is the thing that matters most?' Hughes' answer, 'Well sir – spiritual power is the only thing we have got' was to earn Montgomery's lasting confidence.[178] In earnest of his sentiments, one of Hughes' first steps as assistant chaplain-general of the Eighth Army was to write to all Protestant chaplains presenting their cause as a crusade, averring that 'A soldier who fights for the British Way of Life serves God and us, for he protects the freedom of the Church'.[179]

Naturally, Montgomery's resounding victory at the Second Battle of Alamein served to vindicate his philosophy and methods of command. In consequence, Hughes and the chaplains of the Eighth Army benefited by association. To a large extent, this was due to Montgomery's own version of how his chaplains had contributed to this desperately needed victory, insisting that they had laid its moral and religious foundations. At the thanksgiving service held in Cairo cathedral after the battle, Montgomery asserted that 'I would as soon think of going into battle without my artillery as without my Chaplains'.[180] In March 1944, in a speech delivered at the Mansion House, Montgomery returned to the theme of the religious and moral basis of war-winning morale. Stressing that 'the key to success in battle' was 'the man inside the tank, and the man behind the gun', Montgomery insisted that 'such men must have faith in God and they must think rightly on the moral issues involved'.[181] Before Alamein, he maintained, his 'devoted brotherhood of chaplains' had responded magnificently to his clarion call '"The Lord mighty in battle" will give us the victory.'[182] Indeed, in December 1944, Sir James Grigg, the Secretary of State for War, confirmed to the House of Commons that 'Field-Marshal Montgomery has over and over again impressed upon me the importance of [chaplains'] work, especially upon active service'.[183]

Montgomery's military success and his unambiguous understanding of morale certainly encouraged Hughes to refer to himself as 'General Montgomery's Chief Padre' and their meeting of minds helped to ensure that 'the General–Padre relationship between Montgomery and [Hughes] was one of the most successful and famous of all time'.[184] Certainly, the Eighth Army's chaplains benefited immediately from Montgomery's understanding of their importance. One of the early dividends of Montgomery's favour was the provision of better transport. As the senior chaplain of the 10th Armoured Division recalled:

> When [Hughes] told Monty that the chaplains' work was greatly hindered by the shortage of transport, Monty at once ordered that every chaplain in the 8th Army must be issued with his own truck, so that before the battle of Alamein began, every chaplain was properly equipped and mobile. It was a great boost to our morale as it made us feel that our work was really appreciated.[185]

In view of the success of the Eighth Army in North Africa, Sicily and Italy, by 1943 the work of its chaplains had come to be regarded as setting the standard for the army as a whole. Furthermore, the spiritual state of the Eighth Army was depicted in glowing terms from as early as the autumn of 1942. Just prior to leaving Britain for the TORCH landings in North Africa, a newly returned Eighth Army chaplain told the officers of the 6th Armoured Division 'I believe that in the desert, and under the stars, the men of the 8th Army are a brotherhood and they are coming to see the nearness of God.'[186] By Easter 1943, with Axis forces in North Africa on the verge of surrender, Hughes was publicising the methods of Eighth Army padres, no doubt with an eye to the untried chaplains of the Home Forces and the largely inexperienced chaplains of the newly arrived First Army. In a short paper entitled 'The Chaplain's Duty in Battle', which was published in the *Chaplains' Magazine* at Easter 1943, Hughes systemised the role of the front-line chaplain before, during and after the classic offensive battle. This role involved playing a supportive part in 'The Approach to Battle' and providing 'Eve of Battle Services', 'Voluntary Companionship at Zero Hour', 'Practical Service in Battle', 'Reconstructive Companionship in Thought after Action', 'The Burial of the Dead' and the holding of 'Thanksgiving and Memorial Services' thereafter. Significantly, this advice enjoyed Montgomery's full endorsement, Montgomery writing on a draft version of the paper:

> I have noted the above with great interest and commend it to all chaplains. A chaplain who follows the above advice will have done well, and will earn the love of his men – which is a pearl of very great price.[187]

In 1944, Hughes added to this store of wisdom in a booklet entitled *The Chaplains of the Grand Assault: A Summary of the Experience in the Field of the Eighth Army Brotherhood of Chaplains*, in which he assured his readership that 'The padre's way to an army's heart is through conviction that religion assists its fighting'.[188]

An important symbol of the Eighth Army's perceived superiority in the spiritual and moral realm was Montgomery's continuing patronage of Hughes. When Montgomery was recalled to Britain at the end of 1943 to take command of the 21st Army Group in preparation for the invasion of France, along with his other protégés Montgomery insisted on taking Hughes with him as 'head chaplain'.[189] Some months later, in September 1944, Montgomery successfully lobbied for Hughes' appointment as chaplain-general.[190] Meanwhile, and now as deputy chaplain-general to the 21st Army Group, Hughes, like Montgomery, extended his morale-boosting activities to the civilian population. On 15 June 1944 Hughes' talk on 'The Consecration of our Armies' was broadcast on the BBC Home Service.[191] Later that summer, Hughes also featured in a Sunday morning service which was broadcast live from Normandy. For this memorable co-production of the BBC and the church militant, J.W. Steele (then assistant chaplain-general of the Second Army) organised the music, Hughes preached the sermon and Montgomery read the lesson, pausing only when the service was over-flown by a squadron of British fighters.[192] Four months later, and as the climax of the king's visit to British forces in the field, Hughes led another Sunday service which was broadcast live from a small Protestant church in Holland. In the presence of the king and Montgomery – both of whom were clad in battle dress – Hughes invoked sentiments that were by now very familiar:

> Lord God of Hosts, mighty in battle, stretch forth, we pray Thee, Thine almighty arm, to strengthen and protect our soldiers in the line, endow them with those virtues which draw the sting of perils and with those energies which conquer weariness. Send Thy comfort to the wounded, Thine angels to the dying, and Thy uniting Spirit unto all. That one strong life divine may dare us on to victory through Jesus Christ our Lord.[193]

A major theme which seemed to emerge from the collaboration of Montgomery and Hughes in 1942 was the notion of the consecration of British arms to a higher purpose. In a Christmas sermon, which was broadcast from Bethlehem in the afterglow of the Eighth Army's triumph at Alamein, Hughes endowed the vulnerable image of the Christ-child with a new and urgent militancy:

> In this small town, in baby heart was born the vision of a noble
> Christian culture, full of grace and truth . . . we serve with
> Consecrated Sword the Prince of Peace and guard His flock, that
> of His Kingdom there shall be no end.[194]

This quasi-crusading ideology was very much cultivated and cherished by
leading chaplains as the war was widened in North Africa and taken back to
continental Europe by a series of massive sea and airborne landings that were
in a very real sense reminiscent of the crusades of old. One First Army order
of service from the period 1942–3 emphasised this theme in explaining the
patriotic and religious symbolism of the First Army's field sign. Its shield, it
maintained, represented 'our country . . . a sure and a safe refuge'. 'The
Crusaders' Cross' which it featured was:

> The symbol by which all men shall know the ideals and principles
> for which we stand . . . nothing can be higher than the hope
> expressed by that symbol – persecution, oppression and terror
> banished, and replaced by Christian peace and toleration. No one
> can doubt the intention of those who serve and follow The Cross.

Finally, there was 'The Drawn Sword':

> Long ago a Christian Soldier gave us an example of the cause
> for which the sword should be drawn. This example we of First
> Army endeavour to follow. St. George drew his sword and
> destroyed a dragon which had enslaved a nation. We endeavour
> to destroy a dragon which has arisen in Europe which would
> enslave the whole world. We cannot sheath our sword until our
> task be thoroughly finished.

This exposition was followed by a prayer for victory and by the prayer of
another famous soldier saint, St Ignatius of Loyola:

> Teach us, good Lord, to serve Thee as Thou deservest; to give
> and not to count the cost; to fight and not to heed the wounds;
> to toil and not to seek for rest; to labour and not to ask for any
> reward, save that of knowing that we do Thy will . . .[195]

Perhaps inevitably, this crusading consciousness became inter-woven with
an ersatz Arthurian romanticism. In a revealing insight into the mentality and
self-perception of the most senior army chaplains in the Mediterranean,

A.J. Wilcox, the deputy chaplain-general in the Middle East, wrote to Hughes in December 1943:

> We must keep all these Chaplains together afterwards and must have a wonderful old House, medieval, well-timbered, grand staircase, a haunted room, a wonderful Chapel, 'The Holy Grail' above the altar . . . yes, we must dream, 'tis the only thing that keeps us sane.[196]

With his appointment to the 21st Army Group early in the following year, Hughes was in a position to share these perceptions with a largely new constituency, namely the forces mustered for the invasion of France. In his *Chaplains of the Grand Assault*, Hughes admonished the chaplains under his command:

> Faith transforms the character of military effort, brings men to war for righteousness' sake, sets a just purpose before them and the light of a high calling in them . . . We have full commission to match the men of this great enterprise, on the eve of battle, with King Arthur's Knights of Chivalry.[197]

Quite possibly due to Hughes' influence, in the build-up to D-Day Montgomery seems to have been mesmerised by the idea of a national service of consecration to be held prior to the cross-Channel invasion. In his Mansion House speech of March 1944, Montgomery had made much of the symbolism of the Sword of State and of the words of the coronation service: 'With this sword do justice, stop the growth of iniquity.'[198] At around the same time, and during a lengthy correspondence with Archbishop Temple, Montgomery went on to suggest a possible order of service for a proposed 'Public Hallowing of the Armed Services of the Crown'. Inspired by the coronation service, it was to be a national occasion held in full coronation regalia at Westminster Abbey, the focus of the service being the Sword of State, its sacred symbolism and its present implications.[199] Although this ambitious project was thwarted by a marked lack of government enthusiasm for the idea, a more modest service was held for senior British officers on the eve of OVERLORD. The moving force behind this event was J.W. Steele, who, as assistant chaplain-general of the First Army in 1942–3, no doubt composed the First Army order of service that we have just examined. According to Steele, this 'eve of battle dedication service' was held for the benefit of the senior officers of the Second Army. The inspiration behind the service was Steele's encounter with the new flame-throwing *Crocodile* tanks of the 79th Armoured Division. Stunned by their awful nature, Steele was concerned that their indiscriminate use would vitiate the all-important moral and religious basis of the coming Allied campaign. As he put it to General Sir Miles Dempsey, the GOC of the Second Army, he was

> not very happy about having these things without there being some sort of moral control over them [because] in them lies a great power of revenge. You can let loose troops with these things and the answer isn't very pleasant, it means that you just burn up a lot of Germans . . . these things are there to win the war with, not to take revenge on an enemy.

Interestingly, and in another indication of the moral influence that chaplains wielded at the highest levels of the army, Dempsey was convinced by Steele's appeal to the principles of just war theory. Consequently, the two agreed on a dedication service, its underlying purpose being to ensure that those with 'power of authorisation' over the use of these weapons 'should come and promise to use them for the purpose which is intended'. In the event, and in view of the overwhelming need for secrecy prior to the invasion, a parish church (Christ's Church, Portsdown) was commandeered and its vicar temporarily ejected. Although Steele's original plan had envisaged that the congregation would leave at the end of the service and go 'straight down to the boats', owing to the last-minute postponement of the invasion this final detail had to be omitted. Nevertheless, Steele's taste for the melodramatic extended to a desire to recreate the service 'which the knights [of the Order of the Bath] used to hold in the Tower of London' but, with no details of this service being available, Steele was eventually compelled to devise an order of service from his own fertile imagination.[200] Despite the theatricality of Steele's service, the same mood that prevailed at Christ's Church, Portsdown, was also struck by army chaplains in the aircraft, gliders and ships of the invasion force. In at least one troopship a chaplain echoed the sentiments of Steele and of the founder of the Jesuits, British soldiers leaving aside their pre-battle preparations to recite the dedication prayer of St Ignatius of Loyola.[201]

Despite the chaplains' assiduous efforts to exalt and indeed sacralise the national cause, a notable departure from the methods of 1914–18 appears to have been a conscious avoidance of the visceral belligerence which had been exhibited by so many chaplains in the First World War. This reflected the more pacific mood of the churches in the inter-war period and these sensibilities were also shared, as senior officers recognised, by British soldiers in general. As Montgomery wrote to Sir Alan Brooke in the wake of El Alamein in November 1942:

I am quite certain that the way to deal with the German is to face up to him in battle, and fight him; it is the only way to deal with him, because then you kill him. The trouble with our British lads is that they are not killers by nature; they have got to be so inspired that they will want to kill, and that is what I tried to do with this Army of mine.[202]

As early as 1939, Harry Blackburne had warned chaplains against the temptation to stoke hatred of the Germans, arguing:

War is brutal, but it need not be brutalising. Any attempt to create in the minds of our sailors, soldiers and airmen feelings of hate, must be resisted at all costs, for hate can only have a weakening and depressing effect on all who give way to it.[203]

In 1942, the new GOC of the 43rd (Wessex) Division, Major-General G.I. Thomas (who was widely nicknamed 'von Thoma' for his Teutonic methods and apparent lack of humour),[204] made an unsuccessful attempt to impose a more militant ministry upon his chaplains. As one divisional chaplain remembered, at a meeting held at Canterbury just after Thomas assumed command of the division:

The general, with very few preliminaries, stated that he wished his chaplains to preach a *Jihad* (a Mohammedan word for a war against unbelievers) . . . Furthermore, he laid down during this 'pep' period that the addresses given throughout the Division on each Sunday should be identical; that each chaplain would receive a copy of an approved address and preach or read it verbatim.

This attempt to revive some of the more questionable methods adopted by divisional commanders during the First World War provoked a furious response:

The storm broke . . . It was pointed out that chaplains were individuals who varied considerably in thought and outlook, and that such a method, imposed from above by a layman, was totally unacceptable. They said furthermore that they believed they were commissioned by Christ to preach the Gospel and not a *Jihad*. They conceived that it was their duty to inculcate into the personnel of their units the recognition and acceptance of Christian faith and practice, and also to prepare them to face the strain of battle and, if it should come, death itself. The General, understandably angered by this flat refusal to accept his policy, banged the table with his cane, saying that never before had he encountered such an uncooperative, indeed rebellious, body of chaplains, and stormed out.[205]

Besides finding more appropriate means by which to inspire the army to fight, chaplains continued to play a key role in maintaining morale in other respects. Although faced with increasing competition from ENSA and the NAAFI, chaplains still played a significant role as providers of canteens and other entertainments. As one chaplain, who was put in charge of a regimental canteen in the Western Desert, put it: 'although some poured scorn on the "Holy Grocer", I knew I was making a valuable contribution to the welfare of the troops and their morale, while relieving an officer for more warlike duties'.[206] Again, given the RAChD's collective experience of the First World War, the role of the front-line chaplain remained essentially unchanged from what it had been from 1916 to 1918. As the history of the 52nd (Lowland) Division put it:

> In battle, generally speaking, the padre was up with the doctor at the Regimental Aid Post, though often he was out with the stretcher-bearers under fire. He would take his share of carrying the R.A.P. equipment, and he carried for his own purposes a supply of welfare cigarettes, sweets, stationery – all the little homely things that might help to comfort a wounded lonely lad. The wounded were his first concern, especially the gravely wounded; and it does not need a great deal of imagination to perceive what necessary services the chaplain could perform in the way of writing letters or even recording a dying wish, over and above the sympathy and companionship he could offer a stricken man. His function within the medical organisation of the division, as in a sense the doctor's aide in emergency, was thus clear-cut and significant.[207]

Chaplains also continued to take responsibility for disposing of the human detritus of battle. Although the task of clearing a battlefield in the First World War had proved a common and unpleasant duty for chaplains and burial details alike, the full-scale mechanisation of the British army in the intervening period entailed the additional horror of recovering large numbers of corpses from burnt-out tanks and armoured vehicles. If the consequences of a fatal hit on sealed vehicles loaded with fuel and ammunition were appalling enough, this problem was compounded by a general recognition that British armoured vehicles were often inferior to their German counterparts and were also woefully vulnerable to the dreaded 88mm anti-tank gun. Even a growing reliance on the superior American *Sherman* tank from 1942 did little to offset this situation, the chronic impression of inferiority being exacerbated by the appearance of German *Panther* and *Tiger* tanks in 1943.[208] Certainly, it would be no exaggeration to say that British tank crews fought most of the Second World War with the prospect of a hideous fate if their tanks were hit and with little confidence in the relative merits of their own machines. Indeed, one veteran of the north-west Europe campaign described even the *Sherman* as:

> a self-igniting crematorium . . .
> a self-sealing mausoleum . . . or
> a self-detonating bomb![209]

In view of this situation and its obvious implications for morale, the duty of recovering bodies from burnt-out vehicles often devolved solely upon the chaplains of armoured units. In Tunisia in 1942, for example, Bill Cook was involved in the burial of a German corpse which had been recovered from a burnt-out half-track. Because the ground was hard and rocky, Cook asked an officer of the 1st Derbyshire Yeomanry for a burial party, a request which was 'flatly refused on the grounds that it would be bad for his men's morale'.[210] Similarly, in the wake of a successful British attack in Normandy in 1944, Leslie Skinner, a Methodist chaplain of the Sherwood Rangers Yeomanry, was left to clear up its human debris:

> On to all objectives by lunch time [he noted in his diary] . . .
> 8 men killed, 5 still in tanks . . . Buried . . . 3 dead and tried to
> reach remaining dead in tanks still too hot and burning. Place
> absolute shambles. Infantry dead and some Germans lying about.
> Horrible mess. Fearful job picking up bits and pieces and
> re-assembling for identification and putting in blankets for burial.
> No infantry to help. Squadron Leader offered to lend me some
> men to help. Refused. Less men who live and fight in tanks have
> to do with this side of things the better. They know it happens
> but to force it on their attention is not good. My job. This was
> more than normally sick making. Really ill – vomiting.[211]

Despite many continuities with the First World War, Second World War army chaplains seem to have borne a much greater burden of personal welfare work than did their predecessors of 1914–18. Clearly, the relaxation of Britain's divorce laws in the late 1930s, the far-flung theatres of war to which hundreds of thousands of men were sent for years on end and the greater degree of sexual freedom which the wartime situation engendered on the Home Front entailed terrible emotional strain for a large number of soldiers and other servicemen. Although the army created a new system of local army welfare officers in order to deal with situations such as this,[212] chaplains often found themselves dealing with the bitter and complicated marital problems of men under their care. Bill Cook remembered that, in Italy by the end of 1944, difficulties of this kind had become endemic among his men:

> Chaplains had fewer services to take, but an increasing load of welfare cases. Most of the men had been away from home for over three years and the strains were beginning to take [their] toll. Thousands of families began to break up.

What was true of the 'D-Day dodgers' in Italy was no less true of the men of the 'Forgotten Fourteenth' Army in the jungles of Assam and Burma. In March 1944, A.H. Rodgers wrote of the 2nd Border Regiment at Imphal:

> The men have only two topics these days – Repatriation and trouble with their wives. They come to me – I feel it is often just a mere longing to talk of home and their loved ones. . . . Photographs are passed round – 'That's the boy, Padre – he is 9 years old. This is the girl – I've never seen her' and so on.[213]

Furthermore, the attitudes of the rank and file towards army chaplains during the Second World War were identifiably different in certain key respects from those which had developed between 1914 and 1918. In a lengthy and revealing MO report entitled 'The Chaplain to the Forces', contemporary attitudes towards chaplains were divulged and analysed in detail. Written in June 1943 and based largely on evidence compiled from rear-area units and units that were yet to see active service,[214] the report relied on testimony gleaned from a constituency which many chaplains would have thought unpromising. Nevertheless, and while recognising that their commissioned rank guaranteed their respectful treatment in public, the report presented a broadly sympathetic picture of chaplains' work and of their image within the army. Recognising the difficulty of working within an organisation whose membership represented a cross-section of British society at large, the report conceded that the chaplain's role was intrinsically invidious:

It is difficult [it maintained] for a padre to do anything without getting severely criticised . . . if he is too sheltered and intellectual he is said to be 'other worldly', and if he comes right out and acts as the others do, it is wondered if this is the sort of example that clergymen ought to set. If his sermons are learned, he is accused of talking over the men's heads, if they are simple, he is said to be talking down to them. If he keeps strictly within his own sphere, people wonder what he does all the week, if he is generally helping, here, there and everywhere, he is accused of pushing his nose in.[215]

Nevertheless, the report argued that chaplains were generally well thought of, concluding that 'there is very little criticism of the chaplain's sincerity or goodness. Almost without exception, the chaplains are hard-working, conscientious, good-living men, but without the ability to "get over" to their men.'[216] This lack of 'the common touch' was ascribed to the clergy's natural unworldliness, to their comparatively high level of education and to their status as officers, a status which militated against the development of a closer relationship with the other ranks.[217] If the general attitude of untried soldiers or lines of communication troops towards their chaplains was more or less positive, then the recollections of men who fought in the 43rd (Wessex) Division throughout the north-west Europe campaign indicate that the experience of active service could considerably enhance the stature of chaplains among front-line soldiers. According to Charlie Wakeley of the 1st Worcestershire Regiment, chaplains played 'a very big role in morale':

The chaplain [of the 1st Worcesters] was looked at as a saint, he was. I can only speak for infantrymen, I can, but to see the chaplain – you more or less got faith when you saw the chaplain. And you saw him quite a bit. He wasn't a man that was three miles behind the lines or nothing. He was there – he was administering to the dead and everything. Even in the front line he was.[218]

Likewise, the medical officer of the 7th Somerset Light Infantry noted:

During all the fighting [in Normandy] Padre Richards visited the companies calmly and coolly. A great strain on him because he knew the men intimately, many of the casualties were his friends. Many burials to perform, many graves to dig.[219]

Even out of the line, chaplains proved a welcome source of support. Wally Caines, an officer of the 4th Dorsetshire Regiment, noted with appreciation how, after the survivors of his battalion were pulled out of the line in July 1944, 'Padres met us with cheery smiles, giving us cigarettes, chocolate and sweets'.[220]

Although the chaplain's lot may well have been more difficult among inexperienced or rear-area troops, a degree of cultural distance from ordinary soldiers can hardly be described as a calamitous problem for the work and reputation of British army chaplains during the Second World War. Certainly, their circumstances and performance compared very favourably with that of the generation of 1914–18. Coming from a less militaristic generation, divested of the missionary illusions of 1914 and much less prone to see their war as a divine crucible for earthly improvement, chaplains of the period 1939–45 quite simply had fewer grounds on which to attract criticism and fewer aspirations of their own to disappoint. Moreover, and whereas the cause which they had supported culminated in the utter defeat of Germany, Italy and Japan and in the horrific revelations of Belsen, the cause that their forebears had championed had become mired in the tortured wastelands of the Western Front and had issued in an unstable and temporary peace. Even the post-war situation on the domestic front seemed to vindicate the sacrifices of the citizen soldiers of the Second World War, sacrifices which were on a much-reduced scale in comparison with those of their fathers' generation. Whereas the fruits of victory in 1945 included far-reaching social reform at home, the generation that had endured the Somme and Passchendaele found little to console themselves in the social and economic environment of Britain in the 1920s. In sum, there was very little reason for post-1945 writers to recriminate against army chaplains, a situation that stands in marked and decisive contrast to that which had occurred in the inter-war years.

Whatever the opinion of ordinary soldiers, some of the army's most senior commanders clearly invested considerable faith in the role of chaplains throughout the Second World War. Indeed, and in the aftermath of victory, they hailed the contribution of army chaplains to the recent triumph. In July 1945, for example, Montgomery issued a circular to all chaplains in the 21st Army Group in which he announced that their efforts had been 'crowned with complete success'. In congratulating them on their recent 'magnificent work', Montgomery paused to define the nature of their triumph:

> You have inspired us with that spirit of high endeavour which has
> enlivened all our actions, and you have constantly made us bear
> in mind from whence cometh our strength, 'If it had not been the

Lord who was on our side, when men rose up against us, then they had swallowed us up quick [Psalm 124.3].' The tremendous consciousness among all ranks of the greatness of our task, which has now been blessed with complete victory, is largely the result of your labours.[221]

Despite this paean of praise, it is well nigh impossible to quantify the relative contribution of the army's chaplains to British military success in the Second World War. However, it is worth stressing two important points. First, in terms of their military role, chaplains undoubtedly provided enormous support for soldiers both individually and collectively; they developed a powerful moral and religious idiom with which to inspire them, they entertained them in their idle hours, they offered support in their domestic problems, they prepared them for battle, tended to their wounds and provided a vestige of dignity in death. Furthermore, and despite their status as non-combatants, they demonstrably bore the same risks as other soldiers. Between 1939 and 1945, the British army suffered 126,734 fatal casualties including 96 members of the RAChD, a figure that corresponds almost exactly to the army's wartime ratio of one chaplain to 1,250 soldiers.[222] Second, the growing importance of their role from 1942 onwards was contemporary with an upturn in British military fortunes, the enhanced profile of chaplains being associated with the growing influence of Britain's most flamboyant and significant fighting general, Bernard Montgomery. Clearly, the enhanced role accorded to chaplains in Montgomery's Eighth Army and 21st Army Group was very much part of the army's long ascent to eventual victory.

Conclusion

In common with the rest of the British army, the Chaplains' Department underwent a dramatic transformation during the course of the two World Wars, with the role of its chaplains being viewed very differently in 1945 from what it had been in 1914. Although the military role of army chaplains will always be prone to arouse the suspicion and censure of Christian pacifists and the lurid and even prurient interest of certain historians, the military value of this role and its broader cultural significance needs to be properly appreciated. When one takes into account the liberal, relatively affluent, increasingly democratic and fundamentally Christian ethos of early twentieth-century British society, the highly militarised and belligerent character of its principal adversaries (Imperial Germany and *jihad*-inspired Turkey in the First World War; Nazi Germany, Fascist Italy and Imperial Japan in the Second), the tremendously destructive power of modern weaponry and the offensive posture forced upon the British army and its allies in order to secure victory in its principal theatres of war, the chaplains of the British army clearly played a significant part in assisting its citizen soldiers to eventual victory. The continuing existence (and even the increased prominence) of the army's chaplains in both World Wars was not simply a historic hangover or a function of the foibles of pietistic commanders but it was fundamentally indicative of the abiding importance of religion in contemporary British society and of the military value of religious belief in modern conflicts of unparalleled magnitude.

Chapter 4

THE CHURCH IN KHAKI

Introduction

IN THE LIGHT of Chapter 1 it should already be apparent that the religious cultures of the churchgoer and the non-churchgoer were overlapping rather than distinct realms. While private prayer and a love of hymnody were common to both, voluntary services and the sacraments could attract many soldiers who would have normally avoided them in civilian life. In any case, the British army ensured that most soldiers were turned (however reluctantly) into regular churchgoers by dint of King's Regulations. If the influence of the churches was upheld by military law and custom (and also by the army's more recent real-isation of the importance of religion for good morale) then the religious dynamics of the British army were also profoundly affected from 1914 to 1918 and from 1939 to 1945 by the enlarged constituency of devout soldiers which the two World Wars produced. Although hardly recognised, in both World Wars the British army was subject to a huge injection of churchgoing civilians and was host to significant religious revivals. It is the purpose of this chapter to explore the origins and wider significance of these phenomena.

Church parades, compulsion and controversy

The views and debates surrounding the compulsory nature of public worship in the army (which usually took the form of a parade service) serve as a clear indication of how the beliefs and attitudes of churchgoers and non-churchgoers defy easy differentiation. While some of those who were church members and churchgoers in civilian life cherished the fact that their ability to attend public worship was safeguarded by the army, others, including some chaplains, felt that the principle of compulsion and the chore of inspections discredited the churches and was counter-productive in religious terms. Although it was technically possible to declare oneself an atheist, an agnostic, or a member of any obscure denomination in order to avoid parade services, in practice there was often no alternative for the refractory save the prospect of lengthy and unpleasant fatigues.[1] As one anecdote from the First World War put the situation, the non-Anglicans of one battalion comprised 'sixteen Roman Catholics, twelve Wesleyans, six Primitive Methodists, two Jews and four Peelin' Purtaties'.[2]

For many churchgoers – and particularly for Nonconformists – this situation was intolerable, not least because it was a clear violation of the hallowed voluntary principle in matters of religion. Private William Knott, a Salvationist who joined the Royal Army Medical Corps in 1914, voiced all the strangled rage of the Nonconformist conscience when he wrote:

> Some of these Church Parades are the great hypocrisies of the British nation and I trust we shall soon be privileged to gather again with people who congregate to receive blessing and help not because they are driven to it like slaves.[3]

Similarly, and although an Anglican, Stephen Graham declared:

> I have not the slightest hesitation in saying that I would infinitely rather go to any civil church than to any military one, and that for me the Church parade has been one of the unpleasant parts of this enforced military life.[4]

In fact, so objectionable did Graham find parade services at the Guards Chapel in London that he 'became officially a Presbyterian' in order to avoid them.[5] In addition to those church members and churchgoers who found parade services objectionable, there were also less devout soldiers who found in compulsion and Sunday inspections plenty to grouse about. Frank Richards, an old regular and an associate of Robert Graves, insisted in his memoirs that 'ninety-five per cent' of the 2nd Royal Welch Fusiliers 'thoroughly detested' church parade – a proportion that had remained suspiciously unchanged from the pre-war years.[6] Whether an accurate representation of the situation or not (Richards was vehemently anti-clerical throughout his long soldiering career), one 'chaplain of experience' was prepared to confirm for *The Army and Religion* report that most soldiers appeared to resent the imposition of church parade.[7]

However, and notwithstanding all of this, it would be easy to exaggerate the resentment which church parades inspired among soldiers at large during the First World War. Obviously, the experience of church parade was subject to numerous imponderables such as the charisma and ability of the presiding chaplain, the prominence accorded to hymnody and the degree of formality insisted upon. As one Anglican chaplain testified of his men's attitudes to church parade on the Western Front:

> [O]ut here there is at least no opposition whatever to religion; colossal ignorance no doubt, but many signs of awakening inter-est. Church parades they really like. Perhaps this is due to the omission of most of the tiresome minutiae of Church Parade 'Inspection' as usually conducted at home.[8]

If many Nonconformists should have subscribed to the view that 'The parade service is not altogether a happy thing',[9] this contravention of the voluntary principle clearly posed little problem for hundreds of Noncon-formist chaplains. Indeed, plenty of Nonconformist soldiers also seem to have been untroubled by it. At Whitsuntide 1916, Corporal Ernest Goodridge, a Wesleyan soldier of the 18th King's Royal Rifle Corps, described a joint Nonconformist parade service as 'a most helpful service' from which its participants 'came away stronger in the faith that God is still in Heaven and all is Right with the world'.[10]

The debate over the rights and wrongs of church parade rumbled on in the regular army of the inter-war period.[11] However, the controversy over compulsion gained new momentum during the Second World War, as the volunteers and conscripts of a more recalcitrant generation voiced their dis-satisfaction with church parades, sick parades, pay parades and other mani-festations of army 'bullshit'.[12] Again, there were many churchmen who were willing to endorse their stand in relation to church parades, the Noncon-formist press becoming strident in its condemnation of compulsion.[13] For some clergy and concerned laymen, the pernicious quality of compulsory church parade was all too evident. As Peter Sutton of the Royal Army Service Corps remembered:

> Church Parades were universally resented, perhaps even more by the religious men, who realised how much they alienated the private soldiers from organised religion of any kind. Sunday [was] the one day when we didn't have to get up and dress our beds [and] a Church Parade quite ruined this treasured bit of relaxation.[14]

Such was the opposition to compulsion in some quarters that it could even militate against voluntary services. As one chaplain remembered of an incident in Normandy in July 1944:

> Sunday 30th was quiet – the lull before battle – and voluntary services were held in all Squadron areas. The turn-out was remarkable, with 'B' Squadron 150 strong . . . One of the new men in that Squadron, seeing the number present, suspected a 'Parade', which of course it was not, and said: 'Is this a compulsory service? If so, I'm not coming!'[15]

However, once again the protests of a highly vocal element should not be mistaken for unanimous opposition. Charlie Wakeley, who passed through a succession of infantry battalions during the course of the war, accepted church parade as a non-negotiable aspect of army life. Moreover, Tony Foulds, who served as a private in a Young Soldiers' battalion and subsequently as an officer in the Royal Artillery, was surprised by the lack of resentment which these occasions caused.[16] In any event, the compulsory system was eroded from within as the war progressed, with chaplains themselves heading the retreat from Sunday compulsion and parade ground rigmarole. Long resisted by conservatives on the Army Council, who continued to cite their view of religion as an aid to morale,[17] this retreat was facilitated by the fact that 'Padre's Hour' was providing a new and less controversial forum in which the chaplain could play his vaunted role as a morale raiser. In the spring of 1943, the chaplain-general, C.D. Symons, proposed that each unit should have a compulsory but relatively informal parade service once a month, with soldiers from other units being free to attend voluntarily. This compromise solution was reluctantly accepted by the Army Council but it was not until 1946, with the war safely over, that the principle of compulsion was finally abolished.[18]

Denominations and denominationalism

One of the salient features of the expansion of the British army in the two World Wars was that on both occasions it was accompanied by a massive injection of active churchgoers, often from religious, ethnic and social groups which were under-represented in the regular army. In 1914–15, for example, recruiting for Lord Kitchener's New Army saw an influx of Welsh Nonconformist, Irish Roman Catholic and Ulster Protestant recruits, largely as a result of the raising of ethnic divisions designed to harness national and regional identities to the wider war effort. Furthermore, the recruitment of the New Army and the mobilisation of the Territorial Force led to a much wider social spectrum of British society being represented in the army, with the professions, finance and commerce providing proportionately more volunteers than other sectors of the British economy.[19] After 1916, and once again from 1939, conscription served to consolidate rather than diminish this wartime diversity, preventing the army's rank and file from becoming once again the preserve of the unskilled working class.[20]

If the ethnic and social diversity of the army could be a cause for satisfaction, the religious profile of the army in the First World War proved a sensitive and complicated issue, reflecting the patriotism of different denominations and affecting their relative leverage over the War Office. Although the regular army published the denominational affiliations of its rank and file as late as 1913, such figures were not made available for the army during the First World War. Indeed, it was even reported in *The Globe* in October 1915 that figures of religious attestation were no longer being compiled because of Nonconformist lobbying in high political circles. Allegedly, this pressure had been exerted because of the numerical weakness of the Nonconformist churches that the process was revealing.[21] Just over 70 per cent of the regular army's rank and file were recorded as being Anglican in 1913[22] and Anglican pundits were convinced that this proportion remained constant throughout the First World War. In June 1915, the chaplain-general even informed Archbishop Davidson that between 70 and 75 per cent of the soldiers of most infantry brigades were Anglican, complaining that this predominance was not reflected in the number of Anglican chaplains allotted to them.[23]

However galling such claims may have been for the members of rival denominations, Anglican claims to the nominal allegiance of 70 per cent of British soldiers were substantially correct. If Adrian Hastings was right in estimating that more than 60 per cent of the English population was notionally Anglican at this time,[24] the Church of England appears to have gained a higher proportion of nominal adherents among soldiers because they were effectively obliged to attend church parade and were therefore expected to attest a religious allegiance of some kind. In addition to the Church of England acquiring many of the careless and the uncommitted, soldiers of other denominations also seem to have declared themselves Anglicans for the duration of the war, the English Nonconformist churches in particular finding it difficult to retain the allegiance of pre-war members and adherents. As J.H. Shakespeare, the chairman of the United Board, confessed in 1916: '[The United Board has] made careful and detailed investigations and we have found that a very large proportion, we think not less than 50%, have been registered otherwise than under our Denominations'.[25] Although it is difficult to explain why this phenomenon occurred, it is possible that, separated from their families and placed in a culture which was historically alien to many Nonconformists, some simply identified themselves as Church of England upon enlistment. Given the fractious nature of their religious milieu, motives for this decision could even be theological in origin. As one Anglican chaplain remembered of the Territorials of the 2/1st and 2/3rd London Regiment:

> Seventy per cent of the soldiers wore identification discs with the letters 'C. of E.' imprinted on them. Those who had no definite religious convictions usually counted themselves as belonging to the National Church. One man told me that as a civilian he was a Strict Baptist, but that upon enlistment he thought it better to become a temporary member of the Church of England for fear of falling into the hands of some padre who, though a Baptist, was not Strict.[26]

This trend towards conformity seems also to have applied to British Jews. Although a fear of anti-Semitism may also have been at work, British-born working-class Jews were not renowned for their public observance, a tendency that had not been helped by the social exclusiveness of many British synagogues.[27] Much to the chagrin of the self-appointed leaders of British Jewry, pre-war habits appear to have translated themselves into a large number of temporary defections. According to Michael Adler, the senior Jewish chaplain on the Western Front, Jewish chaplains estimated that they were aware of only two-thirds of the Jewish soldiers then serving in the British army. Indeed, Adler himself confessed his perplexity at finding a number of soldiers 'bearing the names of Cohen, Levy, Isaacs and Solomons who were Christians'. He even remembered one soldier who wore an *Arba Kanfoth* who had given his religion as Roman Catholic.[28]

Another complicating factor in the army's system of denominational record keeping was that officers were not required to divulge their religion and could even find themselves allocated a denomination on a purely arbitrary basis. Hitherto ignorant of the very existence of identity discs, Bernard Martin remembered the following conversation with a quartermaster at Southampton prior to his embarkation for France in 1916:

> 'Why do you put a chap's religion on the disc, sergeant?'
> He laughed. 'Precaution, sir, precaution. In war you never can tell.'
> 'Tell what?'

'Why, sir, if your number *should* happen to come up, you wouldn't want the chaplains to quarrel about who's to bury you.'

'I'm not really C of E.' I observed mildly.

The sergeant said in the tone of a wise man talking to an inexperienced youth, 'You stick to C of E, sir. You wouldn't want to be buried by the Pope I'm sure.'

I laughed. 'I don't suppose it makes any difference.'

'Oh, it does make a difference, sir.' He spoke earnestly. 'It does. RCs go to Hell before they get to Heaven – that's official. RCs call it Purgatory. You're definitely better off as C of E, sir.'[29]

Muddying the waters still further was the fact that the original ethnic and denominational profile of given units could change radically over time. This is especially evident among the army's Scottish, Irish and Welsh divisions, with casualties, transfers and even disbandment of their constituent battalions dramatically altering their initial religious composition. For example, the 38th (Welsh) Division suffered a progressive dilution of its Welsh character as a result of its heavy losses on the Somme.[30] Nevertheless, and despite this loss, the division saw a reduction in the number of its Anglican chaplains and an increase in that of its Welsh Nonconformist chaplains in the closing months of 1916.[31] As Anglican sources sourly noted, 'Mr Lloyd George has declared this 38th Division to be a Nonconformist Division notwithstanding the overwhelming evidence to the contrary',[32] a conceit which the Archbishop of Canterbury labelled 'a pitiable piece of political intrigue'.[33] A similar fate befell the army's three Irish divisions, with massive casualties and a chronic lack of replacements from Ireland reducing their original identities to vestigial form. In 1918, the 10th (Irish) Division lost even its Irish designation when it was compelled to incorporate nine Indian battalions in Palestine.[34] As a result of the bloodletting on the Western Front, the 16th (Irish) and 36th (Ulster) divisions also lost much of their original ethnic and religious character, a factor which caused disquiet and unease for Catholic Nationalists and Protestant Unionists alike.[35] As early as September 1916, and ever watchful of the denominational composition of British divisions on the Western Front, Bishop Gwynne reported to the Archbishop of Canterbury that 'The Headquarters 16th Division informs me that 55% of the Division are of denominations other than R.C.'.[36] If the 16th Division grew increasingly dependent on English conscripts to replace its casualties and ended the war with only one Irish battalion left in its ranks,[37] by the beginning of 1918 the 36th Division had been so badly mauled that it was compelled to incorporate five regular battalions from Irish regiments whose men were very largely Catholics. Indeed, so far had the division deviated from its original character as an extension of the militantly Protestant Ulster Volunteer Force that on St Patrick's Day 1918 Mass was celebrated and shamrock distributed among the division.[38]

Despite the many problems inherent in estimating the army's religious composition during the First World War, it would be reasonable to surmise that, throughout the course of the war, approximately 70 per cent of its soldiers were Church of England. A further 10 per cent were Presbyterian, 7 per cent Roman Catholic and the remaining 13 per cent belonged to a variety of Nonconformist denominations, with a tiny minority being Jews or obdurate atheists.[39] From these statistics, it seems clear that the overall effect of the war years was to halve the proportion of Roman Catholics in the army (which stood at 14 per cent in 1913) while boosting the representation of Presbyterians and Nonconformists (whose representation in the regular army was in the order of 7 and 6.7 per cent respectively on the eve of the war).[40]

In contrast to the situation in the First World War, the denominational profile of the army in the Second was much clearer, a situation aided by the established practice of allocating chaplains to soldiers according to a fixed ratio. In 1942, War Office statistics based on the 2,476,956 men and women then serving in the British army showed that 70.9 per cent of them were Church of England (or belonged to a sister church), 10.1 per cent were Roman Catholic, 8.9 per cent were Church of Scotland or Presbyterian, 5.6 per cent were Methodist and 2.7 per cent were Baptists or Congregationalists, denominations whose interests were still represented to the War Office by a truncated United Board.[41] Salvationists made up a further 0.2 per cent while a clutch of other Christian denominations (Christian Scientists, Unitarians, Plymouth Brethren and Quakers) comprised an additional 0.1 per cent. Of the non-Christian religions, Jews made up 1.1 per cent of the army while Hindus and Muslims comprised 0.04 per cent between them. Significantly, while only a miniscule 0.06 per cent professed to be atheists, a somewhat larger proportion (0.08 per cent) claimed a more outlandish affiliation, among them the army's 677 Christian Brethren and its solitary Druid.[42]

Clearly, these statistics reflected current trends in Britain's demography and religious life. Between 1911 and 1931, population growth in Scotland was more than 5 per cent lower than the British average, a factor that helps to account for the relative decline in the army's Scottish (and therefore Presbyterian) constituency relative to the First World War.[43] However, the number of British Catholics and British Jews was growing in the inter-war period and their presence in the army was boosted after 1939 by volunteers from Eire and by the recruitment of Jewish refugees from continental Europe.[44] Given the widespread practice of Jewish soldiers professing another religion for fear of capture by the Germans, it is in fact quite likely that the proportion of Jews in the army was actually higher.[45] If nominal Anglicans and the religiously indifferent continued to lend buoyancy to Anglican numbers, then the decline of the mainstream Nonconformist churches in England and Wales (and their strong pacifist sympathies in the 1930s) was probably reflected in their smaller representation in the army between 1939 and 1945.[46] Doubtlessly, the army's traditional intolerance of those who professed an outlandish affiliation or no religion at all helped to keep the number of dissenters to a minimum. Nevertheless, Walter Cleveland, a regular soldier who was captured at Singapore in 1942, remained true to his avowed atheism throughout his army career, notwithstanding having to wash up and peel potatoes in the cookhouse in lieu of attending church parade.[47] However, others proved less resilient and, in one instance, a newly declared Spiritualist returned to the bosom of the Church of England after latrine cleaning replaced church parade as his regular Sunday observance.[48]

Religion and the officer corps

Given the regimental organisation of the British army and the historically paternalist ethos of its officer corps, the piety of regimental officers had a major influence on the army as a whole. The significance of this factor was recognised in Roman Catholic quarters by the inclusion of a whole chapter on the religious example of officers in the *Catholic Soldiers* report of 1919.[49] Although both World Wars saw a progressive broadening of the social composition of the officer corps, taken as a whole the army's regimental officers were still very largely drawn from among the comparatively church-going middle and upper classes of British society.[50] Especially in the First World War, many were tempted to view the oversight of the spiritual welfare of their men as a natural part of their duties. As Gary Sheffield has put it, although the primary obligation of the regimental officer was 'to ensure that his men were well fed and clothed and comfortable' it was also widely recognised that 'The soldier's soul and personal happiness were also the responsibility of the diligent officer'.[51] If chaplains were inclined to complain of the way in which public school officers seemed to have little sense of the immediate and personal value of religion for themselves or for their men,[52] even Julian Bickersteth recognised the existence of a breed of officer whose faith was both exemplary and influential.[53] The best-known observer and exponent of this religiously infused style of leadership was Donald Hankey, an old Rugbeian, who was killed on the Somme in 1916 and whose essays on life in the army were published in the *Spectator* and the *Westminster Gazette*. Characteristically mingling fact with fiction, Hankey's essay on 'The Beloved

Captain', which he wrote for the *Spectator* while serving in the ranks of the 7th Rifle Brigade early in the war,[54] gave an idealised portrait of a company officer whose leadership had 'a touch of the Christ about it', even down to the tending of his soldiers' blistered feet.[55] Later in the war, and while serving as a subaltern in the 1st Royal Warwickshire Regiment, Hankey appears to have exemplified this style of leadership and is reputed to have led his men into action with the exhortation, 'If wounded, Blighty – if killed, the Resurrection.'[56]

Celebrated though he was, Donald Hankey was far from being alone in attempting to exert a religious influence upon his men. The pre-war regular army had an established tradition of regimental officers attending to the moral and spiritual welfare of the other ranks and many wartime Territorial and temporary officers likewise displayed the same spirit of religious activism that had animated them in civilian life. In 1917, and as CO of the 6th Connaught Rangers, Rowland Feilding organised the distribution of crucifixes which had been blessed by the pope to the men of his battalion.[57] That Feilding's religious leadership was far from unique among Roman Catholic officers of the time is confirmed by the fact that one Roman Catholic chaplain testified in *Catholic Soldiers*:

> My experience of Catholic officers was very consoling . . . Officers led their men in religious practices as they did when they went 'over the top'. I had only a few Catholic officers in the division I worked with, but they never failed me. They came for Confession with parties of their men, whom they had zealously shepherded to the Sacraments, and were the first to go down by the roadside on their knees for Confession . . . The duty (often self-imposed) of marching their men to Mass was evidently one that they appreciated and with them the 'church parade' was not a 'bore' or 'nuisance', as it is to so many young officers whose junior rank condemns them to tasks for which nobody is likely to volunteer.[58]

Despite clerical grumbling about the religious calibre of 'the average old public school officer',[59] this kind of leadership was also in evidence among Anglicans, with certain officers even being prepared to lead religious services in the absence of commissioned chaplains.[60] A case in point was Colonel J. Purefoy Robinson of the 101st Brigade Royal Garrison Artillery. As William Drury, an Anglican chaplain who encountered Purefoy Robinson in Mesopotamia, recalled:

> [He was] a very sincere Churchman [who] had taken services himself on occasion. Later on in the campaign, when we were

without tents, he never hesitated to kneel and say his prayers in full view of his men. Doubtless the fact that his rank prevented any spoken criticism made this easier at the time; but it was a habit to which he had been faithful throughout his career. He immediately presented me with a list of members of the Church of England's Men's Society amongst the gunners. He was keenly interested in the meetings which we held and made a point of being present and discussing differences of opinion quite frankly and freely with the men, whether members or not.[61]

Such attitudes and behaviour were not confined to crusty old regulars, however, not least because a large number of committed Anglican laymen and even Anglican clergymen became combatant officers during the First World War. One officer of the former stamp was Julian Bickersteth's younger brother, Burgon, who was known in the 1st Royal Dragoons as 'the Bishop' on account of his strongly religious views and interests.[62] However, these laymen also comprised many theological students, among them Captain A.D. Hamer of the 1/8th Manchester Regiment, who was killed in an attack five days before the signing of the Armistice. The son of an Anglican clergyman, Hamer was described by his CO, who had received Holy Communion with him just before his death, as 'an example to all of us' in his dual capacity as 'a soldier and a Christian'. Moreover, one of his junior officers testified to the moral and religious example of Hamer and felt compelled to adduce some theological rationale from his death:

God has taken him unto Himself because he wanted him, because his blameless and exemplary life would satisfy God in a greater degree than most of us, thereby staying the hand of God and shortening the duration of this terrible scourge.[63]

Not surprisingly, the experience of war had a tendency to radicalise the views of men of Hamer's background. Alec De Candole, another prospective clergyman and temporary officer to be killed in the autumn of 1918, betrayed much dissatisfaction with the contemporary Church of England in a series of essays written prior to his death. In these essays, De Candole described the overweening denominationalism of the Church of England as 'a disgrace to Christianity' and argued not only for the universal election of souls but also for a reformed doctrine of purgatory.[64] It was no doubt illustrative of the significant constituency of committed but progressive Anglican officers in the British army at the end of the war that William Temple's visit to France and Belgium in February 1919 attracted large numbers of officers to conferences associated with the reformist Life and Liberty movement.[65]

In addition to these students and other laymen, it was as symptomatic of the missionary zeal of many contemporary clergy as it was of the breadth of the national response to Kitchener's recruitment campaign that hundreds of Anglican clergymen chose to volunteer for combatant as well as non-combatant service during the First World War. Although the former were technically acting in defiance of canon law, some seem to have taken very easily to military life. Without doubt, the most striking example of these clerical warriors was the much-decorated Anglican clergyman Bernard William Vann, a pre-war chaplain and assistant master at Wellingborough School who was posthumously awarded the VC for his exploits leading the 1/6th Sherwood Foresters during the crossing of the Canal du Nord in September 1918, exploits that included the single-handed capture of a German field gun.[66]

Other denominations were also well served by many of their regimental officers. As with the Church of England, many of the Church of Scotland's ministers felt compelled to enlist and, in the summer of 1916, it was even reported that more Church of Scotland ministers were serving in combatant units than had volunteered as chaplains.[67] Although it is not known how many of these ministers were commissioned, it is clear that Scottish Presbyterianism was, in any event, well represented by its commissioned laymen. William Ewing remembered how, on board a transport bound for Gallipoli, a sympathetic officer agreed to treat the reinforcements on board to 'twenty minutes on the fighting in which he had taken part, if they would then listen to me for twenty minutes preaching the gospel'.[68] Similarly, and in his capacity as regimental transport officer of the 1/5th Scottish Rifles, John Reith quickly provided his brigade's Presbyterian chaplain with a horse and groom.[69] In partnership with this minister, and moved by the fact that he felt 'a moral responsibility' for the men under his command,[70] Reith set about the task of turning the men of his section into committed members of the United Free Church. As Reith noted, by Good Friday 1915 it was clear that their combined efforts had borne fruit:

> All the Transport men were nominally Presbyterians but only nine out of about fifty-five were Church members. A dozen more were well past the usual age of joining, but between twenty and thirty had barely reached it on mobilisation. I did not want any of them to join the Church to please me, so [I] had moved delicately, but in the result twenty-two names went to the Minister and he had seen each of the men separately. Today he came to our farm to conduct a special service of admission . . . I was glad that these young fellows – walking in hourly jeopardy as they were – had been brought into this new relationship with God.[71]

English Nonconformist chaplains were no less conscious of the spiritual assistance rendered by sympathetic officers and NCOs. As the Wesleyan chaplain T.L.B. Westerdale noted in 1917: 'A religious C.O. or sergeant-major is a tower of strength to the padre, and where you find such in a battalion you generally find the services well attended.'[72] Moreover, it seems likely that some of the army's smaller denominations were heavily reliant on their officers to act as substitutes for their chaplains. For Michael Adler, the burial of Jewish soldiers according to Christian rites proved a constant cause for concern and even led him to conduct a number of reburials.[73] Consequently, and from early 1915, Jewish officers were requested to supervise the burial of Jewish soldiers whenever possible. As Lieutenant Sydney Frankenburg of the 1/8th Manchester Regiment wrote to his wife in June 1915:

> I went over to GHQ to a Jewish service, the chief Rabbi was there . . . I am to be appointed a sort of Jewish chaplain, that is they have approached me to read the burial service over such Jewish soldiers who die in the hospitals and field ambulances in this area.[74]

If regimental officers clearly played a substantial role in supporting and even sustaining religious life in the army during the First World War, this phenomenon was much less in evidence during the Second. This was a function not only of the improved organisation of army chaplaincy but also of an inter-war decline in church membership and attendance among those social classes from which the officer corps was primarily drawn. As church leaders were uncomfortably aware, the inter-war period in which the increasingly youthful regimental officers of the Second World War were raised were years in which the influence of religious education declined in the nation at large and in which a discernibly secular spirit was abroad in British society. Given these secularising trends and the importance of COs in helping or hindering the chaplain's work at a local level, the wartime fall in the average age of the army's junior officers may have posed something of a generational problem for the RAChD. Partly as a reaction to widespread criticism of the supposedly 'Blimpish' image of the officer corps, from 1941 the army pursued a vigorous policy of promoting younger men to the command of units likely to see action overseas. Consequently, by December 1942 the median age of lieutenant-colonels in the Guards, the line infantry, Royal Engineers and Royal Corps of Signals had fallen to forty-one, with a downward trend still in evidence by 1943, the year in which Montgomery expressed his wish to see men in their early thirties commanding regiments of the Royal Armoured Corps.[75] By 1942, many chaplains were airing grievances against their COs, with 'younger officers' coming in for 'particular criticism'.[76] The issue was simple enough; whatever value general officers may have attached to the work of chaplains, it was up to COs at a local and regimental level to provide a supportive environment for the chaplain's work. As one senior chaplain put the problem in January 1943: 'The greatest difficulty of all is the unlimited power of the C.O. over matters spiritual.'[77] However, even fairly indifferent officers could insist on the observance of army regulations in the contentious matter of church parades. Alastair Menzies, one of the youngest Anglican chaplains in the RAChD, encountered this situation when he was posted to a unit of Royal Engineers in Kent in 1941. At his first parade service, and upon noting that none of the officers had deigned to turn up, Menzies dismissed the men after saying the Lord's Prayer with them. The reaction of their officers was as unexpected as it was disconcerting, for after this incident he was 'put to Coventry in the mess although none of those officers had bothered to come to worship. They cut me dead.'[78]

If many regimental officers were only prepared to ensure the observance of King's Regulations in matters spiritual, others remained convinced of the intrinsic value of religion for their men. As in the First World War, many Roman Catholic officers continued to shepherd their co-religionists to the sacraments. John Scollen, for example, was diligent in ensuring that the Catholic gunners under his command did not neglect their religious duties, securing the use of a truck in which to convey the Catholics of 914 Defence Battery of the Royal Artillery to midnight Mass at Christmas 1941.[79] Likewise, in Normandy in August 1944, Captain Bill Bellamy of the 8th Hussars ensured that he 'attended Mass with as many Catholics as I could muster' in a cornfield on the Feast of the Assumption.[80] Given the strength of regimental tradition in certain units, the importance of Catholic practice could even be upheld by Protestant officers. As Rudesind Brookes, the chaplain of the 1st Irish Guards, remembered of St Patrick's Day 1943:

> [It] was the custom that all officers including the Protestants went to Mass on St. Patrick's Day. The previous day an Anglican chaplain from Brigade had the temerity to ask [the CO] what arrangements he had made for the non-Catholics in his Regiment. Colonel Andrew was furious and replied, 'I would like you to know that I command a Catholic Regiment and on St. Patrick's Day we all go to Mass.' It was fortunate that Andrew was not a Catholic, as it would otherwise have been very embarrassing.[81]

Whether for personal or professional reasons, other COs continued to support the cause of religion in their own units. In marked contrast to

Menzies' debilitating experience with the Royal Engineers, when A.R.C. Leaney was posted as chaplain to the 6th Royal Sussex Regiment in 1939, its CO greeted him with 'the propitious words, "Good morning, padre. You and I are to work together, I think"'.[82] Similarly, and although Norman Jones received a cool reception from the Anglophobic Major-General Wimberley of the 51st (Highland) Division when he was posted to this division as an Anglican chaplain in 1942, he was eventually blessed by the arrival of a new CO of the 7th Black Watch. In stark contrast to his predecessor (who 'simply did not care for chaplains'), this new CO proved to be sympathetic to Jones's work as a regimental chaplain and an elder of the Church of Scotland.[83] More remarkably, the role of regimental officers as leaders of religious worship was not entirely absent from the Second World War. As one tank officer remembered of life and death on campaign in the Western Desert:

> [I]t was not uncommon for me to have to hold a grave digging session after food and before sleep. The padre was a good chap but his place was with the main echelon which could be at bulk-head stores fifty miles behind. Usually some honest believer of an officer recited a garbled form of the committal service over the remains before we closed the shallow grave.[84]

Indeed, and because of a comparable lack of chaplains on vessels of the invasion fleet, many officers appear to have led their men in prayer on the eve of D-Day.[85]

Besides the well-disposed layman who continued to underwrite the importance of religion in the army, the British officer corps of the Second World War also contained a number of priests, ministers and theological students who exerted a religious influence of their own. Although a much rarer phenomenon than in the First World War, a handful of clergymen still succeeded in obtaining commissions in combatant units after the outbreak of war in 1939. The most remarkable of these was Hugh Lister, an Anglican clergyman and senior curate of the Eton College Mission in Hackney Wick, who was serving as a major in the Welsh Guards when he was killed in Belgium in September 1944. Lister developed the habit of holding communion services for the men of his company, services that were well attended because of their informality and because of his reputation as a fighting officer.[86] As in the First World War, many theological students also proved to be good officer material. Hugh Bone, for example, served as a junior officer in the 2nd East Yorkshire Regiment throughout the campaign in north-west Europe and completed his written examinations for the Methodist ministry during a period when his battalion was out of the line.[87] In August 1944, and following his death in Normandy, the edifying correspondence of another theological student was published in *The Times*. Killed at Caen in July, the anonymous author of these letters was described by his CO as 'one of my best officers' who had been killed as a company commander in 'a very difficult attack'.[88]

Religion and the other ranks

As with the officer corps, the level of religious commitment evinced by the other ranks varied considerably in both World Wars. However, and because the army's NCOs and privates were generally drawn from the lower social classes, formal religious commitment was somewhat less in evidence. This, of course, reflected prevailing patterns of churchgoing and church member- ship in civilian society. Nevertheless, and although the other ranks remained largely working class in composition throughout both World Wars, the raising of Kitchener's New Army in 1914–15 entailed a significant broadening of their social profile in comparison with the pre-war regular army. Far from being very largely recruited from the dregs of the unskilled working class, Donald Hankey described Kitchener's army as 'a triumph of democracy'[89] and William Ewing averred that: 'Men from the pulpit, the college, the Bar, and the Exchange rub shoulders with those from the shop and the warehouse, clerks, railwaymen, policemen, and ne'er-do-wells from the streets.'[90]

Given the varied composition of the army at this time and the powerful missionary appeal of serving in the ranks, it was perhaps inevitable that some clergymen who joined the army in the early months of the war should have shunned the opportunity of taking a chaplain's or an officer's commission. As H.A. Thomas, who in 1914 was the Anglican curate of Alsager, wrote of his decision to enlist:

> I saw at once what a gorgeous opportunity was here afforded for the clergy to come into real touch with the People . . . Here was a chance to get amongst men whom the church never sees except as unconscious babes or inanimate corpses. Apart from the justice of our cause, it was a missionary enterprise without parallel.[91]

For the Wesleyan minister J.A. Boullier, whose service (as a reservist) was less a matter of choice than it was for Thomas, the fact that a significant number of clergy and theological students were serving in the ranks of the New Army was full of missionary promise. Writing as a brigade chaplain after the battle of the Somme, Boullier declared that:

Never in the history of our race had the Church been so well represented in the ranks of His Majesty's Army. In one battalion alone I met five students of the Church to which I belong, and while I write these lines three students for the Irish Methodist ministry are serving in units within a radius of six miles . . . In the very unit to which I am attached, there is at present a Presbyterian minister of ten years' standing serving in the ranks . . . To them are granted golden opportunities of exercising a true Christian ministry, for such has been my own experience.[92]

The experience to which Boullier was alluding was the fact that, even while serving as a gunner in Flanders, he had been persuaded to lead services for fellow Methodists during the winter of 1914–15.[93] Stephen Graham remembered the similar case of a sergeant of the 2nd Scots Guards who had returned to the colours on the outbreak of war. A former regular and a veteran of the Boer War, he had left the army, trained at an Anglican theological college and had secured a living in Surrey before volunteering once again for the army. Although he had encountered a degree of anti-clerical prejudice from officers and fellow sergeants alike, Graham remembered that he had slowly won his comrades over, becoming 'greatly admired because he lived what he preached'. In fact, Graham went so far as to claim that this anonymous NCO was 'a great spiritual gain, and that his life, though he never preached or "saved souls," or betrayed by any act that he was a priest, nevertheless made a deep impression on men's minds'.[94] Despite these examples, it is likely that clergymen were most numerous in the RAMC. In 1914, H.A. Thomas found that he was one of three Anglican priests among a batch of sixty recruits for a single field ambulance. Indeed, so strong was the clerical presence in this ambulance that its CO insisted on its 'parson-privates' acting as jobbing curates while in England in order to raise cash 'for the benefit of the Corps and Band Fund'.[95] Similarly, and at roughly the same time, W.E. Sellers noted the existence of a single 'barrack room of the R.A.M.C. at Aldershot' which held no fewer than five Anglican curates and one Wesleyan minister.[96]

This clerical presence in the ranks was reinforced by more theological students for, as Donald Hankey recognised at the time, 'nearly all ordinands of the Church of England, being of the right age and sound of limb, have enlisted or been granted commissions in the Army'.[97] This phenomenon was by no means limited to the Church of England. In 1914, twenty-two Wesleyan students of Handsworth Theological College joined the army. Of these, only three became chaplains, eleven joined the RAMC and eight enlisted in combatant units, with no fewer than six of these finding themselves in

'B' Company of the 14th Royal Warwickshire Regiment (First Birmingham Pals). Indeed, so common was the enlistment of Wesleyan theological students at this time that it provoked a good deal of controversy in the denominational press.[98] In addition to hundreds of clergymen and theological students, the churches' presence among the other ranks was also boosted by hundreds of thousands of committed laymen. To a large extent, the incidence of the latter was dictated by the religious geography of the British Isles and by the strongly regional character of Territorial and New Army units in the first years of the war. Even after conscription was introduced, observers were repeatedly struck by the very different levels of religiosity which obtained from unit to unit. As one Presbyterian chaplain put it in 1917:

> I have known nearly half a battalion profess faith in Christ by sitting down together at His table [and] I have also known of battalions where not 10 per cent would take advantage of any religious privileges offered them.[99]

A high level of religious commitment was regarded as the norm for Roman Catholic soldiers of southern Irish regiments and a strong degree of Catholic fervour was also in evidence among the Kitchener volunteers of the Tyneside Irish Brigade and among the Territorial battalions of the London and Liverpool Irish. If these volunteers and Territorials shared the Catholic character of the 16th (Irish) Division,[100] Cyril Falls confirmed that a militant Protestantism was very much part of the 'group spirit' of the original 36th (Ulster) Division:

> One factor . . . which could not be omitted from a faithful record [of the division] was the element of religion . . . Undoubtedly something of the old covenanting spirit, the old sense of the alliance of 'Bible and Sword', was reborn in these men. It was the easier recreated because of the strength of religious feeling which had existed in times of peace in Protestant Ulster, one of the few parts of the country wherein the reformed churches had not, by their own admission, lost ground in the last thirty years. Religious feeling inspired the men of Ulster in those days of training, and remained with them in the days of war.[101]

If the Orange Order was well-organised and well-represented within the original 36th Division,[102] a spirit of Protestant revivalism also became evident very quickly for, while in training at Ballykinler in 1914–15, the division's 107th (Belfast) Brigade seems to have experienced a large-scale religious revival. According to one female worker at this camp, its men were 'like Cromwell's Ironsides' and she was told that all would die 'in defence of the Bible'. Furthermore, at a crowded watch night service at New Year 1915, a young officer exhorted the congregation with the words, 'Men, before this time next year we may all be killed; but to a Christian, death is only beginning to live.'[103] Such religious fervour appears to have been in evidence throughout the 36th Division prior to its ill-fated attack on the Schwaben Redoubt on 1 July 1916. As Martin Middlebrook has remarked:

> The Ulstermen awaited the attack in a state of emotional, religious fervour. Many were members of the Orange Order and some had sent for the orange sashes of their order and wore these over their bulky equipment. Hymns were sung, prayers were said.[104]

Besides the well-known example of the army's Irish and Ulster units, a strong religious culture was also in evidence in the 38th (Welsh) Division. Despite the fact that its Nonconformist character was strongly contested in Anglican circles, recruitment for the 38th Division was undoubtedly bolstered by appeals from Nonconformist pulpits across the principality and its Nonconformist constituency does appear to have grown significantly during the course of 1915. Although exaggerated claims were made as to the new and astounding moral rectitude of army life[105] (and nothing came of a newspaper proposal that a Welsh 'Pals' battalion should be recruited from among 'religious young men') the men of the division's 113th Brigade proved to be models of good behaviour. Largely recruited from Nonconformist North Wales, its men were conspicuous at local chapel services, Sunday schools and Bible classes while billeted in Llandudno during the winter of 1914–15.[106] Eighteen months later, and prior to the 38th Division's attack on Mametz Wood in July 1916, the men of one of its battalions – the 16th Royal Welch Fusiliers – prepared themselves by singing Welsh hymns and by listening to the admonitions of their CO to make their peace with God.[107]

If the army experienced some early success in harnessing the religious and cultural identity of Irish Roman Catholics, Ulster Protestants and Welsh Nonconformists, it also capitalised on the desire of leading British Jews to have units of their own. An early scheme to raise a Jewish 'Pals' battalion for the New Army foundered through a lack of support among working-class Jews in London's East End[108] but a later attempt to mobilise non-naturalised Jews for the British war effort proved more successful. With the position of Russian Jewish immigrants posing something of a problem after the introduction of conscription in 1916, the decision of the War Cabinet to raise all-Jewish battalions from these immigrants for service in Palestine in

1917 was the best that could have been reached under the circumstances, particularly as the option of repatriation to Russia evaporated following the Bolshevik Revolution of that year. Formed into the 38th, 39th and 40th battalions of the Royal Fusiliers, these battalions consisted of non-naturalised Jewish conscripts, Jewish soldiers transferred from other units of the British army and, after the Balfour Declaration of November 1917, of Zionist volunteers from the United States.[109] Eventually amalgamated into a new Judean Regiment, Jewish sensibilities were further flattered when these battalions were issued with a menorah cap badge bearing the Hebrew inscription *Kadima* (Eastward).[110]

Significantly, and in the interests of recruitment and morale, the military authorities were prepared to go to considerable lengths to encourage and preserve the distinctive cultural and religious character of these ethnic units. If serving Jewish officers and soldiers were allowed to transfer to the Jewish battalions of the Royal Fusiliers,[111] during the early months of the war Catholics in England and Scotland were allowed to enlist for Irish regiments and much was done to ensure that the Irish battalions of the New Army were provided with Catholic officers.[112] Furthermore, and as the recruitment crisis in Ireland deepened in the wake of the Easter Rising, the Army Council decided to reserve the army's small number of Irish Catholic recruits for the regular battalions of southern Irish regiments.[113] If the Tyneside Irish Brigade was not transferred to the 16th (Irish) Division as it requested, the 38th (Welsh) Division was allocated the 15th Royal Welch Fusiliers, a battalion raised from expatriate Welshmen living in London.[114] In a similar fashion, the 36th (Ulster) Division received a draft of Orangemen from Glasgow, men who, in the words of Frank Crozier, 'had expressed a desire to serve in the Division under the red hand of Ulster'. In the event, Crozier, who was charged with collecting this draft, was unimpressed by their boisterous and unruly demeanour:

> I can draw a veil over the scenes at the Clydeside city, and at Ardrossan, save to say that a more drunken orgy I have never witnessed. Bands, banners, booze and blasphemy run riot. At last the ship is reached and with it safety, for a merchant captain has power at sea and a hose pipe! The orange lions become sober lambs.[115]

Even if volunteers were not forthcoming, it appears that the army had certain means of ensuring that its ethnic units were kept up to strength, often through a vigorous and occasionally disconcerting policy of cross posting.[116] According to a story recounted by 'Tubby' Clayton, a detachment of nine hundred putative recruits for a cavalry regiment was paraded and divided according to the following procedure:

> 'Roman Catholics, one pace to your front.'
> 'Church of England, stand fast.'
> 'Other religions, one pace to the rear.'
> The Roman Catholics were drafted into some Irish regiment, the Nonconformists into a Welsh formation, and the five hundred who stood fast found themselves in the [East Kents].[117]

Although large concentrations of the religiously committed were to be found in the army's Ulster, Welsh, Irish and Jewish units, there were even differences between the prevailing religious temper of English and Scottish troops.[118] James Black, for example, the Presbyterian chaplain of two Scottish battalions in a largely English division, claimed: 'On the lowest estimate, I could count on a voluntary service [attendance] that would shame many an English battalion's compulsory parade.'[119] Scottish soldiers in general were widely perceived as having stronger church connections than their English counterparts. As one Scottish chaplain noted:

> Sometimes one finds in the Scottish soldier a wonderful faith, but, much more than with the Englishman, an attachment to the kirk or the minister at home. In fact, the case is exceedingly rare of a Scotsman without Church connection of some kind. If one meets it, the man is usually deeply ashamed, and does not quite acknowledge it.[120]

According to the results of the Church of Scotland's own investigations, some 30 per cent of Scottish soldiers were 'vitally related' to a particular church, a term that The Army and Religion report construed to mean that a man had a love for his church, a regard for its fellowship and its teachings and an active sympathy with its aims. If The Army and Religion report was more pessimistic about the Scottish situation, putting the proportion of Scottish soldiers who were in a 'vital relationship with any of the Churches' at around 20 per cent, the situation among English troops was demonstrably worse. Only 11.5 per cent of English soldiers were classified in this way. Moreover, it was significant that the highest level of church affiliation was to be found among the Territorials of the 51st (Highland) Division,[121] a factor which may have sprung from the fact that, even among Scottish soldiers,

> those who showed the most real attachment and love to their Church were in the majority of cases from the country districts

or smaller towns. The Church was quite evidently the centre of their thoughts and interests, in a way that was not true of the city man.[122]

If unfavourably compared to their Scottish counterparts, even the religious character of English units could vary according to whether they were regular, Territorial or New Army in provenance, from which part of the country they were recruited and, crucially, at what point of the war they were being examined. Territorial and New Army units initially had comparatively high proportions of church members and churchgoers in their ranks. Further-more, and however diluted these connections were by the deepening impact of the war, the regional character of the British army continued to ensure that its English units reflected significant variations in England's religious geography. Finally, it must be borne in mind that *The Army and Religion* report was based on evidence which was collated following the introduction of conscription and after devastating casualties on the Somme in the summer and autumn of 1916, casualties which were largely borne by the Kitchener volunteers, Territorials, regulars and reservists of the early war period. In other words, by the time the compilers of this report were collecting and considering their evidence, the character of the British army between August 1914 and January 1916 had changed considerably, in religious as well as in other respects.

English and Scottish Territorial and New Army units contained – at least in their original form – an unusually high proportion of the religiously committed. Indeed, both the *Catholic Soldiers* and *The Army and Religion* reports agreed that proportions of pre-war churchgoers were much higher among the volunteers of the early war period then they were among the conscripts of 1916–18. If Roman Catholic chaplains were aware of a declining number of their co-religionists in non-Irish units as the war progressed,[123] even David Cairns conceded that 'there are indications that the Kitchener and Territorial forces of the first period of the war were considerably more church-going than the later armies'.[124] In the early stages of the war, an obvious source of volunteers for the army were the senior ranks of the militaristic youth organisations which the British churches and British Jewry had fostered since the creation of W.A. Smith's Boys' Brigade in Glasgow in 1883. Inspired by a common desire among the churches to influence working-class males beyond the years of Sunday school and by the ethos and appeal of the mid-Victorian Volunteer movement, by 1900 the pan-denominational Boys' Brigade numbered more than 900 companies and 44,000 members in the British Isles alone. Its success prompted the creation of more narrowly denominational imitators in the form of the (Anglican) Church Lads' Brigade, the Catholic

Boys' Brigade and the Jewish Lads' Brigade.[125] Such was the significance of
these organisations that in 1910 (when the combined membership of the
Boys' Brigade and Church Lads' Brigade stood at nearly 100,000) the War
Office sought to incorporate them into a national cadet force linked to the
Territorial Force. Although Smith and his Boys' Brigade successfully resisted
these pressures, the Church Lads' Brigade quickly succumbed to them,
obtaining official recognition as a cadet unit for the King's Royal Rifle Corps
and eventually dressing its members in khaki.[126]

These youth organisations were, however, only symptomatic of a much
broader culture of militarism which was current among Britain's churches and
the Anglo-Jewish elite at the beginning of the twentieth century. Among their
other effects, the awkward lessons of the Boer War had prompted fevered
debate over national efficiency and Britain's preparedness for a major war.
Out of this debate emerged the National Service League, a populist and patriotic movement which, from its inception in 1902, campaigned for the creation
of a limited system of compulsory military service and which had strong
support from the Church Lads' Brigade.[127] The appeal of the NSL among
the churches was strengthened from 1906 when Lord Roberts, the most
celebrated Christian soldier of his day, resigned as commander-in-chief in
order to lead the movement. While the cause of the NSL attracted the support of many Anglican clergy, who saw in compulsory military service some
hope for the nation's moral, spiritual and physical regeneration, other leading
churchmen lent their endorsement to kindred movements. Francis Bourne,
for example, the wartime Archbishop of Westminster, wrote a pamphlet for
Lord Meath's 'Duty and Discipline' movement entitled *The Paramount Need
of Training in Youth*.[128] In fact, and despite their high-profile presence in
the international peace movement, their widespread opposition to the Boer
War and their common hostility to demands for conscription, Britain's Nonconformist churches were by no means immune from this militaristic culture.
In terms of Nonconformity's dealings with youth, not only was the Boys'
Brigade well established among Methodists, Congregationalists and Baptists
by the early 1890s[129] but the Religious Tract Society cheerfully sustained the
military interests of millions of adolescent males in the form of its *Boys' Own
Paper*.[130] Moreover, and from the 1860s onwards, Nonconformist culture had
harboured its own military proclivities. Although these were most obviously
reflected in the rise of the quasi-military Salvation Army, they were also
apparent in Nonconformist support for armed liberal causes abroad, in the
currency of the cults of Victorian 'soldier-saints' (such as Sir Henry Havelock
and Gordon of Khartoum) and in a conscious reclaiming of Oliver Cromwell
and Nonconformity's militant seventeenth-century heritage.[131]

Given the militaristic propensities of the British churches prior to the First World War, it is not surprising that their members and adherents should have responded so readily to Kitchener's recruitment campaign of 1914–15. The most obvious illustration of this response was the raising of the 16th and 19th King's Royal Rifle Corps and of the 16th Highland Light Infantry, New Army battalions which were originally recruited from among current and former members of the Church Lads' Brigade in London and the Boys' Brigade in Glasgow.[132] Such was the enthusiasm for the war in the ranks of the Church Lads' Brigade that it was soon being claimed that the movement in the diocese of London (its metropolitan heartland) sent 'practically every officer eligible and nearly every cadet of seventeen years of age to join the regular forces soon after the declaration of war'.[133] However, this enthusiastic response from the churches went far beyond their youth organisations and seems to have been the norm among male church members and church-goers of military age. If loyal members of the established churches of England and Scotland might have been expected to volunteer, the peculiar history and circumstances of Roman Catholics (at least in mainland Britain) and of British Nonconformists also rendered them highly susceptible to the recruiting campaign of 1914–15. For many Roman Catholics, the war offered an opportunity to defend Catholic Belgium and to vindicate Catholic loyalty to a historically Protestant British state. Moreover, for those supportive of Irish Home Rule, it offered the chance to demonstrate the good faith of Irish Nationalists in relation to Ireland's military obligations to the empire.[134] The German invasion of Belgium also struck a very powerful chord in the Nonconformist conscience, a conscience which had long been accustomed to championing the rights of weak and oppressed peoples. Furthermore, and although many Nonconformists had been fiercely opposed to calls for conscription prior to the war, the creation of the New Army seemed a triumph of that voluntarism which they had always championed, a triumph to which they were anxious to contribute. Such was the enthusiasm for volunteering in Nonconformist circles early in the war that congregations eagerly published their enlistment figures in the church press and at least one Baptist minister even lobbied for the raising of a Baptist corps.[135] In fact, and as W.E. Sellers observed, the pre-war suspicion that many Nonconformists were 'unpatriotic' in view of their hostility to compulsory military service was exploded by the fact that the example of the churches showed that voluntarism was equal to the occasion:

> The churches gave of their best. The vicarages and manses of the country were denuded of their sons. In some Sunday-schools the young men's classes volunteered to a man. In many places

it was only with great difficulty that the work of the Sunday-schools was carried on, because the male teachers had enlisted.[136]

Certainly, all this evidence shows that the high-profile recruiting appeals of religious leaders during the early months of the war were not without their effect, that they fell upon responsive ears and that the Bishop of London's claim that 'khaki is the garment of the faithful' was not without foundation.[137] This phenomenon also indicates that attachment to church, chapel or synagogue was an important aspect of the associational character of respectable working-class life, an aspect which the raising of the New Army (with its battalions of 'Pals', 'Commercials' and even 'Sportsmen') exploited to the full.[138] Indeed, it is quite likely that the conspicuously high level of voluntary enlistment among church members and churchgoers in the early months of the war was reflected in the way in which the churches so readily embraced the rhetoric of martyrdom in relation to the sacrifices that these men were to make.[139]

If the predisposition of many church members and churchgoers to enlist clearly influenced the religious character of the army's rank and file during the early stages of the First World War, then the nation's religious geography also played a major and probably longer-term role in this respect. Often compared unfavourably to Irish and Scottish units, even English units reflected significant variations in England's religious geography, with Roman Catholics being especially numerous in Lancashire units and Jews being well-represented in battalions and divisions recruited from London, Manchester, Liverpool and Leeds.[140] Many English units also contained a significant smattering of Nonconformist soldiers who, true to their independent traditions, proved remarkably adept at organising prayer meetings of their own. One Wesleyan chaplain declared as late as 1917: 'Many Wesleyan and Baptist N.C.O.s hold little services in their dug-outs in the trenches and in barns, and without question their influence in their companies is nearly always very great indeed.'[141]

In addition to the presence of significant numbers of Roman Catholics, Jews and Nonconformists in many English units, a conspicuous feature of the character of the pre-war (or 'First Line') Territorial battalions of the London Regiment was the large number of Anglican communicants in their ranks. Whereas informed estimates from later in the war were liable to put the proportion of committed Anglicans at 'about 3 or 4 per cent' of those who were 'nominally C. of E.',[142] Anglican chaplains repeatedly commented on the high levels of sacramental participation evinced by these Territorials, a phenomenon which clearly reflected the pre-war vigour of Anglo-Catholicism in the London suburbs.[143] According to 'Tubby' Clayton, the 1/16th London

Regiment (Queen's Westminster Rifles), whom he first encountered in the winter of 1915–16, was at that time chiefly composed of 'the suburban type', mainly ex-public school boys and bank clerks whose normal but superficial religious apathy had been shaken by their wartime experiences. For these men, so Clayton averred, the need for sacramental religion 'stood as a need confessed'. Consequently, around a quarter of the battalion, or some 200 men, were regular communicants at this time. Moreover, one of its sister battalions, the 1/5th London Regiment (London Rifle Brigade), furnished Talbot House with no fewer than 500 communicants at Christmas 1915.[144] Although there was always a strong connection between Talbot House and this metropolitan Anglo-Catholic sub-culture (Clayton maintained that, even later in the war, the number of communicants at Talbot House 'almost doubled' when London divisions were in the vicinity)[145] its existence was obvious to many others, including E.C. Crosse, who remarked that 'For some reason or another London regiments usually provided the largest numbers of communicants'.[146] According to William Drury, who served with the 56th (1st London) Division in the Somme in 1916, the original London Rifle Brigade contained 'an exceptional proportion of religiously minded men', a fact brought home to him when he was waylaid to lead an impromptu service for the battalion as it came out of the line.[147] Not only this, but in the 56th Division, which was then almost wholly composed of the Territorial battalions of the London Regiment, there were at least three Anglican clergymen acting as stretcher-bearers and the CO of one infantry battalion was 'a silver-haired old clergyman, much beloved and respected by those under him'.[148] Naturally, this was a highly significant reflection of the links between the Church of England and the Territorial Force in the capital, links which had been assiduously cultivated by the Bishop of London, Arthur Winnington-Ingram, who was chaplain to the London Rifle Brigade at the outbreak of war.[149] During his visit to the Western Front at Easter 1915, the bishop made a particular point of visiting battalions of the London Regiment and his trip culminated in an Easter Day service for the men of the London Rifle Brigade.[150] Unsurprisingly, the milieu of the 56th Division proved to be highly congenial for Anglo-Catholic chaplains like Julian Bickersteth who, as senior Anglican chaplain to the division, could reflect in the summer of 1918:

> I think, without undue prejudice, that the boys whom I have found
> do best from the point of view of the Christian religion out here
> are those trained in the Catholic parishes at home. They know
> what they want, and are not ashamed of their faith.[151]

The presence of a leavening (and even substantial pockets) of pre-war churchgoers and church members among the men of the British army in the first two years of the First World War does much to explain the strong impression that many churchmen gained of a religious revival in the British army at this time. Significantly, the revivalist impulse was far from dead in British religious life, as the ongoing cycle of local revivals and parish missions and, most conspicuously, the Welsh revival of the early 1900s very clearly demonstrates.[152] If widespread opposition to the religious terms of the 1902 Education Act has been credited with helping to spark the Welsh revival,[153] it is not hard to see why large numbers of men, assured of the justice of their cause and confronted with the realities of a massive European war, should have quickly turned to religion for spiritual comfort and moral assurance. This was not only true of those who were already religiously committed but also of many whose religiosity had been more exiguous hitherto, a phenomenon illustrated by the sentiments of one soldier who wrote to a wife or sweetheart towards the end of 1916:

> It is miraculous that I have escaped being hit. Well, lass, I place all my trust in our Heavenly Father, and I know He will not fail me. As you know, I never did make a big show of being religious, but it is in my heart all the same.[154]

Outward signs of this revival were fading by the time Cairns, Plater and similar pundits got to work in 1917 but there can be no doubt that it affected many soldiers of the British army in the months between the outbreak of war and the battle of the Somme. Evidence for this diffuse and asynchronous revival is plentiful and comes from almost every denominational quarter. We have already noted the revival which occurred at Ballykinler camp among the men of the 36th Division in the winter of 1914–15. However, by this time a revivalist campaign was already under way among troops training in Scotland. Led by the YMCA and the Pocket Testament League, the campaign claimed no fewer than 12,000 converts and greatly raised the hopes of many Scottish Presbyterians for further success in the future.[155] A significant rise in the devotional temperature of Scottish units also seemed apparent to William Ewing at Gallipoli in 1915. Not only were his voluntary services attended by 'very large companies' but many young soldiers came forward to become members of the United Free Church.[156] In fact, the war appeared to be impressing upon all the value of prayer. As Ewing remembered of his months in the Dardanelles:

> I was struck with the frequency with which clergymen there said to me that one great outcome of this war, and the experiences through which it is bringing us, will be a heightening of the value

attached to prayer. It has led many a man to pray who was not accustomed to pray; for multitudes who have never been prayer-less it has lent a new sincerity and earnestness and a deepened sense of reality to their communion with God . . .[157]

Evidence of military revivals was also keenly collected and recounted by English Nonconformists. As W.E. Sellers claimed in 1915: 'Never before has such deep seriousness fallen upon our men, and in their quiet moments, and even amid the stress of battle, thoughts have turned to Christ and hearts have been surrendered to him.'[158] At a typical Sunday evening service at a Wesleyan church in Aldershot, fifty soldiers had made their 'decision for Christ' and 'Never a night passed but some soldiers gave themselves to Christ in the "Glory Rooms" of the various soldiers' homes'.[159] Signs of a religious revival were also apparent among Roman Catholics, one chaplain even drawing a favourable comparison between the faith of the crusaders and that of the troops to whom he ministered in France, men whom he described as a veritable 'community of saints'.[160] Signs of religious fervour were even apparent to Anglican chaplains, who were, of course, saddled with a much greater proportion of nominal adherents. While serving as a brigade chaplain in France early in 1915, Bishop Gwynne was struck by the piety of the 3rd Coldstream Guards. On one occasion, practically the whole battalion assembled for a voluntary Sunday evening service. Notwithstanding his long missionary experience, Gwynne felt compelled to write: 'I cannot remember a service for years where I felt the Real Presence and attended a heartier service. There must have been 800 present.'[161] Another Anglican chaplain, C.E. Doudney, was greatly impressed by the response which he met with among the men of the 18th Brigade on the Western Front in the summer and early autumn of 1915. According to Doudney's own account of his work among its infantrymen and gunners, his voluntary services were well attended, his congregations keen and many soldiers received Holy Communion.[162] Indeed, during a period of sick leave in July 1915, Doudney assured his Bath parishioners that:

> [R]eligion [has been] put to the severest test which any system could possibly be put to; and we have seen it come out absolutely triumphant . . . instead of the faith of men being shaken, we have seen it getting stronger and stronger . . . Tens of thousands of men, hard, rough working men, who perhaps never attended church at home, and never though of it are finding definitely that God is their close Friend . . . I am talking absolute bedrock truth when I say that a miracle has happened in the hearts of these lads. . .[163]

Although Doudney did not live to feel his confidence ebb, other chaplains did discern the decline of this religious enthusiasm as the war went on. T.L.B. Westerdale, a Wesleyan chaplain and former stretcher-bearer who claimed experience of no fewer than eight different divisions, wrote in 1917:

> In the early days of the war at Aldershot, and later also on Salisbury Plain, one remembers the packed chapels and YMCA huts, the Holy Crusade spirit of the men, the mighty volume of fervent song, the rich, melting after-meetings, the numerous conversions, the many vows of the warriors going forth to fight for the cause of God in a strange land. But the novelty of crusading wore off, and now . . . I feel sure the Holy Crusade spirit has practically evaporated . . . After six months in action or inaction men settle down with a dogged determination to see the thing through with a more or less 'fed up' feeling, but probably few think very deeply now of the great principles for which they came out to fight. A few great preachers with the Cromwellian touch touring the whole field would do us all good at present.[164]

These developments were also perceived by Lauchlan Maclean Watt, an experienced Church of Scotland hut worker and chaplain who wrote in 1917:

> When I was out first, at the beginning of the war, nothing impressed me more than the deep atmosphere of devotion which pervaded the men in the camps . . . Volunteers in every great cause are always idealists. The tide of religion that swept over them was like a vast contagion of enthusiasm; and one can never forget what it meant in the YMCA huts, and places where prayer was wont to be made. But the war has dragged on its weary length, and the mass of humanity in khaki in the Land of War is much more miscellaneous, while religion is much more a matter of the individual to-day than it was then.[165]

However, it must be stressed that this diminishing enthusiasm was not simply a result of the prolonged and enervating effects of trench warfare on the individual. What must also be taken into account are the one million casualties suffered by the British army up until December 1916.[166] Bluntly stated, casualty levels at Ypres, Gallipoli, Loos and the Somme were such that many of the men who experienced either a religious conversion or a deepening of their faith in 1914–15 simply did not survive or remain in the army long enough to become hardened or disillusioned. Death, wounding, transfer and reorganisation destroyed the original character of many units which had once harboured strong religious cultures. In other words, the religious revival of 1914–15, like many other smaller revivals in the British army since the 1740s, could not survive the inevitable attrition and disruption of hard and sustained campaigning.[167]

Influenced by the sober and penitential mood of the Church of England's National Mission of Repentance and Hope (and of the twin commissions on the war convened by Scotland's main Presbyterian churches)[168] from 1916 many Protestant chaplains and laymen began to confront the question of how to nurture interest in religion and the churches among an army whose constituency of pre-war churchgoers and church members had been severely reduced by the trials of the war so far. Despite some discouraging signs, these pundits were greatly heartened by the presence of what they viewed as unconscious but 'profoundly Christian characteristics'[169] among soldiers in general. As the Presbyterian chaplain A.H. Gray put it:

> On closer inspection, the indifferent, irreligious soldier turns out to be a good chap. His language might be sulphuric, but his conduct is often unselfish and even tender. He is plucky and doggedly persevering. He is friendly and jolly and happy even amid mud and shells. He can and does rise to such heights of self-forgetfulness that he makes many religious people seem small and mean . . .[170]

Likewise, in Holy Week 1917, Burgon Bickersteth observed that, among Britain's citizen soldiers:

> There is a marvellous increase of personal philanthropy, if it can be so called – charity and kindness to one's neighbour, willingness to share the last crust, to choose the dangerous post, to help in whatever way possible the lame dog over the stile. It is the so-called practical religion professed by many in peace time.[171]

These perceptions were clarified by another chaplain who wrote:

> The real religion of the Army is expressed in the extraordinary unselfishness of a large proportion of people, and the splendid friendship between men which helps them through. The hopeful sign is the prevalence of an ethic which is essentially Christian.[172]

Virtues such as comradeship, unselfishness, cheerfulness, courage, sincerity and humility co-existed with a general respect for Christ as teacher and exemplar and a strong belief in the value of prayer.[173] The clear challenge for the churches, therefore, was to transform this 'inarticulate faith expressed in deeds'[174] into an informed and committed faith among men 'who have never known or do not understand or have forgotten the Christian religion'.[175] As Neville Talbot concluded his *Thoughts on Religion at the Front*: 'There is everywhere about, over here, a diffused Christianity in men who are better than they know. It seems like so much material that needs just a spark to set it ablaze.'[176]

Among zealous young churchmen, there was naturally no shortage of suggestions as to how this might be achieved. In connection with the work of the National Mission in 1916, J.P. Maud, the Bishop of Kensington, circulated several hundred military and naval chaplains with a view to identifying problems and an agenda for change within the Church of England. Significantly, the report which his inquiries provoked remained confidential because of a widespread suspicion among senior Anglican churchmen that the whole exercise smacked of an Anglo-Catholic conspiracy.[177] If Anglo-Catholics such as Julian Bickersteth claimed to have learned the value of Catholic teaching and sacramental practice, for many liberal churchmen, mesmerised as they were by their desire to forge the kingdom of God on earth, the way ahead for the churches did not simply involve the reform of public worship. Their agenda embraced the wholesale reform of church structures and church life, the popularisation of a new and heroic vision of Christ and the churches' unswerving commitment to a more equitable socio-economic order in the post-war world.[178] Indeed, the whole of the second half of *The Army and Religion* report was devoted to propounding these objectives, with some thought also being spared for the future of religious education and the work of the League of Nations.[179] If the compilers of this report were struck by a correlation between their own findings and those of the Bishop of Kensington,[180] there was no shortage of confidence among progressive chaplains that these ambitious goals could be achieved. In 1917, and with the blessing of Bishop Gwynne, a pamphlet was published by 'An Army Chaplain' which answered in a resounding affirmative the crucial question *Can England's Church Win England's Manhood?* Furthermore, it summoned Anglican chaplains – 'as exponents of the Religion of self-sacrifice' – to 'inspire our people and send them forward in this NEW CRUSADE'.[181]

In and of itself, this far-reaching agenda for reform constituted a difficult and long-term project, not least because it sought to present, in the midst of a war of unparalleled magnitude, a new vision of Christianity to a generation which had scarcely grasped the old. Conceived in the latter period of the war and partly predicated on a particular theology of the kingdom of God, practical circumstances conspired to prevent this agenda from obtaining a significant foothold within the army as a whole. Quite apart from the elusiveness of kingdom theology for the average, theologically illiterate soldier, the military situation on the Western Front in 1917–18 was hardly auspicious for the popularisation of such an ambitious agenda. Not only was April–November 1917 marked by a series of major and costly offensives at Arras, Messines, Ypres and Cambrai but the following year saw the wholesale reorganisation of the BEF and the highest casualties of the war in the eight months of relatively mobile fighting triggered by the German spring offensive of 1918. Moreover, the coming of the Armistice in November, which was followed by a period of rapid demobilisation,[182] ensured that much of the manhood which progressive chaplains and church workers sought to inspire quickly escaped from their tutelage.

Perspectives on the spiritual state of the army in 1939–45 were very different from what they had been in 1914–18. Dealing with a more secular generation and with the experience of the First World War behind them, the churches were much less disposed to hope for spiritual dividends from the war. Certainly, there is no evidence to suggest that at any point in the conflict they apprehended a return to organised religion among the British army at large. The composition of the army and the means by which it was expanded also differed greatly from 1914–18. Not only was there a significant decline in the army's proportion of front-line soldiers, but the expansion of the army was guaranteed by conscription from the outset, a fact which precluded a voluntary recruitment campaign comparable to that led by Kitchener in 1914–15. Particularly when coupled with the army's increasingly centralised and sophisticated system of personnel selection and training, there was clearly much less scope for the creation of new units with strong ethnic, cultural or political identifications. If the army's Irish Catholic component was severely reduced by the creation of the Irish Free State, and the consequent loss of the army's richest Irish recruiting grounds, even loyal Ulstermen were in relatively short supply. Preoccupied with the abiding threat of Republican insurgency, exempt from conscription and largely bereft of a Territorial organisation, Protestant Ulster's most visible contribution to the army in the Second World War was not a neo-Covenanting host like the 36th (Ulster) Division but a modest number of volunteers for the army's Irish line regiments.[183]

Despite these factors, significant aspects of the religious culture of the other ranks in the First World War did re-emerge in the Second. A small number of clergy and ordinands, who were still mindful of the missionary potential of this situation, once again chose to serve in the ranks and particularly, it would seem, as medical orderlies and stretcher-bearers.[184] Moreover, Nonconformist soldiers still retained their capacity for self-organisation.

As Corporal Bill Gould, a Methodist soldier of the 1st Worcestershire Regiment, recalled:

> It is a common misconception that soldiers are averse to religion, that spirituality is not much in evidence in their daily routine, but I found that a number of my colleagues were sincere Christians who were concerned about how they lived their lives in full view of their comrades. After the conflict in [north-west] Europe, 1st Worcestershire Regiment were in occupation of an area near the River Elbe . . . We had lost our official padre and had attended no religious service for some months, when, on inspiration, four or five men of the Signals Platoon got together to organise a meeting whereby – by each contributing a prayer or an act of liturgy from the prayer book – we could jointly perform an act of worship. In fact we held many such meetings and our unaccompanied voices sang the hymns with which we were all familiar.[185]

Wartime issues of the *Methodist Recorder* were, in fact, replete with stories of Methodist soldiers launching successful spiritual initiatives. For example, in February 1943, an ex-officer of the Royal Armoured Corps, recounted the story of a trooper in an armoured regiment who had helped others to find 'a living faith' by leading prayer meetings in the desert prior to his death at El Alamein.[186] The previous month, the paper had published a front-page story on how a Methodist local preacher had inaugurated a revival at a jungle outpost in north-east India. In the absence of a chaplain, and finding that 'half his comrades had been churchgoers before joining the army', his voluntary Sunday evening services attracted '100 to 150 men, half the camp' and their success had persuaded the CO to secure the services of a Methodist missionary as an officiating chaplain.[187] However, such success was not confined to Nonconformists. Eric Gethyn-Jones, an Anglican chaplain, enjoyed considerable success with his unofficial system of 'Padre's Helpers', which he created in the 43rd Reconnaissance Regiment prior to D-Day. As Gethyn-Jones remembered:

> I asked . . . for volunteers (below [staff sergeant major] rank) who would act as 'Padre's Helpers'. They were to be of two grades. The first would gather the men together for prayers and Communion when I wirelessed ahead that I would be with their Squadron at a particular time. The second were to be prepared, in addition, to take prayers once a day in my absence for any who

wished and were off duty. These volunteers were given a book entitled *A Pocket Padre*. It required courage to come forward and have one's name published in Orders as a Padre's Helper, yet over fifty did so, and more than half were prepared to read the daily prayers.[188]

During the course of the subsequent campaign, and despite very heavy losses among them, the efforts of these helpers served to make 'a peace-time priest's normal life appear an uphill task!'[189]

The army carefully avoided repeating the New Army experiment of the First World War but a strong ethnic and religious identity nevertheless survived in some units between 1939 and 1945. Besides the obvious case of the Irish Guards, the army's surviving Irish infantry regiments (namely, the Royal Inniskilling Fusiliers, the Royal Ulster Rifles and Royal Irish Fusiliers) continued to recruit heavily from among Irish Catholics in the inter-war years.[190] Furthermore, and although in large measure a propaganda exercise, the creation of an 'Irish Brigade' with the active support of Winston Churchill in 1942 symbolised the continuing links between the British army and Catholic Ireland.[191] Composed of the 1st Royal Irish Fusiliers, the 6th Royal Inniskilling Fusiliers and the 2nd London Irish Rifles, the brigade served in the Tunisian, Sicilian and Italian campaigns, the latter being marked by an official audience with the pope for 150 officers and men of the brigade.[192] However, and in an echo of the First World War, heavy losses among its original members ensured that the distinctive character of the brigade proved very difficult to maintain.[193] In a similar fashion to the 'Irish Brigade', the army also formed a Jewish brigade group in Italy in September 1944. However, the contribution of British Jews to the 'Jewish Brigade' was limited by the fact that its principal components were three battalions of the Palestine Regiment, a polyglot entity which had been raised with the co-operation of the Jewish Agency and which counted no fewer than fifty-two nationalities in its ranks. Indeed, so limited were its personnel requirements that the only British Jews whose services were readily accepted were those who volunteered from the artillery or from the army's technical corps.[194]

The perennial shortage of peacetime recruits for the regular army meant that many Scottish and Welsh regiments found it difficult to maintain their notional national identity during the inter-war years. The regulars of the Welsh Regiment were, for example, less than two-fifths Welsh in the early 1920s.[195] However, some Scottish regiments did succeed in maintaining a preponderantly Scottish and Presbyterian character in their regular battalions. Among these were the Argyll and Sutherland Highlanders, whose second battalion at the outbreak of the Second World War was very largely composed of Scotsmen 'from the industrial belt stretching between the Forth and Clyde rivers; from Edinburgh, Falkirk, Motherwell, Hamilton, Clydebank, Greenock, Gourock, Port Glasgow and Stirling'.[196] In 1934, the 2nd Argyll and Sutherland Highlanders even revived the regimental kirk which had been established by its forerunner, the 93rd Highlanders, at the Cape of Good Hope in the early 1800s. The reconstituted kirk was recognised by the General Assembly of the Church of Scotland and was active when the battalion went to war in 1939.[197] Furthermore, the 1st Cameronians (Scottish Rifles) observed a heavily contrived regimental tradition which linked them to the days of their radical Covenanting forebears. Prior to parade services held at camp or in the open, the battalion sent out pickets to nearby vantage points in imitation of the vigilance required at the Presbyterian conventicles of the Restoration era. In addition, the battalion held an annual, full-dress 'Conventicle' – complete with armed sentinels – in order to commemorate the creation of the original Cameronian Regiment in 1689.[198] In many 'First Line' Highland Territorial battalions, religion was also very much a regimental affair and one Methodist chaplain noted that the officers of the original 51st (Highland) Division – which had been captured en masse at St Valéry-en-Caux in June 1940 – 'had Scottish religion [to] a very high degree'. Indeed, the Presbyterian chaplain at their prison camp at Eichstatt even conspired to get their dress uniforms sent out from home 'and on Sunday they paraded as though they were in Edinburgh Castle – terrific do'.[199] Similarly, when a Church of Scotland chaplain was attached to the 5th Black Watch – part of the reconstituted 51st (Highland) Division – he was gratified to find that most of its officers and men were already members of the kirk and that officers and other ranks alike acted as elders at communion services.[200]

If religious revivals proved to be much less common in the British army in the Second World War than they had been in the early months of the First, a major context in which these revivals did occur was in the Japanese prisoner-of-war camps of the Far East. Whereas chaplains in German and Italian POW camps noted that a widespread interest in religion seldom survived the earliest and most traumatic stages of captivity,[201] such revivals proved to be more resilient in the Far East. Certainly, and as a general phenomenon, this is not hard to understand. As the Japanese had not ratified the Geneva Convention of 1929 and were disposed to treat prisoners of war not only with contempt but also as 'a vast and expendable labour force',[202] conditions were generally much worse for British prisoners in Japanese camps than they were in those of the other Axis powers. A number of other factors also dictated that this dire situation tended to strengthen the appeal of religion. First, primitive conditions, brutal treatment and a scarcity of relief supplies were reflected in much higher mortality rates among prisoners, a factor which may have encouraged the longer-term survival of 'emergency' religion among prisoners of war. Second, the same factors also conspired to produce a situation in which organised religion had far less competition in the form of alternative recreations and diversions. Third, the circumstances of captivity sometimes lent a new significance to Christian ethical teaching and to traditional perceptions of Christ. Fourth, and finally, because Japan was not historically a Christian nation and because the Japanese did not fully recognise the religious rights of their prisoners of war, organised religion became a focus of resistance and protest to a much greater extent than it did in the prison camps of Germany or Italy.

The most tangible products of these revivals were the numerous churches and chapels which were either built or converted from existing buildings by the voluntary labour of British and other prisoners of war. Within months of the surrender of Singapore, no fewer than seven of these churches had been established in the neighbourhood of Changi, with other sites being regularly used for open-air services.[203] As the concentration of British prisoners of war in Singapore was broken up and dispersed, the construction of new churches continued apace, not only on Singapore island itself but also in Kuala Lumpur and at Kanburi in the Thai jungle.[204] Given their largely self-governing status, religious life in the camps in and around Changi was comparatively unfettered and contemporary statistics of monthly communicants suggest that as many as one-third of all British prisoners of war in these camps were regular Anglican communicants throughout their captivity.[205] In addition to promoting a thriving sacramental life, these prisoners' churches also served as vital centres of recreation, with weekday services, confirmation classes, choir practices and Toc H branches all active by the middle of 1942.[206] In July of that year the Anglican Bishop of Singapore, Leonard Wilson, even confirmed 179 soldiers and ordained a deacon in St George's church.[207] The artistic life which these chapels promoted was certainly diverse and accomplished. Not only were their fixtures and fittings obtained and even manufactured by the prisoners themselves but one makeshift chapel (St Luke's, in Roberts Barracks Hospital) was adorned by the work of Bombardier Stanley Warren of the Royal Artillery, who painted five life-size murals depicting scenes from the life of Christ.[208]

It was not only in the camps at Singapore that religious life flourished. At Tanjong Priok on Java, where services often 'had to be held in secret and in very small numbers',[209] the centrality of religious life for British prisoners of war was reflected in the contents of their camp magazine. In the *WireVille Gazette* dated 9 August 1942, a leading article described the recent consecration of the camp's new church (another St George's), which was the product of three months' work by the prisoners themselves. Significantly, the church was intended to serve not only as a functioning place of worship but also as 'a fitting memorial to "those who have lived, suffered and died out here"'. In addition to its full description of the consecration of St George's, the magazine also reported at length on the activities of the camp's Toc H group.[210] Even in the hellish conditions of the labour camps on the Burma–Thailand railway, organised religion eventually emerged as a strong element of camp life. In addition to the bamboo chapel that was built at the base camp at Kanburi just before Christmas 1943,[211] services were often held in the open air. One prisoner, Douglas Firth of the Royal Army Service Corps, recalled how at Kanu in Thailand two padres were permitted 'to cut out seats in tier fashion which looked like steps on the hillside as an area for P.O.W.s to worship'.[212] For Ernest Gordon of the 2nd Argyll and Sutherland Highlanders, organised religion actually gained in strength and cohesiveness among prisoners at Chungkai after a period in which something akin to 'the law of the jungle' had reigned among them.[213] According to Gordon, this process was part of a wider revolution in camp life after a period in which 'We had no church, no chaplains, no services'.[214] By the end of 1943, and in addition to new camp workshops, laundries and even a library, the camp at Chungkai had its own Bible lending library, Christian discussion groups and open-air chapel. Moreover, prisoners had rediscovered their 'respect for the dead'. As Gordon put it:

> Every man went to a grave of his own, with a cross to mark it. On the cross a friend would carve the facts of his life; his name, regiment and rank, and the dates of his birth and death.[215]

In Gordon's view, much of this reawakened religious interest arose out of a new and urgent appreciation of the practical value of Christian ethics:

> We were seeing for ourselves the sharp contrast between the forces that made for life and those that made for death. Selfishness, hatred, envy, jealousy, greed, self-indulgence, laziness and pride were all anti-life. Love, heroism, self-sacrifice, sympathy, mercy, integrity and creative faith, on the other hand, were the essence of life, turning mere existence into living in its truest sense. These were the gifts of God to men . . . With these principles beginning to manifest themselves to us, we began to notice such forces at work around us. On occasions when we marched into the countryside on labour details we saw them in the actions of Christian natives, in the differences between the Christian way of life and the Oriental one.[216]

As Gordon's analysis implies, much of the appeal of Christianity for British prisoners of war in the Far East lay in the sense of moral superiority over the Japanese which it provided. Although they were seldom, if ever, killed for purely religious reasons, the deaths of British and Commonwealth missionaries at Japanese hands served to create a new generation of Christian 'martyrs' in the Far East and the Pacific.[217] Likewise, and although less widely recognised by contemporaries, it seems clear that executions in Japanese POW camps could also assume the character of Christian martyrdoms. J.N. Lewis Bryan (the most senior British army chaplain to be captured at Singapore) remembered how an Australian prisoner, who was condemned to death for trying to escape from Singapore in September 1942, told him that 'I have my New Testament here, sir, and I am going to read it while they shoot me'. This promise was kept to the letter.[218] Likewise, Ernest Gordon recalled how another Australian was executed at Chungkai for his attempts to procure medicines outside the camp. Beheaded before his fellow prisoners, he prepared himself for his ordeal by reading a passage from the New Testament.[219] Given the primacy of the ethical content of popular Christianity and the wartime concept of a war in defence of Christian civilisation, the significance of such gestures for British prisoners of war in the Far East cannot be overlooked. Furthermore, and as with their fathers' generation on the Western Front in the First World War, for many prisoners of war in the Far East the figure of Christ appears to have become emblematic of victorious suffering, a theme that was reflected in the paintings of Stanley Warren. As Ernest Gordon noted, the members of his discussion groups in the camp at Chungkai tended to focus heavily on this aspect of Christ's life and ministry:

> He was one of us. He would understand our problems, because they were the kind of problems he had faced himself. Like us, he often had no place to lay his head, no food for his belly, no friends in high places. He, too, had known bone-weariness from too much toil; the suffering, the rejection, the disappointments that make up the fabric of life . . . As we read and talked, he became flesh and blood. Here was a working-man, yet one who was perfectly free, who had not been enslaved by society, economics, law, politics or religion. Demonic forces had existed then as now. They had sought to destroy him but they had not succeeded . . . True, he had been suspended on a cross and tormented with the pain of hell; but he had not been broken. The weight of law and of prejudice had borne down on him, but

failed to crush him. He had remained free and alive, as the Resurrection affirmed. What he was, what he did, what he said, all made sense to us.[220]

Despite the exalted nature of such perceptions, the significance of organised religious activity as a form of defiance and resistance was also obvious. Indeed, it is even conceivable that the restrictions which the Japanese sometimes placed on religious services helped to endow them with a seditious quality that they did not wholly warrant. Nevertheless, some religious activities were clearly subversive. As Lewis Bryan noted with satisfaction, national days of prayer were observed by successive 'watches' of volunteers in all prisoners' chapels on Singapore island, notice of them being received through an illegal wireless set. Likewise, successive Armistice Days were marked by 'United Services of all Denominations' whose solemnity compensated for the banning of the 'Last Post' and 'Reveille' by the Japanese authorities.[221] Even the naming and adornments of prisoners' chapels bespoke the strength of a civil religion charged with a new air of defiance. Not only was St George a much-favoured patron of these chapels, but they sometimes lay at the heart of a conscious attempt to create an idealised corner of England in these forsaken foreign fields. At Tanjong Priok, the chapel of St George was fronted by an extensive and well-kept lawn which the prisoners knew as 'the Village Green'.[222] When Changi's original church of St George was converted from a mosque situated in India Lines, it was decorated with a carved plaque of St George and the Dragon and equipped with all the furnishings of a substantial parish church. As one prisoner, Private Stuart Dalton of the Royal Army Ordnance Corps, recalled:

> The form of the mosque made adaptation to a church easy enough for it had nave, chancel, vestry, churchyard and lychgate. Four units worshipped at St. George's – the [Royal Northumberland] Fusiliers and units of the Royal Engineers, the Ordnance Corps and the Service Corps – the last named being three units admirably fitted to carry out the necessary alterations as they comprised mechanics of all kinds . . . The Engineers made the Communion Table, altar rails, pulpit, lectern and wardens' staves while the Ordnance Corps fashioned an altar cross out of a brass shell case and inscribed it with the badges of the four units. They also arranged the lighting, made two candles for the altar and repaired a small harmonium to accompany the choir while the Service Corps undertook to provide every week the bread and wine for the Communion.[223]

The holy warrior

'The best Christian is always the best Soldier; the more of Prayer in my army, the more of Victory.'[224]Ascribed to King Gustavus Adolphus of Sweden, the champion of European Protestantism at the height of the Thirty Years War, these sentiments had been generally accepted in late Victorian society. In this context, the cult of the Christian warrior had enjoyed a considerable renaissance, particularly with the celebrated careers of Sir Henry Havelock, Gordon of Khartoum and Lord Roberts of Kandahar. Given that the truth of this axiom had been endorsed in British society since the mid-Victorian period, civilian religious commentators during the First World War were not slow to reiterate the claim that religious men made better soldiers by definition. Interestingly enough, and although Haig may have been convinced of the decadence of France and of the military worthlessness of the French army by 1917, the French army of 1914–15 had been characterised by its offensive spirit.[225] One Roman Catholic publication of 1916 ingenuously attributed this not to its tactical doctrine but to the fact that 'the great majority' of French soldiers were 'faithful to the Catholic traditions of their country [and] animated with the immortal spirit of St. Louis and the Maid of Orleans'. The same publication also insisted that it was his faith which rendered the Irish Catholic soldier so formidable:

> Those same qualities, too, are the modern Irishman's heritage from a past that tells only of endurance, tenacity and pluck. Not merely have the Irish regiments from Ireland herself won a unique distinction in the war, but the strong Irish strain that runs through the contingents from the British Dominions has potently contrib-uted to the exploits of troops whom many experts consider to surpass all others in dash and bravery.[226]

In a similar vein, and on behalf of British Jewry, Michael Adler expressed considerable pride in the disciplinary record of Jewish soldiers and stressed the credentials of Judaism as a front-line religion:

> [T]he large majority of Jews engaged on active service belonged to the fighting units of the Army, such as the Infantry, Artillery, Tanks, Machine Gun Units, and the special Brigades of the Royal Engineers who were in charge of the gas operations. In the Admin-istrative Departments they appear to have been comparatively few in number.[227]

Despite the partisan nature of such claims, it is significant that John Baynes noted how a personal religiosity was a distinguishing feature of the best and most reliable soldiers of the 2nd Scottish Rifles in 1915.[228] This phenomenon was probably as true of Britain's non-professional soldiers as it was of the regulars and reservists of the early war period. Although the religious backgrounds of VC winners have been impossible to ascertain for the purposes of this study, it may be significant that Britain's only double VC winner for the First World War was Captain Noel Chavasse, the regimental medical officer of the 1/10th King's Liverpool Regiment, who was a staunch churchman, a son of the Bishop of Liverpool and the twin brother of an army chaplain.[229]

In terms of the vaunted link between piety and military prowess, it may be significant that the volunteers of 1914–15 (who mustered a large proportion of churchgoers and church members in their ranks) were regarded as much better military material than were the conscripts of 1916–18. Although the question of the relative effectiveness of British divisions during the First World War is subject to a host of complicating variables, it may be noted that the 9th and 15th (Scottish), 36th (Ulster), 51st (Highland) and 56th (London) divisions (all originally New Army or Territorial divisions with relatively strong church cultures) have been counted among the best British divisions on the Western Front.[230] Certainly, and for the military authorities at least, religious feeling was regarded as a key indicator of high morale.[231] This is particularly evident from two Third Army 'Morale Reports' dated November 1916 and May 1917, documents which were based on samples of soldiers' uncensored letters. On the basis of the sentiments expressed in this correspondence, the first report derived considerable satisfaction from the fact that roughly a quarter of soldiers' letters contained 'a definite expression of religious feeling'. This evidence prompted the author's claim that 'The Cromwellian "Trust God and keep your powder dry", might still be the motto of our Army to-day'. The second report confirmed that 'belief in God . . . the sense of serving a great cause . . . the discipline of the Army [and] the brotherhood of soldiering' were the 'four foundations, with humour as the cement, [which] are the base of a pyramid on which will rise the apex of Victory'.[232] For Philip Gibbs, it was self-evident from his experiences as a war correspondent that religion proved to be an extra source of consolation and courage for the individual soldier:

[M]any men found help in religion, and sought its comfort with a spiritual craving. They did not argue about Christian ethics and modern warfare. Close to death, in the midst of tragedy, conscious in a strange way of their own spiritual being, and of a spirituality present among masses of men above the muck of war, the stench of corruption, and fear of bodily extinction, they groped out towards God. They searched for some divine wisdom greater than the folly of the world, for a divine aid which would help them to greater courage.[233]

Remarkably, it was not only in the difficult conditions of the front line that soldiers found vital sustenance in religion. When recaptured after attempting to escape, Sapper George Waymark, a signaller who had been taken prisoner by the Germans in April 1918, found that hymnody and the Book of Common Prayer enabled him to survive the wretched conditions of solitary confinement. As Waymark remembered: 'Each night I went through the Church service, being Parson, Choir and Congregation, and, strange to say, some of the others in nearby cells joined in the hymns.'[234] More indirectly, the importance of a personal religiosity in helping individuals cope with fear and trauma may be reflected in descriptions given by chaplains of those soldiers who were executed for cowardice and desertion, a common verdict (which echoed parallel cases in the American Civil War) being that they were men whose religious outlook and behaviour were as poor as their military conduct.[235]

If morale was perhaps a more fragile commodity in the British army during the Second World War, religion continued to play an important role in sustaining it. In 1949, a War Office report on the army's wartime morale concluded a survey of factors which had influenced it by emphasising that:

> Last, but not least, religion should be mentioned as a factor capable of deeply influencing morale. There is no doubt that religious faith will increase the powers of endurance and self-sacrifice of soldiers who possess it. There is evidence also that the experience of battle often quickens, for a time at any rate, the religious sentiments that are latent in many soldiers. By fostering these sentiments, and in many other ways, a good chaplain may help to raise and maintain the morale of a unit, particularly in action, as many commanding officers have testified.[236]

Given the very different nature of the expansion and organisation of the British army in the Second World War and the current state of research on the army in this period, it is even more difficult to establish a correlation between the combat effectiveness of given units and their religious configuration. However, on an individual level, the experiences of prisoners of war in the Far East provide some good illustrations of how a personal religiosity continued to sustain and inspire many. For Eric Lomax, who forsook his fundamentalist Baptist beliefs later in life and whose testimony seems fairly objective, his religious background never lost its significance as the principal means whereby he survived the ordeal of captivity and forced labour. With his memoirs prefaced by a passage from the Book of Revelation ('I am alive, and was dead . . . Write therefore the things which thou hast seen')[237] Lomax conceded that:

> In a way, though I feel very distant from the young man who was so easily drawn into that sectarian embrace, the moral conviction of being saved, that I really had found God, helped me to survive what came later. I was still very committed and religious when I went to war . . . If I can be grateful to the Chapel for anything, it is for helping me build that armour of stubbornness that got me through.[238]

In more positive terms, Major P. William-Powlett of the 3rd King's Own Hussars maintained that those who held and practised their religion sincerely were 'the most fortunate' among his fellow prisoners of war. Indeed, he concluded his memoir of captivity with the reflection:

> I have been asked what quality of character is the most powerful to help a man through the experience of prisoner of war life . . . Those who worry about themselves and food, and who think that they will die unless they have a little more to eat than their neighbour, fare worst. Those with strong wills, who force themselves into activity to keep themselves from thinking, do not do badly. Those with equable temperaments, who take things as they come, do better. Those do best, who are kindly, widely tolerant, and interested in their fellow man, who have a steady faith in the fundamental goodness of Providence, and who realise that despite appearances mankind is gradually learning a better way of life. They are those who hold high the royal destiny of man.[239]

Interestingly, this view forms not only the leitmotif of Ernest Gordon's *Miracle on the River Kwai* (which has been unduly belittled on the basis of its 'strong evangelical message')[240] but is also evident in a chaplain's memoir of his long months in a POW camp in Hong Kong. According to G.M.R. Bennett, the experience of captivity ultimately served to supplement mere faith with a profound experiential knowledge of the nature and purposes of God. In particular, the profound truth of the message of St Paul in Romans 8.35 seemed to be emphasised in these severe but ultimately sustainable conditions: 'Neither tribulation, nor distress, nor persecution, nor famine, nor nakedness, nor peril, nor sword can in themselves separate us from the love of Christ or each other.'[241]

If religious considerations provided an interpretative framework for extreme suffering, then they also affected other perspectives on the two World Wars. Given the far-reaching influence of the Romantic movement in diffusing neo-chivalric values in nineteenth-century British society, many educated Britons proved highly susceptible to viewing the First World War in terms of a crusade. This view was particularly encouraged by Germany's apparent lapse into pre-Christian barbarism and by her military alliance with the Ottoman empire, whose entry into the war was accompanied by the declaration of a *jihad* against Britain, Russia and France.[242] Although present in a less explicit form among the ordinary volunteers of 1914–15, neo-crusading views were inevitably marked among the officer class. As late as September 1917, one major-general informed a chaplains' conference on the Western Front that 'we were engaged in a Crusade, not now to snatch the tomb of Christ from infidel hands, but to rescue the life & the Spirit of Christ from the dark forces that would seek to overwhelm it'.[243] If a neo-crusading consciousness could be applied to the struggle against Germany, it is not surprising that it should have been well to the fore in those campaigns in which British soldiers faced the Turks. In fact, it may well have been more than coincidental that the landings on the Gallipoli peninsula took place just after St George's Day 1915. This crusading consciousness seems to have been particularly strong among Roman Catholics, notwithstanding their lack of a crusading indulgence and the controversial neutrality of Pope Benedict XV. For Bryan Cooper, an officer of the 5th Connaught Rangers, his battalion's spiritual preparations for its attack on Hill 60 in August 1915 seemed powerfully reminiscent of earlier centuries, notwithstanding the changed technology of war:

> For the Church of England men, the Revd J.W. Crozier celebrated Holy Communion; and Fr. O'Connor gave absolution to his flock. The bullets of snipers were whistling overhead, and ploughed furrows through the ground as the men knelt in prayer and listened to the message of peace and comfort delivered by the tall khaki-clad figure. In a few hours they were to plunge into a hand-to-hand struggle with the old enemy of Christendom, and their pulses throbbed with the spirit of Tancred and Godfrey de Bouillon, as they fitted themselves to take their places in the last of the Crusades.[244]

Although evident enough at Gallipoli, these sentiments appear to have grown stronger as British forces advanced through the Holy Land in the closing months of 1917. For Lieutenant Noel Chamberlain, an old boy of Ampleforth, the sight of a historic monastery that had been sacked by the retreating Turks proved sufficient to provoke a distinctly atavistic reaction:

> The monastery had been used as quarters for their troops . . . Before leaving, however, they managed to break anything they could not carry away. Some things they had burnt, statues were hurled to the ground, and books torn to pieces . . . Vestments were also lying in shreds . . . As I rode away I could not help wondering whether Ampleforth would ever suffer a similar fate, whether the cloisters would ever ring to the sound of the military, and the library be despoiled by the infidel. That truly was the first time I felt justified in calling the campaign a crusade. Somehow or other the Turk's character had seemed mellow – age had rubbed off his barbarity. I question that now![245]

Naturally, the capture of Jerusalem stirred these emotions to a crescendo. For Fr Bede Camm, a monk of Downside and an army chaplain, the sight of the holy places liberated from the Turks after seven hundred years of Turkish control was truly exhilarating:

> It was always one of the dreams of my life . . . to see Jerusalem. But I never expected to see it as I did; Jerusalem delivered, delivered from the age-long tyranny of the Turk, with the Union Jack flying over her towers, her streets thronged with British soldiers . . . I saw sights at Jerusalem that had never been seen since the days of the Crusaders, saw the victors prostrating themselves, as their forefathers had done . . . before the Tomb of Christ, long processions of Catholic soldiers making the Stations of the Cross along the Via Dolorosa, British Tommies on guard at the doors of the Holy Sepulchre, and in the very cave where Christ was born for us at Bethlehem . . . I heard the vaults of the old Crusading Church of St. Anne echo to the familiar strains of English hymns, the well-known bugle call of our Army ring out from the Mount of Olives, mingling with the hoots of the lorries which in almost ceaseless stream carried supplies and ammunition to our troops in the Jordan Valley, or on the Nablus front.[246]

Although neo-crusading sentiment was clearly evident at certain times and in certain quarters of the British army during the First World War, this consciousness proved somewhat harder to sustain in the Second. Strongly influenced by the salutary experiences of the First World War and by the pacifism of the inter-war years, among the Protestant churches in particular neo-crusading rhetoric tended to have a hollow ring. As Dean Cyril Alington acknowledged in his pamphlet *The Last Crusade* (which was published in February 1940 and which sought to prove that Britain had 'a clear claim' to be fighting a crusade): 'There are some, perhaps many, to whom the title of this little book will give inevitable offence. They will assume that it implies a self-righteousness which is wholly un-Christian, and, in our own case, completely unjustified.'[247] Although the Dean of Durham and former head-master of Eton was known for his persuasiveness,[248] a survey undertaken by MO in August 1940 found that Alington's pamphlet had not been well received. It also established that, if Alington's claims were unappealing for many within the churches, among the population at large the concept of crusading seemed to be devoid of any useful significance. This was an inauspicious conclusion given that the Ministry of Information was poised to use the term extensively in a forthcoming propaganda campaign.[249]

Like the Ministry of Information, the army appears to have done its best to forge a militantly religious and even neo-crusading consciousness among its citizen soldiers during the war years, and not only via the sermons and pronouncements of its chaplains. While various models of cruiser tanks and self-propelled guns were given names such as the *Cromwell*, the *Covenanter*, the *Bishop* and the *Sexton*, in North Africa, where the context of desert warfare lent the notion of crusading a greater resonance, the offensive which success-fully broke Rommel's siege of Tobruk in November 1941 was code-named operation CRUSADER. This name was also bestowed upon the A15 cruiser tank which appeared in the desert earlier that year.[250] The name *Crusader* was also given to the 8th Army's official weekly newspaper that was launched in May 1942.[251] Despite the fact that it was probably becoming somewhat hackneyed even before Alamein, the crusading motif was recurrently employed throughout the remainder of the war, no doubt deriving fresh stimulus from Montgomery's conspicuous brand of militant Christianity. Indeed, it is worthy of note that the insignia of the British First, Second and Eighth Armies and that of the 21st Army Group (all of which saw service in the Mediterranean or north-west Europe) were variations on the theme of a crusader's cross set within a crusader's shield. Moreover, King George VI deliberately invoked 'the crusading spirit' and the 'crusading impulse' in his broadcast address to the British people on the evening of 6 June 1944.[252]

Despite this high-flown rhetoric and various direct and indirect efforts within the British army to stimulate a new and exalted attitude towards the war, it seems clear that Britain's citizen soldiers, though persuaded of the justice of their cause, generally lacked the military and religious zeal to see it in more elevated terms. In his memoirs of the Tunisian campaign, Spike Milligan used the term 'descendant of the Crusaders' with characteristic irony and Raleigh Trevelyan remembered being told by a fellow officer in 1944 that 'All this talk about crusades made him retch'.[253] As for the *Crusader* newspaper, which followed the 8th Army to Italy in 1943, Alec Bowlby compared its contents unfavourably with that of its German counterpart, *Sud Front*. Whereas the former featured full-page spreads of 'luscious German nudes', the *Crusader* was 'so bad no one in the Platoon bothered to read it. We used it for "bumf" [i.e. toilet paper]'.[254] Despite all of this, the concept still had a resonance for some, with Catholics in particular proving susceptible to its appeal. In fact, the left-wing journalist W.N. O'Connor was scathing about Cardinal Hinsley's pronouncement that Britain was 'at the side of truth and justice in this conflict' and sourly noted Catholic enthusiasm for the 'Cardinal's Cross':

> As a token of this conviction, [Hinsley] expressed the wish that every Christian knight of the British cause would wear a little cross under his tunic. Practical measures towards this end were taken and 50,000 bakelite crosses bearing the words: 'The Pledge of Victory' were manufactured. They were duly blessed by Cardinal Hinsley and were distributed to the Forces through Chaplains.[255]

Besides this bakelite echo of the medieval practice of taking the cross, the militant and patriotic overtones of Hinsley's 'Sword of the Spirit' movement ensured that educated Roman Catholics were particularly prone to these neo-crusading ideas. In a personal reflection dated December 1943, Hugh Dormer, an ex-pupil of Ampleforth, a veteran of the Special Operations Executive and an officer in the Irish Guards, wrote:

> [S]hould I die this spring on the battlefields of Europe, I die as a volunteer . . . in a cause that I believe in with ever-increasing certainty. For the ideas of Nazi philosophy are infinitely more far-reaching than those of the French Revolution, and more diabolic than anything yet known in the history of the West . . . God knows we in this country are far from perfect, but this war is far more of a Crusade than the Crusades themselves ever were . . . We fight to-day not against ignorant heathens, or Vandals

who know not the value of what they destroy, but against conscious and calculating anarchists, who strike at national culture and religion, precisely because they know that cathedrals and schools are the nerve centres of that spirit which they aim completely and for ever to destroy. The men who resist this revolution in Europe now with their lives are martyrs to a very real extent.[256]

Conclusion

The consequences of mass military service in the two World Wars were in many respects beneficial for the British churches. Contemporary concerns over morale and the historically privileged position of the churches in the army ensured that more young people (and young men in particular) were regularly exposed to religious influences than would have been the case in civilian life. Apart from the ministry of army chaplains, the work of other religious agencies (which we will examine in Chapter 6), the active support of many general and regimental officers and a significant broadening of the army's composition during the war years clearly served to strengthen the influence of the churches at all levels. Indeed, and as in the eighteenth and nineteenth centuries,[257] a strong leavening of churchgoing soldiers helped to inspire religious activity and even produced some tangible religious revivals among their contemporaries. Although high-flown crusading rhetoric was lost on all but a few, religion nevertheless provided the ultimate moral foundation of Britain's national struggle in both World Wars. If there is also evidence from the war years to suggest that religious sentiment not only strengthened morale but actively enhanced the soldier's fighting abilities, it is beyond doubt that religious activity became a rallying point and focus of defiance for British soldiers in captivity in the Far East during the Second World War. Nevertheless, and acting as a strong countervailing force to all of this, there was the fact that the conditions of war also generated a formidable array of moral problems and threw into question contemporary perceptions of what it was to be religious. These counter-currents and their significance are the subject of our next chapter.

Chapter 5

RELIGION, MORALITY AND WAR

Introduction

FOR A SOCIETY IN WHICH standards of public and private morality were still very much dictated by Christian precepts, and in which Christianity itself was widely conceived as a system of practical ethics, the moral impact of the two World Wars had far-reaching religious implications. As we have seen, one of the main challenges faced by British army chaplains during the First World War lay in preaching the national cause while not appearing to be positively unchristian in doing so. By the same token, many of the chaplains who were keen to endow the British soldier with a sense of religious and moral purpose in the Second World War were anxious to ensure that the rhetoric of hate was avoided and that the principles of the just war were applied. However, the moral dilemmas of war were multitudinous and went far beyond the ethics of killing and the practical corollaries of just war theory. For vast numbers of respectable civilians wrenched from the confines and constraints of home, the whole experience of military service was very much an occasion of sin, the vices to which the British soldier had always been susceptible proliferating in the context of mass mobilisation. Thus, and while the army provided plenty of scope for the churches to bring their influence to bear, the virtuous civilian-in-arms was at the same time liable to be influenced by the brutalities of war and by the viciousness of comrades. It was in the widespread deterioration of civilian moral standards, far more than in a loss of faith per se, that the churches confronted the most significant symptom of religious change in the years of the two World Wars.

Religion and the conduct of war

While it would be true to say that pre-war standards of morality suffered as a result of both World Wars, evidence from their European theatres indicates that a shared Christian culture could at least do something to ameliorate the horrors of modern warfare. The most obvious example of this is the 'Christmas Truce', which was widely observed – and subsequently greatly romanticised – in the British sector of the Western Front in 1914. However, the reasons for this truce cannot be simply attributed to the spontaneous appeal of Christmas to citizen soldiers reacting against the grim experience of trench warfare. What is remarkable about the British units involved in the Christmas Truce of 1914 is that they were largely regular in composition[1] and one of the most convivial aspects of life in Britain's regular army was the manner in which Christmas was celebrated in its barrack rooms. As Horace Wyndham remembered of Christmas Day in the army at the end of the nineteenth century, barrack rooms were invariably decorated and peace and goodwill prevailed therein: 'Old feuds, of long standing, were, for the nonce, annulled (in all probability to be renewed with increased bitterness on the next day) and old friendships cemented.' Defaulters were released from the guardroom in honour of the occasion and 'the bonds of discipline were perceptibly slackened, and breaches thereof openly winked at'.[2] In view of all of this, the famous events of Christmas 1914 strongly suggest that the regulars and reservists who made up most of the British battalions in the line simply chose to extend the spirit of Christmas and of familiar barrack room custom to the Germans in the trenches opposite. However, this widespread truce also provided a much-needed opportunity to bury the dead, an opportunity that Malcolm Brown and Shirley Seaton have recognised as being for many 'the *real* reason' for the Christmas Truce.[3]

In addition to the classic example of the Christmas Truce, religious considerations could influence the conduct of war in other respects. From Italy and north-west Europe during the Second World War there is evidence to indicate that combatants on both sides accepted that churches and other sacred edifices should be respected if at all possible, a concept which was articulated (though all too often ignored on the Western Front in the First World War) in the Hague Convention of 1899.[4] As Sir David Fraser remembered of the Italian campaign of 1943–5, 'the general guidance' in this theatre of war was that Italy's 'shrines should be regarded as sacrosanct unless military necessity demanded otherwise'.[5] For a time at least, this consideration gave the historic Benedictine monastery at Monte Cassino some immunity from the ravages of war but it ultimately failed to save it from destruction in 1944 once the tactical significance of its position had become clear to the Allies.

Fraser recalled that the Allied bombing of Monte Cassino prompted heated debate among his fellow Guards officers as they awaited the invasion of France:

> I can see the emotion on the faces of some friends in that Yorkshire farm kitchen, as they demanded whether those who opposed them would think it right to risk their men's lives to spare some ancient building; while, on the other side, other friends argued that in any war or any circumstances there must be some actions from which it is morally imperative to abstain, even at the cost of operational disadvantage. Was not the destruction of one of the most venerable shrines in Western Christendom just such an example?[6]

In the subsequent campaign in north-west Europe, church buildings were often respected, a factor that made them ideal places of refuge for the wounded. At Etterville in Normandy, the parish church became a dressing station for British and German wounded, an ad hoc arrangement which had been negotiated with the Germans by the chaplain of the 4th Dorsetshire Regiment.[7] Similarly, at Raamsdonk in southern Holland, both British and German troops sought shelter from indiscriminate shellfire within the walls of its great church.[8] In fact, it was the spectacle of the deliberate shelling of a chapel holding British wounded in Italy in 1944 that constituted Alec Bowlby's worst wartime experience, one which seemed to serve as a metaphor of the cosmic struggle between good and evil of which the present war was a part. As Bowlby recollected:

> [T]he enemy gunners were celebrating. They fired happily at nothing until a stray shell hit our [Advanced Dressing Station], a chapel clearly marked with a red cross. Someone inside began ringing the bell. It drew the attention of the German gunners' observer, but not in the way intended. He simply directed *all* the guns on to the chapel. Dumb with horror we watched it struck again and again. The bell continued to ring. The rate of fire increased. Bits fell off the chapel. It seemed only a matter of time before the whole building collapsed. We listened to the bell as if our lives depended on it. God and the Devil suddenly seemed very real. When the shelling died down the bell was still ringing. It continued to ring for minutes after the last shell. We were too moved to say anything. We just grunted, and found pieces of kit that needed attention. But what had happened on the hill no longer seemed so meaningless.[9]

The common religious culture that ensured that truces could be arranged to bury the dead and that religious buildings were accorded a degree of respect could also influence the way in which the enemy was perceived. Negatively speaking, it could inform a perception of enemy apostasy and depravity. This perception was famously reflected in the story of the Canadian sergeant who was allegedly crucified by his German captors during the Second Battle of Ypres in 1915.[10] From the Second World War, it is also apparent in the diary of W.J. Hill, a Methodist chaplain, who had qualms about burying German dead, primarily because he might be giving a Christian burial to an 'avowed pagan'.[11] However, this awareness of a shared religious culture could have more positive corollaries. During the First World War, it was common for German soldiers to brandish pocket Bibles and crucifixes when attempting to surrender[12] and, for at least some British soldiers, an awareness of religious commonality heightened the ethical problems raised by the war. For one such soldier, Sydney Fuller of the 8th Suffolk Regiment, the discovery of a German prayer book in a captured pillbox near Ypres proved something of a watershed:

> The German prayer book found in the pillbox at Poelcappelle –
> on the cover, *Mit Jesus in der Feld*, and inside a coloured picture
> of Christ looking with pity on a dead German soldier. The same
> picture as in our own Field Prayer Book, *With Jesus in the Field*.
> The only appreciable difference being in the uniform of the dead
> soldier – German in one, khaki in the other – and the feeling
> experienced on seeing that picture compared with one of our
> own, that the whole War was a horrible mistake.[13]

If this sense of commonality could moderate attitudes to the Germans in the First World War, a generation later contact with Japanese Christians could do something to moderate general attitudes of fear and loathing towards the Japanese among Far East POWs. Remarkably, one of those who received communion at Bishop Leonard's confirmation service in St George's chapel in Changi in July 1942 was a Japanese officer.[14] Similarly, Douglas Firth remembered holding a limited conversation with a Christian guard on the Burma–Thailand railway, their conversation being prompted by the small cross that Firth had taken to wearing about his neck. However stilted, Firth remembered that 'the exercise . . . proved helpful to us both and gave me a special boost of spirit that I needed'.[15]

If the sense of a shared Christianity caused some British Protestants to adjust their attitudes towards the enemy, it was natural for Roman Catholics – with their much stronger sense of being part of a global church – to feel a particular sympathy for their co-religionists among the enemy. For example, Fr William Doyle of the 16th (Irish) Division was assiduous in ministering to German prisoners during the First World War and he was even known to preach to his men 'on their obligation to respect the lives of prisoners'.[16] If Doyle routinely soothed the fears of captured German Catholics he was also prepared to give absolution to those who were about to die. In June 1917, and minutes before the German positions on Messines ridge disintegrated in what was then the largest man-made explosion in history, Doyle climbed out of his trench in order to give absolution to its distant and unwitting defenders – 'trusting to God's mercy to speed it so far'.[17] Again in the Second World War, British Roman Catholics were keenly aware of the existence of their many co-religionists in Germany and of their difficult relationship with the Nazi regime. In June 1945, Captain Alan Harris of the Royal Engineers wrote to his sister expressing his sympathy for the predicament of Catholics in the diocese of Munster, whose bishop had famously led the attack on the Nazis' euthanasia programme:

> We are still in Catholic Germany. I drove up on Corpus Christi day and every village, however ruined, had its festivity . . . all the wayside shrines and memorials were decorated with flowers, the footpaths were bordered with beech boughs stuck into the ground at every three feet, making them into leafy avenues . . . for the procession of the Blessed Sacrament. Bishop Count Galen of Münster was one of Hitler's most determined opponents, but since those days his cathedral has been bombed, half his diocese obliterated so that most of his churches, seminaries and schools no longer exist. [T]he final victory coincided, they say, with more than a little of the traditional soldierly brutality and licentiousness and then after this he found himself to be included in the non-fraternisation order and was in consequence just a little cool about it all.[18]

These sympathies were still more in evidence in relation to Italian Roman Catholics. Prior to the Badoglio Armistice of September 1943, British and Italian priests had shown a reciprocal interest in the spiritual needs of their co-religionists languishing in POW camps.[19] Later, during the Italian campaign, the Italian clergy were to prove very obliging in their dealings with Roman Catholic army chaplains.[20] It would, in fact, hardly be stretching the point to claim that the presence of large numbers of Roman Catholics in the Eighth Army helped to smooth the path of the victors in Italy's North African empire. Following the Axis evacuation of Libya in the aftermath of Alamein,

John Scollen was struck by the fact that Italian civilians were outnumbered by British and Commonwealth troops at services in the cathedral at Tripoli. Indeed, their presence seems to have helped the Italian ecclesiastical author-ities to take a conciliatory view of defeat, an important factor given the collapse of alternative sources of authority in this former outpost of Musso-lini's empire. As Scollen noted, during a sermon preached by the Bishop of Tripoli he 'made some reference to "soldati Inglesi"' and he seemed to be saying to his Italian congregation 'that the English soldiers, as fellow Catholics, were in a special way their brethren'.[21] In Italy itself, Alec Bowlby was stuck by the marked preference shown to his Roman Catholic comrades by Italian civilians. On one occasion, while at dinner in an Italian farmhouse, an Irish soldier named O'Connor produced a small crucifix and declared himself 'Cattolico':

> The old woman shrieked for joy.
> 'E Cristiano! E proprio Cristiano!'
> She was all over O'Connor, to the extent of producing some-thing special from a small bottle. O'Connor grinned smugly.[22]

If the Christian culture of contemporary British society could serve to ameliorate the brutality and bitterness of war then it also helped to ensure that there was room in the British army for conscientious objectors who were prepared to undertake non-combatant military service. Ranging from polit-ical anarchists through to Jehovah's Witnesses, conscientious objectors proved to be a mixed bag in both World Wars but a great many were motivated (either wholly or in part) by religious considerations. However, these considerations could be more sectarian than altruistic in character and it is notable that, during the First World War, the Christadelphians furnished a far greater number of conscientious objectors than did the comparatively liberal Society of Friends (1,716 as opposed to 750).[23] In both World Wars, the army's principal repositories for conscientious objectors were the RAMC and the specially created Non-Combatant Corps. Conscientious objectors who found themselves serving as stretcher-bearers in the front line gener-ally earned the admiration of their fellow soldiers. As Charlie Wakeley said of the stretcher-bearers of the 1st Worcestershire Regiment in 1944–5:

> A good many people had got in their minds that conscientious objectors was cowards and all that. But whoever got that about was very wrong, they was, because I saw conscientious objectors and I always told people that should all have been given the Victoria Cross . . . In khaki, the same as me, they'd got the Red

Cross on their arms and they was stretcher-bearers . . . As soon as anybody was down and out, a big call would go up, 'Stretcher-bearers!' and these chaps would used to go out and fetch them back in – no 'below ground' like we was, or in 'shallows', they'd got to go out and fetch them in and they did a job that we was all proud of . . . They was probably more braver than us people![24]

Despite the plaudits earned by those conscientious objectors who served as medical personnel in the front line, those who found themselves in the Non-Combatant Corps tended to be viewed in a rather different light. Formed in March 1916,[25] the Non-Combatant Corps was never very large and at no point mustered more than 3,000 conscientious objectors during the First World War.[26] Exempt as it was from front-line duties and from the carrying of arms, the role of its constituent companies was generally confined to labouring duties at home or on lines of communication overseas. Given the scruples of its soldiers and the sometimes marginal (and hence morally debatable) nature of the tasks to which they were assigned, the disciplinary record of the Non-Combatant Corps was hardly exemplary.[27] For their part, its soldiers found themselves discriminated against in terms of pay and were generally held in low esteem as members of what was soon branded the 'No Courage Corps'.[28] If its work remained much the same between 1939 and 1945, the role of the Non-Combatant Corps was at least broadened to include civil defence. However, whether unloading trains or managing smokescreen defences in the Peak District, the 6,000 conscientious objectors who served in the Non-Combatant Corps in the Second World War[29] shared a rather undistinguished service history with their forebears of 1916–18. Committed to dull and menial duties and often resented by their fellow soldiers, some of the more adventurous among them eventually transferred to bomb disposal units or to airborne units of the RAMC.[30] In addition to its unglamorous role and the unenviable light in which it was seen, the Non-Combatant Corps in both World Wars also harboured a strong and decidedly sectarian religious sub-culture, a fact that probably did little to enhance its reputation. During the First World War, Seventh Day Adventists were court-martialled for refusing to work on Saturdays and one of its putative company commanders in the Second World War later confessed that he found the prospect of his new command depressing rather than daunting. He wrote:

I had been warned that in the camp at Glasgow many individual tents held prayer meetings nightly before calling it a day. And I had been further informed that these – shall we say red-hot gospellers – did not by any means believe in hiding their light under a bushel.[31]

War, faith and morals

Because of the supposedly paradigmatic experiences of men such as Wilfred Owen, Robert Graves and Siegfried Sassoon, and the common tendency to view the experience of the First World War through the medium of literature rather than history, the religious impact of the First World War upon the British soldier has often been seen in terms of a loss of religious faith.[32] As Richard Schweitzer has pointed out, this model neatly correlates with a powerful 'modernist' interpretation of the First World War which stresses the dramatic and far-reaching cultural changes that the war effected in British and European society.[33] However, and as Jay Winter argued in his seminal study of private and public mourning in Europe after the First World War, this 'modernist' model is manifestly inadequate, not least because of its failure to take into account the tremendous resilience and adaptability of traditional cultural forms.[34] Crucially, the experience of the First World War does not seem to have had an immediate and negative impact on public religious observance in Britain; indeed, the 1920s appear to have seen a modest increase rather than a decline in the number of the nation's church members and churchgoers.[35] Similarly, the religious experience of British soldiers in the First World War cannot be characterised in terms of an overall loss of faith. In his studies of religious faith and doubt among British soldiers on the Western Front, Schweitzer developed a more flexible 'spectrum model' as a better means of comprehending the range of religious attitudes that existed among his subjects and also of appreciating the movement of individuals from one religious viewpoint to another over the period of the war.[36] However, Schweitzer's own model, in placing 'true believers and pure atheists' at opposite ends of a shifting spectrum of faith,[37] does not do justice to the deeply complex and even paradoxical nature of individual religious faith and practice and nor does it take into account the various meanings which contemporaries attached to the condition of being religious. As Callum Brown has emphasised, nineteenth-century Protestantism encouraged the view that to be religious meant 'to be teetotal, thrifty, churchgoing, respectable [and] "saved"', quite apart from being simply 'a believer in God'. Conversely, to be irreligious meant to be 'drunk, spendthrift, unchurched, "rough", unconverted or a non-believer'.[38] Significantly, *The Army and Religion* report, which was very much informed by these assumptions, was not so much concerned by the low incidence of atheism among soldiers but by other obstacles and solvents to religiosity and how they might be overcome. Similarly, while Charles Plater's *Catholic Soldiers* report failed to discover any widespread loss of faith it too was concerned at the morally corrupting aspects of army life and by their possible implications for the post-war years.[39]

Inevitably, there were those soldiers who not only questioned but ultimately lost their faith in the Christian vision of a loving and merciful God as a result of their experiences in the First World War. Fifty years after the event, Private C. Bartram of the 94th Trench Mortar Battery spelt out his reaction to the tragic slaughter of 1 July 1916 in the following terms: 'From that moment all my religion died. All my teaching and beliefs in God had left me, never to return.'[40] Likewise, for Private W.H.A. Groom of the 1/5th London Regiment (London Rifle Brigade) the experience of an attack at Passchendaele in 1917 had a devastating effect on his belief in the integrity of the Church:

> Where, oh where, was God in this earth covered ossuary, this mud swamp receptacle for the bones of the dead? It was I suppose for me the moment of truth . . . Now on this day, with this traumatic experience, my belief in a Church which condoned killing faded away. I would not again voluntarily attend or take part in the communion or other church services and rightly or wrongly that was that.[41]

However, and to offset these examples, there are many others which illustrate that the perennial problem of evil was not necessarily resolved by a rejection of belief in God or by the dismissal of an apparently discredited Church. The chaplains who informed the *Catholic Soldiers* report were unanimous that adequate religious instruction had ensured that the horrors of war had not widely shaken the faith of Roman Catholics. Although one of their number conceded that discussions on 'God's power and the war' and 'the problem of pain' were endemic in the army, another insisted: 'Our men are not puzzled as non-Catholics are by God's allowing war. They understand it is a consequence of sin, of free-will badly used.'[42] Another soldier of the 1/5th London Regiment, Private Norman Demuth, came to a similar conclusion through his own reflections on the subject. As Demuth remembered:

> Sitting in the front line on a firing step it was very uncomfortable, nothing to do and not very much to talk about. [It] made one sit and think much more deeply than one would have done otherwise . . . I used to sit and think quite deeply about God and I felt perfectly certain that . . . he existed you see and one very often felt something behind one. And I suppose the philosophy was this, that after all . . . it was a very nice world to live in, if we choose to muck it up that's our fault.[43]

What seems to have concerned chaplains and religious observers far more than the problem of soldiers losing their faith was the generally coarsening and brutalising nature of army life in an age of mass mobilisation and industrialised slaughter. On the lesser end of the scale, during the First World War religious commentators voiced their concern at the difficulties faced by many soldiers who tried to pray by their bedsides before lights-out.[44] More seriously, and although E.C. Crosse maintained that a chaplain 'didn't have to worry his head about atheism or agnosticism', he did admit to being deeply troubled by the seedier aspects of life among front-line soldiers. As Crosse lamented:

> The most obvious failing of a soldier was his language. To say the very least of this it was hideous, monotonous and futile. It was not a case of swearing when things went wrong. It was the addition of ugly words to all ordinary conversation which grew so irritating.

Although Crosse could derive some comfort from the fact that sexual incontinence was limited by a sheer lack of opportunity, he found:

> One of the most annoying offences of the war, which no routine orders succeeded in checking to any great extent, and of which the padre necessarily met a good deal, was the looting of the dead . . . nothing one could do seemed able to stop the practice.[45]

Gambling on a large scale was technically prohibited by army regulations but *The Army and Religion* report noted that this particular vice was still 'very prevalent throughout the Army'.[46] Consequently, one Anglican chaplain even devoted half of his published 'Hints to Chaplains' to arguments which could be usefully employed against this 'craving to be everlastingly making more and more money, instead of being content to do a thing for its own sake and be paid for your pains'.[47] Besides gambling, the vaunted generosity and selflessness of the common soldier was belied by a high incidence of petty theft. As Tom Pym said of the vagaries of soldiers' morality:

> A battalion goes over the parapet to the attack leaving packs behind. Another battalion comes up into the same trench in reserve, and, while waiting, rifle the other men's packs, razors being in chief demand. Later in the same engagement the men fight desperately in relief of the very people whose razors have come so strangely into their possession.[48]

The callousness engendered by the war could, of course, take more alarming forms. The war correspondent Philip Gibbs remembered one conversation with a Bantam soldier on the Somme in 1916:

> With ironical laughter, outrageous blasphemy, grotesque imagery, he described the suffering of himself and his mates under barrage fire which smashed many of them into bleeding pulp. He had no use for this war [but] he had no liking for the Germans, and desired to cut them into small bits, to slit their throats, to disembowel them . . . 'Oh,' said that five foot hero, 'there will be a lot of murder after this bloody war. What's human life? What's the value of one man's throat? We're trained up as murderers – I don't dislike it, mind you – and after the war we shan't get out of the habit of it. It'll come nat'ral like!'[49]

If Gibbs was disturbed by this blood-curdling diatribe, as a chaplain William Drury was deeply unsettled by the behaviour of an NCO on the Somme who proved to be the self-appointed custodian of what Drury described as 'a ghastly chamber of horrors in Favière Wood':

> It was an underground tunnel in which thirty or forty dead Germans had been lying for the last two months. This man took a morbid pleasure in his gruesome exhibition. He would stop to comb the hair of one of the corpses. I mention this as a characteristic of a certain ghoulish humour that showed itself sometimes . . . It was an ugly development of that indifference to the horrible and light-heartedness in face of death which were necessary and not unhealthy safeguards of sanity.[50]

Obviously, all of this behaviour was distinctly at odds with what contemporaries associated with the norms of a religious life and its implications for those who came from a religious background in civilian life were all too apparent. We have already noted the brutalising effects of war on many army chaplains but it is clear that this process was not simply confined to members of the clergy. As Burgon Bickersteth wrote to his mother from a machine-gun training school in 1916: 'Under real conditions there must be great satisfaction in hearing the rattle of one's guns and seeing Boches falling, even though in cold blood it could hardly be called an edifying occupation for a respectable Christian.'[51] Undoubtedly, it was this sense of respectability, this key dimension of religiosity, which appears to have been most undermined by the First World War. Stories of otherwise devout and dependable men being led astray in the context of the war are legion and the *Catholic Soldiers* report even devoted a whole chapter to the subject, deploring in particular the evils that flourished in base areas in France.[52] Among Protestants, the evidence was no less depressing. Despite the religious character and susceptibilities of the original 36th (Ulster) Division, Frank Crozier, who commanded the 9th Royal Irish Rifles in 1915–16, admitted that 'The sex question played a large part in my training syllabus of both officers and men'. This policy was largely dictated by the situation and attitudes of the battalion:

> By June, 1915, we were away from Ireland . . . The times were abnormal. Who could tell, might not they all be 'pushing up the daisies' in some foreign field shortly? Why not have a fling and enjoy the pleasures of sexual intercourse while the chance was there?[53]

Similarly, on the Somme in 1916, the chaplain of the 16th King's Royal Rifle Corps (Church Lads' Brigade) was able to locate the battalion's trenches simply by the language that emanated from them:

> I knew where you all were. I couldn't see you but I knew where you were from the language that was coming up. I knew it was the Church Lads' Brigade and I've never heard anything like it in all my life.[54]

The moral decline of former theological students was emblematic of this broader tendency. Bernard Martin, for example, remembered his shock at being ordered to participate in a gas attack at Ypres by an officer named Hardy, particularly as Hardy had at the same time invoked the Mosaic principle of 'an eye for an eye and a tooth for a tooth'. In the event, Hardy transpired to be a clergyman's son who had been studying at 'a parson-factory' in Cambridge prior to the war. When asked by Martin whether he would return to his studies, Hardy simply replied 'disillusioned'.[55] Again, Frank Richards remembered the fate of a theological student who joined the 2nd Royal Welch Fusiliers in 1917:

> A dozen new signallers joined us . . . One of them was a bit religious and told me that he had been studying for the ministry but had joined up at his country's call. I told him that if he was lucky enough to be still alive and with the Battalion in four months time his language would be the same as mine . . . In three months

he was the only one left out of the twelve, and by that time, which was a month less than I had said, nobody would have thought who came in contact with him that he had ever studied for the ministry. His bad language won universal approval and he also became highly proficient in drinking a bottle of ving blong . . . He was killed in December on Passchendaele Ridge.[56]

In addition to the debilitating effects of alcohol, swearing, gambling, petty theft, illicit sex and mass slaughter, many contemporaries were also keenly concerned about the prospects for the Sabbath once peace returned. After decrying the pernicious effects of the army's traditional rum ration, one Presbyterian chaplain confessed his fears for the future of the Scottish Sunday in 1917:

> Sunday doesn't exist in the army. A chaplain holds his services any time and anywhere he can get them, and, speaking person-ally, I have had more services on week-days than on Sundays. What effect will three years of such life have on the Scottish Church? We are proud of our good traditions of church attend-ance. But for three years now Sunday has been only one of the seven days in the week, and little else.[57]

Likewise, at least one Roman Catholic chaplain was also aware that Sundays had not been honoured as in civilian life and he was also very conscious of the fact that, for several years, British Catholics had been exposed to the often poor example of their French co-religionists:

> They have been in countries where people were Catholics in name only. They have been so circumstanced for so long that they have not been able to practise their religious duties regu-larly, and have in consequence come to regard the obligation as less binding: and there is a great danger that they will retain the same tendency at home.[58]

In the event, later pundits had no hesitation in attributing the rise of a more leisure-oriented Sunday (and the corresponding decline of what the 'Radio Padre' described as 'The stuffy, dull Sunday of the so-called "Puritan" and "Victorian" days') to mass military service in the First World War.[59] As John Drewett intoned in 1942: 'The attitude to Sunday has been markedly different since the last war. Continental travel and the effect of the several years which many men passed on the Continent during the war have left their mark.'[60]

Besides the question of Sabbath day observance, a broader problem with army life was that erosion of denominational loyalties which it frequently entailed. As we have already seen, many recruits saw fit to switch their denominational allegiance upon joining the army but the weakness of denominational ties was apparent even among those who remained steadfast. As one Scottish hut worker testified in 1917:

> I am convinced that the vast majority of genuine Anglicans in the army would never dream that it was unseemly for, let us say, a Presbyterian to share with them in their celebration; or that they were committing mortal sin in participating in a celebration according to the Scottish usage.[61]

If these sentiments could be interpreted as indicative of a popular and practical ecumenism which put the churches to shame, some chaplains were intimidated by their sheer prevalence and by their negative implications. In a report written by a Scottish Episcopalian chaplain for an interdenominational conference of chaplains during the First World War, the author admitted:

> As for our devout men: 99 per cent of them regard it as a virtue that they 'don't care where they go as long as they get a good sermon' and their Faith is proportionately nebulous and their esprit-de-corps to correspond.[62]

Interestingly, these debilitating tendencies were not only apparent among the Christian churches. Despite Michael Adler's positive appraisals of the wartime experiences of British Jewry, at least one Jewish chaplain was aware of how military service had eroded the religious standards of many Jewish soldiers. As Arthur Barnett wrote in the *Jewish Chronicle* in February 1919:

> Generally speaking, I believe the effect of war on the Jewish soldier will have been to make him less Jewish in life and outlook. Men who before had lived a fairly Jewish life, will now, after those years of de-Judaising tendencies and influences, find it difficult to recover their faded Jewish consciousness. Army life has produced a sort of Jewish anaesthesia.

As an illustration of this process, Barnett cited a recent experience of his own:

> I have had a good deal to do . . . with certain Labour Units consisting for the most part of [Russian-born] Jews, the majority

of whom come from the East End of London . . . In one of these companies, where the Jews are about 500 strong, they were getting an issue of bacon and pork in their daily rations. I therefore applied to the Army Headquarters for some substitute to be provided, and the request was immediately granted. Imagine my surprise and disgust upon my next visit to their camp at hearing from their Commanding Officer that the men had protested in large bodies and practically threatened to refuse work unless the bacon ration was restored for their breakfast . . . The only reply I received upon remonstrating with them was: 'It's not so bad when you get used to it!'[63]

With respect to the influence of war on religious life between 1939 and 1945, MO surveys repeatedly demonstrated that the impact of war had the net result of strengthening rather than weakening belief in God, a phenomenon that was especially marked among service personnel.[64] As one survey of January 1943 summarised the situation:

[A]mong all the samples studied, never more than a tiny proportion of 1–4% say they have *lost* their faith. In general the effect of war has been to confirm pre-existing attitudes, to strengthen faith where it existed before, but also to confirm and strengthen attitudes of scepticism, agnosticism and indifference.[65]

However, and as in the circumstances of 1914–18, there were inevitably those who questioned their belief in a loving and merciful God. As Spike Milligan remembered of an advanced dressing station in Italy in 1943:

Three jeeps arrived with stretcher cases. Among them is a German, his face almost off. Poor bastard. There was a trickle of wounded all afternoon, some walking, some on stretchers, some dead, the priest went among them carrying out the last rites. Was this the way Christ wanted them to go? The most depressing picture of the war was for me the blanket-covered bodies on stretchers, their boots protruding from the end.[66]

A month later, Milligan declined the opportunity to receive the sacraments:

A Catholic priest visited us this evening and asked if anyone wanted Confession and Holy Communion. I nearly went but since the war started, my belief in God had suffered a reverse. I couldn't equate all the killing by two sides, both of whom claimed to be a Christian society. I was, as Gary Cooper would say, 'kinda mixed up inside'.[67]

If Milligan was liable to misconstrue the Christian character of Nazi Germany, others did not react in the same way to comparable experiences. War liberalised the straight-laced, Prayer Book Anglicanism of Lavinia Orde, an officer in the ATS, but it by no means undermined the basic tenets of her Christian faith. In fact, the site of an air crash in England seemed only to confirm them:

> [T]here was practically nothing left of the two pilots . . . I left thanking God that we had souls and not only bodies to end up like that. If it is true that one only dies when the pattern of one's life is ended, that death is not a tragic misadventure but a final culmination of the point of life, it's so difficult to understand why the point should have come so early in these young men's lives. I suppose they had the job in life of dying for civilisation now, and we should all prepare for that and be glad we might be chosen.[68]

Even reactions to Belsen could affirm the value of faith and religious identity. As a Methodist chaplain of the 15th (Scottish) Division remembered, the sight of the camp filled his CO with righteous indignation: 'Now, Padre, tell me where there are any Christians in Germany.'[69] Similarly, and according to Harry Levy, the senior Jewish chaplain of the British Second Army, Jewish soldiers who witnessed the condition of the camp's inmates after liberation felt a strengthening of their Jewish identity 'because these were our brothers'. Indeed, having been under the impression that all Jews had been exterminated, it was inspiring to find 'hundreds who had survived . . . [because] you had a feeling . . . Israel lives'.[70]

Despite being weakened by the First World War, the mores of Victorian religiosity clearly remained deeply entrenched in British Christianity twenty years later and renewed war once again saw the erosion of pre-war religious values rather than a widespread slide into atheism. Predictably enough, the problem of soldiers praying by their bedsides once again emerged, a problem which was possibly exacerbated by the length of time that many soldiers spent kicking their heels in camps and barracks in Great Britain. If one soldier remembered how 'heroes who knelt by their beds' had been deterred from this practice after being 'showered with boots',[71] Charlie Wakeley experienced a different kind of 'hero' at Whittington Barracks in 1940:

[T]here were thirty or forty of us . . . rough and ready blokes, ex-drunkards, ex-boxers and gentlemen . . . In the next bed to me there was a chap who'd come from Stourbridge [and] his name was Jack Bessey and I always admired the man . . . It was night time the first night in the barracks and he got down at the foot of his bed and knelt down and said his prayers. And you got one or two jeering, 'Gerrup!' and all that sort of thing . . . and every night in that barracks for six weeks Jack Bessey said his prayers and eventually the people admired him that much that all the barracking finished and when Jack used to get down there you could see one or two more get down and say their prayers.[72]

Notwithstanding Bessey's example, hitherto pious men did succumb to the generally lower tone of army life. As a MO survey of 1943 noted:

Reports have shown many cases of people who in 'civvy' street were fairly keen church-goers, and now keep very little connection at all. Many of these people were members of a church dance band, leading lights in the tennis club, regular attenders at the social club, etc. One man, who now goes nowhere near a church, avoids church parades whenever he can [and] swears like a trooper, was the vigorous leader of a Boys Brigade group before joining up – and intends to go back to it after the war![73]

Spike Milligan gleefully traced the spectacular fall from grace of one Bombardier MacDonald, a Jehovah's Witness with whom he shared a hut in England:

Like most fanatics, [MacDonald] didn't enjoy religion, he suffered from it. Every weekend we'd find his pamphlets on our beds. A terrible end they came to. But the pressure was too much and gradually MacDonald became less and less religious: he started drinking and swearing ('I tell you the bloody day is at hand'). The end of the holy man came one revealing night. And it came to pass that Gunner James Devine was on mid-night guard when he was awakened by a rhythmic thumping from the back of the coal shed. Investigation showed Bombardier MacDonald, his trousers round his ankles, having a late-night knee-trembler . . .[74]

If another World War exposed a large part of a second generation of church members and churchgoers to military life in all its coarseness, it also had its brutalising effects on the front-line soldiers among them. As Ken Tout remembered, a fellow trooper who was known as 'a strict Baptist' went on the rampage with other soldiers of the 1st Northamptonshire Yeomanry in a German town early in 1945. Somewhat the worse for drink, and seeing a china shop still standing amidst the ruins, the group systematically destroyed all of its remaining stock, a vengeful culmination of 'months of bitter fighting, frustration, loss of friends, wounding [and] freezing'.[75] Although hardly comparable with the mass rape and pillaging that attended the Red Army's advance into Germany at about the same time, this incident nevertheless serves as a clear example of how the moral constraints of civilian religious life could be dramatically loosened under the conditions of active service.

Conclusion

Britain's historic Christian culture influenced the moral conduct of the two World Wars at a personal and even at a tactical level while also modulating perceptions of the enemy. However, it also suffered in the process. Contrary to popular myth, comparatively few British soldiers found themselves faced with insuperable theological problems as a result of either war. From the perspective of the churches, the problem of those who lost their faith paled in comparison with the fact that mass military service entailed a perceptible and widespread deterioration of pre-war moral and therefore religious standards. Given the perennial moral hazards of army life and the brutalising influence of modern war on those who experienced its effects, accepted models of religiosity inherited from civilian life were subjected to enormous strain and significant erosion, a situation that seems to have hastened the slow retreat from the puritanical standards of the Victorian era in British religious life.

Chapter 6

THE ARMY AND RELIGIOUS PHILANTHROPY

Introduction

IN BOTH WORLD WARS, the huge growth in the number of commissioned army chaplains was paralleled by a massive expansion in civilian
religious work among soldiers, an expansion which amounted to the mobilisation of what Callum Brown has described as the nation's 'salvation industry'.
On both occasions, this mobilisation was driven by two convergent currents
in British religious life. First, there was the ubiquity of the churches' social
and missionary work in civilian society, and particularly in working-class areas
of Britain's towns and cities. Many of the civilian religious organisations which
soldiers encountered while in the army were organisations that were already
familiar to them from civilian life – organisations such as the YMCA and
YWCA, the Salvation Army, the Church Army and (in the Second World
War) Toc H. The second of these convergent currents was the social and
missionary work that civilian religious organisations had sponsored among
the rank and file of the regular army and its reserve forces since the 1860s.
Coming after more than half a century of heavily publicised religious work
among soldiers, the outbreak of war in 1914 and the dramatic expansion of
the British army thereafter prompted massive expansion in this existing field
of church work, the hitherto distinct spheres of civilian and military religious
work converging and fusing with the advent of a mass citizen army. The
motives of civilian religious work among soldiers and civilians had always

been somewhat mixed, representing (to various degrees among its many practitioners) a conflation of missionary, paternalistic, philanthropic, prudential and patriotic concerns. Driving and informing much of this religious work during the First World War was the general conviction that the conflict represented a unique opportunity to influence an entire generation of British men during a highly impressionable period of their lives. If this conviction was less in evidence during the Second World War, what is impressive about both World Wars was the sheer scale and diversity of civilian religious work among soldiers. In both conflicts, the British churches and British Jewry addressed the spiritual, physical and mental needs of millions of British soldiers through activities that ranged from the distribution of religious literature to the provision of convalescent homes and cinema shows. Although the extent and variety of this work precludes an exhaustive treatment of this subject, it is at least possible to address some of the main areas of civilian activity and to assess their impact upon the army as a whole.

Clubs, canteens and centres

The convergence of religious work among soldiers and civilians from August 1914 was clearly illustrated by the extent to which individual parishes and congregations at home were ineluctably drawn into ministering to soldiers. The enormous expansion of the army in 1914–15 led to acute problems in providing suitable accommodation for Kitchener's multitudinous volunteers, a problem which was tackled by the hasty construction of vast new training camps and by the expedient of billeting soldiers upon civilians.[1] The gradual confinement of the regular army to its barracks during the nineteenth century had led to the practical elimination of billeting as a normal practice and had also meant that the practical problems associated with large numbers of young men cut adrift from the restraining influences of home had largely been confined to garrison towns. However, the expansion of the army from the late summer of 1914 meant that these problems became far more common and civilian fears of widespread drunkenness and sexual promiscuity were no doubt instrumental in securing a robust response from the churches. In these circumstances, church-run soldiers' clubs proliferated; by 1916, the Wesleyans alone were claiming to have opened at least 400 clubs since the war began.[2] Faced with similar problems of entertaining troops overseas, even British missionaries adapted their work to present circumstances. In Alexandria, for example, it was observed in 1917 that the Church of Scotland's missionary to the Jews of the city had, along with his wife, 'thrown themselves wholeheartedly into the work among soldiers':

The hall under the church . . . has been transformed into an attractive Soldiers' Rest and Refreshment Room, with facilities for reading, writing, games, and music [and] Dr Mackie said congregational work was largely in abeyance. We found him visiting in the hospital. This work had the first call upon his service, because, as he strikingly put it, Great Britain is to-day identical with the Kingdom of God. Anything done to heighten the efficiency of her fighting men, and to promote the success of her enterprise, is, at present, the most direct service that can be rendered to the Kingdom of God.[3]

This host of local initiatives at home and overseas supplemented the work of larger religious organisations. Some of these, such as the YMCA and Elise Sandes' soldiers' homes, were already very experienced in army work while others, such as the Catholic Women's League, were relative newcomers to the field. However, some of these newer organisations proved more adaptable to wartime conditions than did their more established counterparts. As static institutions situated in imperial camps and garrisons well away from the principal theatres of a prolonged war, the impressive if varied network of late Victorian and Edwardian soldiers' homes was not well placed to deal with the demands of the new situation. In the light of this fact, it was no doubt sobering for the Wesleyan Conference of 1915 to learn that its Army and Navy Board was maintaining thirty-nine homes, at a cost of over £150,000 per annum, in home and imperial stations that were, in many cases, rapidly becoming backwaters.[4] While the Wesleyans busied themselves in creating a new generation of temporary soldiers' homes (of which there were twenty-seven by 1916)[5] it is significant to note that some of the male assistants who had rallied to Elise Sandes' evangelical soldiers' homes in Ireland in the first busy weeks of the war had followed the BEF to the continent by early 1915.[6] Quite apart from the problems attendant on their geographical location, the evangelical work of these homes had evolved around the quiet routines of garrison life in a comparatively small regular army and had been largely based on cultivating long-term relationships with individual soldiers. Naturally, the scale of expansion, disruption and mortality in the British army during the war years threw into relief the shortcomings of this approach and served to prove the veracity of Miss Sandes' opinion that 'peace and not war-time is the best opportunity to reach our sailors and soldiers'.[7]

As with the soldiers' homes, so too with the Army Scripture Readers' and Soldiers' Friend Society, another stalwart of the mid- and late-Victorian mission to soldiers. At its peak during the First World War, the Society was able to field sixty-four full-time scripture readers who served under the direction of

Anglican army chaplains.[8] However, this represented a tiny contribution given the size of the AChD and also the millions of men who passed through the British army during the course of the war. The work of army scripture readers in the pre-war years had, like that of the soldiers' homes, generally been conducted within the settled routines of garrison life, with readers seeking to secure the conversion and development of younger soldiers through assiduous barrack-room visiting. Notwithstanding the advent of YMCA and other huts as an alternative sphere of operations, the circumstances of 1914–18 rendered this approach increasingly difficult.

Of all the civilian organisations which plunged into army work in 1914–18, none attained the size, prominence or level of organisational efficiency achieved by the YMCA. Although the profile and achievements of this avowedly inter-denominational organisation aroused suspicion among some churchmen (and even led to out-and-out rivalry between the Canadian Association and the chaplains of the Canadian Expeditionary Force),[9] relations between the British YMCA, the Protestant churches and their accredited chaplains were generally cordial. During the course of the war the chaplain-general, Bishop John Taylor Smith, gave his public blessing to the YMCA's 'increasing influence' and *The Army and Religion* report of 1919, while being compiled by an inter-denominational steering committee, was financed by the YMCA.[10] Given its experience of regular camp work with the pre-war Volunteers and Territorial Force, and also the work of the Soldiers' Christian Association (a YMCA auxiliary) in South Africa during the Boer War, the YMCA possessed the organisation, the equipment and the expertise to begin work among Britain's expanding army from a very early stage. According to Sir Arthur Yapp, the Association's dynamic national secretary and the principal architect of its wartime mission, the YMCA – or 'Red Triangle' as Yapp re-branded it in August 1914 – opened more than 250 recreational centres in Great Britain within ten days of the outbreak of war.[11] Indeed, the first YMCA secretaries to serve with the BEF arrived in France long before they had received official permission for their work from the War Office.[12]

Confined to the bases and lines of communication in France until the summer of 1915, the YMCA developed an impressive infrastructure of more than 300 centres in camps, hospitals and railway stations. Furthermore, and following its admission to army areas in June 1915, the Association established additional centres closer to the front line and opened its first hostel for the use of relatives visiting dangerously sick or wounded soldiers.[13] When the WAAC was formed in 1917, the YMCA, in conjunction with its sister organisation, the YWCA, opened yet more centres for the benefit of female personnel.[14] In addition to its welfare work, through its Universities Committee (which comprised 'official representatives of all the Universities of

Great Britain') the YMCA became a major provider of adult education for soldiers. In 1918, an official report by the Ministry of Reconstruction's Adult Education Committee noted that, 'throughout the war' and 'under the most difficult conditions' the YMCA had:

> organised lectures and classes among the troops, [to] a greater extent in France and other theatres of war than at home. In addition to its permanent workers a large number of lecturers have visited camps abroad for short periods. In many Y.M.C.A. centres the work has developed beyond the provision of lectures, Classes and study circles have been formed, and the necessary books supplied.[15]

However, the YMCA also eventually acquired a front-line role. By 1917, YMCA centres were being opened near dressing stations and casualty clearing stations on the Western Front and, in the summer of that year, the Association even earned for itself a modest place in the planning of a full-scale British offensive. Prior to the capture of Messines ridge in June 1917, the YMCA and the RAMC arranged for thirty-four temporary centres to be opened near the dressing stations of the attacking divisions so that every wounded man could be provided with food, a hot drink and a postcard that was to be sent to his family.[16] In addition to its work in France and Belgium, the British YMCA was also well represented in the other theatres of war, including Italy, Gallipoli, Salonika, Palestine, East Africa and Mesopotamia. Its representatives even accompanied British forces to north Russia in the wake of the Bolshevik Revolution.[17]

In addition to meeting the enormous financial costs of this vast operation, the YMCA was faced with the formidable task of finding workers for its vineyard. On the Western Front alone, the number of YMCA personnel came to average around 1,500, with numbers occasionally rising to as many as 1,750. Given the constraints of the war, its workers largely consisted of 'men of low medical category or over service age'[18] plus a smattering of female volunteers, their presence representing something of a revolution in an organisation that had hitherto cherished its exclusively male identity.[19] The patriotic and inter-denominational nature of the YMCA's work proved a great draw for many liberal-minded Free Church clergymen who were unable or disinclined to take a chaplain's commission. Indeed, one Wesleyan missionary in India even defied his superiors in London in order to serve a six-month stint with the YMCA in Mesopotamia.[20] During the period of the war, approximately 260 Free Church ministers served overseas as YMCA volunteers, with a further 167 serving at centres in the British Isles.[21]

YMCA centres came in many shapes and sizes, ranging from dugouts in the Ypres salient to purpose-built huts and large marquees in camps, bases and rear areas. However, and whatever the shape of its centres, the YMCA was firmly committed to Christian service in its broadest sense. As one Presbyterian chaplain wrote of the YMCA in Mesopotamia in 1917:

> There was no limit to their beneficent activities. They were there to promote the physical, moral, social, and spiritual well-being of the soldiers; and as far as the interests of the lads were concerned, it may truly be said that 'nothing was alien to them'.

As a result of this, YMCA activities in Mesopotamia (as elsewhere) included the provision of canteens, the organisation of sporting activities, the supply of reading and writing materials and the staging of lectures, concerts and cinema shows.[22] Within this broad remit, the YMCA also sought to influence its many clients in a spiritual sense, its stated purpose being (in the British context at least) not to act as a competitor but as 'an auxiliary to the Churches' by turning soldiers into more committed members of their own denominations.[23] As a YMCA handbook for its workers put it:

> No attempt to detach men from their respective allegiance is sanctioned or authorised. Rather, every encouragement must be given to them to persevere and develop in their allegiance. It is contrary to the whole purpose of the YMCA that the Association should become a substitute for the worship and corporate life of any Church or denomination.[24]

During the war years, this desire to demonstrate its good faith towards the churches was demonstrated by the Association's 'War Roll pledge of allegiance to our Lord Jesus Christ' (a scheme whereby soldiers pledged their Christian commitment for the future)[25] and also by its willingness to provide accommodation for denominational worship, a policy that was even adopted in relation to Roman Catholics and Jews.[26] In fact, it was indicative of the sheer breadth of vision of the Association during the war that it even acquired a Jewish branch in the form of the Jewish Naval and Military Association which ran its own 'temporary rest house' and canteen in central London. Such was Jewish appreciation of 'the liberal spirit' of the YMCA that one of its huts was paid for by subscriptions raised at the Central Synagogue in London.[27]

Besides the ubiquitous and wide-ranging work of the YMCA, there was also that of denominational organisations such as the Salvation Army, the Church Army, the Catholic Women's League and the Scottish Churches Huts

Joint Committee. Of these organisations, the Salvation Army was the first to make its presence felt on the Western Front, dispatching an advance party to Brussels in August 1914. Although this vanguard was forced to beat a hasty retreat in the path of the German advance through Belgium and northern France, by the end of the war there were some forty Salvation Army centres – 'temples of rest and refreshment for body and soul' – in this theatre of war. These were part of a larger Salvation Army presence on the Western Front which also included a fleet of motor ambulances and a hospital visitation service.[28] With the significant exception of the Salvation Army, the work of these denominational organisations seems to have been primarily geared towards meeting the specific needs of their own denominations. The Catholic Women's League, for example, maintained: 'The first object of a Catholic Soldiers' Recreation Hut is to bring Catholic Soldiers into touch with one another in a Catholic atmosphere, and to give them facilities to practise their religion.'[29] By the end of the war, the CWL had opened twenty-six huts in France, each equipped with a chaplain's room and each providing opportunities for daily Mass and other devotions.[30] Comparable to the nature and scale of Catholic organisation was that of the Church of Scotland and Scotland's United Free Church, whose combined efforts at home were extended to France in 1916 under the auspices of the Scottish Churches Huts Joint Committee. Although they also offered opportunities for recreation, like their Catholic counterparts these facilities were primarily geared towards buttressing the faith of their Presbyterian constituency. As a description of worship in one of these centres was careful to emphasise, 'the canvas shook with the singing of the Scottish Psalms', after which a communion service was held and 'about twenty soldiers were received into the fellowship of the Church for the first time'.[31] It was in one of these devotional centres – the Scottish Churches Hut at Montreuil, which doubled as the St Andrews Soldiers Club during the week – that Haig was to derive that 'spirit of peace combined with high resolve' which he found so essential as commander-in-chief of the BEF.[32] By the end of the war, the Scottish Churches Huts Joint Committee was responsible for thirty-four centres and more than 300 workers in France alone.[33]

However, the Church of England's Church Army represented the major denominational rival to the YMCA, claiming 800 centres in operation by March 1917 and over 1,100 by the end of the war.[34] In common with Scottish Presbyterian and CWL activities, Church Army work was firmly subordinated to the direction of army chaplains and responsibility for Church Army work on the Western Front eventually came to lie with Bishop Gwynne.[35] Like the YMCA, the Church Army was partly reliant on a limited pool of clerical volunteers, with those going abroad being expected to serve six months and those serving at home being required to serve for three.[36] Although there was a shortage of clerical volunteers by the autumn of 1917,[37] by January 1918 no fewer than 292 Anglican clergymen had served with the Church Army and a further eighty-five were still working under its aegis.[38] If the sheer size of the nominal constituency of the Church of England blurred the distinction between general evangelistic work among soldiers and work among men of a particular denomination, the question of Anglican prestige certainly placed a special onus on the scale and quality of Church Army work. As Gwynne told Archbishop Davidson in March 1916, the quality of its endeavours over previous months had given cause for concern and the organisation was now faced with intense competition from its rivals. This competition, if not at least matched, would cause the military authorities to 'think less of the Church of England'.[39] Considerations of this kind appear to have weighed heavily for the rest of the war. In March 1917, and in the wake of the German withdrawal to the Hindenburg Line, the Church Army was compelled to make an unexpected appeal for additional funds, one hundred new tents being required to colonise those areas evacuated by the Germans. As the appeal stated:

> Many huts will also now have to be moved nearer the troops. Only those who have seen the men toiling through the mud from the trenches and the open can realise the priceless boon of these cheery 'Homes from Home'. Keen men unsuitable for military duty are only too eager to man the Tents, which cost £200, equip-ment £100. More huts are still needed, now costing £400 . . . £100,000 more will be required very shortly if the Church is to keep [being] represented near the firing line.[40]

Ironically, this policy of being 'represented near the firing line' caused the Church Army problems of its own, especially in the wake of the German spring offensive of 1918. Within a fortnight of the commencement of this onslaught, the Church Army had lost 'at least 55 huts and tents on the Western Front', a significant loss of assets also being incurred by the YMCA.[41]

The massive efforts of the churches' civilian agencies placed acute pressure on their financial resources. Indeed, one of the main reasons for the belated commencement of the Scottish churches' work on the Western Front was a chronic lack of funds.[42] For the Church Army, the costs of bearing the Church of England's share of this work ran to £240,000 in the second year of the war and by 1918 this annual expenditure had risen to around £400,000.[43] Although the YMCA defrayed a substantial amount of its costs through the sale of refreshments and merchandise, the net cost of its work during the

First World War was eventually estimated at a staggering £8,000,000.[44] Furthermore, these organisations inevitably worked in indirect and financially unprofitable competition with each other and also with the army's own regimental institutes and Expeditionary Force canteens. By the end of the war, the degree of competition from the latter can be gauged by the fact that the Expeditionary Force Canteen Committee was running 295 canteens on the Western Front and had shipped goods worth more than £20,000,000 to its overseas depots in the previous eleven months.[45]

What, then, were the fruits of this vast, varied and expensive endeavour on the part of the YMCA and other church organisations, an endeavour which was hailed at the time as being without precedent in the annals of European warfare?[46] In terms of military morale, the churches were undoubtedly indispensable contributors to 'that great welfare network' of canteens and other facilities that buttressed the morale of the British army throughout the bloodiest trial in its history.[47] Sir John French, the commander-in-chief of the BEF from August 1914 to December 1915, said of the work of the YMCA and kindred organisations: 'The old soldiers of the past were splendid, but they certainly never surpassed the splendid courage shown in this war, and one cannot help thinking that perhaps it is to be traced to the work of these institutions.'[48] Certainly, it is worth noting that the French army had no equivalent of this ubiquitous network of practical support, an important consideration given the mass mutinies it suffered in 1917. In moral terms, moreover, the proliferation of clubs, centres and canteens under the aegis of civilian religious agencies provided soldiers with safer and more wholesome opportunities for refreshment and recreation than they might find elsewhere, particularly in common brothels or in the army's *maisons de tolérance*. In more positively religious terms, soldiers could and did respond to the higher goals of these organisations. According to Salvation Army sources: 'In France alone over 20,000 soldiers sought salvation at the penitent-forms in the huts, etc.'[49] Similarly, the YMCA's War Roll pledge had attracted more than half a million signatories by the autumn of 1918.[50] However, it is impossible to tell how many of these military penitents and signatories were already seekers or committed Christians in civilian life and, as for the YMCA's War Roll pledge, even Yapp admitted that 'Many have no doubt forgotten their promise' even before the war was over.[51]

Whatever their missionary success may have been, the YMCA centres and their denominational equivalents were well frequented as providers of entertainment, refreshment and other creature comforts. Although more broadly patronised, they were naturally very much appreciated by soldiers of a more religious disposition. One Methodist soldier, a Sunday school teacher in civilian life, wrote from a YMCA centre at Great Yarmouth in April 1916:

The YMCA is crowded every night with chaps writing home . . .
it is a grand place and every body feels at home as much as is
possible under the circumstances . . . It is grand to come into a
place like this, everybody is welcome & the folks try their best
to make one feel homely. There is also a concert & games room
and about the middle of the evening a hymn is sung & a prayer
offered. It is an excellent institution.[52]

However, and despite such endorsements, hopes for a tangible religious
awakening among the great bulk of the army proved elusive. In December
1917, one Anglican chaplain noted in his diary:

Had cocoa and biscuits at a YMCA hut [at Vlamertinghe] and
talked to the elderly 'conductor' thereof . . . He confessed, in
answer to a question of mine, that as far as his experience went,
the spiritual work of the YMCA out here was practically nil. I
reassured him by saying that the 'cup of cold water' (to say nothing
of the hot cocoa which he gave me gratis, very kindly) would not
be forgotten on earth after the war and might be remembered in
Heaven.[53]

In the long term, this prognosis no doubt proved to be correct. If the
wartime labours of the churches clearly failed to effect the spiritual transformation of a generation of largely working-class soldiers (men who were,
in any case, well accustomed to taking advantage of the churches' social and
recreational offerings in civilian life) then they almost certainly added to a
reservoir of sympathy for organised Christianity among this same group.
Indeed, in view of the fact that the religiosity of the average Briton was
strongly ethical and practical in character, the efforts of these civilian organisations no doubt served as a concrete illustration of exemplary Christian
behaviour for many British soldiers, Yapp even proclaiming that this consideration lay at the heart of the YMCA's 'cup of cold water' missionary
strategy:

The British soldier hates a sham, and instinctively classes the
hypocrite with the Hun. He may not understand our Shibboleths;
he has no use for our controversies, but he can and does understand the Life of the Master, when he sees the beauty of that Life
reflected in some humble follower of His, who day by day is
risking his life at the Front, that he may supply a cup of cocoa
to a wounded soldier . . .[54]

However subtle and indirect their strategies were, the YMCA and its sister organisations certainly exposed their volunteers to enormous risks in pursuing their work. In June 1917, and only days after the capture of the village of Wytschaete near Ypres, Rowland Feilding was surprised to find that a Nonconformist minister had already established his YMCA canteen in the ruins of the village.[55] Similarly, Lieutenant Ulick Burke of the 2nd Devonshire Regiment drew some very favourable comparisons between the church-run canteens and those of the Expeditionary Force canteen service on the Western Front:

> Our own Expeditionary Force canteens as they called them were far back [behind the lines]. But the Salvation Army were well up. And what they call the Church Units. If [they] could find [a] place . . . they'd scrounge some wire netting from the battalions and a piece of wood to make beds . . . And you could always go in there and especially coming from the Front Line. Sometimes troops fell out, couldn't keep up. They were more exhausted than the others. You didn't wait for them because you knew damn well they'd find their way home. But on the way there they'd go into these places where they were given a rest and a hot cup of coffee and told exactly how much further they had to go, and that sort of thing. They were marvellous those people especially the Salvation Army.[56]

George Jameson, who served with the Northumberland Hussars on the Western Front, also singled out the Salvation Army for particular praise:

> One thing I think I'd give full marks to was the Salvation Army. Whenever there was a show they got up as close as they could . . . It was really a Mecca to find these places . . . I can remember one that I used to often drop into. And it was a most unhealthy spot to be in. It was at Vimy [and] was under constant shellfire and at night worse, you see. They reckoned that transport would use that road at night and would keep it under strafing the whole time. But tucked into the side of the hill down that road was the Salvation Army in a hole in the ground. And they used to have tea and whatever going all hours of the day. How they survived there I don't know. Wonderful people.[57]

E.C. Crosse, a particularly astute Anglican chaplain, observed shortly after the end of the war that one of the most subtle but significant indicators of the success of military chaplaincy was that the clergy seemed to be viewed in a more sympathetic light than they had been prior to 1914. As Crosse remarked: 'The title "Padre" has to some extent passed into civilian usage, and in general, wherever it is used, it carries with it a sympathetic connotation which is one of the assets of the war.'[58] Two decades later, the Church Army found that its fundraising efforts for the Second World War were greatly assisted by the appreciation of those who had benefited from its efforts in the First. As a record of the Church Army's work between 1939 and 1945 remarked:

> The work of the Church Army in 1914–1918 still brought its tributes . . . A man sent five shillings 'in appreciation of a welcome given and kindness shown at a Church Army dug-out near Shrapnel Corner, Ypres, during the last War'. And in 1943 a gift was accompanied by the following: 'This in remembrance of a special little bit of service to a few men, including myself, on the Somme at midnight in 1917.'[59]

One MO survey of September 1942 also found that the Salvation Army was still riding high in terms of public esteem and 'enjoying the credit for its good work' between 1914 and 1918.[60] Typical of the favourable remarks made about the Salvation Army was the view that 'it was very good in the last war' and the recollection:

> Wherever you found an S.A. place you knew you would be treated well. As a matter of fact I never thought much of them until I went to France in 1914, and since then I've always thought a lot of the Salvation Army.[61]

Despite the immense efforts of these civilian agencies, the most successful of the temporary soldiers' clubs, homes and institutes to emerge out of the First World War was a chaplain's club opened at Poperinghe in December 1915. The brainchild of Neville Talbot, then senior Anglican chaplain of the 6th Division, the purpose of Talbot House was to serve as 'a kind of Church hut' as close to the front line as possible.[62] Named after Talbot's younger brother, who had been killed near Ypres earlier that year, and widely known as 'Toc H' because of its initials in Morse code, Toc H provided recreational and devotional opportunities in a busy and somewhat tawdry town which was well within the range of heavy German guns. Permanently staffed by Philip ('Tubby') Clayton, who was nominally the garrison chaplain at Poperinghe, Toc H was established in premises rented from a Flemish brewer and was furnished through a successful combination of local foraging and donations from well-wishers in Great Britain.[63] Among the latter, Neville Talbot's father, Bishop E.S. Talbot of Winchester, dispatched 'some splendid old hangings' for its chapel which had once adorned the bishop's chapel at Southwark.[64] Besides the prominence accorded to its permanent chapel, one of the most distinctive features of Toc H was its strongly egalitarian ethos, an ethos reflected in its secondary designation, 'Everyman's Club', and one which was proclaimed by a notice that adorned the door of Clayton's room, 'ALL RANK ABANDON YE WHO ENTER HERE'.[65] In earnest of these sentiments, officers and other ranks mixed freely at Toc H, Clayton hosting tea parties and Sunday suppers which encouraged this practice.[66] It was, indeed, one of Clayton's boasts that the club operated 'on the Robin Hood principle of taking from the rich to give to the poor', only officers being obliged to pay for overnight accommodation.[67] This egalitarian ethos was reflected in the fittings of the chapel which, owing to its unusual location in a large hop loft, was duly christened 'The Upper Room'.[68] Besides those gifts sent from England, the chapel was furnished with a discarded carpenter's bench and with devotional items donated by soldiers themselves. Symbolically, the altar was left without a communion rail in order to emphasise 'the unity between ministrant and recipients'.[69]

In many respects, Toc H represented a curious amalgam of the classic Anglo-Catholic 'slum' mission and the typical pre-war soldiers' home. With regard to the former, its chapel offered the consoling beauty of holiness to soldiers who lived 'not only in danger but in squalor' amidst 'a foreground of filth' and against 'a horizon of apparently invincible menace'.[70] With respect to the latter, and notwithstanding the lack of a woman's touch, every appearance of domesticity was encouraged and to this Clayton ascribed a good measure of the club's popularity:

> The Englishman [he wrote], mainly town-bred, loves light, noise, warmth, overcrowding, and wall-paper, however faded . . . Our wall-paperdom, therefore, was half the secret of the drawing power of Talbot House. It was a house proper – not one large bare hall with a counter at one end and a curtain at the other, but a house, like home, with doors and windows and carpets and stairs and many small rooms, none of them locked . . . the place belonged to you in a home-like way, and relied on your being kind to it in return.[71]

Evidently, the formula proved as successful as it was original, with many thousands of soldiers making use of Toc H during the latter half of the war.

In the late summer of 1917, and at the peak of its activity during the Third Battle of Ypres, 'A test tally of ten minutes' duration . . . revealed the entry of 117 men'.[72]

Apart from its sacred and domestic character and its overtly egalitarian spirit, there were other reasons for the success of Toc H. 'Tubby' Clayton, who had worked extensively with young men as a curate prior to the war,[73] proved a popular and charismatic incumbent. According to William Drury, Clayton had a remarkable personal gift, namely 'the extraordinary power of making an unlimited number of friendships without losing individual interest in the case of any one of them'.[74] Indeed, one of Clayton's many admirers maintained that 'although the bricks and mortar might bear the name "Talbot House," the soul and spirit of the institution was and always will be Philip Clayton'.[75] Besides having a formidable asset in the person of Clayton, Toc H also enjoyed the patronage of some very senior officers. In January 1916, the Earl of Cavan, Clayton's cousin, was appointed corps commander in the area and Cavan was to prove a frequent and conspicuous visitor until his departure for Italy in November 1917.[76] Likewise, General Plumer, the longstanding commander of the Second Army in the Ypres sector, also sought solace in 'The Upper Room' whenever the opportunity arose.[77] Furthermore, Toc H played a significant part in promoting military morale in the last and crucial year of the war. As Clayton noted of the winter of 1917–18: 'An evil spirit for the first time troubled both officers and men; and in the inevitable stagnation the phantom of failure, ridiculed before, walked grimly abroad, and was not always challenged.'[78] Although this broader problem was at the same time being tackled on a higher level by Bishop Gwynne, Talbot sought some interim solutions. As he put it, rather than being soothed by 'a massage of entertainments and longer canteen hours', the thinking soldier – 'and in this Army such men were no negligible number' – needed 'light and leading' and consequently Toc H inaugurated

> a series of informal meetings called 'grousing circles,' to which a nucleus of trustworthy friends brought men with grievances, while a few splendidly helpful officers dropped in to listen and occasionally advise. These meetings were so manifestly good that, when reported to the Army Staff, they were not only sanctioned but several local troubles were quietly adjusted.[79]

If Toc H seems to have had a reputation for being immune from German shelling,[80] the wider importance of Toc H for morale in this notoriously difficult sector of the Western Front was underlined in April 1918. Upon being ordered to close his premises in view of the unfolding German spring offensive, Clayton refused to do so. Remarkably, his defiant stand was endorsed by a senior staff officer who stressed that 'the closing of an institution so well known as Toc H was in a real sense harmful to the general morale' of troops in the Ypres sector.[81]

Toc H gave rise to one of the most successful ex-servicemen's associations to emerge out of the war. Formally inaugurated in 1922, the Toc H movement was conceived as an inter-denominational Christian organisation dedicated to the ideal of 'Unselfish Service'.[82] Its growth was rapid (not least because it sought to perpetuate the unselfishness of the war years by recruiting among members of the younger generation)[83] but it failed to attract significant support from officers and soldiers of the regular army. Indeed, a divergence between the ethos of the citizen army of the First World War and the regular army of the post-war period was evident to 'Tubby' Clayton as early as 1919, when he wrote:

> The two variant attitudes of mind may be summarised in two sentences: the civilian soldier said: 'I don't mind the war so much, but I can't stick the Army'; the regular replied: 'When can we finish with this beastly war and get back to real soldiering?'[84]

Clearly, support for Toc H and its egalitarian brand of Christianity was strong in the former constituency and almost negligible in the latter. In fact, so little support was forthcoming from regular soldiers that, in January 1930, Tubby Clayton informed Plumer (who, since 1918, had become a field marshal, a peer of the realm and a leading supporter of the Toc H movement) that Toc H had, 'apart from a few senior officers and a few young guardsmen, no membership whatsoever in the present Army'. Very much aware of the military origins of the movement, Clayton complained that 'we are faced with the pathetic fact that the Army as a whole is ignorant of Toc H, and, if anything, rather averse to playing its part in what is rapidly becoming the biggest and most wholesome men's Society in the Empire'.[85] Plumer's subsequent intervention on this issue produced a circular from the Army Council which reminded serving officers and soldiers that membership of Toc H was not prejudicial to military discipline.[86] Nevertheless, the fruits of this memorandum proved disappointing, no doubt because the movement's ethos was still seen as being incompatible with the hierarchical sensibilities of the regular army, especially if it involved such improprieties as 'officers and private soldiers calling each other by their Christian names and slapping each other on the back'.[87] Significantly, it was only as the composition of the army began to change with the introduction of conscription in May 1939 that the friends of Toc H made their next high-level bid to reawaken interest in the movement. In July, the Army Council issued another circular which commended 'the objects of the [Toc H] movement to all soldiers and especially to the newly formed militia', that is to all those citizen soldiers so far conscripted.[88]

If the regular army proved stony ground for Toc H during the inter-war years, some of the more established purveyors of religion to the regular army also encountered problems after 1918. For the soldiers' homes in particular, the 1920s and 1930s were difficult years. Whereas the Wesleyan Methodists had run thirty-nine permanent soldiers' and sailors' homes across the empire in 1914, by 1940, the total number of permanent sailors', soldiers' and airmen's homes run by the recently unified Methodist church had fallen to twenty-five, whose cost amounted to less than two-thirds of the £150,000 required in 1914. Furthermore, whereas the Wesleyan homes could provide overnight accommodation for more than a thousand men in 1914, by 1940 this total had fallen to just 443.[89] Given that the Irish garrisons had always been at the centre of their work, the partition of Ireland in 1922 also dealt a devastating blow to Miss Sandes' soldiers' homes, with a dozen being closed or rededicated to work with the army of the Irish Free State.[90] Whereas Elise Sandes had presided over no fewer than thirty-one soldiers' homes in 1913, by the mid-1930s this number had fallen to nineteen.[91] Clearly, the inter-war period appears to have seen the overall decline of evangelical work within the army, a phenomenon which was related to the pacifism of the era as well as to the decline of the patriotic evangelical constituency which had always proved their mainstay. By 1938, the Army Scripture Readers and Soldier's Friend Society had only twenty-five full-time and twenty-two part-time readers, whereas at the peak of its work half a century earlier, no fewer than ninety-five readers had been employed by the Society.[92] By the late 1930s, amalgamation with the Soldiers' and Airmen's Christian Association seemed the only way forward, the amalgamation taking place in September 1938.[93] However, and as in the First World War, the newly created Army Scripture Readers and Soldiers' and Airmen's Christian Association was not ideally placed to capitalise on the expansion of the army from early 1939. Although the Association eventually opened several huts, thirty-five rest rooms and increased its number of readers to around 200 due to the recruitment of part-time volunteers and 'Lady Scripture Readers',[94] this remained a relatively small contribution compared to that of other organisations. Furthermore, it was reflective of the limited appeal of its evangelical ethos that the Association seems to have made its greatest mark in bases in south Wales and Northern Ireland, where considerable help was received from local sympathisers.[95]

Although the inter-war years were unpropitious times for those religious institutions with historic links to the army, the outbreak of renewed European war saw a resurgence of civilian religious work among soldiers by agencies whose mettle and ability had been proved in the First World War. Armed with the support of the Archbishop of Canterbury and the leaders of the Free Churches (who announced at the outbreak of war their confidence in the Association and their recognition of its 'essential experience and leadership')[96] the YMCA greatly expanded its existing work with the armed services. By early 1940, the YMCA was helping to provide lectures and short courses for soldiers via the newly created Central Advisory Council for Education in HM Forces.[97] Furthermore, and within just five months of the outbreak of war, more than 500 YMCA centres had been opened or adapted to work with the armed forces in Great Britain. As Lieutenant-Colonel Sir Henry McMahon, then president of the National Council of Young Men's Christian Associations, put it in February 1940, the Association's aim was 'to emulate YMCA service in the previous campaign . . . "We are here to do all we can for everybody."' Given the wide dispersal of anti-aircraft sites across Britain, a major new weapon in the Association's armoury was the so-called 'YMCA on Wheels', a fleet of seventy-five motor vehicles each carrying 'hot drinks, food, chocolates, cigarettes, games, books, magazines [and] writing-paper' in addition to 'a sympathetic YMCA worker prepared to organise recreation; to give helpful advice and guidance [and] to carry out any useful task such as delivering mail, and shopping in the towns'.[98] While its wartime work in Great Britain got off to a vigorous start, the YMCA's work with the forces abroad was not neglected either. In December 1939, the first YMCA centre for the men of the BEF was opened in France and a YMCA official was dispatched to co-ordinate work in Egypt in February 1940.[99]

The scale of YMCA work with Britain's armed services during the Second World War can be inferred from the proceedings of the fifty-ninth annual meeting of its National Council in July 1942, a meeting which was reported at length in *The Times*. Here it was announced that there were no fewer than 923 mobile canteens operating in Britain in addition to '28 Mobile Libraries and 6 Mobile Entertainment Vans', a substantial and versatile reinforcement to the 1,254 YMCA centres then working with the forces at home. In addition to these mobile and static facilities in Great Britain, there were similar facilities in operation in Iceland, India, the Middle East and Africa. Besides its canteens, centres and a small number of more exclusive officers' clubs, the British YMCA was also involved in other spheres of work, notably in assisting British prisoners of war through the World's Alliance of YMCAs and in running projects such as 'Snapshots from Home'. This was a scheme whereby servicemen serving overseas were sent recent photographs of their families. All of this activity, a great deal of which had been pioneered during the First World War,[100] was facilitated by the efforts of more than 100,000 volunteers of the Association's National Women's Auxiliary and was financed by the Association's War Service Fund whose revenue was generated by donations and by trading surpluses. By the end of November 1941, donations had totalled more than £1,000,000 since the war began, with donations coming from the USA and Malaya as well as from individuals, businesses and trades unions in Great Britain.[101]

By all accounts, many of the YMCA's counterparts were equally active. Although high-level Anglican support for the YMCA may have led to a decline in the relative importance of the Church Army in the Second World War,[102] the Salvation Army, the Church of Scotland and the Methodist church rose to the challenge of the new conflict with gusto. According to Salvation Army sources, at the peak of its wartime activity there were 450 Salvation Army centres in Great Britain alone, these centres being supplemented by a further 200 mobile canteens. In terms of its overseas service, the Salvation Army credited itself with working with British troops in Norway, France, the Low Countries, Germany, Austria, North Africa, Greece, Italy and Iraq.[103] Similarly, and under the aegis of the Huts and Canteens sub-committee of its Committee on Church and National Service, by 1942 the Church of Scotland was responsible for 260 huts and canteens in Great Britain and the Middle East and for a further forty-five mobile facilities.[104] By the same year, the Methodist church in Great Britain was claiming responsibility for 700 canteens for servicemen.[105]

Unlike the situation which had prevailed in the First World War, this huge religious and philanthropic endeavour had the major advantage of being centrally co-ordinated. In 1939, and at the instigation of the Army Council, the War Office had prudently created a Council of Voluntary War Work, a body that was chaired throughout the war by Lieutenant-General Sir John Brown and which included representatives of the armed forces, the YMCA, the YWCA, the Church of Scotland, the Salvation Army, the Church Army, Toc H, the CWL and the United Board.[106] Although the Women's Voluntary Services were also represented at the Council's meetings, 'full membership was confined to those national bodies which had a religious as well as a philanthropic background'.[107] Characterised by a spirit of co-operation, the CVWW eventually established sub-committees in each military command and worked at a local level with local army welfare officers. This degree of co-ordination naturally served to prevent 'over-lapping, competition and waste of effort and scarce materials' among its constituent organisations.[108] According to the general secretary of the YMCA, by the summer of 1942 'The Council had made possible great economy in effort [and] had effected a striking achievement in Christian unity'.[109] A clear example of how the Council for Voluntary War Work was able to co-ordinate and channel the efforts of the churches came in July 1944, when it dispatched a fleet of thirty mobile canteens to Normandy.[110] Not only were its personnel the recipients of special training prior to embarkation but, according to a *Times* report, this initial convoy represented the combined efforts of the YMCA, the YWCA, the Salvation Army, the Church of Scotland, the Church Army and the CWL. Although all of the workers in the convoy wore the overseas uniform of their respective organisations, all wore a shoulder flash bearing the letters CVWW.[111] By the end of August, and in addition to some static facilities, the total number of CVWW mobile canteens in north-west Europe had reached sixty, and it was perhaps a fitting tribute to the work of the CVWW in this theatre of war that a mobile YMCA canteen was present at Luneberg Heath when Montgomery took the surrender of German forces in north-west Europe on 8 May 1945.[112]

If the element of competition between religious organisations was reduced during the Second World War, the YMCA and its sister organisations still faced a number of major problems, some of which were recurrences of those faced in the First World War. First, there was inevitably a degree of indirect competition from secular organisations such as the NAAFI (the consolidated Forces' canteen service created in 1920) and ENSA, which provided tens of thousands of cinema and variety shows in partnership with the NAAFI.[113] Second, volunteers for overseas work were hard to come by and this shortage was particularly acute in India and the Far East where, as a War Office report noted: 'The philanthropic bodies could not recruit enough helpers, and organisations like the YMCA, YWCA and Toc "H" relied mainly upon the U.S.A. for reinforcements.'[114] Third, finance remained a daunting problem. By the end of November 1940, a year of massive expansion had seen the expenditure of the YMCA's War Service Fund rise by nearly £100,000 over its income. Although this deficit was eliminated by the end of the following year, commitments continued to accumulate and sources of funding remained uncertain. As Lord Athlone pointed out in 1942, the donations and trading surpluses which maintained its War Service Fund 'were subject to constant fluctuation' and substantial donations from the United States and Malaya seemed set to evaporate in the wake of American and Japanese entry into the war. In more ways than one, therefore, the Association's 'service to the Nation' remained very much 'a venture of faith'.[115]

Part of the financial problem experienced by the YMCA and its equivalents stemmed from the fact that the relative costs of their facilities had increased since the First World War. Whereas the Church Army had estimated in 1917 that fully equipped tents and huts cost in the region of £300 and £400 respectively, YMCA sources put the cost of a hut at 'between £1,500 and £3,000' by 1940. Apparently, this was 'due not only to higher prices but also to the need for better facilities', the generation which had experienced the inter-war boom in commercialised leisure being more difficult to please in this respect than their fathers' generation had been. In fact, and in order to satisfy these higher expectations, the YMCA even re-designated its huts as 'clubhouses'.[116] Fourth, a series of military defeats and evacuations during the first years of the war brought with them staggering losses in terms of equipment and stores. As a result of the German rampage through France and the Low Counties in May and June 1940, the Church of Scotland left more than £20,000 worth of assets in the hands of the victors. Similarly, in the wake of the Dunkirk evacuation, the YMCA estimated its own losses on the continent as amounting to £70,000,[117] or, in material terms, 'thirteen canteens, six other motor-vehicles, three huts, fifteen centres in various buildings, a large quantity of stores and equipment, four railway truckloads of stores already at railheads, and other property'.[118] Nevertheless, despite these losses, the Salvation Army, the Church Army and the YMCA could derive a measure of comfort and cachet from the fact that the stocks of their centres and mobile canteens were distributed free of charge to Allied soldiers awaiting evacuation at Dunkirk, Boulogne, Nantes and St Malo.[119] The last major problem faced by these organisations came in the form of the very different situation of the Home Front in the Second World War. Quite apart from sudden and secretive military movements that could render once flourishing canteens and centres redundant overnight,[120] there were competing demands from the civilian domain, mobile canteens being routinely deployed in heavily bombed areas of Britain's towns and cities. As Mrs Sydney Marsham of the YMCA's National Women's Auxiliary put it in 1942: 'More than 900 YMCA Mobile Canteens, complete with their staffs of women, were ready to turn out at a moment's notice to meet any emergency.'[121]

Notwithstanding the secular alternatives of the NAAFI and ENSA shows, there can be no doubt as to the ubiquity and popularity of church-based facilities. In 1943, one MO report described the scale and diversity of the work undertaken by civilian religious organisations on behalf of the army:

> [The] YMCA, YWCA, Toc H, The Red Shield (Salvation Army), the Church Army [and] The Church of Scotland Huts are all concerned with religious aspects of life . . . In a great many areas, local churches run canteens in church halls, and usually make special arrangements for Sunday evenings. Red Shield and Church Army canteens invariably run Sunday services. Toc H, created in the last war especially for the serving men, between wars had considerably

expanded its activities, but now is once again concentrating on the Forces. Groups for service and discussion are being formed in all types of units and most Toc H canteens are backed by a club and almost invariably by a special room used as a chapel.[122]

In January 1944, it was reported that, in the year ending 30 November 1943, no fewer than one million servicemen had patronised just seven YMCA facilities in Greater London alone.[123] Indeed, in 1944 a War Office survey found that forty out of sixty-one soldiers' hostels in London were run by religious organisations.[124] Without doubt, the efforts of the churches and of church organisations were greatly appreciated in many quarters. Montgomery, for example, was so convinced of their beneficial effects for the ordinary soldier that he allowed his name to be used in the YMCA's fundraising campaign for 1944. If Montgomery had 'nothing but the highest praise' for the work of the YMCA, lesser mortals also saw the enormous practical value of the Association and its wartime work. As part of the same radio broadcast which invoked the approval of Montgomery, the Lord Mayor of London, Sir Frank Newson-Smith, cited the case of a sergeant in a prison camp in Germany who had remitted the sum of £30 to the Association in recognition of its efforts on behalf of prisoners of war.[125] However, this appreciation on the part of the other ranks also extended to other organisations. In his vivid memoir of the war in Burma, George MacDonald Fraser remembered with great affection the work of a certain mobile canteen which was always present in his battalion's transport lines:

> I can see it now, a jungle clearing and two smiling douce old ladies from Fife, with their battered tea-urn and tray of currant scones. 'Mai guidness, Ennie, we're running out of sangwidges! Did I not say we needed anither tin of spem? Dearie me! More tea, boys?' And afterwards, they would rattle off in their truck (*'Furst* gear, Ennie – and don't rev the motor, woman! Oh, mai, take a hemmer to it! Bay-bay, boys!') beaming and waving and adjusting their hair-pins, with Japs just up the road. There are heroines; I've seen them.[126]

Although David Coulter has argued for the success of the work of the Church of Scotland's huts and canteens, particularly in providing a host of civilian ministers and church workers to assist Presbyterian chaplains in their work,[127] this actually represents a very modest achievement in overall terms. As in the First World War, such facilities no doubt helped morale, especially (it would seem) in the Far East where army welfare provision was often lacking and where, according to South-East Asia Command, philanthropic bodies 'proved invaluable to the morale of soldiers tired out by long campaigning'.[128] Furthermore, facilities such as these provided wholesome refreshment and recreation for soldiers during wartime conditions of increased sexual opportunity and relaxed sexual mores.[129] However, there is very little evidence to suggest that the huts, canteens and centres of the Church of Scotland – or of any other organisation for that matter – elicited much of an overtly religious response outside of their natural constituency of existing churchgoers and church members. Indeed, even as a very subtle means of evangelisation among the broader masses of the army, this work appears to have borne very little fruit, a phenomenon that was probably related to short-term and long-term factors. First, those religious organisations working under the auspices of the CVWW were expected to provide facilities that were open and welcoming to all service personnel, an imperative which precluded overt proselytism on the part of their representatives.[130] Consequently, and despite the co-existence of chapel and counter in thousands of their huts and centres during the Second World War, the primacy of the latter was inevitable from the outset. Second, and as Jeffrey Cox has argued, the Protestant churches' established preoccupation with Christian social work was an intrinsically broad and incoherent phenomenon, embracing and conflating very different inspirations and objectives.[131] In its many and ubiquitous manifestations, this work ultimately served to produce in the long term several generations of working-class Britons who were inclined to take a utilitarian and opportunistic view of the range of services that the churches had to offer.[132] Consequently, and although the philanthropic work of the churches in providing for the needs of soldiers between 1939 and 1945 was impressive in scale, self-sacrificing in nature and widely recognised and appreciated, it was no more likely to result in a significant religious revival than was the churches' ongoing work among the civilian population. Indeed, and with the experience of 1914–18 in mind, the best prospect that the Church Army could hope for in the light of its work in the Second World War was that:

> Many a suburban vicar in days to come, calling without much hope on a new ex-Serviceman resident, will find his welcome a little warmer because Sergeant Smith remembers the heroic arrival of a Church Army Mobile Canteen in the middle of a sandstorm at Mersa Matruh when the world seemed full of dust and defeat, or because Captain X, on a sweltering day in Baghdad listened patiently to Private Brown's sad tale of a wife and a lodger, and gave just the bit of sound advice that saved a home.[133]

Mobile churches, bishops and Bibles

It is indicative of the colossal commitment of the British churches and of British Jewry that the efforts of the YMCA and similar bodies by no means exhausted the spirit of enterprise which sought to bring religious influences to bear upon the British soldier during the two World Wars. In addition to promoting the cause of the mobile canteen, the mechanisation of the army before and during the Second World War even resulted in the provision of motorised churches. The first of these appears to have been an improvisation that saw service in the closing stages of the North African campaign. As a *Times* report put it: 'A mobile church, in the form of a converted lorry, accompanied the Eighth Army during the campaign in Africa, and the Commander-in-Chief, General Montgomery, was much interested in it.'[134] However, and in order to serve the 'spiritual needs' of the 21st Army Group in north-west Europe, specially manufactured vehicles were made available. The two 'motor-churches' of St Paul and St George were consecrated in July 1944, duly recognised by the War Office and St Paul's subsequently arrived in Normandy aboard a tank landing craft.[135] Clearly, these were vehicles whose provision reflected a close collaboration between the civilian church and the military authorities. Consecrated by Archbishop Temple and staffed by members of the RAChD, each was a product of 'the devoted work, often in their spare time, of R.E.M.E. and civilian craftsmen, and A.T.S. officers'. As *The Times* described them, these vehicles were

> tiny but very beautifully fitted and furnished places of worship, lined with polished oak. The altars, with their cloths and hangings of satin and velvet, in the blue and red colours of the Army Group flash, are movable, so that each vehicle can either accommodate in itself a little congregation of perhaps a dozen or, with the altar moved to the open rear end, and the use of a microphone and public address system which will be carried, be made the centre of a service for the largest possible number in the open air. The vehicles carry poles and canvas to form penthouse extensions for use as 'vicarages' when the chaplains' camps are pitched. The chaplains for these moving churches will be able when required to go on tours of the Army Group area fully equipped to live in the field for weeks together, and thus make up in some measure for the present acute shortage of unit chaplains among the armies.[136]

If motorised churches were a remarkable new departure, a longstanding duty of civilian clergymen had been to minister to the religious needs of their co-religionists who were not under the direct charge of army chaplains. During the two World Wars, the number of these 'officiating' chaplains grew exponentially, with the Anglicans and Wesleyan Methodists providing over a thousand of them by 1916.[137] In theory at least, all of these chaplains were subject to the approval and supervision of senior army chaplains and they were paid by the War Office on a weekly basis according to the number of soldiers under their care.[138] Although the work of officiating chaplains was relatively inconspicuous, the contact of other civilian clergy with the troops was definitely otherwise. On the grounds of their feasibility and their considerable propaganda value, official tours and visitations of the Western Front became a much-favoured activity for British religious leaders during the First World War. At Easter 1915, the Bishop of London, Arthur Winnington-Ingram, made a much-publicised visit to the BEF,[139] to be followed in due course by the Bishop of Birmingham, the Bishop for Northern and Central Europe, the Archbishop of Armagh, the Archbishop of Canterbury,[140] the Archbishop of York and the Bishop of Kensington.[141] Even in far-off Mesopotamia, where the Indian Ecclesiastical Establishment assumed responsibility for spiritual matters, the Anglican communion did not neglect episcopal visitations. Indeed, so frequent were episcopal visits to Mesopotamia from India that the chaplain-general was able to use this argument as a means of fending off the proposal that a bishop be permanently appointed to this theatre of war as well.[142] In addition to Anglican and Roman Catholic bishops, other civilian visitors to the BEF included the Moderator of the Church of Scotland[143] and the Chief Rabbi, who, like many of his episcopal counterparts, was cordially received at GHQ.[144] Although the hospitality which was extended to various religious dignitaries by the military authorities was emblematic of the value that they placed upon religion, these visits could try the patience of the army's commanders, particularly when visitors went home to air their amateur opinions on military matters.[145] Shows of military and ecclesiastical solidarity could be as contrived as they were inconvenient. During the pioneering visit of the Bishop of London in 1915, for example, troops were collected from far and wide in order to ensure a suitably impressive turnout at church parade.[146] Similarly, during the Archbishop of York's extended visit to the Western Front in 1917, the army appears to have been at pains to provide the 62nd (2nd West Riding) Division for a large parade service, the reason being, as Bishop Gwynne observed, that it was 'a Yorkshire Division'.[147]

Even for the likes of Haig, the constant stream of ecclesiastical visitors could prove tiresome. According to G.S. Duncan, Haig eventually developed 'an instinctive dislike . . . to visitors from civilian life, and not least to churchmen, unless they came on a highly responsible mission'.[148] Significantly, Haig was particularly unimpressed by Cardinal Bourne, whom he met on the cardinal's second visit to the Western Front in October 1917 and whom he considered 'neither eminent in appearance nor in conversation'.[149] Similarly, at a thanksgiving service held at GHQ in August 1918, Haig refused to countenance the suggestion that the visiting Bishop of Kensington be allowed to lead the service, insisting that 'This was to be an official army service; it ought therefore to be conducted by the official army chaplains, and not by a visitor from outside'.[150] If they were not accorded the increasingly strained official welcomes extended to accredited denominational leaders, other prominent religious figures also made their way to France, among them being the famous revivalist preacher 'Gypsy' Smith who worked for a time at the base at Le Havre.[151] According to W.E. Sellers:

> The Government heartily backed the efforts of the churches. In addition to the chaplains of all denominations, others for whom no appointments could be found were allowed to go to France at their own or their friends' expense, to render to the soldiers what spiritual help they could.[152]

A case in point was R.J. Campbell, the distinguished if somewhat maverick Congregationalist minister who made no fewer than three visits to France in 1915. For his third visit, by which time he was preparing for ordination in the Church of England, he was even allowed to bring his own car.[153]

During the Second World War, episcopal visits to troops serving overseas were much more constrained by issues of distance, particularly as the Mediterranean rather than northern Europe was the centre of gravity for the army's operations throughout much of the war. However, 1943 saw the Archbishops of York and Canterbury endeavour to overcome this situation by addressing a special message to the army that was to be read at church services on the Sunday nearest to New Year's Day.[154] Furthermore, in August 1944, Cardinal Griffin, the new Archbishop of Westminster, visited the garrison of Malta en route to Italy and newly liberated Rome.[155] For the Church of England, the need for episcopal visits of this kind was apparently quite acute, particularly in view of the fact that no Anglican bishop was acting as a commissioned chaplain in the RAChD. However, for Anglicans in Egypt, immediate episcopal oversight was at hand in the form of the formidably experienced Bishop Llewellyn Gwynne, formerly the BEF's deputy chaplain-general and now bishop in Egypt and the Sudan. Although acting in a civilian capacity, to all intents and purposes Gwynne's role in Egypt from 1940 to 1945 appears to have been very similar to his role in France between 1915 and 1918. Besides visiting and confirming troops of the Western Desert Force in November 1940,[156] Gwynne used the pulpit of the newly consecrated

Anglican cathedral of All Saints, Cairo, as a platform for direct and morale-boosting homilies worthy of the First World War. In 1957, Field-Marshal Lord Wilson, who had been commander-in-chief of British troops in Egypt throughout 1940, remembered that:

> During the dark days of June 1940 when France collapsed and Italy declared war on us, things were very difficult for those serving in Cairo as our country was regarded by both Egyptians and foreigners as beaten. At the time the sermons of the Bishop at evening service in the Cathedral were a source of strength, courage and inspiration to all who heard them. He expounded the righteousness of our cause and the steadfastness of our race in a manner that produced spiritual support to our efforts.[157]

In addition to providing thousands of officiating chaplains and the occasional high-profile visitor, the churches also worked to provide useful religious activities for the troops. In both World Wars, Catholic chaplains and clergy proved active in providing Catholic soldiers with short retreats, with the opportunity to go on pilgrimage and even with the chance to see the pope. Pioneered by Fr Charles Plater, a promoter of the retreat movement in civilian life, the first 'epoch-making' retreat for Catholic soldiers was held at Isleworth in December 1915.[158] By the end of the war, Plater estimated that 460 Catholic soldiers had made retreats of this kind in English retreat houses.[159] During the years of the Second World War, it was, indeed, expected that the military authorities would prove co-operative in releasing soldiers to go on retreat, or on a 'Refresher Course in Christianity' as retreats were conveniently renamed. As Fr Gerard Lake remembered, for COs 'the word "Retreat" had a sinister meaning. Hence, very early on, the name was changed to "Refresher Course in Christianity", and this rang a bell in the military mind; a rose by any other name . . .'[160] Indeed, it is striking to note the extent to which COs were prepared to indulge these Catholic activities and also their Protestant counterparts, namely confirmation classes and the newer breed of church membership courses which flourished during the Second World War. Few events, however, rivalled the Army Catholic Congress that was held in Jerusalem on 15 August 1918, the Feast of the Assumption. Conceived by the senior Catholic chaplain of the EEF in conjunction with its deputy adjutant-general, more than 1,500 British and Imperial troops were released and transported from across the Middle East for the occasion, the highlight of which was a soldiers' procession around the city's holy sites.[161] Similarly, the Allied liberation of Rome, Christendom's second most holy city, in June 1944 afforded the opportunity to meet Pope Pius XII in audience. Again, the military authorities proved more than accommodating, as the following report from *The Times* dated 20 June 1944 illustrates:

> The Pope this morning received in audience soldiers of the Eighth Army mostly Catholics, who had previously attended Mass . . . After bidding them welcome, the Pope said that God had willed that he should be Vicar of Christ at a period of human history when the world was filled as never before with suffering and distress unmeasured. He spoke to them as some of his children for whom he had prayed . . . As is frequently his custom when receiving British pilgrims, the Pope referred to British martyrs, Saints Edward, Thomas à Becket, John Fisher, and Thomas More, to whose protection he commended his audience . . . The party was accompanied by a general officer representing the army commander, General Leese, and the chief army chaplains.[162]

Although more modest in scale, comparable Protestant activities were equally indulged. As an MO report noted in 1943, COs 'frequently' allowed soldiers time off for confirmation classes.[163] One striking example of this indulgence was the case of the 15th (Scottish) Division's 'Pre-Confirmation Schools', three of which were held in the six months prior to D-Day. As week-long residential courses, these schools enjoyed the full backing of the divisional commander, Major-General G.H.A. Macmillan, and were jointly organised by the division's Anglican and Presbyterian chaplains. Clearly a success in numerical terms, by May 1944 no fewer than 1,400 men of this division had been instructed and confirmed into the Church of England or the Church of Scotland.[164] Given the emphasis that was placed on religion as a foundation for good morale in both World Wars, the attitude of COs to such activities is easily explicable. As Fr Lake put it:

> I think that most commanding officers felt that there was some connection between morale and morals; that religion and patriotism support and strengthen each other; and that the happiness of the individual soldier could be destroyed by the lack of practical religious living and a fundamental morality based on the Ten Commandments.[165]

If senior officers had a definite confidence in the ability of special religious activities to promote military efficiency, soldiers of a more junior rank often evinced a different reaction. Bernard Martin, who served as a young officer on the Western Front, remembered being disabused of his hopes for church reform when his battalion was addressed by the Archbishop of York in 1917:

> I don't remember even his subject and I doubt if anyone in the battalion paid much attention – just another boost of morale . . . as I watched his dignified performance with several attendant chaplains, my thoughts wandered amongst my war experiences . . . all leading me to believe the war would inevitably bring changes in the established Church. Now I had doubts sufficient to stir again the disillusion I thought I'd overcome. What did Establishment leaders living in safety and comfort, know about war or any need for reconsidering beliefs . . . In bitterness I fancied the Archbishop back in Blighty, telling the House of Lords 'I've just returned from a visit to the Front . . . our boys in high spirits . . . won't be long before we have good news . . . very soon now'.[166]

Among most soldiers, however, the reaction to various forms of religious junketing was probably more prosaic. Significantly, Fr Charles Plater had warned his very first batch of military retreatants that 'A retreat is not an idle holiday, but a serious business demanding hard work, earnestness and generosity'.[167] Although it would be foolish to deny that such activities attracted a solid core of sincere believers, self-interested exploitation of the churches' activities was endemic in civilian religious life and there can be no reason to doubt that, among those soldiers who availed themselves of retreats and confirmation classes in the army, there was a significant element of skivers whose primary motivation was to escape their normal duties. The same MO report that noted the willingness of COs to release soldiers for confirmation classes also noted that the number of confirmation candidates among soldiers was artificially high – 'for confirmation in the Army is something of a racket'.[168] In a similar vein, it would appear that for at least one Irish soldier in Italy in 1944, an artful declaration of intent to see the pope gave him sufficient leverage over his company commander to win a contested application for local leave.[169]

As in many earlier conflicts, during both World Wars an immense effort was also devoted to distributing religious literature to the men and women of the British army. Notwithstanding the fact that the War Office had for decades issued portions of scripture and approved prayer books to soldiers as a matter of policy, there were many civilian agencies who were more than willing to augment this official provision. According to Arthur Yapp, the YMCA alone distributed 'Millions of Testaments and gospel portions' free of charge to serving soldiers during the First World War.[170] Moreover, in May 1919 it was noted that the Church of England's venerable SPCK had spent in excess of £400,000 in 'liberally and ungrudgingly' providing religious literature for the armed services.[171] One magazine article from 1916 observed how the SPCK, the Religious Tract Society, the British and Foreign Bible Society, the Scripture Gift Mission, the Pocket Testament League and the Trinitarian Bible Society had each donated an 'ample supply' of their publications for distribution through Anglican chaplains alone.[172] In this respect, the work of the Scripture Gift Mission was no doubt aided by the fact that the chaplain-general, Bishop Taylor Smith, was a member of its governing committee. Chaplains were, of course, an important medium for this kind of work and Taylor Smith seems to have ensured that the Scripture Gift Mission produced a special edition of the Book of Proverbs for soldiers, its thirty-one chapters enabling them to read 'a chapter for each day of the month'.[173] However, chaplains were not inclined to distribute everything that pious civilians sent to them for the edification of the soldier and one Presbyterian chaplain, the Revd J.M. Connor, noted in his diary how, in November 1914, he had felt obliged to destroy an inappropriate 'Parcel of Tracts from Woking'.[174] Nevertheless, the friends and associates of Bishop Taylor Smith donated no fewer than 200,000 prayer cards which were distributed among the first elements of the BEF to arrive on the continent,[175] prayer cards that were presumably copies of his own *Soldier's Prayer* which was printed in 'millions of copies of the Scriptures and prayer books distributed between 1914–1918'.[176]

During the Second World War, evangelically minded chaplains remained active in promoting the reading and study of scripture. One Anglican chaplain, for example, remembered his success in introducing the work of the Bible Reading Fellowship to the Guards' training camp at Pirbright:

> I suggested to the Guardsmen that as they were fighting for a Christian country and for Christian principles it would be sound for them to train themselves in the knowledge of the New Testament by daily reading of a brief but orderly kind; the [Bible Reading] Fellowship had brought out a Service Edition of notes for the purpose, with the Bible passage printed at the top of each page. The response was beyond my expectations. In a few weeks 800 Guardsmen were buying the notes; a man in each hut took the names of those who wanted them and obtained the number required each month from me.[177]

Chaplains' ingenuity was also demonstrated in North Africa, where chaplains of the Eighth Army had produced thirty-four publications of their own by the end of 1942, including 'a printed Form of Service' that 'could be seen in the dark without the use of artificial light.[178] Despite such innovation, plain scripture continued to be in demand among soldiers, with no fewer than 30,000 New Testaments being distributed to British soldiers by British chaplains during the course of the Normandy campaign.[179] However, and as in the Victorian era, there was still plenty of scope for the keen layperson to present the word of God directly to the necessitous Tommy. As units of the BEF prepared to sail from Irish ports in August 1914, many were visited on their transports by workers from Elise Sandes' soldiers homes, who distributed hundreds of testaments and tracts among them.[180] Likewise, soldiers who were churchgoers or church members could expect to receive Testaments and prayer books from relatives and co-religionists at home. At Christmas 1917, for example, the servicemen of St Michael's and St John's parish, Clitheroe, each received a copy of the newly published *Catholic Soldiers' and Sailors' Prayer-Book*, which was dispatched to them with 'Best Xmas Wishes from the Fathers and Congregation'.[181]

In addition to religious literature, British Catholics were also active in ensuring that their soldiers received a plentiful supply of other devotional aids. In October 1914, and in response to an appeal by a chaplain in France, *The Tablet* announced its intention of supplying Catholic soldiers with a complete 'devotional outfit' comprising a Catholic prayer book, a Catholic pamphlet, a rosary, a scapular and a Sacred Heart Badge.[182] In 1917, the devoutly Catholic wife of Lieutenant-Colonel Rowland Feilding of the 6th Connaught Rangers arranged that his men should receive miniature crucifixes that had been blessed by the pope and brought back to England by Cardinal Bourne. These crucifixes were distributed with great ceremony during a church parade at Locre.[183] As we have already seen, early in the Second World War Cardinal Hinsley introduced the 'Cardinal's Cross', a cross which was designed and blessed by Hinsley himself and that he intended every Catholic soldier to carry. Devised in conjunction with the Sword of the Spirit movement which he had also inaugurated, supplies of the Cardinal's Cross were procured and distributed to Catholic soldiers by their own chaplains.[184] For many Catholic soldiers, however, home was still the principal source of items of this kind. Spike Milligan, for example, noted of one parcel sent to him by his mother in 1943:

> A parcel from home! 2/3rds of which are Holy Medals of St Patrick and St Therese. I only need St Andrew and I've got the set, if I had worn every one sent me I'd have weighed 20 stone. Had I died, men searching for my identity disc might have said, 'Christ, he *is* St Patrick.'[185]

In view of the scale and duration of the two World Wars, and the number and diversity of their purveyors, it would be impossible to estimate the total number of testaments, tracts, magazines, prayer books and other religious artefacts which were distributed to soldiers during these years. However, what is beyond doubt is that the total ran into tens of millions. Indeed, Alan Wilkinson has estimated that, between 1914 and 1916 alone, some 40 million Bibles, prayer books, hymnbooks and tracts were distributed to British troops by civilian religious agencies.[186] Although most may have remained unread or unused, been thrown away or even sent home as souvenirs,[187] many still fell into appreciative hands. Despite a widespread tendency to treat Bibles as talismans, there were soldiers who made full and orthodox use of Holy Writ and, on the basis of the British army's experience, there seems little reason to doubt Richard Schweitzer's verdict that 'the Bible was the most widely read book among Great War soldiers'.[188] In 1917, W.E. Sellers wrote of a certain Bible which had been found on the body of a 'Christian soldier' of the Dorsetshire Regiment who had been killed on the Somme the previous year. Sellers averred that:

> The owner has marked many pages of the book with blue, red and green pencils, has drawn sketches, written comments on chapters and texts that had brought comfort and strength to him. The margins contain almost a complete diary of the war. Chapters and texts are associated with each movement, each battle, each deliverance.[189]

According to Cyril Falls, who served with the 36th (Ulster) Division during the First World War, popular Protestantism stimulated and perpetuated personal habits of Bible-reading among these Ulstermen. As Falls recollected: 'The General commanding the 4th Division, to which the 36th was attached for instruction after its arrival in France, spoke of his astonishment at finding so many Ulstermen reading their Bibles.' Furthermore, Falls himself testified from personal experience that:

> it was not uncommon to find a man sitting on the fire-step of a front-line trench, reading one of the small copies of the New Testament which were issued to the troops by the people at home. The explanation was that, on the one hand, religion was near and real to them; on the other, that they were simple men. They saw no reason to hide or disguise that which was a part of their daily lives.[190]

Similarly, William Ewing, a United Free Church minister and a Scottish Territorial chaplain at Gallipoli and in Mesopotamia, wrote:

> In hospital it was a common thing to see a lad on his stretcher, quite unobtrusively, but with evident appreciation, reading his New Testament. I handled a great number of these books, and found them not, as a rule, simply dog-eared from carrying in the pocket, but well thumbed, which sufficiently testified to the use made of them.[191]

Undoubtedly, the words of scripture could offer very real comfort to those in a state of anxiety or distress. Just before an attack in November 1917, Private H.L. Adams of the 6th Royal West Surreys consulted a book of texts with a like-minded comrade, both deriving considerable comfort from the text for the day: 'The Lord will fight thy battles for thee.'[192] In certain cases, scripture could even become a source of comfort which united soldiers on active service with their relatives at home. At the height of the battle of the Somme, for example, E.G. Routley, a subaltern in the 6th East Kents, wrote to his mother:

> I came across a Bible in the trenches and opened it at random and turned to the 23rd Psalm, & I want you to read it whenever you feel depressed. I am always thinking of that lovely verse ('Yea though I walk through the valley of the shadow of death I will fear no evil' &c) whenever I am given any dangerous job . . .[193]

Among Roman Catholics, prayer books also seem to have offered comfort to many, a fact that was particularly evident among southern Irish units. As one Anglican chaplain, William Drury, recalled of the Somme in September 1916:

> An officer of the [16th] Irish Division told me that, coming down after the taking of Guillemont . . . he noticed the dead body of an Irishman lying with his hand held above his face and something white clasped in it. On going closer he saw that it was a Roman Catholic book of prayers. After that he looked particularly at the bodies he passed and saw three more in Trônes Wood who had died whilst reading the prayers.[194]

Similarly, rosaries and scapulars were often quite properly used as devotional aids and as emblems of trust in God and in the intercessory power of the saints. As one Catholic soldier wrote in an account of a barrage on the Western Front in 1917: 'I was thinking at the time that it was like hell. But I felt, somehow, that Our Lady would see us through, so I just gripped my rifle with my one hand, and said my beads with the other.'[195]

The churches and medical care

In considering the involvement of pious civilians in providing for the sundry needs of the British soldier, it is important to remember the supplementary medical facilities that civilian religious organisations provided for the army, especially during the First World War. Again, this was a natural extension of charitable medical work in pre-war civilian society, church-run dispensaries, nursing associations, ambulances and hospitals being important features of contemporary health care for Britain's working classes.[196] While the Church Army briefly took responsibility for a fleet of fifty motor ambulances on the Western Front,[197] the Salvation Army ran its own section of motor ambulances in France for most of the war, both initiatives stemming from the 'entire lack' of such conveyances in the autumn of 1914. By the end of the war, 'The Salvation Army Section' comprised no fewer than thirty vehicles with their attendant drivers. These vehicles were employed (like all civilian ambulances operating under the aegis of the Red Cross) at the base hospitals of the BEF.[198] In addition to this, numerous church-based hospitals and convalescent homes either opened their doors to wounded soldiers or were established for the duration of the war.

Perhaps the largest provider in this respect was the St John Ambulance Association, an organisation which had been founded by the English branch of the Order of St John in 1877. Although it worked in collaboration with the Red Cross in both World Wars and no doubt possessed a broader philanthropic appeal, the Anglican character of the St John Ambulance movement was unmistakeable and was common to the Order, the Association and the St John Ambulance Brigade. Established in 1887, as late as 1929 it was admitted in the Brigade's official history that 'It is a noteworthy fact that throughout its existence Church Parades have always appealed strongly to members of the Brigade'.[199] In any event, by November 1918 the St John Ambulance Association was running no fewer than 245 auxiliary hospitals in England with beds for more than 16,000 sick and wounded. In addition to these hospitals, which included the largest voluntary hospital in Great Britain, a St John Ambulance Brigade hospital had also been established at Etaples in September 1915, a hospital which held 520 beds in prefabricated huts brought over from England and that was virtually destroyed by German air raids in May 1918.[200] Besides the contribution of the St John Ambulance movement, among the new convalescent homes to be established in Great Britain was the Duchess of Norfolk's home for the 'totally incapacitated and incurable', a facility that was opened in 1917 for the care of unmarried Catholic men.[201] British Jews were no less active in providing for the army's wartime medical needs and in September 1914 an entire auxiliary hospital was presented to the War Office by Sir Marcus Samuel, to which more than 400 'seriously wounded non-commissioned officers' were admitted before its closure in December 1918.[202]

In addition to providing their own hospitals, the St John Ambulance Brigade and its progenitor, the St John Ambulance Association, also furnished a substantial cadre of trained personnel for the RAMC. Created in the aftermath of Edward Cardwell's far-reaching reforms of the British army in the early 1870s, one of the original tasks of the St John Ambulance Association was to provide 'a civilian reserve for [the] Army Medical Department'.[203] Consequently, during the Boer War, the St John Ambulance Brigade provided a quarter of the army's medical personnel in South Africa.[204] With the creation of the Territorial Force in 1908, the War Office delegated much of the training of Territorial medical personnel to the Brigade and it also organised Voluntary Aid Detachments from the membership of the St John Ambulance movement. In the event of war, these medical units were to be mobilised for home service and Brigade personnel would replace the RAMC staff of military hospitals in Great Britain.[205] If the St John Ambulance movement was therefore an integral part of the army's reserve forces prior to the outbreak of war, then its importance was fully vindicated after August 1914. By April 1920, the number of Voluntary Aid Detachments organised by the St John Ambulance movement had reached 945, amounting to more than 30,000 trained civilian medical staff who, from 1915, served overseas as well as in Great Britain.[206] Furthermore, over 17,000 Brigade personnel served in the army between 1914 and 1918, a number that was almost the equivalent of its entire male membership in 1914.[207] In keeping with the spirit of the times, it was not unknown for members of the Brigade to volunteer en masse for Kitchener's New Army. One of the three field ambulances of the 38th (Welsh) Division was composed entirely of Welsh members of the Brigade's No. 11 district, these men being granted the distinction of wearing St John's Ambulance insignia on their army uniform.[208] As the history of the 38th Division put it:

> The whole of the men who formed this unit had had three or four years' training in first-aid, stretcher work, and nursing before enlistment and, being mostly miners, had had frequent opportunity of putting their training into actual practice under most difficult conditions before war began.[209]

Although dwarfed by the efforts of the St John Ambulance movement, the Quaker-inspired Friends Ambulance Unit was another civilian organisation that made a notable contribution to medical work in the British army during both World Wars. Unlike the St John Ambulance movement, which was arguably eclipsed by the Red Cross in the Second World War, the FAU also succeeded in retaining a distinct identity.[210] On the Western Front between 1914 and 1918, the FAU helped in the evacuation of the wounded and ran a hospital at Dunkirk in addition to providing help at dressing stations in forward areas.[211] At home, members of its General Service Section also assisted in the care of disabled soldiers.[212] In the Second World War, members of the recreated FAU provided various forms of assistance for the RAMC in Egypt, Greece, Italy, the Dodecanese and north-west Europe.[213] However, as an expression of 'practical pacifism',[214] the FAU's work with the army was fraught with ambiguity, a situation that entailed soul-searching within its ranks, problems with the army (John Hick remembered that there were always 'great rows over saluting') and pointed criticism from more hard-line pacifists at home.[215] However, and notwithstanding the FAU's awkward situation in relation to the military hierarchy on the one hand and to more extreme pacifists on the other, the organisation appears to have earned the respect of ordinary soldiers. While FAU members in the Western Desert stoically endured the rigours of desert warfare and enjoyed good relations with their RAMC colleagues,[216] no fewer than sixteen FAU members were captured in Greece in 1941.[217] One of these, Michael Mounsey, was subsequently elected to act as *Vertrauensmann*, or liaison officer, between the German authorities and his fellow prisoners of war at Stalag XX A near Thorn. As David Wild, a British army chaplain, observed of this remarkable election:

> Seven hundred combatant Warrant Officers and N.C.O.s and a hundred and fifty Australians proceeded to elect as their representative a conscientious objector. Michael was a fluent German speaker and, being shrewd and scrupulously fair to all, he carried out the job with distinction for over a year. I cannot imagine soldiers of another army making such a choice.[218]

Conclusion

In the course of the two World Wars, the British churches and British Jewry made gigantic and even heroic efforts to provide for the spiritual, moral, mental, physical and medical needs of the British soldier. Although partly driven by patriotic concerns, these wartime labours at the same time represented the development of a diverse array of peacetime work among soldiers and civilians. Clearly, such efforts did little to promote overt religiosity among the majority of soldiers who were not already church members or active churchgoers. Moreover, and while no doubt earning the gratitude of many individuals and the marked appreciation of the military authorities, they had no single overarching religious rationale or motivation. In fact, they tended to perpetuate an existing tendency among soldiers and civilians to take advantage of the churches' philanthropic work while remaining aloof from closer association. Indeed, it is quite probable that, in the peculiar circumstances of wartime, many aspects of church work unintentionally encouraged popular heterodoxy. This was not only with respect to promoting an unhealthy view of Bibles and other religious artefacts but also in reinforcing an ingrained popular conviction that true Christianity was not about theological orthodoxy or active church membership but was fundamentally expressed in an individual's good works.

CONCLUSION

THIS STUDY OF RELIGION and the British soldier in the two World Wars throws up a host of insights into the religious state of Britain and into the religious outlook of the army and its commanders in the first half of the twentieth century. If we turn first of all to the state of religion in contemporary British society we are confronted with a situation that, at first sight, may appear paradoxical. The First and Second World Wars were fought against a backdrop of religious decline, particularly in terms of formal and regular religious practice in civilian life. Although contemporary churchmen inherited and rehearsed a pessimistic appraisal of the religious state of the nation, the indications are that British society as a whole was indeed experiencing a downward trend in terms of church and Sunday school membership and attendance. Moreover, and partly because of the First World War, inter-war society also saw significant changes in the moral and religious outlook of the nation. These changes were reflected in new divorce laws, in a tangible shift in sexual and reproductive morality and in the retreat from Victorian patterns of Sabbath day observance. All of this naturally encouraged consternation and a certain mood of despondency within the churches. Nevertheless, and even in statistical terms, the picture was not universally bleak. The symptoms of religious decline were most in evidence in specific churches, in certain social classes and in particular parts of the country, with mainstream urban and suburban English Protestantism being principally affected. However, and despite the major implications of decline in this quarter, for British Jews and

Roman Catholics, for the newer and more fundamentalist Protestant churches, for the 'Celtic fringes' of the British Isles and even for rural England the picture was much healthier and was even one of significant growth in the former cases.

Despite shifting moral paradigms and a downward trend in formal religious attachment and observance in mainland Britain, Christianity continued to exert a powerful and even defining influence on national and individual life. The British state retained its established or national churches and its semi-sacralised view of the monarchy. It subsidised denominational schooling and it promoted the cause of religion both in and through national institutions such as the armed services and the BBC. In fact, the nation's civic religion was no doubt boosted by the development of a national cult of remembrance during the inter-war years, public religious services becoming a staple feature of Armistice Day at a local and national level. Furthermore, and although British society's puritan sensibilities may have been eroded in certain respects during the inter-war years, the ongoing debate over Sunday observance showed that they were still very much in evidence in certain regions and in many localities. Indeed, they were still sufficiently strong at a national level to ensure the abdication of Edward VIII in 1936 as well as the continuing illegality of abortion and of homosexual practices.

Crucially, and amidst the collective trauma of the two World Wars, Britain's historic Christian identity continued to console and support the nation. Quite apart from the pronouncements of throngs of patriotic church-men, Britain's Christian identity and heritage were evidenced in the wartime activities of the monarchy, national days of prayer being called by George V and George VI, with the latter also acquiring some distinction as a religious broadcaster in the Second World War. Moreover, the famous wartime eloquence of David Lloyd George and Winston Churchill derived much of its force from its invocation of religious themes and motifs that were deeply embedded in the history and culture of Protestant Britain. However, this strongly religious dimension to contemporary British patriotism was not purely militaristic and atavistic. Indeed, centuries old notions of elect nationhood (and more recent concepts of Britain as the crusading champion of Christian civilisation against the neo-paganism of Imperial and Nazi Germany) also influenced wartime discourse as to Britain's post-war future. While powerful concepts of the nation's religious identity informed and fuelled debate on social reconstruction in both World Wars, a growing awareness of the moral dangers of secular ideologies during the Second provided new purpose and impetus to religious education in Britain's schools, a development that was marked by the religious provisions of the Education Act of 1944. Obviously, and notwithstanding the force of popular supposition and academic conjecture, the experience of the two World Wars cannot be described as a secularising influence in relation to British public life for religion clearly remained close to the centre of British national consciousness.

Moving from the national to the individual level, we can again see how religious concepts and beliefs continued to inform British society to a profound extent. Although, in overall terms, regular religious practice and formal religious adherence were becoming the preserves of a decreasing minority of the British public, a strong personal religiosity remained very widespread. In fact, it is quite possible that this continuing move towards a more personal and autonomous model of religion was positively if unintentionally encouraged by the rise of religious broadcasting in the inter-war years. This dominant form of religiosity, which appears to have been particularly prevalent among the working classes, clearly owed more to formative childhood influences than to regular contact with the churches, these influences being the product of the home and of the Sunday or denominational elementary school. During the early twentieth century, this pattern seems to have become increasingly common among the middle and upper classes, with grammar and public schools playing a comparable role to that of elementary and Sunday schools for the working classes. Although this autonomous form of adult religion reflected different denominational influences, its broad characteristics appear to have been a respect for the Christian rites of passage, a knowledge of basic prayers and devotions, an often impressive familiarity with hymnody and a strong emphasis on the ethical dimensions of Christianity and on the value of personal prayer. Furthermore, and among the middle and upper classes, with their longer exposure to scriptural studies and to regular chapel going at school, this form of religion could also embrace an extensive if fairly unsophisticated knowledge of Holy Writ. Evidently, and however estranged from habits of regular churchgoing 'diffusive Christianity' may have been, this ubiquitous and autonomous form of religion was by no means independent of the churches and by no means wholly divorced from the culture and outlook of the regular churchgoer, communicant or church member.

From a clerical point of view, this phenomenon of diffusive Christianity was further complicated by common and unsettling symptoms of popular heterodoxy, a situation that is probably endemic to Christian cultures but which nevertheless tended to flatter the clergy's professional – and not to say perennial – capacity for disappointment. Although fatalism, divination and more recent phenomena such as Spiritualism clearly encroached upon the supernatural outlook of many Britons (including churchgoers) in the war years, their significance should not be overstated. Not only did these miscellaneous beliefs rarely constitute an articulate and alternative world-view but they often derived their currency from a belief in ghosts and a concept of personal providence that were very much traditional aspects of British popular and religious culture. Moreover, such selectivity and eclecticism was also very much in evidence in other spheres of popular religious life, not least in a pragmatic and widespread non-denominationalism and in an essentially utilitarian recourse to church welfare agencies among the working classes.

If religion in civilian society appears to have been in better shape than many contemporaries allowed, this situation was fully reflected by the state of religion in the British army during the war years. As a vastly expanded force composed largely of non-professional soldiers, the army essentially reproduced the contours of contemporary religious life, with all their social, ethnic, regional and generational differences. Certainly, a strongly religious outlook seems to have prevailed among the army's most senior general officers, most of whom were products of upper- or middle-class backgrounds and had served as junior officers in the late Victorian and Edwardian regular army. For a combination of professional and personal reasons, religious concerns were also in evidence among many of the army's regimental officers during the two World Wars, these officers tending to come from those social classes in which levels of religious knowledge and religious practice remained relatively high. Similarly, patterns of religiosity among the army's rank and file reflected significant variations in religious practice and affiliation between different regions and between different social and ethnic groups. However, and although the army clearly sustained some vibrant religious sub-cultures, it was the phenomenon of diffusive Christianity that characterised the religious outlook of the army's overwhelmingly English and working-class rank and file. As in civilian life, this diffusive Christianity was manifested in numerous and often subtle ways. Significantly, and notwithstanding the army's customary intolerance of the professedly godless, most soldiers quietly submitted to the state-sponsored religion to which they were subjected by the army. Indeed, they also betrayed little inclination towards atheism, which remained a marginal and even precarious phenomenon. While many soldiers held distinctly heterodox beliefs, these were essentially eclectic and pragmatic in character and very seldom amounted to a coherent alternative to the Christian orthodoxy of the mainstream churches. Finally, soldiers also made extensive, pragmatic and even unorthodox use of the vast machinery of religious philanthropy that was developed for their benefit, its existence and ethos tending to confirm the popular conviction that Christianity was above all else a religion of good works and practical service.

If all of these facts substantially qualify the assumption that younger working-class men were (of all sections of British society) least susceptible to religious influences, we must also reconsider whether the experience of industrialised warfare in the first half of the twentieth century acted as a secularising influence on the millions of Britons who served in the British army. Clearly, the evidence we have examined suggests that it did not. While religious manners and habits were no doubt coarsened and questions of theodicy proved troubling for many, there is no indication of a widespread drift towards atheism. Moreover, and while military service brought hundreds of thousands of regular churchgoers into contact with the morally challenging context of army life and modern warfare, it also brought millions of non-churchgoers into prolonged contact with an institution in which the churches enjoyed a privileged and influential position. Furthermore, the fearsome prospect and circumstances of active service (and, for tens of thousands, the anxieties and hardships of captivity) accentuated some key aspects of civilian religious life. Clearly, and no doubt because the majority of adult British males believed in God, prayed occasionally and shared a national weakness for hymnody, soldiers often proved highly susceptible to what their chaplains and other representatives of the churches had to offer in difficult times. Although this susceptibility was most marked among convalescents, prisoners of war and front-line soldiers (who represented a declining proportion of the army during the two World Wars) there were even occasions when a spirit of revivalism was evident throughout the army, notably during the heady if bloody months of 1914–16. Furthermore, and while religious revivals among soldiers did occur during the war years, it was in civilian life that this revivalist spirit was most lastingly felt, notably in the form of the Toc H movement that thrived among veterans of the First World War during the inter-war period.

What is certainly very significant is the fact that the army's most senior and influential commanders in both World Wars shared the apparently reasonable and well-founded conviction that religion was a crucial and sustaining force for the morale of their citizen soldiers. However, and because this conviction chiefly stemmed from an appreciation of the importance of morale in winning the war, the functional priorities of the army's commanders clearly diverged from the missionary aspirations of many in the churches. Whereas Haig and Montgomery were concerned with using the army's chaplains to sustain a vigorous sense of purpose and righteous enthusiasm, the churches were liable to view the army as a mission field. Such missionary ambition was frustrated by the circumscribed terms within which their chaplains and agencies operated and also by the prevalent religious outlook which they encountered, the diffusive Christianity of the ordinary soldier serving to inoculate him against greater involvement in church life while encouraging him to make full and appreciative use of the spiritual, material and moral comforts that organised religion had to offer.

In broad historiographical terms, the significance of these conclusions seem threefold. First, and in terms of the long-running debate over secularisation, in addressing the religious dynamics of class, gender, war, patriotism, ethnicity, regionality and age they show that the situation of religion in British society in the first half of the twentieth century was more robust than has often been realised. However, and while largely confirming the cultural strength of contemporary Christianity as perceived by Callum Brown in his groundbreaking *Death of Christian Britain*, they demonstrate that male religiosity was not so dependent on female influence as Brown imagines. Furthermore, they demonstrate that the religious culture of Britain did weaken perceptibly on several fronts in the inter-war period, a conclusion that throws into question Brown's claim that the collapse of Britain's Christian culture was a sudden and dramatic phenomenon precipitated by the burgeoning feminism of the 1960s. Second, and in terms of the historiography of British religion in the two World Wars, they demonstrate the inadequacy of the existing focus on leading churchmen, church affairs and conscientious objectors. This focus has remained unchanged since the 1970s, years in which the academic climate induced by A.J.P. Taylor, the Cold War, the Vietnam War and *Oh What a Lovely War* afforded plenty of opportunity for the preferences and perspectives of Christian pacifists to crystallise into subject boundaries and historical orthodoxies. Third and finally, these conclusions constitute an important wake-up call for military historians of the two World Wars, a breed that has too readily subscribed to the supposed obsolescence of religion as a significant force in contemporary British society and culture. In the light of this presumption, and in the absence of earlier correctives, army chaplains tend to be treated as peripheral figures with a hazy and slightly dubious role. Moreover, the ubiquitous philanthropic work of civilian religious organisations is unexplained (even when it is acknowledged) and religious conviction is regarded as either an ethnic peculiarity or as a suspect personal foible. Clearly, and perhaps for military historians most of all, this study shows that it is time to think again.

NOTES

Preface

1 Schweitzer, 2003, xxiii
2 Schweitzer, 2003, xxv
3 Holmes, 2004, 503

Introduction

 1 Milligan, 1972, 49
 2 Cited in Mews, 1973, 174
 3 See Currie *et al.*, 1977 and McLeod, 1993, 1–13
 4 Brown, 2001, 156
 5 See, for example, Milligan, 1972, 49, 63, 93; 1976, 41, 163, 178–9, 181–2, 202; 1978, 40, 43, 102; 1980, 13, 32–3, 57, 83, 105–7, 112–13, 168–9, 174–5, 190, 209, 231
 6 Brown, 2001, 9
 7 Brown, 2001, 57
 8 Brown, 2001, 166
 9 Brown, 2001, 156
10 Brown, 2001, 105
11 Brown, 1999, *passim*; Brown, 2001, *passim*
12 See, for example, Brown, 1994; Ceadel, 1980; Chandler, 1993; Chandler, 1994; Goodall, 1997; Hastings, 1991; Hoover, 1989; Hoover, 1999; Lawson, 2003; Marrin, 1974; Mews, 1973; Robbins, 1985; Thompson, 1983; Wilkinson, 1978; Wilkinson, 1986

13   Wickham, 1957, 206
14   Currie *et al.*, 1977, 30, 113–15, 123
15   Snape and Parker, 2001, *passim*; Weight, 2002, 28–33; Wolffe, 1994, 236–53; Hastings, 1991, 382–400
16   Becker, 1998, *passim*; Miner, 2003, *passim*
17   Dewey, 1997, Table 3.7, 59
18   *Statistics of the Military Effort of the British Empire*, 1992, 30, 363
19   Shaw, 1996, *passim*
20   Carver, 1998, 310
21   *Statistics of the Military Effort of the British Empire*, 1992, 192, 206
22   Danchev, 1994, 314
23   Spiers, 1985, 44–5; French, 2000, 49
24   Beckett, 1985 (b), 145–6; French, 2000, 53–5
25   Beckett, 1985 (b), 128–9; French, 2000, 53
26   Simpson, 1985, 79–82; French, 2000, 73–5
27   Jeffery, 1985, 218–19
28   *Statistics of the Military Effort of the British Empire*, 1992, 363
29   Jeffery, 1996 (b), 116–17
30   Jeffery, 1985, 219
31   Jeffery, 1996 (a), 431–2
32   Jeffery, 1996 (a), 438
33   PRO, WO 365/62
34   Wood, 1997, 82–3
35   PRO, WO 365/62
36   Middlebrook, 2000, 63–84
37   French, 2000, 53
38   Crang, 2000, 2
39   Calder, 1996, 51–3; French, 2000, 64
40   Calder, 1996, 51, 234, 249
41   Calder, 1996, 249; French, 2000, 67
42   French, 2000, 67–8
43   French, 2000, 12–47
44   French, 2000, 43, 66
45   Barnett, 1970, 441
46   French, 2000, 113–14
47   Harvey, 1994, 561
48   Ellis, 1993, 157
49   Ellis, 1993, 156
50   Harvey, 1994, 561
51   Carver, 1998, 310
52   Calder, 1996, 249–50
53   French, 2000, 147
54   *Statistics of the Military Effort of the British Empire*, 1992, 243; Woodburn Kirby, 1965, 461
55   Ellis, 1993, 181

56 Ellis, 1993, 182. For a broader discussion of the development of British medical practice in the two World Wars see Bosanquet and Whitehead, 2000, *passim*

57 Ellis, 1993, 169–74

1 'Diffusive Christianity' and the religion of the soldier

1   Cox, 1982, 47, 99–100
2   McLeod, 1996, 12–13; Brown, 1997, 43–4
3   These figures are derived from Currie *et al.*, 1977, 31–2
4   Gregory, 1994, *passim*; Parsons, 2002, 26–41; Montgomery-Massingberd, 1989, 162
5   Cox, 1982, *passim*; Williams, 1999, 126–39
6   Machin, 1998, 53–107
7   Grimley, 2004, 189–90
8   Cox, 1982, *passim*; Williams, 1999, 148–54; Nicholas, 2002, 118
9   DeGroot, 1996 (b), 39
10 Wolfe, 1984, 3
11 Robbins, 1993, 122–3
12 Gorer, 1955, 237
13 Snape and Parker, 2001, 398
14 Currie *et al.*, 1977, 31–2
15 Currie *et al.*, 1977, 157–9
16 Cox, 1982, 42–4
17 Hempton, 1988, 183; Brown, 2001, 156–9; Cox, 1982, 32; Snape and Parker, 2001, 397
18 Snape and Parker, 2001, 406–7; Currie *et al.*, 1977, 31–2
19 Drewett, 1942, 82
20 Cox, 1982, 93
21 Brown, 2001, 8
22 Drewett, 1942, 84
23 Drewett, 1942, 85
24 Drewett, 1942, 87
25 Reay, 1998, 71–100
26 Cox, 1982, 92
27 Drewett, 1942, 89
28 MacNutt, 1917, 350
29 MacNutt, 1917, 358
30 Cox, 1982, 96; Murphy, 1971, 93–4
31 Murphy, 1971, 125
32 Williams, 1999, 129–41
33 MacNutt, 1917, 352–5
34 Cairns, 1919, 108
35 Cairns, 1919, 119
36 Cairns, 1919, 121
37 Snape, 2002, 345

38 Machin, 1998, 54–8; Drewett, 1942, 83
39 Mayhew, n.d., 1
40 MO, FR 2274
41 MO, FR 2274
42 MO, FR 2274
43 MO, FR 2274
44 MO, FR 2274
45 *Methodist Recorder*, 2 September 1943, 3
46 Holmes, 1994, 240–1
47 Snape, 2005
48 Pym and Gordon, 1917, 186
49 Liddle Collection, D.J.B. Wilson
50 McLean and Sclater, 1917, 144
51 Black, 1917, 82
52 Selwyn, 1989, 362
53 Skinner, n.d., 18–19
54 Author's collection, Tony Foulds
55 Quoted in Simpson, 1993, 117
56 Moynihan, 1988, 61–2
57 Quoted in Wilkinson, 1978, 277
58 IWM documents, Owen Eva
59 Quoted in Carpenter, 1996, 77
60 Thomas, 1991, *passim*; Williams, 1999, 75–8
61 Malden, 1917, 7
62 Author's collection, Colin Starkie
63 IWM sound, Alastair Menzies
64 IWM documents, H.L. Adams
65 Malden, 1917, 6
66 Malden, 1917, 16
67 Malden, 1917, 25–6
68 Rogers, 1941, *passim*
69 Lloyd, 1942, *passim*
70 Plater, 1919, 19
71 Maclean Watt, 1917, 76
72 IWM documents, E.C. Crosse
73 Pym and Gordon, 1917, 186
74 Treves, 1916, 183
75 Cairns, 1919, 162, 165
76 Studdert Kennedy, 1918 (a), 49–50
77 Gordon, 1972, 69
78 Ewing, 1917, 158–9
79 Liddle Collection, Arthur Smith
80 Tiplady, 1939, 83
81 Ewing, 1917, 159
82 Selby Wright, 1942, 79
83 Plater, 1919, 26

84   IWM documents, J.B. Scollen
85   *The Tablet*, 20 February 1915, 234
86   O'Rahilly, 1932, 497
87   IWM exhibits and firearms, Troops' Mascots 1914–1917
88   Plater, 1919, 25
89   Trevelyan, 1985, 24, 68, 77–8
90   Author's collection, Charlie Wakeley
91   Plater, 1919, 30–2
92   Plater, 1919, 26
93   IWM exhibits and firearms, Troops' Mascots 1914–1917; Williams, 1999, 67; Weeks, 1920, 85; Gibbs, 1920, 117; Atkinson, 2003, 230
94   IWM exhibits and firearms, Troops' Mascots 1914–1917
95   Gorer, 1955, 265
96   Vaughan, 1981, 193
97   Reith, 1966, 108
98   Graves, 1960, 100
99   Author's collection, MacPherson Knowles
100 Bowlby, 1999, 141
101 Chapman, 1985, 196
102 Author's collection, MacPherson Knowles
103 O'Rahilly, 1932, 432, 460, 474, 505
104 IWM documents, R. Bulstrode
105 Graves, 1960, 161–2
106 Bowlby, 1999, 64
107 Cairns, 1919, 160
108 Quoted in Fuller, 1990, 157
109 Malden, 1917, 14
110 Plater, 1919, 26
111 Brown, 1986, 134
112 Winter, 1992, 190–1; Winter, 1998, 64–6
113 Nelson, 1969, 155–62; Hazelgrove, 2000, 14
114 Jones, 1920, x–xi
115 Cairns, 1919, 19–20; Clarke, 2004, 183–93
116 Nelson, 1969, 154; Hazelgrove, 2000, 80
117 Graves, 1960, 191–2
118 Graves, 1960, 102, 191–2
119 Hazelgrove, 2000, 14 and 33
120 Mews, 1973, 97
121 Mews, 1973, 97–104; Winter, 1992, 191–2; Fussell, 1977, 115–16; Clarke, 2004, *passim*
122 Forbes, 1918, 3–4
123 IWM documents, T.B. Butt
124 Brown, 1994, 88–9; Porter, 2002, 43
125 Horne, 1995, 152
126 Lever, 1971, 56
127 Tout, 1987, 58

128 Bowlby, 1999, 122
129 *The Times*, 5 August 1944, 2
130 Author's collection, Charlie Wakeley; Tony Foulds
131 Cairns, 1919, 43, 46
132 Williams, 1999, 132–4
133 Cairns, 1919, 42
134 Liddle Collection, F.M. Chance
135 Liddle Collection, J.F.R. Modrell
136 Liddle Collection, J.F.R. Modrell
137 Middlebrook, 1984, 55–6; M. Brown, 1996, 6–7
138 Feilding, 2001, 45
139 Tiplady, 1939, 74
140 Tiplady, 1939, 78
141 Middlebrook, 1984, 56; M. Brown, 1996, 157; Fussell, 1977, 131–5
142 Martin, 1987, 82
143 M. Brown, 1996, 317
144 Bickersteth, 1996, 168
145 O'Rahilly, 1932, 463, 473, 494–5; Dempsey, 1947, 7–9, 13–14; Wheatley, 1983, 132–3
146 Plater, 1919, 50
147 Cairns, 1919, 172–7
148 Studdert Kennedy, 1918 (a), 118–19
149 Knight, 1995, 36
150 Knight, 1995, 36, 53–4
151 IWM documents, W.M. Murray
152 Gethyn-Jones, 1988, 106, 118–19
153 MacDonald Fraser, 2000, 163
154 IWM documents, W.H. Miller
155 Pym and Gordon, 1917, 186–7
156 Cairns, 1919, 166–8
157 Barber, 1946, 79
158 Author's collection, Charlie Wakeley
159 IWM sound, Cecil Macauley Johnston
160 Ewing, 1917, 128–9
161 Black, 1917, 82
162 Pym and Gordon, 1917, 187–8
163 Studdert Kennedy, 1918 (b), 224
164 Studdert Kennedy, 1918 (b), 225–6
165 Steel and Hart, 2001, 91
166 Bickersteth, 1996, 169
167 Cairns, 1919, 12
168 Cairns, 1919, 7–8
169 Williams, 1999, 142–3, 149
170 Snape and Parker, 2001, 403
171 MO, FR 1566
172 Gorer, 1955, Table 85, 452

173 Talbot, 1917, 69
174 Plater, 1919, 107–23; Cairns, 1919, 42–3; Dempsey, 1947, 57; Sime, 1952, *passim*
175 RAChD, F.L. Hughes, 8th Army Papers, 'Some Advice on the Chaplain's Duty in Battle'
176 Bowlby, 1999, 82
177 Delaforce, 1999 (b), 114
178 Liddle Collection, Walter Shaw
179 ABA, P1/53
180 Montgomery-Massingberd, 1989, 162
181 Gethyn-Jones, 1988, 82
182 Ryan, 1999, 415
183 Sime, 1952, 344
184 Wolffe, 1997, 64, 83
185 Williams, 1999, 148–54
186 See Arthur, 2001; Brophy and Partridge, 1969
187 Richards, 1983, 85
188 Liddle Collection, J.M. Hill. See also Graham, 1919, 108–9
189 IWM documents, E.C. Crosse
190 Bickersteth, 1996, 193
191 Nicholas, 2002, 118; Wolfe, 1984, 273
192 Author's collection, Tony Foulds
193 Ryan, 1999, 414–15; IWM documents, W.H. Miller
194 White, 2002, 201
195 Sime, 1952, 346
196 Firth, 1995, 21
197 Gordon, 1972, 164
198 Montague, 1922, 57
199 Cairns, 1919, 175
200 Cairns, 1919, 143
201 MO, FR 1870 A
202 Dempsey, 1947, 63–6
203 Cairns, 1919, 156; Wilkinson, 1978, 161
204 MO, FR 23; FR 622; FR 769; FR 1268; FR 1525; FR 1566; FR 1572; FR 2017; FR 2190E; FR 2112; FR 2274; TC Religion 3/B
205 Whitehouse and Bennett, 1995, 107–8

2 God and the generals

1 Winter, 1992, 164–5
2 Holmes, 2004, 505–6; Bickersteth, 1996, ix
3 McLeod, 1996, 21
4 Norman, 1976, 205
5 Drewett, 1942, 85
6 Fraser, 2003, 97
7 Baynes, 1987, 202

8 Baynes, 1995, *passim*
9 Potter and Matheson, 1936, 32
10 Cave, 1999, 248–9
11 Duncan, 1966, 21; Charteris, 1929, 60
12 Duncan, 1966, 130–2; Cave, 1999, 244
13 Cooper, 1935, 114
14 DeGroot, 1991, 193
15 Cooper, 1935, 282
16 DeGroot, 1996 (a), 277
17 Charteris, 1929, 297
18 Duncan, 1966, 17–18
19 Duncan, 1966, 19
20 Duncan, 1966, 60; *Haig's Autograph Great War Diary*, 30 March 1916, 21 May 1916
21 *Haig's Autograph Great War Diary*, 2 and 9 January 1916
22 *Haig's Autograph Great War Diary*, 2 January 1916
23 DeGroot, 1996 (a), 319
24 Duncan, 1966, 20
25 Duncan, 1966, 40
26 Duncan, 1966, 37
27 DeGroot, 1996 (a), 378–9
28 DeGroot, 1996 (a), 379
29 DeGroot, 1996 (a), 350, 367
30 Duncan, 1966, 54, 105
31 Duncan, 1966, 30
32 Terraine, 1990, 175
33 DeGroot, 1996 (a), 387
34 Duncan, 1966, 76
35 Charteris, 1929, 346
36 Duncan, 1966, 120; Cooper, 1935, 328
37 DeGroot, 1996 (a), 292
38 Duncan, 1966, 70
39 Duncan, 1966, 72; Charteris, 1929, 297
40 Duncan, 1966, 122
41 DeGroot, 1996 (a), 364–5
42 Duncan, 1966, 114
43 Duncan, 1966, 120, 124; Charteris, 1929, 316
44 DeGroot, 1996 (a), 405
45 Duncan, 1966, 126
46 Cave, 1999, *passim*
47 Charteris, 1931, 274, 314; Cave, 1999, 247
48 DeGroot, 1993, 62–3
49 DeGroot, 1991, 199
50 DeGroot, 1993, 62–3
51 DeGroot, 1993, 66
52 DeGroot, 1991, 209

53 Bond, 2002, *passim*
54 DeGroot, 1991, 205
55 Winter, 1992, 165
56 Jackson, 1960, 165–6
57 Harington, 1935, xi
58 Jackson, 1960, 168–9
59 Harington, 1935, 103
60 Harington, 1935, 319–20
61 Cave, 1999, 248; Jackson, 1960, 166
62 Gwynne, 1917, 47–8
63 DeGroot, 1996 (a), 392
64 CMS, Diaries of L.H. Gwynne, 17 September 1917
65 Gwynne, 1917, 49
66 IWM documents, E.C. Crosse
67 Crosse, 1917, 8
68 Gwynne, 1917, 48
69 Savage, 1925, 19–20
70 Gwynne, 1917, 44
71 Barrett, 1919, vii
72 Sheffield, 2000 (b), 445
73 Bourne, 2001, 163
74 Lever, 1971, 61
75 DeGroot, 1996 (a), 392
76 Iremonger, 1948, 266
77 Denman, 1992, 56–7
78 Denman, 1992, 57
79 Martin, 1987, 132–3
80 Bourne, 2001, 234
81 Dunn, 1994, 319
82 Richards, 1983, 217
83 Hamilton, 2002, 4–18, 784
84 Hamilton, 2002, 24
85 Montgomery, 1958, 90
86 Fraser, 1999, 99
87 Barnett, 1970, 474
88 Hamilton, 2002, 631
89 Montgomery, 1946, *passim*
90 Montgomery, 1946, n.p.
91 Montgomery, 1946, n.p.
92 Barclay, 1956, 218
93 Hamilton, 1983, 79
94 Gethyn-Jones, 1988, 63
95 Quoted in Gethyn-Jones, 1988, 80
96 Gethyn-Jones, 1988, 81
97 French, 2000, 150
98 Ambrose, 1998, 218

 99   Kirby, 1995, 108, 110
100   Gethyn-Jones, 1988, 81
101   Picot, 1994, 260–1
102   Gordon, 1995, *passim*
103   Royle, 1995, 3
104   Allen, 2000, 119, 121–2, 319
105   Woodburn Kirby, 1958, 505
106   Rooney, 2000, 111
107   *Oxford Dictionary of National Biography*; Dobbie, 1944, 49
108   MO, FR 1870 A
109   Dobbie, 1944, 87
110   Selby Wright, 1941, 19–21
111   Colville, 1972, 231–2
112   Guinness, 1945, 29
113   Atkinson, 2003, 173–4, 262
114   Danchev, 1989, 29–30
115   Drury, 1968, 337
116   Hamilton, 2002, 305–9
117   Danchev and Todman, 2002, 295
118   Danchev and Todman, 2002, 689
119   IWM documents, A.L. Bird
120   Danchev, 1989, 30; Danchev and Todman, 2002, 48
121   Wheatley, 1983, 29
122   Wheatley, 1983, 154–5
123   Atkinson, 2003, 422
124   Gethyn-Jones, 1988, 4

3 Command and the clergy: generals, chaplains and morale

 1   Graves, 1960, 158–9
 2   Chapman, 1985, 117
 3   Bond, 2002, *passim*
 4   See, for example, Purcell, 1983, *passim*
 5   Robinson, 1999, 74–5
 6   Zahn, 1969, 262
 7   Wilkinson, 1981, 251
 8   Louden, 1996, *passim*
 9   Louden, 1996, 120
10   Schweitzer, 2003, *passim*
11   Bourke, 1999, 304–5
12   See Thompson, 1990; A.M. Brown, 1996; Coulter, 1997; Robinson, 1999
13   A.M. Brown, 1996, 226
14   Robinson, 1999, Table 9.1, 234
15   Whitlow, 1938, 46–52, 65–74, 89
16   Whitlow, 1938, 88
17   Adler, 1922, 12

18 LPL, Davidson Papers, Vol. 345, Great War: Clergy 1917–19, 36
19 This table excludes the army's non-commissioned acting chaplains in post in August 1914
20 Drury, 1922, 45
21 LPL, Davidson Papers, Vol. 343, Great War: Clergy 1914–15, 41
22 LPL, Davidson Papers, Vol. 343, Great War: Clergy 1914–15, 207
23 *Statistics of the Military Effort of the British Empire*, 1992, 191
24 Wilkinson, 1978, 126; Marrin, 1974, 206–7; Purcell, 1983, 97
25 Robinson, 1999, 31
26 IWM documents, E.C. Crosse
27 Holmes, 2001, 599–600; Sheffield, 2000 (a), 180–1; Baynes, 1987, 97–100
28 Baynes, 1987, 108
29 Sheffield, 2000 (a), 178–9
30 Fuller, 1990, 175
31 Bowman, 2003, 21–31
32 Englander, 1997, 130; Bowman, 2003, 21
33 Travers, 1987, 38
34 Travers, 1987, 38, 62
35 Porch, 1975, 138
36 Quoted in Travers, 1987, 96
37 Ashworth, 2000, 177–85; Barnett, 1970, 392
38 Marrin, 1974; Wilkinson, 1978; Wilkinson, 1986; Hoover, 1989; Snape, 2002
39 Summers, 1989, *passim*
40 Shattuck, 1987, *passim*
41 Travers, 1987, 87
42 Travers, 1987, 95
43 MacKenzie, 1990, 216–18
44 Jackson, 1960, 164
45 Wilkinson, 1978, 127; Duncan, 1966, 21
46 Blackburne, 1955, 48
47 Harington, 1935, 231
48 *Haig's Autograph Great War Diary*, 15 January 1916
49 Edmonds, 1932, 138
50 Blackburne, 1955, 51
51 LPL, Davidson Papers, Vol. 583, Visit to the Front May 1916, 3–4
52 LPL, Davidson Papers, Vol. 583, Visit to the Front May 1916, 70–1
53 *Haig's Autograph Great War Diary*, 21 May 1916
54 LPL, Davidson Papers, Vol. 583, Visit to the Front May 1916, 55–6
55 Adler, 1922, 46–7
56 LPL, Davidson Papers, Vol. 344, Great War: Clergy 1915–17, 146
57 Thompson, 1983, 337–50; Gwynne, 1917, 55–9
58 Gwynne, 1917, 60
59 Gwynne, 1917, 47
60 Gwynne, 1917, 54
61 Creighton, 1920, 166

62 Crosse, 1917, 32
63 Blackburne, 1932, 115
64 Harington, 1935, 232–3
65 IWM documents, E.C. Crosse
66 IWM documents, E.C. Crosse
67 IWM documents, E.C. Crosse
68 Smyth, 1968, 184–5
69 LPL, Davidson Papers, Vol. 345, Great War: Clergy 1917–19, 200
70 Bickersteth, 1996, 228
71 O'Rahilly, 1932, 455
72 LPL, Davidson Papers, Vol. 344, Great War: Clergy 1915–17, 218, 228
73 LPL, Davidson Papers, Vol. 345, Great War: Clergy 1917–19, 4
74 Thompson, 1990, 390
75 Bickersteth, 1996, 145
76 Quoted in Steel and Hart, 2001, 104
77 Richards, 1983, 288, 301–3; Dunn, 1994, 556
78 IWM documents, E.C. Crosse
79 IWM documents, E.C. Crosse
80 Moynihan, 1983, 65
81 IWM documents, E.C. Crosse
82 O'Rahilly, 1932, 522, note 2. Larkin was Ireland's leading trades unionist and a celebrated public orator
83 Moynihan, 1983, 156
84 Moynihan, 1983, 166
85 Forbes, 1918, 44–5
86 Terraine, 1986, 165
87 Quoted in Marrin, 1974, 209
88 Liddell Hart Centre for Military Archives, GB 99 KCLMA Beddington. I am grateful to Mr Alun Thomas for this reference
89 Purcell, 1983, 99
90 Studdert Kennedy, 1918 (b), *passim*
91 Griffith, 1994, 61, 186; Middlebrook, 2000, 87–91
92 Purcell, 1983, 108; Vaughan, 1981, 91; Cave, 1993, 15–16
93 Griffith, 1994, 188
94 Purcell, 1983, 143–5
95 Gibbs, 1920, 92
96 Wilkinson, 1978, 136
97 Gibbs, 1920, 93
98 Steuart, 1931, 50
99 LPL, Davidson Papers, Vol. 344, Great War: Clergy 1915–17, 193–4
100 Englander, 1997, 139; MacKenzie, 1992, 8, 13–14; Bowman, 2003, 156
101 CMS, Diaries of L.H. Gwynne, 17 October 1917
102 CMS, Diaries of L.H. Gwynne, 18 October 1917
103 CMS, Diaries of L.H. Gwynne, 19 October 1917
104 CMS, Diaries of L.H. Gwynne, 22 December 1917
105 Jackson, 1960, 160

106 CMS, Diaries of L.H. Gwynne, 5 February 1918
107 CMS, Diaries of L.H. Gwynne, 15 February 1918
108 Jackson, 1960, 160
109 MacKenzie, 1992, 3–31
110 Crerar, 1995, 143
111 Montague, 1922, 74–5
112 IWM documents, E.C. Crosse
113 Callan, 1917, 5
114 MacNutt, 1917, 379–80
115 Gibbs, 1920, 116–17
116 Graham, 1919, 256–7
117 Graham, 1919, 257–8
118 Gibbs, 1920, 364
119 Sheffield and Inglis, 1989, 40
120 Plater, 1919, 10
121 ABA, FHD/A5 Francis H. Drinkwater – War Diaries 1915–18, 10 August 1915
122 ABA, FHD/A5 Francis H. Drinkwater – War Diaries 1915–18, 2 July 1916
123 Terraine, 1979, 145
124 DeGroot, 1996 (a), 407
125 *Statistics of the Military Effort of the British Empire*, 1992, 190; Smyth, 1968, 216
126 Jackson, 1960, 169
127 Edmonds, 1932, 135–8
128 Croft, 1919, 24–5
129 Marrin, 1974, *passim*
130 Bond, 2002, 7
131 Sheffield, 2000 (a), 180–1
132 Williamson, 1921, 59–60
133 DeGroot, 1996 (a), 349
134 Croft, 1919, 291
135 Keegan and Holmes, 1985, 51
136 Baynes, 1987, 217
137 *Statistics of the Military Effort of the British Empire*, 1992, 37, 190
138 Middleton Brumwell, 1943, 19
139 Smyth, 1968, 220; Robinson, 1999, 56, 104; Coulter, 1997, 73; PRO, WO 365/62
140 Robinson, 1999, 104
141 Middleton Brumwell, 1943, 30
142 Ellis, 1968, 405
143 French, 2000, 15–16
144 Fraser, 1999, 147
145 Calder, 1996, 273–4; French, 2000, 138
146 Crang, 1997, 61
147 Quoted in French, 2000, 1–2

148 Calder, 1996, 248–9
149 Quoted in Crang, 1997, 61
150 Crang, 1997, 60–74
151 Hastings, 1984, 57
152 MO, FR 1870 A
153 *Parliamentary Debates (Hansard)* Fifth series, 388, House of Commons, 22 April 1943, Column 1893
154 Hoover, 1999, *passim*; Snape and Parker, 2001, *passim*
155 Crang, 2000, 120–1; Lindsay, 1944, 376, 379
156 Anon., 1940, 112
157 Bussby, 1967, 23
158 Selby Wright, 1941, 7
159 Hoover, 1999, 97–120; Robbins, 1985, 279–99; Weight, 2002, 27
160 Selby Wright, 1941, 106–9
161 Coghlan, 1942, 16
162 Middleton Brumwell, 1943, 59
163 Middleton Brumwell, 1943, 63
164 Middleton-Brumwell, 1943, 55–70
165 Smyth, 1968, 244–5; Dempsey, 1947, 143
166 Dempsey, 1947, 144
167 Smyth, 1968, 244; Robinson, 1999, 145; MO, FR 1870 A
168 Selby Wright, 1942, 86
169 Murphy, 1971, 10–11; Green, 2000, *passim*; Hastings, 1991, 417–22; MO, FR 2017
170 McKenzie, 1992, *passim*; Calder, 1996, 250–1; Crang, 2000, 116–20
171 Quoted in Calder, 1996, 251
172 LPL, Davidson Papers, Vol. 583, Visit to the Front May 1916, 56–7
173 Hamilton, 1983, 175
174 Hamilton, 1983, 79
175 Robinson, 1999, 170
176 Montgomery, 1958, 114
177 RAChD, Nye, 1981
178 Smyth, 1968, 232
179 Louden, 1996, 75
180 Hamilton, 1986, 804
181 Montgomery, 1958, 227
182 Montgomery, 1958, 229
183 *Parliamentary Debates (Hansard)* Fifth series 406, House of Commons, 7 December 1944, Column 896
184 Louden, 1996, 3; Smyth, 1968, 232, 234
185 Oliver, 1986, 100
186 Cook and Cook, 1988, 271
187 RAChD, F.L. Hughes, 8th Army Papers, 'Some Advice on the Chaplain's Duty in Battle'; Robinson, 1999, 168
188 Robinson, 1999, 226
189 Montgomery, 1958, 204

190 Hamilton, 1986, 118–19
191 Smyth, 1968, 233–4
192 Hawkins, 1994, 40–3
193 IWM sound, Frederick Llewelyn Hughes
194 RAChD, F.L. Hughes, 8th Army Papers, 'Christmas, 1942 Sermon Broadcast from Bethlehem'
195 Lucas, 1989, between 86 and 87
196 RAChD, Nye, 1981
197 RAChD, R. Rudgard, 'The Very Revd Frederick Llewelyn Hughes . . . Address by the Venerable Richard Rudgard, Archdeacon of Basingstoke, at the Memorial Service held in the Guards Chapel, Wellingon Barracks, on Wednesday 21 June 1967'
198 Montgomery, 1958, 230
199 Hamilton, 1983, 552–3
200 IWM sound, John William Steele
201 IWM sound, Anon. chaplain *et al.*
202 Brooks, 1991, 90
203 Salisbury Woodward and Blackburne, 1939, 47
204 Hills, 2002, 118–19
205 Gethyn-Jones, 1988, 68–9
206 Oliver, 1986, 77–8
207 Blake, 1950, 216
208 French, 2000, 96–106
209 Tout, 1992, 11
210 Cook and Cook, 1988, 87
211 Skinner, n.d., 48–9
212 Crang, 2000, 91–3
213 IWM documents, A.H. Rodgers
214 MO, FR 1870 A
215 MO, FR 1870 A
216 MO, FR 1870 A
217 MO, FR 1870 A
218 Author's collection, Charlie Wakeley
219 Delaforce, 2002, 101
220 Delaforce, 2002, 99
221 RAChD, B.L. Montgomery, 'To All Padres in 21 Army Group', 1 July 1945
222 Smyth, 1968, 307; Ellis, 1993, 396

4 The church in khaki

1 Warner, 2003, 184–5
2 Sellers, 1915, 45
3 IWM documents, W. Knott
4 Graham, 1919, 103
5 Graham, 1919, 102

6 Richards, 1983, 84

7 Cairns, 1919, 39

8 Forbes, 1918, 67

9 Spurr, 1916, 55

10 Goodridge and Goodridge, 2000, 94–5

11 Robinson, 1999, 73

12 Crang, 2000, 78–9

13 Robinson, 1999, 99–100

14 Liddle Collection, Peter Sutton

15 Gethyn-Jones, 1988, 106

16 Author's collection, Charlie Wakeley; Tony Foulds

17 Middleton Brumwell, 1943, 42

18 PRO, WO 32/14687; Robinson, 1999, 100–1

19 Beckett, 1985 (a), Table 1.2, 9

20 French, 2000, 64–6

21 Mews, 1973, 181

22 *General Annual Report of the British Army*, 1914, 93

23 LPL, Davidson Papers, Vol. 343, Great War: Clergy 1914–15, 211

24 Hastings, 1991, 40

25 LPL, Davidson Papers, Vol. 344, Great War: Clergy 1915–17, 141

26 Drury, 1968, 63

27 Englander, 1988, 254–5

28 Adler, 1922, 3–4, 36, 46

29 Martin, 1987, 34

30 Hughes, 1985, 114–22

31 LPL, Davidson Papers, Vol. 344, Great War: Clergy 1915–17, 203

32 LPL, Davidson Papers, Vol. 344, Great War: Clergy 1915–17, 233

33 LPL, Davidson Papers, Vol. 344, Great War: Clergy 1915–17, 235

34 Middlebrook, 2000, 50

35 Bowman, 2003, 153–5

36 LPL, Davidson Papers, Vol. 344, Great War: Clergy 1915–17, 208

37 Middlebrook, 2000, 146; Westlake, 1998, 76

38 Johnstone, 1992, 216–18, 345–6

39 The estimate of professed Presbyterians is based on the total number of Scottish regulars and reservists in 1913 and the number of Scottish enlistments during the war. These totalled just over 580,000, or 10 per cent of the men who served in the British army between 1914 and 1918. Although only 85 per cent of the population of Scotland could be identified as Presbyterians at this time, Presbyterian numbers would have been augmented by recruits from the English and Irish Presbyterian churches and by the tendency of the religiously uncommitted to profess the religion of the majority. See *General Annual Report of the British Army*, 1914, 91, 93, 118; *Statistics of the Military Effort of the British Empire*, 1992, 363. Brown, 1997, 50. For a further discussion of Catholic numbers see Snape, 2002, 325

40 *General Annual Report of the British Army*, 1914, 93

41 Of this 2.7 per cent, nearly two-thirds were Baptists
42 PRO, WO 365/39
43 Dewey, 1997, 120
44 Lipman, 1954, 167; Forty, 2002, 136
45 Rosen, 2004, 26–28
46 Currie *et al.*, 1977, 143, 151; Wilkinson, 1986, *passim*; Hoover, 1999, 37
47 IWM sound, Walter Cleveland
48 Whiteman, 1985, 116–17
49 Plater, 1919, 129–34
50 Sheffield, 2000 (a), 31–3; French 2000, 73
51 Sheffield, 2000 (a), 82–3
52 MacNutt, 1917, 355–8
53 Bickersteth, 1996, 83
54 Sheffield, 2000 (a), 108
55 Hankey, 1918, 60
56 Wilkinson, 1978, 12
57 See Chapter 1
58 Plater, 1919, 131–2
59 Bickersteth, 1996, 83
60 Drury, 1968, 62; Sheffield, 2000 (a), 83
61 Drury, 1968, 207–8
62 Bickersteth, 1996, 255
63 IWM documents, A.D. Hamer
64 De Candole, 1919, *passim*
65 Iremonger, 1948, 266–9
66 O'Creagh and Humphries, 1923, I, 308
67 Anon., 1916 (b), 333–4
68 Ewing, 1917, 7
69 Reith, 1966, 102–3
70 Reith, 1966, 108
71 Reith, 1966, 154
72 Westerdale, 1917, 85
73 Adler, 1922, 43–4
74 Liddle Collection, Sydney Frankenburg
75 French, 2000, 79; Crang, 2000, 52; Forty, 2002, 96–8
76 MO, FR 1870 A
77 MO, FR 1870 A
78 IWM sound, Alastair Menzies
79 IWM documents, J.B. Scollen
80 Delaforce, 1999 (a), 71
81 Wheatley, 1983, 126–7
82 IWM documents, A.R.C. Leaney
83 IWM documents, N.F. Jones
84 Latimer, 2003, 68–9
85 Author's collection, Tony Foulds
86 Hein, 2000, *passim*

87 IWM documents, H.T. Bone
88 *The Times*, 5 August 1944, 2
89 Hankey, 1918, 21
90 Ewing, 1917, 136
91 Moynihan, 1983, 92
92 Boullier, 1917, 13, 288
93 Boullier, 1917, 42
94 Graham, 1919, 250–4
95 Moynhian, 1983, 93–4
96 Sellers, 1915, 10; see also Sellers, 1918, 210
97 Hankey, 1918, 171, footnote
98 Robinson and Hair, 2001, 3–6
99 Gray, 1917, 13
100 Denman, 1992, 41–2
101 Falls, 1922, 16
102 Bowman, 2003, 28–9
103 Potter and Matheson, 1936, 75
104 Middlebrook, 1984, 174
105 Mews, 1973, 123–4
106 Hughes, 1985, 116–17
107 Hughes, 1990, 105
108 Adler, 1922, 9
109 Adler, 1922, 9–11; Westlake, 1998, 170; Englander, 1994, 314
110 Adler, 1922, 10
111 Adler, 1922, 9–10
112 Callan, 1987–90, 46; Feilding, 2001, xii
113 Denman, 1992, 139
114 Hughes, 1985, 115
115 Crozier, 1930, 33
116 Bowman, 2003, 23–4
117 Clayton, 1920, 59
118 For a discussion of the place of religion in the experience of the Scottish soldier in the First World War see Spiers, 1996, 325
119 Black, 1917, 81
120 Maclean Watt, 1917, 95
121 Cairns, 1919, 189–90
122 Black, 1917, 82
123 Plater, 1919, 42
124 Cairns, 1919, 190
125 Springhall, 1977, 13–52; Wilkinson, 1969, 4–7
126 MacKenzie, 1997, 242–3
127 MacKenzie, 1997, 154–5, 242
128 Snape, 2002, 316
129 Springhall, 1977, 28
130 MacKenzie, 1997, 203–4
131 Summers, 1989, 250; Howkins, 1989, 82–3

132   Simkins, 1994, 259; MacDonald, 1983, 139; Springhall, 1977, 47
133   Sellers, 1915, 11
134   Snape, 2002, *passim*
135   Clements, 1975, *passim*; Hendry, 1985, *passim*
136   Sellers, 1915, 4
137   Wilkinson, 1978, 32–6; Moorhouse, 1993, 146–7; Wilson, 1988, 178–9;
      Brown, 1994, 84; Snape, 2002, 322–3; Rae, 1970, 193, note 4
138   Bourne, 1996, 342–7; Liddle, 1996, 6
139   White, 1993, *passim*
140   Snape, 2002, 326; Adler, 1922, 4
141   Westerdale, 1917, 84–5
142   Forbes, 1918, 86
143   Yates, 1999, 287
144   Clayton, 1920, 29–30
145   Clayton, 1920, 82
146   IWM documents, E.C. Crosse
147   Drury, 1968, 106
148   Drury, 1968, 91
149   Wilkinson, 1978, 35–6
150   Vernon Smith, 1915, *passim*
151   Bickersteth, 1996, 261
152   For a local study of the revivalist tradition, see Green, 1996, 256–89
153   Currie *et al.*, 1977, 78
154   IWM documents, M. Hardie
155   Brown, 1994, 89
156   Ewing, 1917, 69–70
157   Ewing, 1917, 128–9
158   Sellers, 1915, xii
159   Sellers, 1915, 13
160   *The Tablet*, 12 December 1914, 796
161   CMS, Diaries of L.H. Gwynne, 28 February 1915
162   Horne, 1995, 143–4, 166
163   Horne, 1995, 151–3
164   Westerdale, 1917, 86–7
165   Maclean Watt, 1917, 72–3
166   *Statistics of the Military Effort of the British Empire*, 1992, 241
167   Snape, 2005
168   Thompson, 1983, *passim*; Brown, 1994, 97–101
169   Talbot, 1917, 30
170   Anon., 1917, 37
171   Bickersteth, 1996, 168
172   Cairns, 1919, 133
173   Cairns, 1919, *passim*
174   Talbot, 1917, 8
175   Talbot, 1917, 30
176   Talbot, 1917, 91

177   Bell, 1916, *passim*; Mews, 1973, 199–203; Cairns, 1919, 447–9
178   Talbot, 1917, *passim*; Gray, 1917, *passim*; Anon., 1917, *passim*
179   Cairns, 1919, 238–418
180   Cairns, 1919, 447–9
181   Anon., 1917, 28
182   Jeffery, 1985, Table 8.1, 214
183   Jeffery, 1996 (a), 433–4, 437–8
184   Fellowes, n.d., 32
185   Fellowes, n.d., 40
186   *Methodist Recorder*, 4 February 1943, 4
187   *Methodist Recorder*, 14 January 1943, 1
188   Gethyn-Jones, 1988, 82
189   Gethyn-Jones, 1988, 160
190   Jeffery, 1996 (a), 433
191   Wood, 1997, 82
192   Jeffery, 1996 (a), 443–4; Wood, 1997, *passim*; Doherty, 1993, 157–60
193   Wood, 1997, 84
194   Beckman, 1998, 66–73
195   French, 2000, 123
196   Gordon, 1972, 19
197   Stirling, 1936, 90; Moffatt and McCormick, 2003, 61–2
198   Edwards, 1954, 214–15
199   IWM sound, Douglas Thompson
200   Coulter, 1997, 144–5
201   IWM documents, W.A. Lathaen
202   Woodburn Kirby, 1969, 532
203   Lewis Bryan, 1946, 9
204   Lewis Bryan, 1946, *passim*
205   Lewis Bryan, 1946, 8–9, 18–19; Woodburn Kirby, 1969, 535
206   Lewis Bryan, 1946, 9; *Toc H Journal*, December 1945, 181–5
207   Lewis Bryan, 1946, 24
208   Lewis Bryan, 1946, 42; Mitchell, 1997, 38
209   Lewis Bryan, 1946, 44
210   IWM documents, E.J. Hazel, 'WireVille Gazette', 9 August 1942
211   Lewis Bryan, 1946, 47
212   Firth, 1995, 15
213   Gordon, 1972, 88
214   Gordon, 1972, 91
215   Gordon, 1972, 133–77
216   Gordon, 1972, 121
217   Moriarty, 1993, *passim*
218   Lewis Bryan, 1946, 10
219   Gordon, 1972, 118–19
220   Gordon, 1972, 133–4
221   Lewis Bryan, 1946, 13
222   IWM documents, E.J. Hazel, 'WireVille Gazette', 9 August, 1942

223 IWM documents, S. Dalton. Identity changed at family's request.
224 Walford, 1915, 5
225 Porch, 1975, *passim*
226 Anon., 1916 (a), 8
227 Adler, 1922, 26. See also 6 and 45
228 Baynes, 1987, 203
229 Gummer, 1963, *passim*
230 Griffith, 1994, 80–1
231 Englander, 1997, 137
232 IWM documents, M. Hardie
233 Gibbs, 1920, 439–40
234 Moynihan, 1978, 148
235 Snape, 2004, *passim*; Plater, 1919, 125–8; Shattuck, 1987, 24, note 24
236 PRO, WO 277/16
237 Revelation 1.18–19
238 Lomax, 1996, 35–6
239 IWM documents, E.J. Hazel
240 Flower, 1996, 228
241 Bennett, 1967, 30
242 Marrin, 1974, 119–42; Siberry, 2000, 87–98; Girouard, 1981, 276–93; Peters, 1979, 90–4
243 DeGroot, 1996 (a), 392
244 Cooper, 1993, 106–7
245 *Ampleforth Journal*, 1918, 299
246 *Downside Review*, July 1919
247 Alington, 1940, 5
248 Fraser, 2003, 99
249 MO, FR 363
250 Forty, 2002, 234; French, 2000, 98–9
251 Bayliss, 1989, 8–9
252 Forty, 2002, Annex A, 46–7; Montgomery-Massingberd, 1989, 162
253 Milligan, 1976, 24; Trevelyan, 1985, 75
254 Bowlby, 1999, 93–4
255 'Cassandra', 1941, 41
256 Dormer, 1998, 108
257 Snape, 2005

5 Religion, morality and war

1 Brown and Seaton, 2001, 225–8
2 Wyndham, 1899, 71–2
3 Brown and Seaton, 2001, 69
4 http://www1.umn.edu/humanrts/instree/1899b.htm, Convention (II) with Respect to the Laws and Customs of War on Land and its annex [1899], Article 56, consulted 13/02/2003
5 Fraser, 2003, 185

6 Fraser, 2003, 185
7 Delaforce, 2002, 70–1
8 Tout, 1992, 87
9 Bowlby, 1999, 104
10 Fussell, 1977, 117
11 Carver, 2001, 54
12 Winter, 1979, 213
13 Steel and Hart, 2001, 313
14 Lewis Bryan, 1946, 24
15 Firth, 1995, 18
16 O'Rahilly, 1932, 431, 501
17 O'Rahilly, 1932, 511
18 IWM documents, Alan Harris
19 Dempsey, 1947, 39, 198–200; Thompson, 1955, 92–3
20 Dempsey, 1947, 45, 106
21 IWM documents, J.B. Scollen
22 Bowlby, 1999, 62
23 Rae, 1970, 77
24 Author's collection, Charlie Wakeley
25 Rae, 1970, 190, note 3
26 Rae, 1970, 71
27 Rae, 1970, 192–3
28 Rae, 1970, 194
29 Goodall, 1997, 116
30 Brock, 2004, *passim*; Goodall, 1997, 116–33
31 Rae, 1970, 193; Goodall, 1997, 118
32 For the religious impact of war on Owen and Graves see Stallworthy, 1998, *passim* and Graves, 1960, *passim*. Largely because of his sexuality, Siegfried Sassoon was already alienated from the Church of England. See Moorcroft Wilson, 1998, *passim* and J.S. Roberts, 1999, *passim*
33 Schweitzer, 1998, 33–6
34 Winter, 1998, 1–11
35 Currie *et al.*, 1977, 31
36 Schweitzer, 1998, *passim*; Schweitzer, 2003, *passim*
37 Schweitzer, 1998, 36
38 Brown, 2001, 33
39 Cairns, 1919, *passim*; Plater, 1919, *passim*
40 Middlebrook, 1984, 316
41 Steel and Hart, 2001, 313
42 Plater, 1919, 10–11
43 IWM sound, 'Great War'
44 Sellers, 1918, 30–5
45 IWM documents, E.C. Crosse
46 Cairns, 1919, 141–2
47 Forbes, 1918, 75–81
48 Pym and Gordon, 1917, 51

49   Gibbs, 1920, 330–1
50   Drury, 1968, 101
51   Bickersteth, 1996, 80
52   Plater, 1919, 72
53   Crozier, 1930, 48
54   MacDonald, 1983, 139–40
55   Martin, 1987, 59–61
56   Richards, 1983, 239
57   Black, 1917, 82
58   Plater, 1919, 149
59   Selby Wright, 1943, 73
60   Drewett, 1942, 83
61   McLean and Sclater, 1917, 253
62   Forbes, 1918, 83
63   Englander, 1994, 351
64   MO, FR 23; FR 622; FR 1566
65   MO, FR 1572
66   Milligan, 1980, 33
67   Milligan, 1980, 83
68   IWM documents, Lavinia Orde
69   Author's collection, Frank Ockenden
70   IWM sound, H. Levy
71   Liddle Collection, Peter Sutton
72   Author's collection, Charlie Wakeley
73   MO, FR 1870 A
74   Milligan, 1972, 63
75   Tout, 1992, 177–8

6 The army and religious philanthropy

1   Simkins, 1985, 166–78
2   Anon., 1916 (b), 346
3   Ewing, 1917, 122–3
4   *Minutes of* [the Wesleyan] *Conference 1915*, 1915, 509
5   Anon., 1916 (b), 346
6   Potter and Matheson, 1936, 42–3
7   Potter and Matheson, 1936, 25
8   Dobbie, 1988, 36
9   Crerar, 1995, 75–80
10   Yapp, 1918, 195; Cairns, 1919, v
11   Yapp, 1927, 58
12   Yapp, 1927, 67
13   Campbell, 1916, 40–6
14   McKenzie, 1918, 419–20
15   *Ministry of Reconstruction Adult Education Committee. Report on Education in the Army*, 1918

16 Edmonds, 1932, 139–40
17 *The Red Triangle Bulletin*, 6 June 1919, 3
18 Edmonds, 1932, 139
19 Yapp, 1918, 63
20 IWM documents, J.G. Bennett
21 Thompson, 1990, 377
22 Ewing, 1917, 254
23 IWM documents, J.G. Bennett
24 Cairns, 1919, Appendix II, 451
25 Yapp, 1918, 211–12
26 Anon., 1916 (b), 343; *Catholic Federationist*, May 1917, 1
27 Adler, 1922, 18
28 Copping, 1917 (a), 181; Edmonds, 1932, 142–3; McKenzie, 1918, 420–1
29 Anon., n.d., *C.W.L. Soldiers' Recreation Huts*
30 Edmonds, 1932, 142
31 *The Record of the Home and Foreign Mission Work of the United Free Church*, April 1917, 80
32 Duncan, 1966, 127
33 Edmonds, 1932, 141
34 LPL, Davidson Papers, Vol. 254, Church Army, 234; Edmonds, 1932, 141
35 LPL, Davidson Papers, Vol. 254, Church Army, 240, 'Instructions for Workers at the Front', 217
36 LPL, Davidson Papers, Vol. 254, Church Army, 221
37 LPL, Davidson Papers, Vol. 254, Church Army, 315
38 LPL, Davidson Papers, Vol. 254, Church Army, 368
39 LPL, Davidson Papers, Vol. 254, Church Army, 224
40 LPL, Davidson Papers, Vol. 254, Church Army, 234
41 LPL, Davidson Papers, Vol. 254, Church Army, 388
42 Edmonds, 1932, 141
43 McKenzie, 1918, 422; LPL, Davidson Papers, Vol. 254, Church Army, 380
44 McMahon, 1940, 308
45 Edmonds, 1932, 134, footnote; Miller, 1971, 20; *Statistics of the Military Effort of the British Empire*, 1992, 875
46 Anon., 1916 (c), 185
47 Beckett, 1985 (a), 25
48 Sellers, 1918, 14
49 Sandall, 1955, 293
50 Yapp, 1918, 211
51 Yapp, 1918, 212
52 Liddle Collection, Gilbert Mortimer
53 IWM documents, M.W. Murray
54 Yapp, 1918, 198, 200–1
55 Feilding, 2001, 118
56 IWM sound, Ulick Burke
57 IWM sound, George Jameson
58 IWM documents, E.C. Crosse

59   Barber, 1946, 8
60   MO, FR 1421
61   MO, FR 1421
62   Lever, 1971, 40–1
63   Clayton, 1920, 27
64   Clayton, 1920, 69
65   Clayton, 1920, 38
66   Clayton, 1920, 38, 103
67   Clayton, 1920, 28
68   Lever, 1971, 48–9
69   Lever, 1971, 44–5, 49
70   Clayton, 1920, 72–3
71   Clayton, 1920, 3
72   Clayton, 1920, 52
73   Lever, 1971, 31–4
74   Drury, 1968, 336
75   Clayton, 1920, 150
76   Lever, 1971, 43–4, 60–2
77   Lever, 1971, 58
78   Clayton, 1920, 95
79   Clayton, 1920, 96
80   Clayton, 1920, 35
81   Lever, 1971, 70
82   Drury, 1968, 339
83   Wilkinson, 1978, 307–8
84   Clayton, 1920, 97
85   Lever, 1971, 164
86   Harington, 1935, 331–2
87   Harington, 1935, 334
88   Lever, 1971, 165
89   *Minutes of the Methodist Conference 1941*, 1941, 229
90   *Minutes of the Methodist Conference 1941*, 1941, 58–9
91   Potter and Matheson, 1936, 12–13
92   Dobbie, 1988, 42
93   Dobbie, 1988, 72–3
94   Dobbie, 1988, 81–4
95   Dobbie, 1988, 83–5
96   McMahon, 1940, 310; *The Times*, 15 July 1942, 8
97   Crang, 2000, 115
98   McMahon, 1940, 310
99   McMahon, 1940, 311
100 Yapp, 1927, 57–89; Anon., 1916 (c), 179–200
101 *The Times*, 15 July 1942, 8
102 Barber, 1946, *passim*
103 Sandall, 1955, 296
104 Coulter, 1997, 267, 271

105 Robinson, 1999, 166
106 Barber, 1946, 11; Morgan, 1953, 12
107 Morgan, 1953, 12
108 Barber, 1946, 11–12; Morgan, 1953, 12; Crang, 2000, 93
109 *The Times*, 15 July, 1942, 8
110 Morgan, 1953, 148
111 Barber, 1946, 86; *The Times*, 29 August 1944, 6
112 Morgan, 1953, 148
113 Miller, 1971, 29, 74–6
114 Morgan, 1953, 119
115 *The Times*, 15 July 1942, 8
116 *The Times*, 3 September 1940, 7
117 *The Times*, 6 July 1940, 7
118 *The Times*, 5 June 1940, 3
119 *The Times*, 19 June 1940, 3; 6 July 1940, 7; Barber, 1946, 22–3
120 Barber, 1946, 46
121 *The Times*, 15 July 1942, 8
122 MO, FR 1870 A
123 *The Times*, 4 January 1944, 2
124 Robinson, 1999, 166
125 *The Times*, 17 April 1944, 2
126 MacDonald Fraser, 2000, 34–5
127 Coulter, 1997, 280
128 Morgan, 1953, 154–8
129 See Costello, 1985, for a wide-ranging survey of this phenomenon
130 Barber, 1946, 8–9
131 Cox, 1982, 87, 89
132 Entwistle, 2001, 32–5
133 Barber, 1946, 6
134 *The Times*, 26 July 1944, 2
135 *The Times*, 26 July 1944, 2; RAChD, F.L. Hughes, 8th Army Papers; Bussby, 1967, *passim*
136 *The Times*, 26 July 1944, 2
137 LPL, Davidson Papers, Vol. 344, Great War: Clergy 1915–17, 91; Anon., 1916 (b), 344
138 Coghlan, 1942, 27–8, 45–6
139 Vernon Smith, 1915, *passim*
140 Anon., 1916 (b), 328–30
141 Duncan, 1966, 129
142 LPL, Davidson Papers, Vol. 345, Great War: Clergy 1917–19, 235–37, 264
143 Reith, 1966, 182
144 Adler, 1922, 36
145 Campbell, 1916, 15–16
146 LPL, Davidson Papers, Vol. 583, Visit to the Front May 1916, 21 May 1916

147 CMS, Diaries of L.H. Gwynne, 29 July 1917
148 Duncan, 1966, 130
149 *Haig's Autograph Great War Diary*, 21 October 1917
150 Duncan, 1966, 130
151 Boullier, 1917, 68
152 Sellers, 1915, 11
153 Campbell, 1916, 17–20
154 MO, FR 1870 A
155 Dempsey, 1947, 91
156 Jackson, 1960, 222
157 Jackson, 1960, 218–19
158 Plater and Martindale, 1919, 1–7
159 Plater and Martindale, 1919, 17
160 Dempsey, 1947, 172
161 Johnstone and Hagerty, 1996, 151–4
162 *The Times*, 21 June 1944, 3
163 MO, FR 1870 A
164 Coulter, 1997, 144–8
165 Dempsey, 1947, 172
166 Martin, 1987, 146–8. Martin wrongly remembered this speaker as the Archbishop of Canterbury
167 Plater and Martindale, 1919, 3
168 MO, FR 1870 A
169 Bowlby, 1999, 164
170 Yapp, 1918, 212
171 *The Record*, 22 May 1919, 2
172 Anon., 1916 (b), 331
173 Whitlow, 1938, 101
174 IWM documents, J.M. Connor
175 Anon., 1916 (b), 317
176 Whitlow, 1938, 101–2
177 Woolley, 1963, 141
178 Bussby, 1967, 24
179 Hastings, 1984, 417
180 Potter and Matheson, 1936, 30–1
181 Casgrain, 1917, author's collection
182 *The Tablet*, 10 October 1914, 513; 17 October 1914, 547
183 Feilding, 2001, 105–7
184 Coghlan, 1942, 10–11
185 Milligan, 1978, 43
186 Wilkinson, 1978, 153
187 Vernon Smith, 1915, 13–14
188 Schweitzer, 2003, 31
189 Sellers, 1918, 101
190 Falls, 1922, 16–17
191 Ewing, 1917, 159

192   IWM documents, H.L. Adams
193   Liddle Collection, E.G. Routley
194   Drury, 1968, 99
195   *The Tablet*, 2 June 1917, 695
196   Cox, 1982, 76–8
197   McKenzie, 1918, 423
198   Edmonds, 1932, 142–3; Macpherson, 1923, 41
199   Fletcher, 1929, 37
200   Macpherson, 1923, 74; Fletcher, 1929, 70–1
201   *The Harvest*, April 1917, 69
202   Adler, 1922, 14
203   Fletcher, 1929,12
204   Fletcher, 1929, 42
205   Fletcher, 1929, 54–6, 59; Cole-Mackintosh, 1986, 47
206   *Statistics of the Military Effort of the British Empire*, 1992, 193
207   Fletcher, 1929, 75, Appendix IV, 97
208   Munby, 1920, 10
209   Munby, 1920, 10
210   Cole-Mackintosh, 1986, 66; St George Saunders, 1949, *passim*
211   Goodall, 1997, 62–8
212   Rae, 1970, 197
213   Tegla Davies, 1947, 76–109, 133–56
214   Tegla Davies, 1947, 3
215   Author's collection, John Hick; Tegla Davies, 1947, 107–8, 142; Crozier, 1969, 156
216   Tegla Davies, 1947, 98, 103
217   Tegla Davies, 1947, 90
218   Wild, 1992, 66; Smith, 1998, 349

BIBLIOGRAPHY

Archival sources

Archdiocese of Birmingham Archives, St Chad's Cathedral

FHD/A5 Francis H. Drinkwater, War Diaries 1915–18
P1/53 St Chad's War Memorial

CMS Archives, University of Birmingham

XCMSACC 18/F1/50–4 Diaries of L.H. Gwynne

IWM, Department of Documents

83/50/1	H.L. Adams
97/33/1	J.G. Bennett
92/28/1	A.L. Bird
87/31/1	H.T. Bone
87/10/1	R. Bulstrode
90/18/1	T.B. Butt
87/10/1	J.M. Connor
80/22/1	E.C. Crosse
95/9/1	S. Dalton [pseudonym]
93/17/11	O. Eva
88/27/1	A.D. Hamer

84/46/1	M. Hardie
91/43/1	A. Harris
85/42/1	E.J. Hazel
96/38/1	N.F. Jones
P 305	W. Knott
95/30/1	W.A. Lathaen
PP/MCR/206	A.R.C. Leaney
80/49/1	W.H. Miller
77/106/1	W.M. Murray
96/34/1	L. Orde
96/38/1	A.H. Rodgers
80/38/1	J.B. Scollen

IWM, exhibits and firearms

Troops' Mascots, 1914–1917

IWM, sound archive

1605	Anon. chaplain *et al.*
569/18	Ulick Burke
17348/4	Walter Cleveland
4077/C/B	'Great War'
11572	Harry Levy
1891	Frederick Llewelyn Hughes
7363/21	George Jameson
12553/3	Cecil Macauley Johnston
13519/3	Alastair Menzies
10660/4	John William Steele
4650	Douglas Thompson

LPL

Davidson Papers, Vol. 254, Church Army
Davidson Papers, Vol. 343, Great War: Clergy 1914–15
Davidson Papers, Vol. 344, Great War: Clergy 1915–17
Davidson Papers, Vol. 345, Great War: Clergy 1917–19
Davidson Papers, Vol. 583, Visit to the Front May 1916

Liddell Hart Centre for Military Archives, King's College London

GB99 KCLMA Beddington

Liddle Collection, University of Leeds

F.M. Chance
S. Frankenburg

J.M. Hill
J.F.R. Modrell
G. Mortimer
E.G. Routley
W. Shaw
A. Smith
P. Sutton
D.J.B. Wilson

MO Archive, University of Sussex

FR 23 'Church – Religion in Wartime' (1940)
FR 363 'Report on the Word "Crusade"' (1940)
FR 622 'R.A.F. Trends' (1941)
FR 769 'Mass Astrology' (1941)
FR 1268 'The Traditional English Sunday' (1942)
FR 1421, 'Report on Feelings about the Salvation Army' (1942)
FR 1525 'Religion and the Future' (1942)
FR 1566 'Religion and the People' (1942)
FR 1572 'Religion and the People' (1943)
FR 1870 A 'The Chaplain to the Forces' (1943)
FR 2017 'Religious Education in Schools' (1944)
FR 2112 'Superstition' (1944)
FR 2190E 'Spiritual Trends in Films' (1944)
FR 2274 'Religious Attitudes in a London Borough' (1945)
TC Religion 3/B

PRO

WO 32/14687 Compulsory Church Parade
WO 277/16 J.H.A. Sparrow, *The Second World War 1939–1945. Army. Morale*, 1949
WO 365/39 British Army – religious denominations
WO 365/62 Nationalities – British Army and Auxiliary Territorial Service
WO 365/149 Officers – Average Age of Officers on Promotion

RAChD Archive, Amport House

F.L. Hughes, 8th Army Papers
B.L. Montgomery, 'To All Padres in 21 Army Group', 1 July 1945
R. Nye, 'The Very Reverend F. Ll. Hughes CB, CBE, MC, TD, MA. A Biographical Essay', 1981
R. Rudgard, 'The Very Revd Frederick Llewelyn Hughes . . . Address by the Venerable Richard Rudgard, Archdeacon of Basingstoke, at the Memorial Service held in the Guards Chapel, Wellington Barracks, on Wednesday 21 June 1967'

Author's collection

Tony Foulds
John Hick
Macpherson Knowles
Colin Starkie
Michael Sutton
Charlie Wakeley
The papers of Frank Ockenden

PP and government publications

The General Annual Report of the British Army for the year ending 30 September 1913,
    London: HMSO, 1914
Ministry of Reconstruction Adult Education Committee. Report on Education in the Army,
    London: HMSO, 1918

Newspapers and periodicals

Ampleforth Journal
Catholic Federationist
The Chaplains' Magazine Middle East
The Church Times
Downside Review
The Harvest
House of Commons Debates
Methodist Recorder
Parliamentary Debates (Hansard)
Picture Post
The Record
The Record of the Home and Foreign Mission Work of the United Free Church
The Red Triangle Bulletin
The Tablet
The Times
Toc H Journal

Published primary sources

Adler, M. (ed.), 1922, *British Jewry Book of Honour*, London: Caxton.
Alington, C., 1940, *The Last Crusade*, Oxford: Oxford University Press.
Anon., n.d., *C.W.L. Soldiers' Recreation Huts*.
Anon., 1916 (a), *Catholics of the British Empire and the War*, London: Burns and
    Oates.
Anon., 1916 (b), 'The Churches and the Armies', *The Times History of the War*,
    8: 313–52.
Anon., 1916 (c), 'The Work of the Y.M.C.A.', *The Times History of the War*,
    9: 179–200.
Anon., 1917, *Can England's Church Win England's Manhood? A Study in Camp, Field
    and Hospital of the Spiritual Condition of English Soldiers*, London: Macmillan.

Anon., 1940, 'The Royal Army Chaplain's Department', *Hutchinson's Pictorial History of the War, 20 December 1939–13 February 1940*, London: Hutchinson: 109–12.

Barber, D.H., 1946, *The Church Army in World War II*, London: SPCK.

Barrett, J.W., 1919, *The War Work of the YMCA in Egypt*, London: H.K. Lewis and Co.

Bell, G.K.A., 1916, *The National Mission of Repentance and Hope. A Report on the Chaplain's Replies to the Lord Bishop of Kensington*, London: Church Army Press.

Bennett, G.M.R., 1967, 'The Value of Faith to Prisoners of War', *RAChD Journal*, 20: 26–31.

Bickersteth, J. (ed.), 1996, *The Bickersteth Diaries, 1914–1918*, London: Leo Cooper.

Black, J., 1917, 'Our Soldiers: the Influence of the War on their Religious Ideas', *The Record of the Home and Foreign Mission Work of the United Free Church*, April: 81–2.

Blackburne, H., 1932, *This Also Happened on the Western Front*, London: Hodder and Stoughton.

Boullier, J.A., 1917, *Jottings by a Gunner and Chaplain: Being the Experiences of a Gunner who for Twenty Months Served with the 28th Brigade R.F.A., 5th Division, and Afterwards as Chaplain to the Forces in the 32nd Division with the 96th Infantry Brigade*, London: Charles H. Kelly.

Bowlby, A., 1999, *The Recollections of Rifleman Bowlby*, London: Cassell.

Brooks, S. (ed.), 1991, *Montgomery and the Eighth Army: a Selection from the Diaries, Correspondence and Other Papers of Field Marshal the Viscount Montgomery of Alamein, August 1942 to December 1943*, Stroud: Publications of the Army Records Society, 7.

Bussby, F., 1967, 'The Chaplains' Club: from Cairo to Brussels', *RAChD Journal*, 20: 22–5.

Cairns, D.S., 1919, *The Army and Religion: an Enquiry and its Bearing on the Religious Life of the Nation*, London: Macmillan.

Callan, J., 1917, *With Guns and Wagons*, London: SPCK.

Campbell, R.J., 1916, *With Our Troops in France*, London: Chapman Hall.

Casgrain, Fr, 1917, *The Catholic Soldiers' and Sailors' Prayer-book*, London: R. and T. Washbourne, copy in author's collection.

'Cassandra', 1941, *The English at War*, London: Secker and Warburg.

Chapman, G., 1985, *A Passionate Prodigality*, Southampton: Ashford, Buchan and Enright.

Charteris, J., 1931, *At G.H.Q.*, London: Cassell.

Clayton, P.B., 1920, *Tales of Talbot House: Everyman's Club in Poperinghe and Ypres 1915–1918*, London: Chatto and Windus.

Coghlan, J., 1942, *Memorandum for Catholic Army Chaplains and Officiating Chaplains to the Forces*, London: United Services Catholic Association.

Cook, H. and Cook, B., 1988, *Khaki Parish: Our War – Our Love*, Worthing: Churchman Publishing.

Cooper, B., 1993, *The Tenth (Irish) Division in Gallipoli*, Dublin: Irish Academic Press.

Copping, A.E., 1917 (a), *Souls in Khaki*, London: Hodder and Stoughton.

—— 1917 (b), *Tommy's Triangle*, London: Hodder and Stoughton.

Creighton, L. (ed.), 1920, *Letters of Oswin Creighton, C.F. 1883–1918*, London: Longmans, Green and Co.

Croft, W.D., 1919, *Three Years with the 9th (Scottish) Division*, London: John Murray.

Crosse, E.C., 1917, *The God of Battles: A Soldier's Faith*, London: Longmans, Green and Co.

Crozier, F.P., 1930, *A Brass Hat in No Man's Land*, London: Cape.

—— 1969, *The Men I Killed*, Bath: Cedric Chivers.

Danchev, A. and Todman, D. (eds), 2002, *War Diaries 1939–1945: Field Marshal Lord Alanbrooke*, London: Phoenix.

De Candole, A., 1919, *The Faith of a Subaltern: Essays on Religion and Life*, Cambridge: Cambrdge University Press.

DeGroot, G.J. (ed.), 1996 (a), 'The Reverend George S. Duncan at G.H.Q., 1916–1918' in A.J. Guy, R.N.W. Thomas and G.J. Degroot (eds), *Military Miscellany I*, Publications of the Army Records Society, 12.

Dempsey, M. (ed.), 1947, *The Priest among the Soldiers*, London: Burns and Oates.

Dobbie, W., 1944, *A Very Present Help*, London: Marshall, Morgan and Scott.

Dormer, H., 1998, *War Diary*, Sevenoaks: Fisher Press.

Drewett, J., 1942, 'Diffused Christianity: Asset or Liability?', *Theology*, 45, July–December: 82–92.

Drury, W.E., 1968, *Camp Follower: a Padre's Recollections of Nile, Somme and Tigris during the First World War*, Dublin: Exchequer Printers.

Duncan, G.S., 1966, *Douglas Haig as I Knew Him*, London: George Allen and Unwin.

Dunn, J.C., 1994, *The War the Infantry Knew 1914–1919*, London: Abacus.

Edmonds [Carrington], C., 1984, *A Subaltern's War*, London: Anthony Mott.

Englander, D. (ed.), 1994, *A Documentary History of Jewish Immigrants in Britain, 1840–1920*, Leicester: Leicester University Press.

Ewing, W., 1917, *From Gallipoli to Baghdad*, London: Hodder and Stoughton.

Feilding, R., 2001, *War Letters to a Wife: France and Flanders, 1915–1919*, Staplehurst: Spellmount.

Fellowes, R. (ed.), n.d., *Fragments of Battle*, Matlock: Newton Mann.

Firth, D., 1995, *The Spirit of the River Kwai*, Keighley: Richard Netherwood.

Forbes, E.A., 1918, *Vermelles: Notes on the Western Front*, Edinburgh: The Scottish Chronicle Press.

Fraser, D., 2003, *Wars and Shadows: Memoirs of General Sir David Fraser*, London: Penguin.

Gethyn-Jones, E., 1988, *A Territorial Army Chaplain in Peace and War: a Country Cleric in Khaki 1938–61*, East Wittering: Gooday Publishers.

Gibbs, P., 1920, *Realities of War*, London: Heinemann.

Goodridge, E.N. and Goodridge, J.A., 2000, *The Same Stars Shine: The Great War Diary and Letters of Corporal Ernest Goodridge*, Loughborough: Teamprint.

Gordon, E., 1972, *Miracle on the River Kwai*, London: Collins.

Gorer, G., 1955, *Exploring English Character*, London: Cresset Press.

Graham, S., 1919, *A Private in the Guards*, London: Macmillan.

Graves, R., 1960, *Goodbye To All That*, London: Penguin.

Gray, A.H., 1917, *As Tommy Sees Us: a Book for Church Folk*, London: Edward Arnold.

Guinness, P., 1945, *We Pledge Our Lives: a Post-war Manifesto from a War-time Prison*, London: Hodder and Stoughton.

Gwynne, L., 1917, *Religion and Morale: the Story of the National Mission on the Western Front*, London: SPCK.

Haig's Autograph Great War Diary [microfilm], 1987, Brighton: Harvester.

Hankey, D., 1918, *A Student in Arms*, London: Andrew Melrose.

Hawkins, D. (ed.), 1994, *D-Day to VE Day*, London: BBC Books.

Hills, S., 2002, *By Tank into Normandy: a Memoir of the Campaign in North-west Europe from D-Day to V.E. Day*, London: Cassell.

Horne, J. (ed.), 1995, *The Best of Good Fellows: The Diaries and Memoirs of the Revd Charles Edmund Doudney, M.A. C.F.*, London: Jonathan Horne Publications.

Jones, E.H., 1920, *The Road to En-Dor*, London: Bodley Head.

Kirby, N., 1995, *1100 Miles with Monty: Security and Intelligence at Toc HQ*, Stroud: Alan Sutton.

Lewis Bryan, J.N., 1946, *The Churches of the Captivity in Malaya*, London: SPCK.

Lindsay, A.D., 1944, 'What More is Needed of the Citizen?', *The British Way and Purpose Consolidated Edition of B.W.P. Booklets 1–18*, London: Directorate of Army Education.

Lloyd, R., 1942, 'Cults of Today. II. The Heresy of Fatalism', *Expository Times*, 54: 229–31.

Lomax, E., 1996, *The Railway Man*, London: Vintage.

MacDonald Fraser, G., 2000, *Quartered Safe out Here*, London: Harper Collins.

McKenzie, F.A., 1918, 'Welfare Work for the Soldiers from Base to Battlefield: a Record of Splendid Achievement', *The Great War*, 11: 401–24.

McLean, N. and Sclater, J.R.P., 1917, *God and the Soldier*, London: Hodder and Stoughton.

Maclean Watt, L., 1917, *In France and Flanders with the Fighting Men*, London: Hodder and Stoughton.

McMahon, H., 1940, 'The YMCA and the War', *Hutchinson's Pictorial History of the War, 20 December 1939–13 February 1940*, London: Hutchinson: 307–11.

MacNutt, F.B. (ed.), 1917, *The Church in the Furnace: Essays by Seventeen Temporary Chaplains on Active Service in France and Flanders*, London: Macmillian & Co.

Malden, R.H., 1917, *Fatalism*, London: SPCK.

Martin, B., 1987, *Poor Bloody Infantry: a Subaltern on the Western Front 1916–17*, London: John Murray.

Mayhew, P., n.d., *The Ministry of an Army Chaplain*, London: Pax House.

Middleton Brumwell, P., 1943, *The Army Chaplain*, London: Adam and Charles Black.

Milligan, S., 1972, *Adolf Hitler: My Part in His Downfall*, London: Penguin.

—— 1976, *'Rommel?' 'Gunner Who?'*, London: Penguin.

—— 1978, *Monty: His Part in My Victory*, London: Penguin.

—— 1980, *Mussolini: His Part in My Downfall*, London: Penguin.

Minutes of the Methodist Conference 1941, London: Methodist Publishing House.

Minutes of [the Wesleyan] *Conference 1915*, London: Wesleyan Conference Office.

Mitchell, R.K., 1997, *Forty-two Months in Durance Vile. Prisoner of the Japanese*, London: Robert Hale.

Montague, C.E., 1922, *Disenchantment*, London: Chatto and Windus.

Montgomery, B.L., 1944, *21 Army Group: Some Notes on the Conduct of War and the Infantry Division in Battle*, Belguim: 21st Army Group.

—— 1946, *Forward to Victory*, London: Hutchinson.

—— 1958, *The Memoirs of Field-Marshal the Viscount Montgomery of Alamein*, London: Collins.

Montgomery-Massingberd, H. (ed.), 1989, *Daily Telegraph Record of the Second World War*, London: Sidgwick and Jackson.

Morgan, M.C., 1953, *The Second World War 1939–1945 Army: Army Welfare*, London: War Office.

Moynihan, M. (ed.), 1978, *Black Bread and Barbed Wire: Prisoners in the First World War*, London: Leo Cooper.

—— 1983, *God On Our Side: the British Padres in World War One*, London: Leo Cooper.

—— 1988, *People at War 1914–1918*, Newton Abbot: David and Charles.

Oliver, K., 1986, *Chaplain at War*, Chichester: Angel Press.

O'Rahilly, A. (ed.), 1932, *Father William Doyle S.J.: a Spiritual Study*, London: Longmans, Green and Co.

Picot, G., 1994, *Accidental Warrior: in the Front Line from Normandy till Victory*, London: Penguin.

Plater, C., 1919, *Catholic Soldiers*, London: Longmans, Green and Co.

Plater, C. and Martindale, C.C., 1919, *Retreats for Soldiers in Wartime and After*, London: Harding and More Ltd.

Pym, T.W. and Gordon, G., 1917, *Papers from Picardy*, London: Constable and Co.

Reith, J., 1966, *Wearing Spurs*, London: Hutchinson.

Richards, F., 1983, *Old Soldiers Never Die*, London: Anthony Mott.

Robinson, A.C. and Hair, P.E.H. (eds), 2001, *Reflections on the Battlefield: from Infantryman to Chaplain, 1914–1919*, Liverpool: Liverpool University Press.

Rogers, C.F., 1941, *Astrology in the Light of Science and Religion*, London: Student Christian Movement.

Salisbury Woodward, C. and Blackburne, H., 1939, *Clergy in War-time*, London: Hooder and Stoughton.

Selby Wright, R., 1941, *Front Line Religion: the Padre Preaches*, London: Hodder and Stoughton.

—— 1942, *The Average Man: Broadcast Addresses by the Radio Padre*, London: Longman.

—— 1943, *Let's Ask the Padre: Some Broadcast Talks*, Edinburgh: Oliver and Boyd.

Sellers, W.E., 1915, *With Our Fighting Men*, London: Religious Tract Society.

—— 1918, *With Our Heroes in Khaki*, London: Religious Tract Society.

Sheffield, G.D. and Inglis, G.I.S. (eds), 1989, *From Vimy Ridge to the Rhine: the Great War Letters of Christopher Stone DSO MC*, Ramsbury: Crowood Press.

Sime, J.A., 1952, 'Battle Exhaustion', *RAChD Journal*, 7: 343–9.

Skinner, L., n.d., *The Man Who Worked on Sundays: the Personal War Diary June 2nd 1944 to May 17th 1945 of Revd. Leslie Skinner RAChD Chaplain, 8th (Independent) Armoured Brigade attached the Sherwood Rangers Yeomanry Regiment*, Stoneleigh: Plus Printing.

Spurr, F.C., 1916, *Some Chaplains in Khaki: an Account of the Work of Chaplains of the United Navy and Army Board*, London: H.R. Allenson.

Steuart, R.H.J., 1931, *March, Kind Comrade*, London: Sheed and Ward.

Studdert Kennedy, G.A., 1918 (a), *The Hardest Part*, London: Hodder and Stoughton.

—— 1918 (b), *Rough Talks by a Padre*, London: Hodder and Stoughton.

Talbot, N., 1917, *Thoughts on Religion at the Front*, London: Macmillan.

Terraine, J. (ed.), 1979, *Sir Douglas Haig's Despatches*, London: J.M. Dent.

—— (ed.), 2000, *General Jack's Diary: War on the Western Front 1914–1918*, London: Cassell.

Thompson, D., 1955, *Captives to Freedom*, London: Epworth Press.

Tiplady, T., 1939, *The Cross at the Front*, London: Epworth Press.

Tout, K., 1987, *Tanks, Advance!*, London: Robert Hale.

—— 1992, *To Hell With Tanks!*, London: Robert Hale.

Trevelyan, R., 1985, *The Fortress*, London: Buchan & Enright.

Treves, F. (ed.), 1916, *Made in the Trenches*, London: Allen and Unwin.

Vaughan, E.C., 1981, *Some Desperate Glory*, London: Warne.

Vernon Smith, G., 1915, *The Bishop of London's Visit to the Front*, London: Longmans, Green and Co.

Walford, C., 1915, *Christ's Sentry: a Manual of Prayers for Soldiers*, London: SPCK.

Westerdale, T.L.B., 1917, *Messages from Mars: a Chaplain's Experiences at the Front*, London: C.H. Kelly.

Wheatley, A (ed.), 1983, *Father Dolly the Guardsman Monk: the Memoirs of Captain the Right Reverend Dom Rudesind Brookes OBE MC TD OSB, Titular Abbot of Sherborne, Sometimes Irish Guards, Monk of Downside, and Army and Royal Air Force Chaplain as Narrated to Anthony Wheatley*, London: Henry Melland.

White, P., 2002, *With the Jocks: a Soldier's Struggle for Europe 1944–45*, Stroud: Sutton.

Whitehouse, S. and Bennett, G.B., 1995, *Fear is the Foe: a Footslogger from Normandy to the Rhine*, London: Robert Hale.

Wild, D., 1992, *Prisoner of Hope*, Lewes: The Book Guild.

Williamson, B., 1921, *'Happy Days' in France and Flanders*, London: Harding and More.

Woolley, G.H., 1963, *Sometimes a Soldier*, London: Ernest Benn.

Wyndham, H., 1899, *The Queen's Service: Being the Experiences of a Private Soldier in the British Infantry at Home and Abroad*, London: Heinemann.

Yapp, A.K., 1918, *The Romance of the Red Triangle*, London: Hodder and Stoughton.

—— 1927, *In the Service of Youth*, London: Nisbet and Co.

Electronic primary sources

University of Minnesota Human Rights Library

Convention (II) with Respect to the Laws and Customs of War on Land and its annex [1899], http://www1.umn.edu/humanrts/instree/1899b.htm (accessed 12 August 2005).

Secondary sources

Adams, R.J.Q., 1987, *The Conscription Controversy in Great Britain, 1900–18*, Basingstoke: Macmillan.

Allen, L., 2000, *Burma: the Longest War, 1941–45*, London: Phoenix.

Ambrose, S.E., 1998, *Citizen Soldiers: the U.S. Army from the Normandy Beaches to the Bulge to the Surrender of Germany*, New York: Simon and Schuster.

Arthur, M., 2001, *When this Bloody War is Over: Soldiers' Songs from the First World War*, London: Piatkus.

—— 2002, *Forgotten Voices of the Great War*, St Helens: The Book People.

Ashworth, T., 2000, *Trench Warfare 1914–1918: the Live and Let Live System*, London: Pan.

Atkinson, R., 2003, *An Army at Dawn: the War in North Africa, 1942–1943*, London: Little, Brown.

Audoin-Rouzeau, S. and Becker, A., 2002, *1914–1918: Understanding the Great War*, London: Profile Books.

Barclay, C.R., 1956, *The History of the 53rd (Welsh) Division in the Second World War*, London: William Clowes and Sons.

Barnett, C., 1970, *Britain and Her Army: a Military, Political and Social History of the British Army 1509–1970*, London: Allen Lane.

Bayliss, G.M., 1989, *Union Jack: a Scrapbook. British Forces' Newspapers, 1939–1945*, London: HMSO.

Baynes, J., 1987, *Morale: a Study of Men and Courage. The Second Scottish Rifles at the Battle of Neuve Chapelle 1915*, London: Leo Cooper.

—— 1995, *Far From a Donkey: the Life of General Sir Ivor Maxse KCB, CVO, DSO*, London: Brassey's.

Becker, A., 1998, *War and Faith: the Religious Imagination in France, 1914–1930*, Oxford: Berg.

Beckett, I., 1985 (a), 'The Nation in Arms, 1914–18' in I.F.W. Beckett and K. Simpson (eds), *A Nation in Arms: a Social Study of the British Army in the First World War*, Manchester: Manchester University Press.

—— 1985 (b), 'The Territorial Force' in I.F.W. Beckett and K. Simpson (eds), *A Nation in Arms: a Social Study of the British Army in the First World War*, Manchester: Manchester University Press.

Beckman, M., 1998, *The Jewish Brigade: an Army with Two Masters*, Staplehurst: Spellmount.

Blackburne, H., 1955, *Trooper to Dean*, Bristol: J.W. Arrowsmith.

Blake, G., 1950, *Mountain and Flood: the History of the 52nd (Lowland) Division 1939–1946*, Glasgow: Jackson, Son and Company.

Bond, B., 2002, *The Unquiet Western Front: Britain's Role in Literature and History*, Cambridge: Cambridge University Press.

Bosanquet, N. and Whitehead, I., 2000, 'Casualties and British Medical Services' in P. Liddle, J. Bourne and I. Whitehead (eds), *The Great World War 1914–45 1. Lightning Strikes Twice*, London: HarperCollins.

Bourke, J., 1999, *An Intimate History of Killing: Face-to-face Killing in Twentieth-century Warfare*, London: Granta.

Bourne, J., 1996, 'The British Working Man in Arms' in H. Cecil and P. Liddle (eds), *Facing Armageddon: The First World War Experienced*, London: Leo Cooper.

Bowman, T., 2003, *The Irish Regiments in the Great War: Discipline and Morale*, Manchester: Manchester University Press.

Brock, P., 2004, '"Excellent in Battle": British conscientious objectors as medical paratroopers, 1943–1946', *War and Society*, 22: 41–57.

Brophy, J. and Partridge, E., 1969, *The Long Trail: Soldiers' Songs and Slang 1914–18*, London: Sphere.

Brown, C.G., 1997, *Religion and Society in Scotland since 1707*, Edinburgh: Edinburgh University Press.

—— 1999, 'Piety, Gender and War in Scotland in the 1910s' in C.M.M. Macdonald and E.W. McFarland (eds), *Scotland and the Great War*, Phantassie: Tuckwell Press.

—— 2001, *The Death of Christian Britain*, London: Routledge.

Brown, M., 1986, *Tommy Goes to War*, London: J.M. Dent.

—— 1993, *The Imperial War Museum Book of the Western Front*, London: Sidgwick and Jackson.

—— 1996, *The Imperial War Museum Book of the Somme*, London: Sidgwick and Jackson.

Brown, M. and Seaton, S., 2001, *Christmas Truce: the Western Front December 1914*, London: Pan.

Brown, S.J., 1994, '"A Solemn Purification by Fire": Responses to the Great War in the Scottish Presbyterian Churches, 1914–19', *Journal of Ecclesiastical History*, 45: 82–104.

Calder, A., 1996, *The People's War: Britain 1939–1945*, London: Pimlico.

Callan, P., 1987–90, 'Recruiting for the British Army in Ireland during the First World War', *Irish Sword*, 17: 42–56.

Carpenter, H., 1996, *Robert Runcie: the Reluctant Archbishop*, London: Hodder and Stoughton.

Carver, M., 1998, *Britain's Army in the Twentieth Century*, London: MacMillan.

—— 2001, *The Imperial War Museum Book of the War in Italy 1943–1945*, London: Sidgwick and Jackson.

Cave, N., 1999, 'Haig and Religion' in B. Bond and N. Cave (eds), *Haig: a Reappraisal 70 Years On*, Barnsley: Pen and Sword.

Cave, T., 1993, 'The 42nd (East Lancashire) Division', *'Stand To!' The Journal of the Western Front Association*, Spring: 12–19.

Ceadel, M., 1980, *Pacifism in Britain 1914–1945: the Defining of a Faith*, Oxford: Clarendon Press.

Chandler, A., 1993, 'The Church of England and the Obliteration Bombing of Germany in the Second World War', *The English Historical Review*, 108: 920–46.

—— 1994, 'Munich and Morality: the Bishops of the Church of England and Appeasement', *Twentieth Century British History*, 5: 77–99.

Charteris, J., 1929, *Field-Marshal Earl Haig*, London: Cassell.

Clarke, D., 2004, *The Angel of Mons: Phantom Soldiers and Ghostly Guardians*, Chichester: Wiley.

Clements, K.W., 1975, 'Baptists and the Outbreak of the First World War', *Baptist Quarterly*, 26: 74–92.

Cole-Mackintosh, R., 1986, *A Century of Service to Mankind: a History of the St. John Ambulance Brigade*, London: Century Benham.

Colville, J.R., 1972, *Man of Valour: the Life of Field-Marshal The Viscount Gort, VC, GCB, DSO, MVO, MC*, London: Collins.

Cooper, D., 1935, *Haig*, London: Faber and Faber.

Costello, J., 1985, *Love Sex and War*, London: Collins.

Cox, J., 1982, *The English Churches in a Secular Society: Lambeth 1870–1930*, Oxford: Oxford University Press.

Crang, J.A., 1997, 'The British Soldier on the Home Front: Army Morale Reports, 1940–45' in P. Addison and A. Calder (eds), *Time to Kill: The Soldier's Experience of War in the West 1939–1945*, London: Pimlico.

—— 2000, *The British Army and the People's War 1939–1945*, Manchester: Manchester University Press.

Crerar, D., 1995, *Padres in No Man's Land: Canadian Chaplains and the Great War*, Montreal: McGill-Queen's University Press.

Currie, R., Gilbert, A. and Horsley, L., 1977, *Churches and Churchgoers: Patterns of Church Growth in the British Isles since 1700*, Oxford: Clarendon Press.

Danchev, A., 1989, 'Field Marshal Sir John Dill: the Early Years', *Journal of the Society for Army Historical Research*, 67: 28–39.

—— 1994, 'The Army and the Home Front 1939–1945' in D. Chandler and I. Beckett (eds), *The Oxford Illustrated History of the British Army*, Oxford: Oxford University Press.

DeGroot, G., 1988, *Douglas Haig, 1861–1928*, London: Unwin Hyman.

—— 1991, '"We are safe whatever happens" – Douglas Haig, the Reverend George Duncan, and the Conduct of War, 1916–1918' in N. MacDougal (ed.), *Scotland and War AD 79–1918*, Edinburgh: John Donald.

—— 1993, 'Haig's Secret Weapon', *Army Quarterly and Defence Journal*, 123: 60–7.

—— 1996 (b), *Blighty: British Society in the Era of the Great War*, London: Longman.

—— 1997, 'Whose Finger on the Trigger? Mixed Anti-aircraft Batteries and the Female Combat Taboo', *War in History*, 4: 434–53.

Delaforce, P., 1999 (a), *Churchill's Desert Rats: from Normandy to Berlin with the 7th Armoured Division*, London: Chancellor Press.

—— 1999 (b), *The Polar Bears: from Normandy to the Relief of Holland with the 49th Division*, London: Chancellor Press.

—— 2002, *The Fighting Wessex Wyverns: from Normandy to Bremerhaven with the 43rd (Wessex) Division*, Stroud: Sutton.

Denman, T., 1992, *Ireland's Unknown Soldiers: the 16th (Irish) Division in the Great War, 1914–1918*, Dublin: Irish Academic Press.

D'Este, C., 1994, 'The Army and the Challenge of War 1939–1945' in D. Chandler and I. Beckett (eds), *The Oxford Illustrated History of the British Army*, Oxford: Oxford Universtiy Press.

Dewey, P., 1997, *War and Progress: Britain 1914–1945*, Harlow: Longman.

Dobbie, I., 1988, *Sovereign Service: the Story of SASRA 1838–1988*, Aldershot: SASRA.

Doherty, R., 1993, *Clear the Way! A History of the 38th (Irish) Brigade, 1941–47*, Blackrock: Irish Academic Press.

Drury, W., 1922, 'The Initial Organisation of the Army Chaplains' Department in the British Expeditionary Force, 1914–1915', *RAChD Journal*, April: 45–9.

Edmonds, J.E., 1932, *History of the Great War Based on Official Documents. Military Operations France and Belgium, 1916: Sir Douglas Haig's Command to the 1st July: Battle of the Somme*, London: HMSO.

Edwards, T.J., 1954, *Military Customs*, Aldershot: Gale and Polden.

Ellis, J., 1993, *The Sharp End: the Fighting Man in World War II*, London: Pimlico.

Ellis, L.F., 1968, *History of the Second World War. Victory in the West II: the Defeat of Germany*, London: HMSO.

Englander, D., 1988, 'Anglicized not Anglican: Jews and Judaism in Victorian Britain' in G. Parsons (ed.), *Religion in Victorian Britain Volume I: Traditions*, Manchester: Manchester University Press.

—— 1997, 'Discipline and Morale in the British Army, 1917–1918' in J. Horne (ed.), *State, Society and Mobilization in Europe during the First World War*, Cambridge: Cambridge University Press.

Entwistle, D., 2001, '"Hope, Colour and Comradeship": Loyalty and Opportunism in Early Twentieth-century Church Attendance among the Working Class in North-west England', *Journal of Religious History*, 25: 20–38.

Falls, C., 1922, *The History of the 36th (Ulster) Division*, Belfast: McCaw, Stevenson and Orr.

Fletcher, N.C., 1929, *The St. John Ambulance Association: its History, and its Part in the Ambulance Movement*, London: The St John Ambulance Association.

Flower, S.J., 1996, 'Captors and Captives on the Burma–Thailand Railway' in B. Moore and K. Federowich (eds), *Prisoners of War and their Captors in World War II*, Oxford: Berg.

Forty, G., 2002, *British Army Handbook 1939–1945*, Stroud: Sutton.

Fraser, D., 1999, *And We Shall Shock Them: the British Army in the Second World War*, London: Cassell.

French, D., 2000, *Raising Churchill's Army: the British Army and the War against Germany 1919–1945*, Oxford: Oxford University Press.

Fuller, J.G., 1990, *Troop Morale and Popular Culture in the British and Dominion Armies 1914–1918*, Oxford: Clarendon Press.

Fussell, P., 1977, *The Great War and Modern Memory*, Oxford: Oxford University Press.

Gilbert, A.D., 1976, *Religion and Society in Industrial England: Church, Chapel and Social Change 1740–1914*, London: Longman.

Girouard, M., 1981, *The Return to Camelot: Chivalry and the English Gentleman*, New Haven: Yale University Press.

Goodall, F., 1997, *A Question of Conscience: Conscientious Objection in the Two World Wars*, Stroud: Sutton.

Gordon, J.W., 1995, 'Wingate' in J. Keegan (ed.), *Churchill's Generals*, London: Warner Books.

Green, S.J.D., 1996, *Religion in the Age of Decline: Organisation and Experience in Industrial Yorkshire, 1870–1920*, Cambridge: Cambridge University Press.

—— 2000, 'The 1944 Education Act: a Church–State Perspective' in J.P. Parry and S. Taylor (eds), *Parliament and the Church, 1529–1960*, Edinburgh: Edinburgh University Press.

Gregory, A., 1994, *The Silence of Memory: Armistice Day 1919–1946*, Oxford: Berg.

Grieves, K., 1997, 'C.E. Montague and the Making of *Disenchantment*, 1914–1921', *War in History*, 4: 35–59.

Griffith, P., 1994, *Battle Tactics of the Western Front: the British Army's Art of Attack, 1916–18*, New Haven: Yale University Press.

Grimley, M., 2004, *Citizenship, Community, and the Church of England: Liberal Anglican Theories of the State between the Wars*, Oxford: Clarendon Press.

Gummer, S., 1963, *The Chavasse Twins*, London: Hodder and Stoughton.

Hamilton, N., 1981, *Monty: the Making of a General 1887–1942*, London: Hamish Hamilton.

—— 1983, *Monty: Master of the Battlefield 1942–1944*, London: Hamish Hamilton.

—— 1986, *Monty: the Field Marshal 1944–1976*, London: Hamish Hamilton.

—— 2002, *The Full Monty Volume 1: Montgomery of Alamein 1887–1942*, London: Penguin.

Harington, C., 1935, *Plumer of Messines*, London: John Murray.

Harrison, M., 1999, 'Sex and the Citizen Soldier: Health, Morals and Discipline in the British Army during the Second World War' in R. Cooter, M. Harrison and S. Sturdy (eds), *Medicine and Modern Warfare*, Amsterdam: Rodopi.

Harvey, A.D., 1994, *Collision of Empires: Britain in Three World Wars, 1793–1945*, London: Phoenix.

Hastings, A., 1991, *A History of English Christianity 1920–1990*, London: SCM.

Hastings, M., 1984, *Overlord: D-Day and the Battle for Normandy 1944*, London: Michael Joseph.

Hazelgrove, J., 2000, *Spiritualism and British Society between the Wars*, Manchester: Manchester University Press.

Hein, D., 2000, 'Hugh Lister (1901–44): A Modern Saint?', *Theology*, 103: 339–46.

Hempton, D., 1988, '"Popular Religion" 1800–1986' in T. Thomas (ed.), *The British: Their Religious Beliefs and Practices 1800–1986*, London: Routledge.

Hendry, S.D., 1985, 'Scottish Baptists and the First World War', *Baptist Quarterly*, 31: 52–65.

Holmes, R., 1994, *Firing Line*, London: Pimlico.

—— 2004, *Tommy: the British soldier on the Western Front 1914–1918*, London: Harper Collins.

Hoover, A.J., 1989, *God, Germany, and Britain in the Great War: a Study in Clerical Nationalism*, New York: Praeger.

—— 1999, *God, Britain and Hitler in World War II: the View of the British Clergy, 1939–1945*, Westport, CT: Praeger.

Howkins, A., 1989, 'Dare to be a Daniel' in R. Samuel (ed.), *Patriotism: the Making and Unmaking of British National Identity Volume II: Minorities and Outsiders*, London: Routledge.

Hughes, C., 1985, 'The New Armies' in I.F.W. Beckett and K. Simpson (eds), *A Nation in Arms: a Social Study of the British Army in the First World War*, Manchester: Manchester University Press.

—— 1990, *Mametz: Lloyd George's 'Welsh Army' at the Battle of the Somme*, Norwich: Gliddon Books.

Iremonger, F.A., 1948, *William Temple Archbishop of Canterbury: His Life and Letters*, Oxford: Oxford University Press.

Jackson, H.C., 1960, *Pastor on the Nile*, London: SPCK.

James, D., 1954, *Lord Roberts*, London: Hollis and Carter.

James, L., 2001, *Warrior Race: a History of the British at War*, London: Little, Brown and Co.

Jeffery, K., 1985, 'The Post-war Army' in I.F.W. Beckett and K. Simpson (eds), *A Nation in Arms: a Social Study of the British Army in the First World War*, Manchester: Manchester University Press.

—— 1996 (a), 'The British Army and Ireland since 1922' in T. Bartlett and K. Jeffery (eds), *A Military History of Ireland*, Cambridge: Cambridge University Press.

—— 1996 (b) 'The Irish Military Tradition and the British Empire' in K. Jeffery (ed.), *'An Irish Empire'? Aspects of Ireland and the British Empire*, Manchester: Manchester Universtiy Press.

Johnstone, T., 1992, *Orange, Green and Khaki*, Dublin: Gill and MacMillan.

Johnstone, T. and Hagerty, J., 1996, *The Cross on the Sword: Catholic Chaplains in the Forces*, London: Geoffrey Chapman.

Keegan, J., 1998, *The First World War*, London: Hutchinson.

—— 1994, *Six Armies in Normandy: from D-Day to the Liberation of Paris*, London: Pimlico.

Keegan, J. and Holmes, R., 1985, *Soldiers: a History of Men in Battle*, London: Hamish Hamilton.

Knight, F., 1995, *The Nineteenth-century Church and English Society*, Cambridge: Cambridge University Press.

Latimer, J., 2003, *Alamein*, London: John Murray.

Lawson, T., 2003, 'The Anglican Understanding of Nazism 1933–1945: Placing the Church of England's Response to the Holocaust in Context', *Twentieth Century British History*, 14: 112–37.

Leonard, J., 1986, 'The Catholic Chaplaincy' in D. Fitzpatrick (ed.), *Ireland and the First World War*, Dublin: Trinity History Workshop.

Lever, T., 1971, *Clayton of Toc H*, London: John Murray.

Liddle, P., 1996, 'The British Soldier on the Somme in 1916', *Strategic and Combat Studies Institute Occasional Publications*, 23: 1–32.

Liddle, P. and Mackenzie, S.P., 2000, 'The Experience of Captivity: British and Commonwealth Prisoners in Germany' in J. Bourne, P. Liddle and I. Whitehead (eds), *The Great World War 1914–45 1. Lightning Strikes Twice*, London: HarperCollins.

Lipman, V.D., 1954, *Social History of the Jews in England 1850–1950*, London: Watts and Co.

Louden, S.H., 1996, *Chaplains in Conflict*, London: Avon Books.

Lucas, J., 1989, *Experiences of War: the British Soldier*, London: Arms and Armour Press.

MacDonald, L., 1983, *Somme*, London: Michael Joseph.

Machin, G.I.T., 1998, *Churches and Social Issues in Twentieth-century Britain*, Oxford: Clarendon Press.

MacKenzie, J.M., 1997, *Propaganda and Empire: the Manipulation of British Public Opinion 1880–1960*, Manchester: Manchester University Press.

MacKenzie, S.P., 1990, 'Morale and the Cause: the Campaign to Shape the Outlook of Soldiers in the British Expeditionary Force, 1914–1918', *Canadian Journal of History*, 25: 215–32.

—— 1992, *Politics and Military Morale: Current-Affairs and Citizenship Education in the British Army, 1915–1950*, Oxford: Clarendon Press.

McLeod, H., 1974, *Class and Religion in the Late Victorian City*, London: Croom Helm.

—— 1984, *Religion and the Working Class in Nineteenth-century Britain*, London: Macmillan.

—— 1993, *Religion and Irreligion in Victorian England*, Bangor: Headstart History.

—— 1996, *Religion and Society in England, 1850–1914*, Basingstoke: Macmillan.

—— 2000, *Secularisation in Western Europe, 1848–1914*, Basingstoke: Macmillan.

Macpherson, W.G., 1923, *History of the Great War Based on Official Documents. Medical Services General History Volume II: the Medical Services on the Western Front and during the Operations in France and Belgium in 1914 and 1915*, London: HMSO.

Marrin, A., 1974, *The Last Crusade: the Church of England in the First World War*, Durham, NC: Duke University Press.

Mews, S., 1992, 'Music and Religion in the First World War' in D. Wood (ed.), 'The Church and the Arts', *Studies in Church History*, 28: 465–75.

—— 1994, 'Religious Life between the Wars, 1920–1940' in S. Gilley and W.J. Sheils (eds), *A History of Religion in Britain: Practice and Belief from Pre-Roman Times to the Present*, Oxford: Blackwell.

Middlebrook, M., 1983, *The Kaiser's Battle, 21 March 1918: the First Day of the German Spring Offensive*, Harmondsworth: Penguin.

—— 1984, *The First Day on the Somme*, Harmondsworth: Penguin.

—— 2000, *Your Country Needs You: Expansion of the British Army Infantry Divisions 1914–18*, Barnsley: Leo Cooper.

Miller, D.W., 1973, *Church, State and Nation in Ireland 1898–1921*, Dublin: Gill and MacMillan.

Miller, H., 1971, *Service to the Services: the Story of Naafi*, London: Newman Neame.

Miner, S.M., 2003, *Stalin's Holy War: Religion, Nationalism, and Alliance Politics, 1941–1945*, Chapel Hill: University of North Carolina Press.

Moffatt, J. and McCormick, A.H., 2003, *Moon Over Malaya: a Tale of Argylls and Marines*, Stroud: Tempus.

Moorcroft Wilson, J., 1998, *Siegfried Sassoon: the Making of a War Poet*, London: Duckworth.

Moorhouse, G., 1993, *Hell's Foundations: a Town, its Myths and Gallipoli*, London: Sceptre.

Moriarty, R., 1993, 'Vivian Redlich, 1905–1942: a Martyr in the Tradition' in D. Wood (ed.), 'Martyrs and Martyrologies', *Studies in Church History*, 29: 453–63.

Munby, J.E., 1920, *A History of the 38th (Welsh) Division*, London: Hugh Rees.

Murphy, J., 1971, *Church, State and Schools in Britain, 1800–1970*, London: Routledge and Kegan Paul.

Neillands, R., 1999, *The Great War Generals on the Western Front 1914–18*, London: Robinson.

Nelson, G.K., 1969, *Spiritualism and Society*, London: Routledge and Kegan Paul.

Nicholas, S., 2002, 'Being British: Creeds and Cultures' in K. Robbins (ed.), *The British Isles 1901–1951*, Oxford: Oxford University Press.

Norman, E., 1976, *Church and Society in England, 1770–1970: a Historical Study*, Oxford: Clarendon Press.

Parsons, G., 2002, *Perspectives on Civil Religion*, Aldershot: Ashgate.

Peters, R., 1979, *Islam and Colonialism: the Doctrine of Jihad in Modern History*, The Hague: Mouton Publishers.

Porch, D., 1975, 'The French Army and the Spirit of the Offensive, 1900–14' in B. Bond and I. Roy (eds), *War and Society: a Yearbook of Military History*, London: Croom Helm.

Porter, P. 2002, 'The Sacred Service: Australian Chaplains and the Great War', *War and Society*, 20: 23–52.

Potter, E. and Matheson, W., 1936, *Elise Sandes and Theodora Schofield: Twenty-one Years of Unrecorded Service for the British Army, 1913–1934*, London: Marshall, Morgan and Scott.

Purcell, W.E., 1983, *Woodbine Willie: an Anglican Incident*, London: Mowbray.

Putkowski, J. and Sykes, J., 1989, *Shot at Dawn: Executions in World War One by Authority of the British Army Act*, London: Leo Cooper.

Rae, J., 1970, *Conscience and Politics: the British Government and the Conscientious Objector to Military Service*, London: Oxford University Press.

Reay, B., 1998, *Popular Cultures in England 1550–1750*, London: Longman.

Robbins, K., 1985, 'Britain, 1940 and "Christian Civilization"' in D. Beales and G. Best (eds), *History, Society and the Churches: Essays in Honour of Owen Chadwick*, Cambridge: Cambridge University Press.

——— 1993, *History, Religion and Identity in Modern Britain*, London: Hambledon.

Roberts, J.S., 1999, *Siegfried Sassoon*, London: Richard Cohen Books.

Rooney, D., 2000, *Wingate and the Chindits: Redressing the Balance*, London: Cassell.

Royle, T., 1995, *Orde Wingate: Irregular Soldier*, London: Weidenfeld and Nicholson.

Ryan, C., 1999, *A Bridge Too Far*, Ware: Wordsworth Editions.

St George Saunders, H., 1949, *The Red Cross and the White: a Short History of the Joint War Organisation of the British Red Cross Society and the Order of St. John of Jerusalem during the War, 1939–1945*, London: Hollis and Carter.

Sandall, R., 1955, *The History of the Salvation Army Volume III 1883–1953: Social Reform and Welfare Work*, London: Thomas Nelson.

Savage, R., 1925, *Allenby of Armageddon*, London: Hodder and Stoughton.

Schweitzer, R., 1998, 'The Cross and the Trenches: Religious Faith and Doubt among some British Soldiers on the Western Front', *War and Society*, 16: 33–57.

—— 2003, *The Cross and the Trenches: Religious Faith and Doubt among British and American Great War Soldiers*, Westport, CT: Praeger.

Selwyn, V. (ed.), 1989, *More Poems of the Second World War*, London: J.M. Dent.

Shattuck, G.H., 1987, *A Shield and Hiding Place: the Religious Life of the Civil War Armies*, Macon, GA: Mercer University Press.

Shaw, D., 1996, 'The Forgotten Army of Women: Queen Mary's Army Auxiliary Corps' in H. Cecil and P. Liddle (eds), *Facing Armageddon: the First World War Experienced*, London: Leo Cooper.

Sheffield, G.D., 1996, 'Officer–Man Relations, Discipline and Morale in the British Army of the Great War' in H. Cecil and P. Liddle (eds), *Facing Armageddon: The First World War Experienced*, London: Leo Cooper.

—— 2000 (a), *Leadership in the Trenches: Officer–Man Relations, Morale and Discipline in the British Army in the Era of the First World War*, Basingstoke: Macmillan.

—— 2000 (b), 'Reflections on the Experience of British Generalship' in P. Liddle, J. Bourne and I. Whitehead (eds), *The Great World War 1914–45 1. Lightning Strikes Twice*, London: HarperCollins.

Siberry, E., 2000, *The New Crusaders: Images of the Crusades in the Nineteenth and Early Twentieth Centuries*, Aldershot: Ashgate.

Simkins, P., 1985, 'Soldiers and Civilians: Billeting in Britain and France' in I.F.W. Beckett and K. Simpson (eds), *A Nation in Arms: a Social Study of the British Army in the First World War*, Manchester: Manchester University Press.

—— 1988, *Kitchener's Army: the Raising of the New Armies, 1914–16*, Manchester: Manchester University Press.

—— 1994, 'The Four Armies 1914–1918' in D. Chandler and I. Beckett (eds), *The Oxford Illustrated History of the British Army*, Oxford: Oxford University Press.

Simpson, A., 1993, *Hot Blood and Cold Steel: Life and Death in the Trenches of the First World War*, London: Tom Donovan.

Simpson, K., 1985, 'The Officers' in I.F.W. Beckett and K. Simpson (eds), *A Nation in Arms: a Social Study of the British Army in the First World War*, Manchester: Manchester University Press.

Smith, L., 1998, *Pacifists in Action: the Experience of the Friends Ambulance Unit in the Second World War*, York: William Sessions Ltd.

Smith, M.A., 1995, *Religion in Industrial Society: Oldham and Saddleworth 1740–1865*, Oxford: Oxford University Press.

Smyth, J.G., 1968, *In This Sign Conquer: the Story of the Army Chaplains*, London: Mowbray.

Snape, M.F., 2002, 'British Catholicism and the British Army in the First World War', *Recusant History*, 26: 314–58.

—— 2004, 'British Army Chaplains and Capital Courts-Martial in the First World War' in K. Cooper and J. Gregory (eds), 'Retribution, Repentance and Reconciliation', *Studies in Church History*, 40: 357–68.

—— 2005, *The Redcoat and Religion: the Forgotten History of the British Soldier from the Age of Marlborough to the Eve of the First World War*, London: Routledge.

Snape, M.F. and Parker, S.G., 2001, 'Keeping Faith and Coping: Belief, Popular Religiosity and the British People' in J. Bourne, P. Liddle and I. Whitehead (eds), *The Great World War 1914–45 2. The People's Experience*, London: Harper Collins.

Spiers, E.M., 1985, 'The Regular Army in 1914' in I.F.W. Beckett and K. Simpson (eds), *A Nation in Arms: a Social Study of the British Army in the First World War*, Manchester: Manchester University Press.

—— 1992, *The Late Victorian Army 1868–1902*, Manchester: Manchester University Press.

—— 1996, 'The Scottish Soldier at War' in H. Cecil and P. Liddle (eds), *Facing Armageddon: The First World War Experienced*, London: Leo Cooper.

Springhall, J., 1977, *Youth, Empire and Society: British Youth Movements, 1883–1940*, London: Croom Helm.

Stallworthy, J., 1998, *Wilfred Owen*, Oxford: Oxford University Press.

Steel, N. and Hart, P., 2001, *Passchendaele: the Sacrificial Ground*, London: Cassell.

Stirling, P., 1936, 'The Ninety-third Highlanders' Church', *RAChD Journal*, January: 190–3.

Strachan, H., 1999, 'The Boer War and its Impact on the British Army, 1902–14' in P.B. Boyden, A.J. Guy and M. Harding (eds), *Ashes and Blood: the British Army in South Africa 1795–1914*, London: National Army Museum.

—— 2001, *The First World War Volume 1: To Arms*, Oxford: Oxford University Press.

—— 2003, *The First World War: a New Illustrated History*, London: Simon and Schuster.

Summers, A., 1989, 'Edwardian Militarism' in R. Samuel (ed.), *Patriotism: the Making and Unmaking of British National Identity Volume I: History and Politics*, London: Routledge.

Tegla Davies, A., 1947, *Friends Ambulance Unit: the Story of the F.A.U. in the Second World War, 1939–1946*, London: Allen and Unwin.

Terraine, J., 1986, *To Win a War: 1918, the Year of Victory*, Basingstoke: MacMillan.

—— 1990, *Douglas Haig: the Educated Soldier*, London: Leo Cooper.

Thomas, K., 1991, *Religion and the Decline of Magic*, London: Penguin.

Thompson, D.M., 1983, 'War, the Nation, and the Kingdom of God: the Origins of the National Mission of Repentance and Hope, 1915–16' in W.J. Sheils (ed.), 'The Church and War', *Studies in Church History*, 20: 337–50.

Travers, T., 1987, *The Killing Ground: the British Army, the Western Front and the Emergence of Modern Warfare, 1900–1918*, London: Allen and Unwin.

—— 1994, 'The Army and the Challenge of War 1914–1918' in D. Chandler and I. Beckett (eds), *The Oxford Illustrated History of the British Army*, Oxford: Oxford University Press.

Urquhart, G., 1998, 'Negotiations for War: Highland Identity under Fire' in B. Taithe and T. Thornton (eds), *War: Identities in Conflict, 1300–2000*, Stroud: Sutton.

Warner, P., 2003, *Field Marshal Earl Haig*, London: Cassell.

Weeks, W.S., 1920, 'Further Legendary Stories and Folk-lore of the Clitheroe District', *Transactions of the Lancashire and Cheshire Antiquarian Society*, 38: 35–86.

Weight, R., 2002, *Patriots: National Identity in Britain 1940–2000*, London: Macmillan.

Westlake, R., 1998, *Kitchener's Army*, Spellmount: Staplehurst.

White, G., 1993, 'The Martyr Cult of the First World War' in D. Wood (ed.), 'Martyrs and Martyrologies', *Studies in Church History*, 29: 383–8.

Whiteman, C.H., 1985, *Patriot, Padre and Priest: a Life of Henry Whiteman*, Worthing: Churchman Publishing.

Whitlow, M., 1938, *J. Taylor Smith K.C.B., C.V.O., D.D.: Everybody's Bishop*, London: Religious Tract Society.

Wickham, E.R., 1957, *Church and People in an Industrial City*, London: Lutterworth Press.

Wilkinson, A., 1978, *The Church of England and the First World War*, London: SPCK.

—— 1981, 'The Paradox of the Military Chaplain', *Theology*, 84: 249–57.

—— 1986, *Dissent or Conform? War, Peace and the English Churches 1900–1945*, London: SCM.

Wilkinson, P., 1969, 'English Youth Movements, 1908–1930', *Journal of Contemporary History*, 4: 3–23.

Williams, S.C., 1999, *Religious Belief and Popular Culture in Southwark, c.1880–1939*, Oxford: Oxford University Press.

Wilson, T., 1988, *The Myriad Faces of War: Britain and the Great War, 1914–1918*, Cambridge: Polity Press.

Winter, D., 1979, *Death's Men: Soldiers of the Great War*, London: Penguin.

—— 1992, *Haig's Command: a Reassessment*, London: Penguin.

Winter, J., 1992, 'Spiritualism and the First World War' in R.W. Davis and R.J. Helmstadter (eds), *Religion and Irreligion in Victorian Society*, London: Routledge.

—— 1998, *Sites of Memory, Sites of Mourning: the Great War in European Cultural History*, Cambridge: Cambridge University Press.

Wolfe, K.M., 1984, *The Churches and the British Broadcasting Corporation 1922–1956: the Politics of Broadcast Religion*, London: SCM.

Wolffe, J., 1994, *God and Greater Britain: Religion and National Life in Britain and Ireland 1843–1945*, London: Routledge.

—— 1997, '"Praise to the Holiest in the Height": Hymns and Church Music' in J. Wolffe (ed.), *Religion in Victorian Britain Volume V: Culture and Empire*, Manchester: Manchester University Press.

Wood, I.S., 1997, '"Twas England Bade Our Wild Geese Go": Soldiers of Ireland in the Second World War' in P. Addison and A. Calder (eds), *Time to Kill: The Soldier's Experience of War in the West 1939–1945*, London: Pimlico.

Woodburn Kirby, S. (ed.), 1958, *History of the Second World War. The War Against Japan: Volume II India's Most Dangerous Hour*, London: HMSO.

—— 1965, *History of the Second World War. The War Against Japan: Volume IV The Reconquest of Burma*, London: HMSO.

—— 1969, *History of the Second World War. The War Against Japan: Volume V The Surrender of Japan*, London: HMSO.

Yates, N., 1999, *Anglican Ritualism in Victorian Britain 1830–1910*, Oxford: Oxford University Press.

Zahn, G.C., 1969, *Chaplains in the RAF: a Study in Role Tension*, Manchester: Manchester University Press.

Reference works

Bourne, J.M., 2001, *Who's Who in World War One*, London: Routledge.

Holmes, R. (ed.), 2001, *The Oxford Companion to Military History*, Oxford: Oxford University Press.

O'Creagh, M. and Humphries, E.M. (eds), 1923, *The V.C. and D.S.O.*, London: The Standard Art Book Co (3 vols).

Oxford Dictionary of National Biography, 2004, Oxford: Oxford University Press.

Statistics of the Military Effort of the British Empire during the Great War, 1914–1920, 1992, London: The London Stamp Exchange.

Unpublished dissertations

Brown, A.M., 1996, 'Army Chaplains in the First World War', St Andrews: PhD thesis.

Coulter, D.G., 1997, 'The Church of Scotland Army Chaplains in the Second World War', Edinburgh: PhD thesis.

Mews, S.P., 1973, 'Religion and English Society in the First World War', Cambridge: PhD thesis.

Parker, S.G., 2003, 'Faith on the Home Front: Aspects of Church Life and Popular Religion in Birmingham, 1939–1945', Birmingham: PhD thesis.

Robinson, A., 1999, 'The Role of British Army Chaplains during World War Two', Liverpool: PhD thesis.

Rosen, B., 2004, 'The Participation and Experiences of Jewish Servicemen and Women in the British Armed Forces 1939–45', Birmingham: BA dissertation.

Thompson, J.H., 1990, 'The Free Church Army Chaplain 1830–1930', Sheffield: PhD thesis.

INDEX

Routledge History
Christianity and Society in the Modern World
General Editor: Hugh McLeod

The Redcoat and Religion: The Forgotten History of the British Soldier from the Age of Marlborough to the eve of the First World War
Michael Snape

In *The Redcoat and Religion* Michael Snape argues that religion was of significant, even defining, importance to the British soldier throughout the eighteenth and nineteenth centuries, and reveals the enduring strength and vitality of religion in contemporary British society, challenging the view that the popular religious culture of the era was wholly dependent upon the presence and activities of women.

Hb 0–415–37715–3

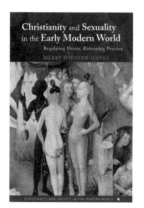

Christianity and Sexuality in the Early Modern World
Merry E Wiesner-Hanks

In this lively and compelling study, Professor Wiesner-Hanks examines the ways in which Christian ideas and institutions shaped sexual norms and conduct from the time of Luther and Columbus to that of Thomas Jefferson. Providing a global overview, and including chapters on Protestant, Catholic and Orthodox Europe, Latin America, Africa, Asia and North America, this volume examines marriage, divorce, fornication, illegitimacy, clerical sexuality, witchcraft and love magic, homosexuality and moral crimes.

Hb 0–415–14433–7
Pb 0–415–14434–5

Available at all good bookshops
For ordering and further information please visit:
www.routledge.com

Routledge History

Women and Religion in Early America, 1600-1850
Marilyn J Westerkamp

Women in Early American Religion, 1600-1850 explores the first two
centuries of America's religious history, examining the relationship
between the socio-political environment, gender, politics and
religion. Drawing its background from women's religious roles and
experiences in England during the Reformation, the book follows
them through colonial settlement, the rise of evangelicalism, the
American Revolution, and the second flowering of popular religion
in the nineteenth century. Tracing the female spiritual tradition
through the Puritans, Baptists and Shakers, Marilyn Westerkamp
argues that religious beliefs and structures were actually a strong
empowering force for women.

Hb 0–415–09814–9
Pb 0–415–19448–2

The Reformation of Ritual: An Interpretation of Early Modern Germany
Susan Karant-Nunn

In The Reformation of Ritual Susan Karant-Nunn explores the
function of ritual in early modern German society, and the extent to
which it was modified by the Reformation. Employing
anthropological insights, and drawing on extensive archival research,
Susan Karant-Nunn outlines the significance of the ceremonial
changes. This comprehensive study includes an examination of all
major rites of passage: birth, baptism, confirmation, engagement,
marriage, the churching of women after childbirth, penance, the
Eucharist, and dying. The author argues that the changes in ritual
made over the course of the century reflect more than theological
shifts; ritual was a means of imposing discipline and of making the
divine more or less accessible. Church and state cooperated in using
ritual as one means of gaining control of the populace.

Hb 0–415–11337–7

Available at all good bookshops
For ordering and further information please visit:
www.routledge.com